American Eden

American Eden

FROM MONTICELLO TO CENTRAL PARK
TO OUR BACKYARDS:
What Our Gardens Tell Us About Who We Are

Wade Graham

HARPER PERENNIAL

NEW YORK • LONDON • TORONTO • SYDNEY • NEW DELHI • AUCKLAND

HARPER ● PERENNIAL

A hardcover edition of this book was published in 2011 by HarperCollins Publishers.

AMERICAN EDEN. Copyright © 2011 by Wade Graham. All rights reserved. Printed in the United States of America. No part of this book may be used or reproduced in any manner whatsoever without written permission except in the case of brief quotations embodied in critical articles and reviews. For information address HarperCollins Publishers, 10 East 53rd Street, New York, NY 10022.

HarperCollins books may be purchased for educational, business, or sales promotional use. For information please e-mail the Special Markets Department at SPsales@harpercollins.com.

First Harper Perennial edition published 2013.

The Library of Congress has catalogued the hardcover edition as follows:

Graham, Wade.
  American Eden: from Monticello to Central Park to our backyards: what our gardens tell us about who we are / Wade Graham. — 1st ed.
    p. cm.
  Includes bibliographical references and index.
  ISBN 978-0-06-158342-1
    1. Gardens—United States—History. 2. Landscape architecture—United States—History. I. Title. II. Title: from Monticello to Central Park to our backyards: what our gardens tell us about who we are.
  SB451.3.G718 2011
  712.0973—dc22

ISBN 978-0-06-158343-8 (pbk.)

13   14   15   16   17   OV/GQF   10   9   8   7   6   5   4   3   2

For Ben and Plum,
intrepid explorers and thoughtful gardeners

"Little joy has he who has no garden," said Saadi. Montaigne took much pains to be made a citizen of Rome; and our people are vain, when abroad, of having the freedom of foreign cities presented to them in a gold box. I much prefer to have the freedom of a garden presented me. When I go into a good garden, I think, if it were mine, I should never go out of it. It requires some geometry in the head, to lay it out rightly, and there are many who can enjoy, to one that can create it.

—RALPH WALDO EMERSON, "COUNTRY LIFE—CONCORD," 1857

CONTENTS

THE POLITICS AND PASSIONS OF GARDENS

To see another's garden may give us a keen perception of the richness or poverty of his personality, of his experiences and associations in life, and of his spiritual qualities.

—*CHARLES DOWNING LAY, A Garden Book, 1924*

This book is a history of gardens in America, from the colonial and revolutionary periods to the present. It is about the form, feel, and life of gardens and the lives of the people who make them, but also about much more. It starts from my conviction that our gardens are meaningful—that they say a lot, and that we can read in them stories, not only about their makers but about ourselves as a people—*our people*, in Emerson's words: we Americans. It is informed by the several sides of my work: designing gardens, all over the country, for all kinds of people and all manner of situations; and studying and writing about America's cultural and environmental history.

Though born of agriculture, gardens are not farms. One definition from 1839 serves reasonably well: a garden is "land . . . laid out as a pleasure ground . . . with a view to recreation and enjoyment, more than profit."[1] Its function is essentially social: a garden is in effect a miniature Utopia, a diorama of how its makers see themselves and the world. Anyone who creates a garden draws a map of their mind on the ground, whether consciously or not. If we take time to read them, carefully situating them in the matrix of architecture, art, literature, and social and economic circumstances in which they are embedded, gardens may tell us about the wealth, power, status, sex lives, ethnicity, religion, politics, passions, aspirations, delusions, illusions, and dreams of their creators. Always rooted in their time and place, even the most unique gardens are indicators and traces of the tensions and energies in a constantly changing society. They can express political theories, aesthetic preoccupations, scientific and religious ideas, cultural inheritances, and sheer force of personality. Thomas Jefferson's layered landscape at Monticello in Virginia expressed all of these things and more, providing us with a map, not only of his deep engagement with the ideas and values of the Enlightenment, but of his own, often deeply conflicted mind as a statesman, businessman, slave owner, farmer, and lover. All his life he worked to reconcile his democratic ideals with his love of luxury and the trappings of aristocracy, and his vision of an egalitarian, agrarian society with the harsh realities of the economic system that underpinned his own status—plantation slavery. Inspired by new British styles in gardens as well as by new ideas about rights, government, and society coming from Great Britain, yet wanting no more to do with that mother country, he struggled to adapt them to the new nation that he contributed so much to conceiving. His garden, every bit as much as his celebrated writings, is a testament to this seminal work of creating something unprecedented: an American character, and an American landscape to go along with it.

Jefferson's dilemmas are still with us: we love to ogle the ostentatious houses and gardens of come-lately billionaires; at the same time we take pride in Michelle Obama's kitchen garden at the White House, planted by schoolchildren with two hundred dollars' worth of supplies. As a people, and as individuals, we want to express our values and virtues, and our sense of responsibility to community and the natural environment, while allowing space for our dreams and aspirations to flower, and, for some of us, our wealth. We must reconcile life, liberty, and the pursuit of happiness, as the founder described them in the Declaration of Independence. Like Jefferson, we look abroad, to Europe, Asia, or elsewhere for models and inspiration, and we seek to transform those borrowed styles into a distinctively American form. For some of us the preferred expression in the garden is no-holds-barred ostentation in imitation of European royalty, like George Washington Vanderbilt's Biltmore Estate; for some it is a "Grandmother's" humble cottage garden of flowers and vegetables; for most, though, it is an amalgam, a middle ground, that weaves the different, competing strands of our heritage into a cultural fabric that is generally middle-class but keeps one eye faithfully on an agricultural past and one, perhaps hopefully, on the dream of one day making it big. Just as Jefferson's house and garden drove him deeply into debt as he built and rebuilt them obsessively until the end of his life, chasing the evolving image of perfection he held in his mind's eye, our gardens reveal the economic volatility and dynamism that have fueled American social mobility, and attendant anxieties about class and status, from the beginning. In every age, old money and new, established social groups and ascendant ones, try to negotiate their shared spaces in part through questions of taste, style, display, and the narratives that are spun around them. What was true in Jefferson's time was true in the Gilded Age at the end of the 19th century and remains true in our era of Hamptons hedge fund billionaires and reality TV makeover shows. Martha Stewart has nothing on our Founding Gardener.

The musician Jack Johnson sings, "I've got a symbol in my driveway," as a comment on how we use things like cars to speak for us, often assigning them certain lines in the play that we write about ourselves that we are hesitant to utter in our own voices. The drama of self-creation isn't straightforward, but full of deviations, diversions, dodges, and impersonations. What makes gardens especially interesting (versus, say, buying cars, houses, clothes, art, companies, or sports teams to show the world who we are) is that making one constitutes the creation of a new world—

our own world, often nearly from scratch, an Eden where outside stresses, failures, and compromises can't enter (at least in theory).

The comparison to drama isn't far-fetched: since ancient times gardens have been compared to stages and used as settings for plays, masked balls, and myriad entertainments; sibling arts, stage and garden are each dramatizations of life and lives. Like theater, our gardens also tell of deeper, personal stirrings: of romantic love, of nostalgia for lost times and places, certainties, dreams, securities, and especially for childhood, that place of refuge, real or imagined. American gardens frequently evoke Arcadian agrarian landscapes, expressing our yearnings for the supposedly simpler lives of a rural time past, even as we have inexorably become an urban people living in an industrialized world churned by war, economic and social upheaval, and the displacement of communities in the face of the constant movement our system voraciously feeds on.

Emerson liked to quote Saadi, the 12th century Persian traveler-poet who chronicled the people and gardens he met on his peregrinations through the Middle East, Central Asia, and India. The gardens Saadi wrote about descended from ancient Persia: the *paradeiza*, or walled kings' hunting grounds, which passed into Greek as *paradeisos*, which was the model for the biblical Garden of Eden in the book of Genesis. Like ancient desert cities, gardens were walled to keep out the bad and shelter the good, in all senses. This is why, as Emerson said, one longed for the freedom of a garden: the keys, permission to enter the bounded refuge of a space apart—separate from other people's lives, separate from the tumult of the city and the vicissitudes of nature alike, since a garden isn't nature but rather an entwining of nature and culture in a highly promiscuous, productive pas de deux.

Every good garden is a window—into the individual mind or minds of its makers, owners, inheritors, or inhabitants, and, through their stories layered on top of one another, a window to the collective mind, our common experience. To recognize what is visible there we have to learn the language of gardens: the vocabulary consists of plants, stone, wood, and water, the syntax a series of conjunctions of parterres and topiary, woodlands and meadows, terraces and pergolas, sculptures and staircases, pools and fountains, hedges and borders, flowers and gravel, straight lines and curves, geometry and wildness, sunlight and shadow, wet places and dry ones. Like DNA, the message can be hard to follow, as it is often carried in a jumble of bits borrowed and retained from here and there, words and phrases from a mix of garden languages, foreign, ancient, and dead, strung together, some of it possibly meaning nothing, but much of it coding for bone structure, color, and character—the way gardens express people's thoughts and statements about life, politics, aesthetics, and matters of the heart.

Yet, looking at the progress of our gardens through time, patterns emerge, and we can see that we share fundamental ambitions, dilemmas, and pleasures over four hundred years of making gardens in the part of North America that has become the United States. The story is one of borrowing, and from a dizzying mix of sources: England, France, Italy, Spain, Persia, China, Japan, India, Mexico, or the South Pacific. The ideas and forms borrowed seem incongruous, even ridiculous: aristocratic styles are adopted by egalitarian republicans, pagan by Christians, English by revolutionary Americans even during the fight for independence, Catholic by Protestants, medieval Gothic by 20th century industrialists, and ancient Asian religious ones by secular modernists. There are all manner of strange combinations, uneasy bedfellows, and improbable convergences. Yet over and over, by the prosaic alchemy of the American melting pot, which works on cultural memes as much as on race, ethnicity, or religion, all of these forms are eventually transformed into middle-class American ones—modest, suburban houses unself-consciously garbed as Greek temples, Scottish castles, storybook cottages, or futuristic space modules, surrounded by miniature versions of the gardens of Versailles, Blenheim Palace, the Villa Medici, or the temple of Ryoan-ji. It is this borrowing and recombining that accounts for the extraordinary visual variety of the American-built environment—so jumbled and outrageous in places that a visitor from elsewhere might think us a kind of house and garden cargo cult. But it also reveals our particular genius: by digesting pieces from all over the world we have created an American style—several, to be exact. At their best ours are looser, freer, more idealistic, and more optimistic than the originals, and unapologetically ecumenical, unafraid to mix and match: thus, in 1960s California, a new universal style was born by merging orthodox modernism, South Pacific pastiche, and the Mexican rancho. Repeatedly, seeming opposites, whether modernist and historicist or formal and picturesque, intermingle, cross-pollinate, and bear hybrid offspring. These mixings are not simply products of American naïveté—there is deep truth to them, since careful historical work reveals that each of these poles shares a common antecedent in the Western tradition—they are branches of the same tree, though with very different leaves and flowers; thus their affinity is a natural consequence of their common heredity. They are surface styles, and divergent ones at that, which nevertheless reveal common psychological and cultural topographies beneath them, just as clothes reveal the contours of the skin and body below.

The newest wave in the garden is in many ways also its oldest: a return to agriculture, as makers of gardens seek to put back some of the links to the farm that were lost as America became overwhelmingly urban and suburban—both aesthetically and in the actual, intensive growing of food. Along with a movement toward more natural and environmentally friendly designs and practices in the garden, these represent a renewed effort toward reintegrating the split parts of our world: on one hand, the Arcadian, agrarian dream of small-town or rural life, with its self-sufficiency, slower pace, and connection to the imagined simplicity of the past; and on the other, the breathless rush and stress of our exurban, postindustrial reality in the 21st century. Paradoxically, or unsurprisingly, depending on how you look at it, for all our sophistication and the distance we have fortunately traveled from the harsh realities of his era, we American gardeners still face the same basic quandaries and enjoy the same rewards and pleasures as Thomas Jefferson did in his own patch of earth.

American Eden

One

FOUNDING GARDENS (1600–1826)

f the United States of America has a founding garden, it is without question the one Thomas Jefferson laid out on a hilltop near Charlottesville, Virginia, which he called Monticello ("little mountain" in Italian), during the era of the American Revolution. The house at the center of the garden is as familiar to most Americans as their own, even if we're unaware of it—it looks out at us from the nickel. Its graceful, white classical columned porch holding up a triangular Greek pediment defines what we think of as "Federal" architecture, that quintessentially American style that was transposed from Jefferson's home in his lifetime to the U.S. Capitol building, the White House, and since to countless tens of thousands of sober courthouses, libraries, and banks across the land, and probably millions of houses, modest and grand alike, all proudly announcing their upstanding American-ness with white columns and pediments—architectural details borrowed, unwittingly, from ancient pagan temples dedicated to rituals of sex and death.

I went to see Thomas Jefferson's garden early on a June morning, and rather than wait for the first shuttle bus to leave the parking lot, I walked alone along the path that leads up the hill through a mature forest of oaks and tulip poplars—Jefferson's favorite tree. The woods were dark and quiet, and there was a dense mist shrouding the ground, blown upslope by a cool southeasterly breeze. It was an appropriately literary way to arrive, worthy of a scene from an 18th century bildungsroman, or one of the moody druidic poems by Ossian that Jefferson liked to recite after dinners with friends. Emerging from the trees I confronted a dank graveyard fenced in black iron with a large obelisk marking the owner's grave, then stepped onto the gravel walk where the slave quarters and workshops once stood; through the cinematically rising mist I caught a glimpse of the perfect rows of multicolored vegetables growing in the thousand-foot-long kitchen garden. Finally, through a gap in the trees, in an opening shaft of sunlight, I recognized the façade of that singular house, with its squat dome and its stately, iconic white columns, just like on the coins in my pocket.

The house and its two parallel outbuilding wings embrace the ur-American backyard: a wide expanse of lawn surrounded by a lazily curving walk between lush, colorful flower borders, shaded by towering broadleaf trees planted in an apparently random, natural disorder. Carefully framed views of distant prospects open between trees and the various outbuildings of the house: a bit of a slowly winding river, a hilltop, a far-off, hazy ridge. A grassy meadow falls away in the distance under more trees, gradually thickening to dense forest as the flanks of the hill steepen. Like his house, Jefferson's garden also became a model for what an American garden ought to be: a relaxed composition of trees, lawn, shrubs, and flowers, informal yet self-assured, large but not palatial, eschewing the tight, clipped geometries of earlier colonial gardens that had been copied from the gardens of the European aristocracy. With the Revolution that Jefferson helped spark and guide, all that formality went out the window, along with the tyranny of the British king and his redcoats and taxes. Jefferson's garden was robust, free, and natural, a paean to the wild American continent, a new kind of garden for a new, democratic age. It has remained a model after more than two centuries and effusions of all manner of styles and incursions of every conceivable foreign influence, and still serves as the unconscious template for many of our contemporary American gardens.

If Monticello is our blueprint, it only makes sense that Jefferson should have designed it, since he was the architect of so many of our national institutions, on paper and in stone. Thomas Jefferson could do just about everything, better than just about anybody. President John F. Kennedy famously welcomed a group of American Nobel laureates to dinner at the White House in 1962 by saying, "I think this is the most extraordinary collection of talent and of human knowledge that has ever been gathered together at the White House—with the possible exception of when Thomas Jefferson dined alone." In turn Jefferson was a member of colonial Virginia's legislature, delegate to the Second Continental Congress, writer of the Declaration of Independence, governor of Virginia, minister to France, secretary of state under President George Washington, vice president under President John Adams, third president of the United States (serving two terms), purchaser of Louisiana from Napoleon, designer and patron of Lewis and Clark's expedition to explore the new territory, and founder and architect of the University of Virginia, the Virginia state capitol, and Monticello—for starters.

In the garden, he proved no less a visionary and pioneer; he was the greatest garden designer in this country of his generation, and among the most disciplined gardeners of any. From the age of twenty-three, the year he got out of college, until 1824, two years before his death, he kept up almost daily entries in his *Garden Book* whenever he was at Monticello.[1] He maintained a lifelong, meticulous record of what he planted, when, in what soil, when he transplanted, when he harvested, what failed, and what thrived. In the Enlightenment spirit of the times, he recorded the time of first flowering of plants all around him, native and cultivated, the first appearance of migrating birds, and, every day of his adult life, the temperature and other meteorological conditions wherever he found himself. Throughout his life, in the midst of war, travel, and decades of public service, he carried on a steady exchange of seeds, bulbs, and plants with correspondents all over America and Europe. He experimented endlessly with new varieties: he grew 150 fruit trees, and up to 350 vegetables at one time, including some 50 varieties of peas, 44 of beans, and upwards of 30 cabbages.[2] He wrote in his *Autobiography* that "the greatest service which can be rendered any country is to add a useful plant to its culture."[3]

And he worked diligently at it: he introduced five hundred olive trees imported from Italy (they failed), the Lombardy poplar, European grapes (they didn't make very good wine), and new vegetables and varieties of rice from all over. In preparation for the expedition to the newly acquired Louisiana Territory, Jefferson arranged for Captain Meriwether Lewis to study botany in Philadelphia for nine months before embarking, so that he would be able to collect specimens of what he came across and bring them back for the benefit of the nation.[4]

Along with the house, the garden at Monticello was Jefferson's life work: he began planning it when barely out of college, built it and revised it between stints, some nearly a decade long, of service to the young country, and kept working in it near daily until his death in 1826. Later in life, when he was finally able to retire from the White House to his beloved home, the garden was a solace and a long-sought and hard-earned refuge from the stresses of the world. Most every day he rode out to survey his farm and garden operations, took pleasure in strolling with friends, family, and visitors from far and wide, and most of all, playing with his grandchildren. As he wrote to his friend, the painter Charles Willson Peale, on August 20, 1811, "I have often thought that if heaven had given me choice of my position and calling, it should have been on a rich spot of earth, well-watered, and near a good market for the productions of the garden. No occupation is so delightful to me as the culture of the earth, and no culture comparable to that of the garden. Such a variety of subjects, some one always coming to perfection, the failure of one thing repaired by the success of another, and instead of one harvest a continued one through the year. . . . [T]hough I am an old man, I am but a young gardener."[5]

In a long life, his youthful passion for gardens was as undiminished by age as his youthful tastes were unchanged by it: the romantic, sentimental, and sometimes fey garden scenes he imagined in his twenties he built in his sixties and proudly showed off to the luminaries of the age. His garden style would seem at odds with the image of gravitas we have of him as a founding father of our nation—but this alone tells us a great deal about his temperament and vision. Gardens were also the scenes of some of his most passionate moments. During the heated run-up to the French

Revolution, he found time in Paris to redesign, on paper, the gardens of his lodging house, and to play hooky from his diplomatic rounds while visiting gardens in the company of a beautiful, seductive, and married young woman. He took them seriously; he considered the art of gardens, as he defined it—"not horticulture, but the art of embellishing grounds by fancy"—to likely deserve a place among the fine arts: "Painting, Sculpture, architecture, music & poetry."[6]

Making gardens for him was part of the larger project of building a new world in America, a real Utopia where men (let's make no mistake, he meant white men, exclusively) could enjoy liberty and the pursuit of happiness free from the oppressions of European societies. Gardens at their best were for Jefferson an expression of the spirit and optimism of a new age in a new country. But the legacy of Jefferson's garden is complex, full of odd pairings and contradictions, like the new country he helped midwife, and like the man himself. Monticello today strikes a visitor as a bald paradox: the flowing, naturalistic garden, the height of modernity at the time, enveloping the severe formality of neo-ancient Roman architecture. Jefferson meant Monticello as a symbol for a new nation, and he based it purposefully on the glorious Roman past—by which he meant the young, republican Rome of the Senate, not the decadent and cruel imperial Rome of the Caesars. It was intended as a symbol of an emerging world that harked back to a golden age of equality and virtue, untainted by the corruptions of the present; but his Utopia on the mountaintop was of course already corrupted, since it was built by slaves. The garden fashion he embraced and executed with as much flair as any designer on either side of the Atlantic was, more even than the architectural fashion, a consummately English form—an odd choice for a man who otherwise hated everything English. And the indulgence and ostentation of it, the sheer luxury and fashionability must have seemed at least a little bit disconcerting in a man famous for his dislike in others of gentility and signs of class, who even as president of the United States went around in plain dress (some would say a calculated dishevelment). For a man obsessed with paring down the national debt when he served as president, it is uncomfortable to consider how he knowingly accumulated so much debt himself—in no small part due to his fancy tastes and his high living—that everything he owned had to be sold on his death, including the slaves, their families broken up.

Some see hypocrisy in the life of Jefferson; his reputation has lately eroded, especially since the confirmation by genetic evidence that he fathered at least one child with his slave, Sally Hemings, even as he railed against miscegenation. But it remains true that Jefferson gave us some of the highest achievements and most inspiring ideals of our culture. He was so purely self-contradictory that his life can be read in starkly opposite senses. While he was alive, and ever since, he has been used as an expert witness by every conceivable political persuasion: fiscal conservatives, labor radicals, abolitionists, states' rights extremists, and by independence movements all over the world. The historian Joyce Appleby has written of him, charitably one might argue: "Jefferson was not a man of contradictions so much as a man of rarely paired qualities."[7] As a garden maker, he presents another paradox: in spite of how accomplished, talented, and singular he was, in his addiction to real estate Jefferson was a lot like us. He loved elegance and grandeur but had to try to square them with the republican conviction that simplicity and function are spiritually and morally superior to luxury. His favorite word was *useful,* but by this he sometimes just meant "beautiful." He wanted to live the good life and make a perfect home, and he dug himself deeply, irresponsibly into debt to do it. Like a lot of us later Americans, real estate was for him an all-consuming activity, an engine for investing money, time, energy, and hopes, and an engine for spending them on unsustainable, conspicuous consumption.

Monticello provides a map of all these tensions, hopes, dreams, aspirations, and contradictions, diagrammed on the ground by Thomas Jefferson for all to see. It is a kind of diorama of what he thought Utopia should look like, and for all its flaws, it is a powerfully beautiful, idealistic, and inspiring spot. To make a pilgrimage to see the place is both to go back to the beginning point of the American garden and to witness the culmination of thousands of years of garden making in the Western tradition. Looking at Jefferson's garden is a way to see ourselves and our history from a different angle, from the garden path, so to speak, taking a walk up the serpentine path of American self-creation.

Though he was born in a distant colony of England, much of it still a rude, violent, thinly settled frontier, Thomas Jefferson was born into the English family; Virginians, especially those from the gentry, kept themselves as close as they could to the motherland, listening raptly for the latest news, opinions, and fashions from home, and sending their sons back across the Atlantic for schooling and business opportunities. Garden making was a big part of being English, and even on an American frontier, the role of English gardens as markers of grace, education, social status, and social climbing formed an important part of the warp and weft of Virginia life. Virginians saw themselves squarely within a European culture then in the grip of an awakening of multiple dimensions—the philosophical, scientific, and artistic revolution of the Enlightenment— gathering force in tandem with the huge economic, demographic, and political transformations of capitalism and colonial expansion that were remaking the globe in the 18th century. Jefferson grew up in the crest of this wave, rose with it, and executed an amazing number of its crowning expressions, in an astonishing breadth of fields.

Jefferson was born April 13, 1743, the first son and third of ten children on the family plantation Shadwell, in Albemarle County, among the ranges of steep hills that rear from the sloping piedmont as it rises to meet the knife edge of the Blue Ridge Mountains to the west. His father, Peter, farmed wheat and tobacco on 1,900 acres, with the labor of thirty black slaves. Peter Jefferson served as a local magistrate, parish vestryman, and member of the Virginia House of Burgesses, the colonial legislature. He was also a capable surveyor and mapmaker, skills that Thomas learned early, coming to know the local countryside well. The young Jefferson was good at math, language, and music. In 1757, when he was fourteen, his father died, leaving him about five thousand acres and a large slave workforce, and the direction that he continue his education at the College of William & Mary, established in the capital, Williamsburg, in 1693.[8] He matriculated at the age of seventeen, in 1760. There are no images from these years, but the famous characterization of him later in life must have applied then: he was tall, at six feet, two and a half inches, big-boned, with sandy hair and a freckled complexion; he wasn't especially handsome, but was vigorous and cut an impressive figure. At college he studied mathematics, the classics, and law, and loved music, playing violin some evenings as part of a foursome that included the lieutenant governor of the colony, Francis Fauquier.[9] He must have frequented the college library, and probably also the one at the governor's palace, both of which included books on gardens and architecture. He would have walked under and noted the double allée of catalpa trees along the Palace Green and would have rambled in the palace gardens, laid out by an earlier lieutenant governor, Alexander Spotswood, thirty-five years before. As Williamsburg was a very small place, he would have been aware of the notable town garden of John Custis (Martha Washington's future father-in-law), begun in 1717, occupying four acres, an entire town block, likely also Custis's plantation at Queen's Creek, a mile north of town, and the celebrated garden at Westover, Custis's brother-in-law, William Byrd II's nearby plantation on the James River.[10] Both Custis and Byrd were noted gardeners and collectors of the native flora, and carried on plant exchanges with some of England's leading horticulturalists, enriching British gardens with American species, and vice versa, and extolling the virtues of their new world.

These weren't the first American pleasure gardens. The earliest colonists, though most concerned with their own agricultural survival, brought with them a gardening culture and stocks of seeds, plants, and plans to root it in the New World. Within the limits of ships and weather, they kept in touch with European fashion and practice. Most 17th century gardens in America were primarily practical: enclosed by walls, fences, or hedges to keep roaming livestock out, mixes of herbs for medicine and cooking, fruit trees, and flowers, arrayed in simple geometric layouts. But even then the wealthier were anxious to demonstrate some refinement in their wilderness outposts, and gardens played a big part. In 1642, a list of flowers in New Amsterdam (Manhattan) gardens included tulips—tulip mania had only reached a frenzy in Holland in the 1630s. By 1660, New Amsterdam gardens had parterres—designs in low hedging and flowers or herbs then all the rage in continental gardens.[11] By 1698, the best pleasure gardens in New Jersey and Pennsylvania were being favorably compared to celebrated European ones.[12]

In the late 1640s, Virginia governor Sir William Berkeley built Green Spring, his house and garden at a plantation midway between Jamestown and Williamsburg. It had an orchard stocked with 1,500 trees, flower gardens, plant nurseries, and a fashionable bowling green, which served as a locus of elite social life—socializing, cricket, horse racing, and fencing—for many years under different owners.[13] In 1665, construction on Bacon's Castle was begun on the James River, an imposing brick manor house surrounded by large formal gardens. Nearby, at Westover, William Byrd II, whose father was a prominent Virginia planter in the 1680s and '90s but who resided in England for most of the first half of his life, helped stoke a vogue for Virginia plants among high-society British gardeners in the 1690s, and he was elected to the illustrious Royal Society for his trouble. Back in the colony after his father's death in 1705, he cultivated a cross-Atlantic reputation as a wilderness sage by publishing an account of an expedition to survey the North Carolina–Virginia boundary through uncharted terrain (Jefferson's father, Peter, helped complete this survey after Byrd's death) and by carrying on a flourishing botanical exchange with various English worthies, including the head of the Physic Garden at Oxford University and Dr. Hans Sloane, who would found the British Museum.

It is hard to imagine from our vantage point, but plants were potent status symbols in the 18th century, living booty sent back from the constant stream of European overseas exploring and colonizing expeditions by swashbuckling botanist-adventurers, dispatched with instructions from kings and queens to bring back the most wonderful and lucrative species from the corners of the world. Botany was the most chic science of the age: its best scientific as well as practical expression, at the forefront of the new and daring sexual system of classification of the plant world initiated by the Swedish taxonomist Linnaeus. Concerned with the fundamental economics of farming and trade that underpinned family, nation, colony, and empire, the discipline of botany pushed far into the exotic, romantic, and sometimes still-savage lands that bestowed upon the day-to-day, violent business of the Age of Discovery its heady poetry and excitement. Even John Locke, the English philosopher whose ideas would serve as a bedrock influence for the Declaration of Independence and later for the framers of the Constitution, and who wrote, "In the beginning, all was America," asked friends in Virginia to send him plants.[14]

In fact, Virginia was not initially at the forefront of colonial gardening. An early governor, Robert Beverley, waxed in his 1705 *History and Present State of Virginia* (in what was frankly an effort to recruit colonists from England) that the colony was "Paradise it self" and was "reckon'd the Gardens of the World," where "a Garden is no sooner made than there, either for Fruits, or Flowers."[15] "Yet," he complained, "they han't many Gardens in the Country, fit to bear that name." He made a point of praising Byrd's Westover and the College of William & Mary, which boasted gardens in the latest style, but on the whole, the gulf between the garden country that nature offered in Virginia and the cultivated gardens that the colonists had committed the resources to create was still wide. Colonial Virginia, by all accounts, was still mostly raw forest when other colonies, especially in New England, were places of bustling cities, orderly townscapes, and an intensively cultivated countryside. Travelers praised Philadelphia, which had been planned as a garden city, as a "greene Country Towne,"[16] and admired Charleston, South Carolina, for its urbanity—it supported an ornamental plant nursery in 1701.[17] Yet Virginia, the first and most populous colony in British North America, had no town worth the name: Jamestown, its capital for the colony's first century, was little more than a nearly abandoned collection of low wooden buildings, while most of the colony's forty thousand or so inhabitants at mid-17th century were dispersed across a vast landscape of low-lying forests and slow, meandering rivers, here and there dotted by small plantations growing tobacco to feed Europe's newest bad habit.

Tobacco's peculiar qualities combined with the geography of tidewater Virginia yielded a unique settlement pattern. Tobacco is a hungry crop, which quickly sucks nutrients out of the soil and is laborious to cut and cure. Land was cheap, granted easily as inducement to settlers; growers, at first relying on their own muscle and that of indentured Europeans, cleared small patches of forest, farmed tobacco for a couple years, and then moved on. Virginia's cultivated landscape had the same ragged, singed look as the slash-and-burn landscape visible today in the Amazon or Borneo. Because many of the rivers and estuaries that segment the tidewater region are navigable, the Virginians found it more profitable to sell directly to ships calling at their plantation docks, often in return for finished goods, than to haul their crops to town, in the bargain avoiding middlemen and tax collectors. Frustrated authorities complained, to no avail, that the Virginia planters preferred "to seate in a stragling distracted Condition."[18]

In the Virginia of Jefferson's early life, a century and a half after the first colonization at Jamestown in 1607, the western frontier lay just over the Blue Ridge, still bloodied by conflict with Indians as well as populated by a rough breed of European, including many recent, battle-hardened refugees from the violent English-Scottish borderlands.[19] More refined European visitors to the western fringes remarked on the scandalous drinking, swearing, fighting, and general uncouthness.[20] Throughout the 18th century, gentility or "refinement" was spread very thin over the dispersed plantations of the country, which made it all the more precious to those Virginians with the money, education, or aspiration to value such things. Nevertheless, by the 1750s, Virginia had grown prosperous and populous, with perhaps four hundred thousand people, 35–40 percent of them blacks. A huge increase in slavery had created economies of scale in the tobacco business and great wealth at the top of the pyramid. Virginia society was more isolated and stratified than in any other North American colony: made up mostly of bonded people—slaves, all black, plus whites in various states of indenture, lasting from one year to perhaps seven, typically to pay off the cost of their transport and maybe buy land and a grubstake of their own—then a thin layer of small planters, topped by a very slender upper crust. Some of these big planters built manor houses based on the latest English styles, first arrayed along tidewater rivers like the James and the Potomac, and later, in the 18th century, moving up into piedmont hills, in sight of the Blue Ridge. But the grand manors didn't sit comfortably: instead they underscored a raw and brutal contrast between the few and the many, protruding like bejeweled fingers from calloused hands. Isolated in what was still a mostly untracked wilderness, they were surrounded by the yards, outbuildings, wharves, slave quarters, barns, and smells and sounds, human and animal, of the quasi-industrial production of tobacco, a luxury drug for foreign consumption. Such conditions were shared with many European colonies, especially those set up for export agriculture, and notably the slave-sugar islands of the Caribbean, where fabulous wealth was being created for a small slice of adventurous, entrepreneurial planters willing to brave the nasty and violent reality that prevailed on the uncivilized margins of the globe.

Wealth, after all, was the point of the Virginia enterprise—this was no principled religious asylum like its Puritan counterpart in New England, but a speculative frontier, where high-status persons came to make fortunes, alongside a motley host of entrepreneurs, dreamers, and misfits, all equally eager for the chance to rise that the colonies afforded them—a chance not available at home.[21] English fashions and imports were sought after from the very beginning: those who could spent money on plates, silver, clothing, paintings, and books, mostly as objects to display inside their houses to demonstrate to visitors and neighbors their ties to and level in English society. Before long, the house itself became a focus, not just among the upper crust but even among what we would call the middle class: wood was replaced by brick, one story became two, then three, reaching upward to be noticed along the road by neighbors and passersby. By the 1720s, "mansionization" was under way all over the colonies.[22]

To UNDERSTAND WHAT Jefferson was doing with his house and garden, we need to go back to 1710, when Alexander Spotswood arrived in Virginia from London to take up the post of the lieutenant governor at Williamsburg, where the seat of government had been relocated in 1699, from moribund Jamestown. The new capital was more like a frontier out-post than a town, barely carved from the woods, with few permanent residents and no landmark other than the small College of William & Mary, which had burned down in 1705 and hadn't been fully rebuilt. But in the imagination of its planner Williamsburg would be as fine and elegant as any in the colonies. A town plan had been conceived and was being laid out by Francis Nicholson, formerly Virginia's governor and later Maryland's, who also designed the town of Annapolis.[23] He had brought with him from England a head full of new techniques and values in city planning, derived from Renaissance Italy and its acolytes in France and proposed as models for rebuilding London after the Great Fire of 1666 by John Evelyn, the architect and garden designer, and Christopher Wren, the architect of St. Paul's Cathedral. These included adding garden elements to towns, such as street trees, green squares, closes, and parks, as well as public open spaces, separation between buildings, and street plans emphasizing prospects and vistas from key intersections and buildings, often on diagonal angles. At Williamsburg, on a narrow plateau fingered on both sides by a filigree of shallow ravines, Nicholson laid out a main avenue, Duke of Gloucester Street, three-quarters of a mile long, with the capitol at one end and the College of William & Mary at the other. Between the two was a market square to be lined with important buildings; nearby at a right angle to the avenue was the Palace Green, at the head of which was to be the governor's palace. (Long on enthusiasm and short on execution, Nicholson laid out two circles with radiating streets in an attempt to make Annapolis grand, but he failed to align the streets with the centers of the circles or with one another, so that the intended vistas are kinked; at Williamsburg, he laid out two diagonal streets passing the college, evidently in order to create a W and [inverted] M to honor its namesakes, but the grid that would connect the letters remained unfinished.)[24]

When Spotswood arrived, the building was unfinished, and it fell to him to complete it. Williamsburg was a quiet place, mostly woods striated by some dirt roads and half-acre lots plotted on paper, uncleared and unbuilt, as most of the owners lived on plantations in the vicinity.

But the promise of the place evidently satisfied him. "The life I lead here is neither in a Crowd of Company nor in a Throng of Business, but rather after a quiet Country manner," he wrote to his brother in Scotland, "and now I am sufficiently amused with planting Orchard & Gardens, & with finishing a large House which is design'd (at the Country's Charge) for the reception of the Governours."[25]

The last detail may explain his pleasure at his situation: what he was doing was setting himself up with a fine country "seat"—what every gentleman in England then aspired to, but which Spotswood couldn't have afforded at home. In Virginia, the king paid the tab. Spotswood threw himself into it, finishing the palace then starting in on the gardens in 1715, again at the colony's expense. The main courtyard held a formal garden enclosed by a four-foot-high brick wall (visible in the Bodleian

Bodleian Plate. (Colonial Williamsburg Foundation)

Plate engraving dating from 1736–40), and the north front of the building was adorned with a parterre garden. Beyond it were sixty-three acres in orchards and pasture, apparently fenced with a "ha-ha," the newest garden fad in England—a fence sunk out of sight in a ditch, like a kind of dry moat meant to keep cattle and sheep away from the house gardens while preserving an impression of seamless continuity between them and the surrounding countryside. In order to open a "visto" or view from the palace, Spotswood asked John Custis in 1717 if he might cut some trees belonging to him: "nothing but what was fitt for the fire, and for that he would pay as much as anyone gave for firewood," Custis reported, and agreed. Spotswood had the trees in question felled, and then, to make himself a second visto, proceeded to hack another swath of Custis's woods: "As to the clearing his visto, he cut down all before him such a wideness as he saw fitt," Custis wrote, indignant.

Spotswood had more plans, including converting a ravine with a brook running in it west of the palace into a "falls" garden: a series of grass terraces with stone steps cut into the slope leading down to a canal and fish pond at the bottom—a rather trendy move borrowed from Dutch gardens, much emulated on grand English estates in the 17th century. The expense, if not sheer ostentation of it, seems to have shocked the House of Burgesses, who were footing the bill. In November 1718, the Burgesses requested an accounting and an estimate of how much more money the project would swallow. Spotswood brooded for some months, then bridled: "I am loath to offer any valuation of my own gardeners . . . performances." A spat over money followed, with the governor insisting that his expenditures were low, pointing out that he was acting (moonlighting?) as landscape gardener, saving them one hundred pounds a year. The Burgesses were unmollified and eventually confronted Spotswood, who promptly walked off the job; the assembly in turn quashed the garden work, allocating "an insulting 1 pound for the completion of a 'bannio'—some sort of ornamental Italianate bathhouse," and fifty-two pounds to wrap up work on the house.[26] Spotswood turned his attention to a speculative real estate venture he had cooked up nearby. Before too long, he was replaced in office. Nevertheless, he had succeeded: accounts of visitors in later years marveled at the elegance of the palace and its grounds in a colony where such luxury was rare, calling it "a magnificent structure, finished and beautified with gates, fine gardens, offices, walks, a fine canal, orchards."[27] Anyone who goes to Williamsburg today can tour the carefully re-created palace and walk through the gardens, and appreciate the genuine artistry and ambition Spotswood brought to his work: the perfectly clipped boxwood parterres, the hedge maze and the mount, the sight lines through doorways and gates that separate each rectilinear space from the next, and the shady path around the canal that offers respite from the sun on a hot day.

To understand what Spotswood was up to in his garden, we have to go back even further, to the Elizabethan England of Shakespeare in the 16th century, then to the 14th and 15th century Italy that Shakespeare himself looked to, and then even further, to the ancient Rome that the Italians of the quattrocento and cinquecento looked to. This centuries-old DNA is discernible both in the garden's design and in his intentions. At the level of design, his garden was exclusively concerned with structure: courtyards, walks, terraces, canal, and clipped green hedges and parterres, all serving to define geometric spaces that are separate from one another yet flow into each other in sequence, with carefully controlled views from one to another, creating a sense of scale and extension. All of this careful delineation and geometry, not least the vistos, served to focus the viewer's attention back on the owner of the garden. The palace and gardens were constructed like a miniature Versailles, the vast landscape King Louis XIV of France had built in the 1660s to symbolize his absolute power over a unified France, with Spotswood himself a kind of miniature Sun King, splendid at the center of his carefully structured Virginia universe.[28]

If it sounds grandiose, it was, but it was at the same time merely a run-of-the-mill kind of striving to impress that would have seemed unremarkable in contemporary England. The lieutenant governor had executed the project in the up-to-the-minute formal mode, adopted from the Italian Renaissance, which had been influencing much of the rest of Europe since the late 16th century, as the northern countries gradually made the transition out of the medieval period to the (early) modern. In Elizabethan England, this process was richly captured by William Shakespeare's plays, which showcased the energies and ideas of the Renaissance as they reached Olde England, where business was booming and a rising commercial class was busy building new towns and cities as fast as it could and savoring the new intellectual freedoms brought by the Protestant Reformation, with its loosening of church control over learning, culture, and government. Much of it, as the plays advertise so fulsomely, was tinged with the colors and flavors of Italy—think of *Romeo and Juliet*, *Othello*, *The Two Gentlemen of Verona*, *The Merchant of Venice*, *Much Ado About Nothing*, or *The Taming of the Shrew*. (Shakespeare and his contemporaries were also deeply impressed by the discoveries streaming in from the New World: savage peoples, wild landscapes, unknown animals and plants, and these too found expression in their art: *The Tempest* is a particularly good example, with a setting inspired by the New World and personnel drawn from Italy, starting with Prospero, the Duke of Milan.)

And so it was in the garden. The medieval European garden was for the most part simple and utilitarian, planted with fruit trees, vegetables, herbs, and flowers in simple, squared beds, enclosed by high walls or thorn hedges and decorated with a minimum of apparatus, perhaps a bench, a bower, and a small source of water. Rarely was a garden open to or visible from the outside. But the Italian Renaissance changed all that. A new, rich, and assertive class of merchants and nobility built ostentatious villas outside of cities and towns, sited to maximize their views of the surroundings—and the surroundings' view of them. The garden walls came down, or were lowered, to reveal carefully framed views. Elaborate geometries of terraces, staircases, pergolas, walks, hedges, and parterres "embellished nature with art," as the stock phrase went, striating the land around the houses with architectural and horticultural form. The French word *renaissance* of course translates literally into "rebirth," and people living at the time felt that they were working toward the rebirth of the glories of classical Roman and earlier Greek civilization after the torpor of the Dark Ages. As the ancient world was properly obsessed with gardens (from the walled Persian *paradeisos,* or king's hunting garden, on), so were gardens a renewed obsession in the Renaissance. In Italy especially, the ruins of the Roman Empire and Rome itself were all around, and so became direct models for buildings and gardens. Builders imitated what they could see and unearth: loggias, courtyards, walls, colonnades, balustrades, exedras, porticos, stairs, fountains, and frescoes.

What they couldn't dig up they could read about, in the newly rediscovered books of the ancient authors, from Aristotle to Xenophon—books that had been lost to Europe for centuries but were now being copied from libraries in the Muslim world, where they had been carefully preserved, and with which Europe enjoyed a growing trade. Pliny's description of his villa near Vesuvius, Horace's of his in the Sabine Hills, and Ovid's *Metamorphoses* all became blueprints, loosely interpreted, for re-creating them with their effusion of sculpture, fountains, water staircases and rills, hidden grottoes, and *boschetti,* or groves. The classical myths and epics provided the grist for "histories" of deities, nymphs, and heroes, played out in gardens in clever, often humorous dramaturgy of temples, statues, inscriptions, topiary, mirrors, trompe l'oeil paintings, aviaries filled with singing birds, automata (early robots), and *giocchi d'acqua*—water games, waterworks that squirted and jetted and delighted visitors. An interest in natural objects and curiosities—another revival of classical science—was indulged in collections of things with intriguing textures and forms: tufa, pumice, coral, mother of pearl, stalactites, pebbles, shells, minerals, and rocks. The Cabinet of Curiosities that every discerning person of means displayed for visitors to their houses moved outside into gardens and grottoes. This astonishing diversity was echoed in the garden structure: formal, geometric spaces around buildings gave way to irregular spaces, paths, and woods farther away—contrasting art and nature, smooth with rough, close with far, light with shade. The most-visited Italian Renaissance gardens, such as the Villa d'Este, Villa Lante, Pratolino, and Villa Aldobrandini, were animated, learned, and

witty entertainments as well as demonstrations of and enticements to erudition. And they were pitched wholeheartedly as re-creations not only
of the splendor of Rome and the knowledge of Athens, but of the biblical garden of Eden, with collections of the most exotic fruits—especially
oranges and lemons, herbs and plants, many from the East of the Bible
and beyond.

Italian villas and gardens captured, for contemporaries, the genius of
the age as much as did the new tastes in poetry, painting, and theater
that the Renaissance produced. Admired by an ever-increasing stream of
travelers from abroad who came to see the wonders of this newly reborn
world, Italy was deemed "the world's great Garden"[29] as well as the world's
great vacation resort for the footloose rich. As of the mid-1500s, many of
those travelers were English, and they liked what they saw, and brought
some of it home as souvenirs: Roman statues and other antique bric-a-
brac, and paintings with which to decorate the houses and gardens they
increasingly built in the Italian style. By 1575, some Elizabethan English
gardens that had been medieval a generation before had sprouted terraces, loggias, fountains, obelisks, and marble statues of Roman emperors. Nonesuch Palace sported a grove and a "wilderness." By the 1600s,
oranges grew in coal-heated conservatories all over Britain.[30]

The country villa became de rigueur among those who could afford
it, and more and more could; with reform of land laws and rising prices
for grain and other farm products, many gentry landowners moved from
the city to their country estates and managed them for profit, expanding their farming operations by "enclosing" or seizing common lands and
woods. (This posh back-to-the-land movement was given a head start by
a series of vexed marriages and a fight with the pope—that is, by King
Henry VIII, when he seized the Roman Catholic Church's property in
England in 1542 and handed it out to his supporters.)[31] In the first half
of the next century, Inigo Jones, architect to King Charles I, imported
the newest Italian mode in villas, which he copied from Andrea Palladio, architect to the Venetian nobility in the mid-16th century, who
had in turn copied details from Roman law courts and attached them
to the new suburban mansions he designed for rich Venice merchants.

Jones also brought movable stage scenery and the proscenium arch into English theater, and staged several famous "masques" for the playwright Ben Jonson, Shakespeare's contemporary, set in gardens complete with painted perspectives, ornate iron gates, and cool grottoes.[32]

A trickle of aristocrats and upper gentry touring Italy became a flood of lower gentry and bourgeoisie in the late 17th century, known as the age of the Grand Tour, ravenous to visit the ancient Roman sites they read about in their newly trendy classics—Ovid, Seneca, Cicero, and Virgil—as well as the modern marvels of Italy, and toting encyclopedic guidebooks like Richard Lassels's 1670 *The Voyage of Italy: With the Characters Of The People, and the description of the chief Townes, Churches, Monasteries, Tombes, Librairies, Pallaces, Villas, Gardens, Pictures, Statues, Antiquities: As Also Of The Interest, Government, Riches, Force &c of all the Princes.* They were eager to translate these myriad wonders into English, and they did, prompting even more interest in Rome and Italy.

What was the urgency? Having taste *worked*. In Italy, from the beginning, villas and gardens were important weapons in the Machiavellian PR battles that accompanied the jockeying for power and prominence between ever-shifting factions of princes, dukes, and popes—for which Machiavelli wrote the bestselling script, *The Prince,* the modern world's first self-help bestseller, widely read by the English. British elites readily adopted the practice. Aristocrats and gentry had their portraits painted in their gardens, dined ostentatiously in them, and threw masques and balls in them.[33] All factions—Protestants and Catholics, Crown and Parliament, Tudor and Stuart—had their prescriptions for the right garden, and garden design took on a sharply political valence. Royalists used the formal elements of Italian gardens, the elaborate geometries of terraces, beds, and parterres, long walks and vistas, to advertise their dominion.

During the English Civil War of 1642, many royalist gardens in this vein were destroyed, but the style was revived when the exiled Charles II, hosted in France by Louis XIV, returned across the channel in 1660.[34] The opposing forces of Parliament derided these "absolutist" gardens as symbols of royal arrogance, but also as impractical, wasteful uses of land that ought to be made productive. They instead prescribed a different, more modest, *true* Italian garden, unpolluted by French inventions or gigantism, patterned on Roman models of the *latifundia*, the farmed estates of the patrician elite, with an emphasis on (profitable) agriculture and a vision of a genteel retirement to the country eagerly cribbed from Virgil's *Georgics* and Horace's *Odes*. They extolled the supposed Roman virtues of simplicity and productivity, and variety, as contrasted with the corruption of the city and the court.

From this fundamental conflict arose an enduring alignment in British politics, society, and culture: Court versus Country parties, representing pro-monarchy and Anglican church and pro-mixed government and dissenting faith factions, which clashed, in one form or another, back and forth through the long oscillation of revolutions and restorations of British history. The garden became a kind of battleground of opposing ideas, and the "right" garden style rose along with the ascendant faction. The sole constant was the claim that designers were returning to classical models. The Country party interpreted this in a predictable way: anti-royalist, which meant anti-France, inevitably held up as a misinterpretation of Italy—too uniform, barren, inflexible, too autocratic in short. Country intellectuals and artists countered with a rising appreciation for "nature" as the embodiment of British freedoms, more appropriate to a British garden, and not by chance in synch with their economic base in agrarianism and landholding. Better to mix the variety of formal gardens with informal groves, in sympathy with the belief in mixed government and limited monarchy, to express the balance of power, the checks and balances the Country party advocated.[35] (The specific formula changed with every generation. So, with the ascension of Protestant King William and Queen Mary in 1689, an anti-France, pro-Dutch political alignment was translated directly into the garden in the form of the more compact, compartmentalized Dutch version of Italy, featuring topiary, hedged enclosures, canals, fish ponds, and "falls" or grass terraces.)

All of this jockeying for the aesthetic high ground spawned considerable anxiety and fanned a deep, constant line of criticism of house and garden aspiration: that is, the *faux pas* and *mal gout* of the *nouveaux riches*— words that ironically still cut more cleanly in French. In the new commercial society, people from lower than aristocratic stations, and perhaps less than perfectly pure blood lines, made money, some of them piles of it, in manufacturing, banking, real estate, foreign trade, tobacco, sugar plantations, or shipping. And they spent it to fit in with the established elite. (This phenomenon—the nouveaux riches trying to buy access to the club through demonstrations of taste—was not new, not even in the Renaissance: the ancient Greeks and Romans loved to talk about it, after they had covered the topics of war and sex and political intrigues.) In Britain, all political loyalties were sensitive to social climbing, badly done. From the beginning new gardens might be criticized: as too big, too gaudy, trying too hard. The phrase "gild the lily" is usually attributed to Shakespeare, but the actual line from Shakespeare's play *King John* is "To gild refined gold, to paint the lily / To throw a perfume on the violet. . . . / Is wasteful and ridiculous excess." Even John Evelyn, the leading garden designer in England from the 1640s to 1700, though a royalist and an admirer of French gardens, believed there was too much luxury and expense in Roman ones—harbingers of its decline, in his estimation. English gardens instead should be both "natural and magnificent,"[36] a balance of nature and art.

This English fretting about how best to imitate the true Italian, classical garden is how the English arrived at their own, modern garden—and, surprisingly, it is how, in imitating formal Italian gardens, the English garden became curiously informal and studiously "natural." It is also, by another twist of the double helix of imitation and inspiration, how America arrived at its own free, democratic garden—the one many of us instinctively hew to today. Between the time Governor Spotswood laid out his grounds at Williamsburg and Jefferson laid out his at Monticello, a sea change was visited on the English garden—so much so that the latter appeared completely unrelated to the former, its direct ancestor. It was an astonishing turn of the garden path, a shift that seemed at the time like a revolution, and young Thomas Jefferson, characteristically, was in its vanguard.

Even in college at William & Mary, Jefferson had design on the brain, planning how to make his own house and garden while keeping abreast of European trends. He began acquiring books on the subjects, including one on classical architecture (either Leoni's edition of Andrea Palladio or James Gibbs's *Book of Architecture*, 1728, Palladio-inspired).[37] When he came home to Shadwell plantation in 1766, instead of focusing on it he set about leveling the mountaintop at Monticello, an undeveloped section of his inheritance. He became a magistrate and parish vestryman and in 1767 was admitted to the bar. Two years later he started building the house. It was Palladian, two stories with a central portico of two stacked colonnades supporting a triangular pediment, clearly inspired by plate 41 of the Leoni Palladio volume.[38] Palladio was all the rage in England at the time among the cognoscenti. Even Dr. Morgan at the College of Philadelphia, whom Jefferson visited for a smallpox inoculation, waxed enthusiastically about the buildings he'd seen on a recent trip to England. While there were a handful of Palladian-inspired plantation houses around—Byrd's Westover boasted some Palladian details, and Mount Airy in Richmond County, Virginia, was copied from Palladian books like Gibbs's—there was nothing nearly so sophisticated and au courant.[39] Jefferson hated the buildings of Virginia, which were nearly all wooden, vulnerable to fire, and generally poorly constructed. Indeed, his childhood home at nearby Shadwell burned down during construction of the new house at Monticello, in 1770. On his little mountain in the Virginia hills, young Thomas Jefferson was making an unambiguous statement about who Thomas Jefferson was and would be.

The garden he had in mind was, if anything, even more rarefied. As with the house, he had been planning it from early on. In 1767, two years before beginning to build the house, he was already planting fruit trees on the slope south of the site. In 1771, as the house itself neared completion, he turned his attention to the landscape, making notes on the back of his pocket-size Memorandum Book. He laid out an astonishing landscape vision: somewhat lugubrious, fairly decadent, and shamelessly romantic for someone who is celebrated as a master of sober and statesmanlike nonfiction prose. It was also in the latest taste, which is not surprising in a smart, passionate young man taken with cutting-edge fashion in things intellectual and material—yet it is totally unlike the no-nonsense Jefferson most Americans think we know. He began his plan with a graveyard, to be hidden away in "some unfrequented vale in the park, where there is 'no sound to break the stillness but a brook, that bubbling winds among the weeds; no mark of any human shape that had been there, unless the skeleton of some poor wretch, Who sought that place out to despair and die in.'" (He took the lines from a popular English play, *The Fair Penitent*, by Nicholas Rowe.) "Let it be among antient and venerable oaks," he specified, and added: "intersperse some gloomy evergreens." The "burying ground" would be a sixty-foot-diameter circle, surrounded by "an untrimmed hedge of cedar, or of a stone wall with a holly hedge on it in the form below," and he sketched two labyrinths for an approach: one with straight paths, one a spiral, with four-foot-wide paths, by design too narrow for two people walking abreast. "In the center of it erect a small Gothic temple of antique appearance, appropriate one half to the use of my own family, the other of strangers, servants, etc. erect pedestals with urns, etc., and proper inscriptions." He went on: "on the grave of a favorite and faithful servant might be a pyramid erected of rough rock-stone; the pedestal made plain to receive an inscription. Let the exit of the spiral . . . look on a small and distant part of the blue mountains. In the middle of the temple an alter, the sides of turf, the top of plain stone. Very little light, perhaps none at all, save only the feeble ray of a half extinguished lamp." Jefferson proceeded to describe another temple, to be built on the steep hillside north of the house near a natural spring. It was to be part of an elaborate water feature built by first leveling the ground below spring level, so that the water would fall onto a terrace by the temple "in the form of a cascade," before dropping off another terrace into a cistern, then led westward to fall off another terrace. Over the cistern, "which may be a bath or anything else," he wrote, would be built a two-story temple, with a roof that "may be Chinese, Grecian, or in taste of the Lantern of Demosthenes at Athens."

Near the temple would be a sleeping figure reclined on a plain marble slab, which was inscribed with four lines of pseudo-classical Latin that

Jefferson knew to be associated with water and grottoes.[40] The whole arrangement would be planted with native beech and aspen trees, and the surrounding forest cut to open a vista to the mill pond, the Rivanna River in the valley below, and perhaps the town of Charlottesville farther west. All around would be low, fragrant plants: "abundance of Jessamine, Honeysuckle, sweet briar, etc." And beneath the temple, hidden from view and rain, would be an Aeolian harp, played mournfully by the shifting winds, unseen. He immediately thought twice, though, probably in view of the expense of leveling the slope and building the structure, and proceeded to sketch a less labor-intensive but no less baroque grotto to be dug into the hill: "build up the sides and arch with stiff clay. Cover this with moss. spangle it with translucent pebbles from Hanovertown, and beautiful shells from the shore at Burwell's ferry. pave the floor with pebbles. let the spring enter at the center of the grotto, pretty high up the side, and trickle down, or fall by a spout into a basin, from which it may pass off through the grotto."[41]

In addition, Jefferson planned a zoological garden as "an asylum for hares, squirrels, pheasants, partridges, and every other wild animal (except those of prey) . . . procure a buck-elk, to be, as it were, monarch of the wood; but keep him shy, that his appearance may not lose its effect by too much familiarity. A buffalo might be confined also." And he made a note that his neighbor, in exchange for some unspecified legal work, had agreed to deed him the peak and flank of the hill that rises four hundred feet above Monticello to the south. On it he planned to erect a tower five stories high, with superposed architectural "orders," that is, types of columns—a Palladian move meant to illustrate the hierarchy of social and spiritual orders. He would call it "Montalto," high mountain, and likely had in mind a "sham" constructed on only one side, like a Hollywood stage set, meant to catch the visitor's eye.

Where did these visions come from? The moody, poetic graveyard, the spangle of pebbles in the grotto, the Chinese roof, and the Gothic temple, bizarrely juxtaposed with his sober, strict Palladian house? The simple answer: right out of Jefferson's European books, as had the house. The temples were taken straight from Gibbs's plates 67 and 69. The

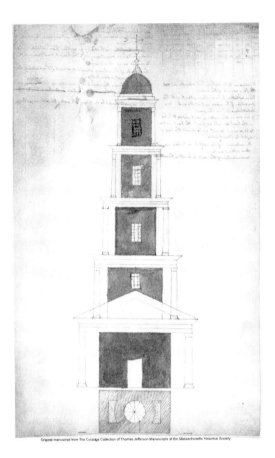

Thomas Jefferson, observation tower, probably 1771. (Massachusetts Historical Society)

Original manuscript from The Coolidge Collection of Thomas Jefferson Manuscripts at the Massachusetts Historical Society.

Lantern of Demosthenes (now called the Choragic Monument of Lysicrates) was illustrated in Dutch artist Jacob Spon's 1679 *Voyage d'Italie*, a copy of which Jefferson owned.[42] On the garden side, the evidence is equally clear. In 1865 he bought a copy of William Shenstone's *Works*, published just a year before, which offered the latest in the new English garden style. Shenstone wrote: "GARDENING may be divided into three species—kitchen gardening—parterre gardening—and landskip, or picturesque-gardening. . . . It consists in pleasing the imagination with scenes of grandeur, beauty and variety. Convenience merely has no share here; any farther than as it pleases the imagination."[43] He was interested in series of scenes that would stimulate the mind with ideas and associations. At the Leasowes, his house near Birmingham, Shenstone created a bucolic landscape of lawns, a lake, and woods, studded with urns bearing memorial inscriptions to his friends, a grotto with a Latin poem about the Nereids, and a grove dedicated to Virgil.

The classical allusions were standard by this time. What was different was the form—or lack of form—in the garden. There were no hedges, no parterres, no straight drives, everywhere simply the artful appearance of unreconstructed nature—an intentional paradox that Shenstone elevated to a rule, as in this example: "THE side-trees in a vista should be so circumscribed as to afford a probability that they grew by nature."[44] Shenstone hadn't invented this exacting naturalism; he was expressing a new British consensus for "a much more Natural and Promiscuous Disposition" of garden elements, in the words of his colleague Joseph Switzer.[45] The new naturalism had been evolving on the margins of the formal garden over perhaps 150 years, and by the time Shenstone wrote, art had been programmatically subordinated to nature, as he made clear: "Art, indeed, is often requisite to collect and epitomize the beauties of nature, but should never be suffered to set her mark upon them: I mean in regard to those articles that are of nature's province: the shaping of ground, the planting of trees, and the disposition of lakes and rivulets." The exception was architecture: "buildings, useful or ornamental," and even "RUINATED" ones, all of which Shenstone felt made "nature appear doubly beautiful by the contrast her structures furnish." And Jefferson read him clearly.

Shenstone's philosophy reflected a general drift in Western Europe toward looking at "nature," which had once meant human nature or the nature of God, and seeing wild nature, outside of us, in much the way we think about it now.[46] Throughout the 17th and 18th centuries, there were three major forces working in this direction in Britain, reshaping the models glimpsed on the Grand Tour and evoked in the classical texts into a distinctively English garden, reflecting ideas of correct English character and nationhood. One was bald politics: the ongoing struggles imposed their symbolisms on the shapes of gardens and the attitudes of their makers. To the ascendant Country faction, which came in the 18th century to be called the Whig party, a truly English garden must be more "natural" and free to reflect the freedom of English subjects. The Whigs, who subscribed to a view of history that holds that the progress of civilization is inevitably onward toward greater liberty and justice—a view to which Jefferson most of the time also subscribed—adopted naturalism as their totem, since doing so implied that their claims to power were "natural." And, naturally, the nature depicted in Whig gardens resembled the English countryside that provided these landowners' living.

Another force was natural science, which, by the 17th century in Britain had taken on a distinctive form known as empiricism, based on a conviction that true knowledge can only derive from the physical examination of things themselves, and through experiment when possible, as opposed to the abstract reasoning advocated by René Descartes, the French philosopher. This was the legacy of Isaac Newton, Francis Bacon, and Robert Boyle, the three English giants of the 17th century scientific revolution.

The third force transforming the role of nature was aesthetic and philosophical. As the Renaissance gave way to the Enlightenment, reason replaced faith and religion as the central organizing principle, making the natural world a worthy object of artistic and philosophical contemplation. Increasing European contact with the rest of the world, including the Americas, stoked a fascination with the savage, untamed, and uncivilized. Again, the geographical locus of these changing representations was Italy, while their forms moved from poetry into painting and then, belatedly, as the pattern has always been, into the garden. English tourists traipsed through the Italian countryside with their copies of Ovid and Horace and Virgil, seeking, in the words of the landscape theorist Joseph Addison, to compare "the natural face of the country with the lanskips that the Poets have given us of it." What they encountered, thousands of years after some of the books they carried were written, were modern Italian arrangements on the same ground described in the texts—no ancient gardens survived anywhere. But no matter; what they saw they sketched, captured, remembered, and re-created at home.

And they looked at pictures of the same landscapes drawn and painted by the Italian masters and by a new vanguard of northern European artists who came to imitate them, especially Claude Lorrain and Nicolas

Gaspard Poussin, *The Falls of Tivoli*, 1661. (Wikimedia Commons)

Poussin early in the first part of the 17th century, and somewhat later Peter Paul Rubens, Jacob van Ruisdael, and Gaspard Dughet, aka Gaspard Poussin, the elder Poussin's pupil and brother-in-law. By cross-pollination, these "landskips"—meaning "painted landscapes" (an Anglicization of the Dutch word for a description of land, *landschap*)—became models for how Englishmen ought to read Latin poetry to discern within it blueprints for their gardens.[47] What they saw in these canvases looked more and more "natural" or wild by the year, emphasizing nature's unruly grandeur, ruggedness, and chiaroscuro more than its orderly settlement or productivity. Later, in Britain, wars with France and economic depressions redirected many would-be British tourists to Italy to have a look at the more remote parts of their own country, especially the mountains of Wales, the Lake District, and Scotland, with their misty and rugged peaks, cascades, and defiles. The imagery in British paintings and poems followed suit, and obediently, so too did the taste in gardens, looking directly to painting to lead the way. As Shenstone wrote: "landskip should contain variety enough to form a picture upon canvas; and this is no bad test, as I think the landskip painter is the gardener's best designer."[48] The "landscape garden" style that developed eventually came to be called "picturesque," which, in the words of William Gilpin, one of the style's evangelists and popularizers, meant "that kind of beauty which would look well in a picture."[49] Gardens became pictures—of nature.

As influential as Shenstone's theories no doubt were, Jefferson's early vision for Monticello derived from a single English garden: the estate of the poet Alexander Pope, at Twickenham, Middlesex, outside London on the Thames River, where all the many strands of the picturesque garden were plaited into a single braid for the first time. Pope had begun his garden in 1719, and in the next half century it became a model for legions of other enthusiasts of the new style, including Shenstone. (We know that in August 1771, Jefferson recommended a list of garden books to his friend Robert Skipwith, including Shenstone's *Works*, Alexander Pope's *Works*, and William Chambers's *Chinese Designs*.)[50] Pope was the 18th century's most important English satirist, essayist, and translator, and his versions of Homer made him wealthy enough to take up an estate and remake it into his own translation of the classical paradise. The garden he designed retained some of its existing elements, such as formal gardens near the house, including a kitchen garden, and orchards, but he also added most of the standard baroque English-Italian knickknacks of his time: a "mount" or conical mound of earth with a circular path to the top, an orangery, a grove with meandering paths, and a grotto Pope had excavated that had multiple rooms, a flowing spring, and decorations made out of his collection of unusual minerals, crystals, rocks, and shells.

Pope was part of a circle of English literati and cognoscenti of Italy that formed around another ardent fan of Palladio, Lord Burlington, who had built, at his estate in Chiswick, a series of noticeably scaled-down re-creations of Palladian villas, themselves tarted-up imitations of Roman ones. The very wealthy Burlington was a patron of the history painter turned garden designer William Kent, with whom he collaborated on a garden filled with homages to favorite scenes visited on Burlington's two Italian Grand Tours (one trip an impressive ten years long, from 1715 to 1725). In addition to the Palladian villas he had built several temples and a "bagnio," all juxtaposed with a hodgepodge of "Gothick" structures: ruins, castles, abbeys, some original, most shams, strewn about an expan-

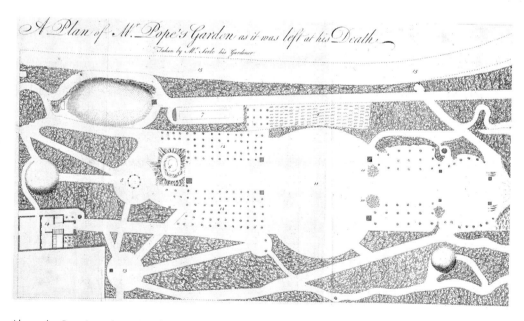

Alexander Pope's garden at Twickenham, plan by John Searle. (Beinecke Rare Book and Manuscript Library, Yale University)

sive picturesque landscape garden of woods striated with radiating and serpentine walks.[51] The Gothic irruption was a direct result of a growing appreciation for ancient British history among Burlington's Whig political set, thought to provide local analogues to Roman and Greek antecedents without the taint of French or English royal power.

As the influence of Twickenham, Chiswick, and a growing number of other estates grew, the new English garden, called the *jardin anglais* on the Continent by enthusiastic imitators—continued to metastasize, soaking up influences as fast as it could, prefiguring the imperial eclecticism of the Victorians in the 19th century and the constant raiding of cultural margins by successive 20th century avant-gardes. The garden at Twickenham was thick with Roman allusions in the form of temples, urns, statues, inscriptions, and an obelisk to honor Pope's mother. He planned to install a series of statues along the riverfront: two Roman river gods joined by a pantheon of illustrious mortals—Virgil, Homer, Marcus Aurelius, and Cicero—all flanked by a pair of swans.[52] Pope searched his library for inspiration: in Pliny's accounts of his villas, Cicero's of his Villa Tusculum, at Frascati, outside Rome, in Homer, in Horace, and in Virgil's *Georgics* above all. He had never been to Italy, but this didn't stop him from borrowing choice bits from Italian gardens he had read about. What resulted was a kind of garden fusion cuisine, an amalgamation of ancient Greek and Roman, Renaissance and modern Italian imitations of these, and English imitations of those, thrown together without concern for chronology or style. What was distinctive about it, though, was what was absent: gone were most of the formal elements, especially topiary. Pope replaced these with a loose knitting together of fields, orchards, woods, and meandering paths, all composed to form a series of pictures of pastoral landscape scenes (complete but for the shepherds who lend the pastoral genre its name), as though one were walking through an art gallery by stepping into each canvas and proceeding to the next one.

Pope's new, natural style was cutting-edge. It was in no small part motivated by disdain for the fact that people of a middling sort had by that time taken up the Italian-Dutch fashion in the garden, eagerly acquiring topiaries from the local "town-Gardiner," thus requiring elite tastemakers like Pope to move on to something less common. Shenstone shared this disdain of that presumptuous nouveau-riche he called "the citizen" and formulated a crisp warning to those who considered themselves au courant that they were not:

> *The taste of the citizen and of the mere peasant are in all respects the same. The former gilds his balls; paints his stonework and statues white; plants his trees in lines or circles; cuts his yew-trees foursquare or conic; or gives them, what he can, of the resemblance of birds, or bears, or men; squirts up his rivulet in jetteaus; in short, admires no part of nature, but her ductility; exhibits every thing that is glaring, that implies expence, or that effects a surprize because it is unnatural. The peasant is his admirer.*[53]

This trend jibed with another, increasingly popular inclination, drawn directly from classical writers but supporting the contemporary fantasy of a virtuous rural retirement. This idea appealed to genteel members of Pope's generation who were critics of the ruling aristocracy and the government (and who possessed rural lands to retire to). Pope the poet loved the idea of a Virgilian self-sufficiency for its overall aesthetic glow, but, luckily for his career, it also meshed nicely with the real-world need of Whiggish landowners to make money at farming. The era saw a massive campaign for promoting "improvement" or "husbandry": the rational, capitalist exploitation of agricultural lands for profit ("utility") married to a concern with pleasure and taste (called "beauty"). The union of utility and beauty was dubbed the *ferme ornée,* the ornamented farm (a concept, again, for some reason most appealing to the English *en français*), which became in the opinion of leading authors the patriotic duty of all enlightened landlords. Joseph Switzer admonished good landowners to practice "Rural and Extensive Gardening" with "woods, pasture, land, etc . . . open to all view, etc."[54] As enclosure pushed common people off their ancestral lands and industrialization with its satanic mills pulled them from it, husbandry became an improbably attractive avocation among the landed classes: engravings of pedigreed cows, pigs, and hens and prints of gentry men in frock coats plowing fields took over parlor walls.[55]

The irony is that Pope's estate was too small to operate as a real farm, even had he tried, and was for all intents and purposes little more than a plush suburban escape for a wealthy city dweller—as had been the case with the Roman and Italian baroque villas. And in fact, Pope and his garden became famous and attracted just such people, with no interest in farming, making the village of Twickenham a trendy spot, a posh garden suburb for the late 18th century A-list.[56]

Even at the tender age of twenty-eight, Jefferson was already powerfully attracted to the notion of a genteel country retirement; in his 1771 reverie he also planned an inscription, taken from Horace's second epode:[57]

> Blessed is he—remote, as were the mortals
> Of the first age, from business and its cares—
> Who plows paternal fields with his own oxen
> Free from the bonds of credit or of debt
> His life escapes from the contentious forum,
> And shuns the insolent thresholds of the great
> Free to recline, now under aged ilex,
> Now in frank sunshine on the matted grass,
> While through the steep banks slip the gliding waters,
> And birds are plaintive in the forest glens,
> And limpid fountains, with a drowsy tinkle,
> Invite the light wings of the noonday sleep.

This heady brew is what Jefferson was drinking when he recorded his 1771 vision for Monticello. It was impressive, especially for someone so young who had traveled so little. But it wasn't unknown, even in the colonies. Most rich landowners, in America as in Britain, stuck with the traditional formal taste—such as the lavish formal garden built at Henry Middleton's Middleton Place, near Charleston, South Carolina, in 1741. But some progressive American gentlemen who had seen the new style in England were constructing notable examples at home—including Middleton's brother William, who had built at his 1730 house, Crowfield, a pond with a mount in it crowned by a Roman temple.[58] As early as 1730 there was a ha-ha at Stratford Hall plantation in Virginia; a little later, picturesque-style gardens were reported at country houses around Philadelphia, including William Hamilton's The Woodlands, an estate Jefferson would have known of, and perhaps visited. By the 1760s, ads for Gothic and Chinese-style garden buildings ran in several American newspapers. Richard Stockton, who had seen Pope's garden at Twickenham, more or less copied it at his estate Morven, in Princeton, New Jersey. In 1762, Mrs. Anne Grant, author of *Memoirs of an American Lady*, recalled how she watched the British garrison of Fort Oswego, New York, under the command of a Major Duncan, kill time by building a landscape garden in the middle of the northern woods: "To see the sudden creation of this garden, one would think the genius of the place [Ah Virgil! Ah Pope!] obeyed the wand of an enchanter; but it is not every gardener who can employ some hundred men. A summerhouse in a tree, a fishpond, a gravel walk, were finished before the end of May."[59]

Nevertheless, none of Jefferson's 1771 ideas were ever built. In 1772 he married the widow Martha Wayles Skelton and moved into the still-unfinished house. The next year her father died, doubling the couple's holdings.[60] Jefferson planned flower beds: two rectangular ones at the west front (the "back" of the house, facing the lawn and the serpentine path), and at the east front a semicircle to plant with shrubs and trees. Neither was built, though he did plant flowers, as his *Garden Book* attests. Seventeen seventy-four was Jefferson's best gardening year to that point (and would be for a long time, as things turned out). He had leveled out his first vegetable garden, 668 feet by 80 feet, on the south slope below Mulberry Row—the line of buildings along a drive named for an allée of mulberry trees he had planted in 1771 to screen the structures from the house, and which eventually numbered nineteen, including the stable, plantation office, joinery, nail factory, log houses for the slaves, and "necessaries" or outhouses. His lists reflect a heavy Italian influence in the vegetables planted that spring, sowed in rows "and distinguished them by sticking numbered sticks in the beds. Aglio di Toscania. Garlic . . . No. 15. Radicchio di Pistoia. Succory, or Wild Endive . . . 26. Cipolle bianche . . . 41. Salvastrella di Pisa . . . 42. Sorrel. Acetosa di Pisa . . . 46. Coclearia di Pisa . . . 47. Cavol Capuccio Spanola di Pisa . . . 56. Prezzemolo. parsely."

One factor may have been that in 1773, a Tuscan gentleman named Philip Mazzei had called on Jefferson looking for land on which to start a farm, for which he had brought a dozen or so indentured Italians and seed stocks. Jefferson, who loved Italy (though he'd never seen it), was excited and offered him the use of two thousand acres nearby, where Mazzei planted olives, grapevines, and vegetables.[61] The Revolution interrupted everyone's plans. (Later in life, Jefferson would ask Mazzei to send to Europe for four vignerons, each one able to play a different instrument, to come to Monticello to make wine.) In the fateful year 1775, Jefferson, then a rising talent in the Virginia House of Burgesses, was drafted to represent his colony at the Second Continental Congress in Philadelphia. Observers in that city were astonished at the young man's entrance into town in a fancy phaeton with four liveried footmen, his black slaves, hanging on the corners. "Yet another of the Sultans of the South has deigned to arrive," read a local newspaper.[62] From then on, Jefferson had little time for gardening. (Though in 1778, with the war still raging, he bought books on the latest English architecture and gardens, including Thomas Whately's *Observations on Modern Gardening* and George Mason's *Essay on Design in Gardening*.) He was elected governor of Virginia in 1779 and managed to add landscape gardening to the William & Mary curriculum[63] before the war came to the region and he was literally run out of the capital by pursuing British troops, in 1781. That year his daughter died; the next year, his wife. In 1783 and '84, he was a delegate to the new U.S. Congress, in Philadelphia and New York, from where he still managed to design additions to the Monticello house (the two long wings or "dependencies"—which were eventually built) as well as a series of projected garden buildings: domed temples after Palladio and Burlington, a Chinese tower after one in Chambers, and various octagonal schemes (which were never built).[64]

In 1784, Jefferson sailed to Europe to join John Adams and Benjamin Franklin, the American minister to France, in seeking French support for the war. Inside a year, Adams was transferred to London and Franklin returned to Philadelphia, with Jefferson succeeding him.[65] He found Paris a revelation, like a dream world, with its elegance, sophistication, wealth, buildings, art, and background hum of erotic excitement, added to its feverish, idealistic political discussions—just his kind of place. Besides his formal diplomatic duties, he mingled with progressive parts of the aristocracy that were in favor of the American republican experiment, attending rounds of parties and dinners hosted by social shakers and studded with brilliant artists, writers, architects, scientists, and philosophers, and where ideas and aesthetics were passionately and elegantly debated. He was living in the windup to the French Revolution—exhilarating days for the author of the Declaration of Independence. Indeed, he was in the thick of it: hosting dinners with some of the leading intellectuals in the French opposition and composing the first draft of the Declaration of Rights that the American Revolutionary War hero the Marquis de Lafayette would submit to the French National Assembly in 1789.[66]

Yet it seems that he spent most of his time in gardens: the royal forest at Marly, the Tuileries, the Jardin du Roi, the Jardins de Luxembourg, the Bois de Boulogne, and many private gardens, including that of Madame de Tessé, the aunt of Lafayette. In addition to the celebrated formal gardens of André Le Nôtre, the Paris region was absolutely thick with *jardins anglais*, which Jefferson lapped up: the gaggle of picturesque follies in the Bois de Boulogne, the wooden bridges, temples, and towers at the Comte d'Artois' Bagatelle, the "anglo-chinois" garden at Simon-Charles Boutin's Tivoli, and the incredible Désert de Retz, built by the Baron de Monville beginning in 1774, with its Temple of Pan, grotto, pyramid, Chinese house, and Ruined Column, a four-story house built inside an enormous, ersatz fluted column, designed to look as though its top had ominously cracked off.[67] At his own residence on the Champs-Elysées, the Hôtel de Langéac, Jefferson grew American corn (which he ate green), sweet potatoes, and watermelons, and toyed with relandscaping the grounds in the picturesque style, actually drawing two plans depicting meandering paths in place of the formal layout (these are the oldest surviving picturesque garden plans by an American). That he even considered revamping the garden is illuminating: the place was big—a three-story house with three separate suites, stables, and a full-time gardener (to say nothing of the maids, cooks, and coachman) to tend the extensive grounds; the rent on the whole lot cost more than his annual salary.[68]

Beginning in early August of 1786, Minister Jefferson permitted himself to spend nearly every day for six weeks visiting gardens, architecture, and art with a young married woman named Maria Cosway, the

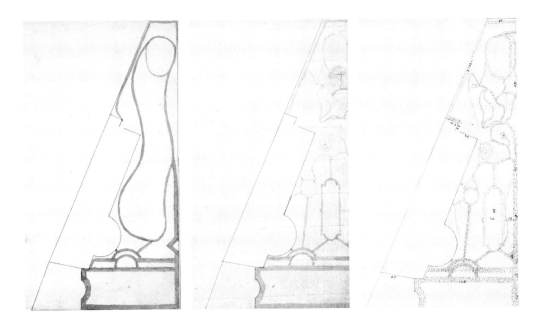

Jefferson's sketches for the Hôtel de Langéac, Paris. (The Huntington Library, San Marino, California)

twenty-seven-year-old Italian-born wife of a prominent English min-iature portraitist. Maria was reportedly irresistible: flirtatious and gor-geous, with blue eyes and curly blond locks, an accomplished musician and painter herself. (Born to a British father and an Italian mother in Florence, Maria studied art in Florence, Rome, and London; exhibited at the Royal Academy; and became a well-known figure, apart from her unfaithful husband, twenty years her senior.)[69] Jefferson was smitten. He sometimes didn't show up for meetings, sending an underling instead. The pair jaunted all around Paris and beyond, to Versailles, to Marly, or to the *jardin anglais* at St.-Germain-en-Laye. In one garden, Jefferson vaulted over a fountain and broke his right—writing—wrist. This gambol laid him up and effectively ended the affair; before he was back in action, the Cosways had returned to London. (The two carried on a somewhat tortured correspondence for a while after, including Jefferson's famous "Head and Heart" letter, with its staged dialogue between the intellect and the emotions—the wellspring of many books, novels, and films.)[70] Even with winsome Maria out of the picture, Jefferson continued his af-fair with his other love interest—gardens. He traveled everywhere, and everywhere he went he looked at architecture and toured gardens: Hol-land, Germany, the south of France, and of course Italy, which he visited with the stated object of researching rice culture and other agricultural topics of potential economic interest in the United States. He sent back olive trees, vines, and rice varieties. Though he never made it south of Florence or saw Rome itself, what he did see in Italy stirred him: he "took a peep into Elysium," he wrote.[71]

In March and April of 1786, he traveled to England, ostensibly on mat-ters of diplomacy, but spent a great deal of his time touring estate gardens with John Adams and his wife, Abigail. He hated English architecture, even though much of it was inspired by Palladio, calling it "the most wretched style I ever saw,"[72] but was deeply impressed by the gardens. In a letter to his close Virginian friend John Page he wrote: "The gardening in that country is the article in which it surpasses all the earth. I mean their pleasure gardening. This, indeed, went far beyond my ideas." As a guidebook he consulted a copy of the Thomas Whately book he'd bought in 1778, in which each of the sixteen gardens they saw was described: Chiswick, Hampton Court, Twickenham, Esther-Place, Claremont, Painshill, Woburn, Caversham, Wotton, Stowe, the Leasowes, Hagley, Blenheim, Enfield Chase, Moor Park, and Kew. Jefferson found Whately's descriptions "remarkable for their exactness" and so made few additional notes. "My inquiries were directed chiefly to such practical things as might enable me to estimate the expense of making and maintaining a garden in that style," he wrote. Accordingly, he made a point of counting the gardeners (two hundred at Blenheim, Oxfordshire), inquiring into the cost of things (seven thousand pounds for the grotto at Painshill, Surrey),[73] and took notes on shortcomings and whether they were due to limitations of topography or of design. He universally disliked straight walks and drives: at Stowe, he wrote, "the straight approach is very ill"; at Caversham, "This straight walk has an ill effect."[74] On the whole he was dispassionate but picky. At Burlington's Chiswick, likely one of his inspirations when first imagining Monticello, he wrote only: "A garden of about six acres; the octagonal dome has an ill effect, both within and without; the garden still shows too much of art. An obelisk of very ill effect; another in the middle of the pond useless."

At the Leasowes, almost certainly a model for his 1771 plans, Jefferson was not impressed:

> *Now the property of Mr. Horne by purchase. One hundred and*
> *fifty acres within the walk. The waters small. This is not even an*
> *ornamented farm—it is only a grazing farm with a path round*
> *it, here and there a seat of board, rarely anything better. Archi-*
> *tecture has contributed nothing. The obelisk is of brick. Shenstone*
> *had but three hundred pounds a year, and ruined himself by what*
> *he did to this farm. It is said that he died of the heartaches that*
> *his debts occasioned him.*[75]

This dismissiveness reveals the level of his expectations, and his intentions for Monticello. He was aiming higher. And, characteristically, he failed to see in Shenstone's fate the clear warning of what that aspira-

View of William Shenstone's Leasowes and Priory by H. F. James. (The British Library)

tion might cost him. His companion, on the other hand, found that the Leasowes "is the simplest and plainest, but the most rural of all."[76] Adams grasped the political and social costs that the ostentation in front of them incurred on a society as a whole—namely, monarchy and monopoly; he would have been aware that at that time about four hundred families owned one-quarter of the agricultural land in England. He remarked sarcastically: "a national debt of two hundred and seventy-four millions sterling accumulated by jobs, contracts, salaries, and pensions, in the course of a century might easily produce all this magnificence of architecture and landscaping."[77] Adams's attitude was properly republican, but it was also regional—a New England dislike of aristocratic ostentation that was not shared by southern would-be aristocrats like Jefferson. He wrote in his diary: "It will be long, I hope, before Ridings, Parks, Pleasure Grounds, Gardens and ornamented farms grow so much in fashion in America." Yet Adams took a kind of Jeffersonian solace in the idea that the natural endowment of the new continent might save Americans from the temptations of garden fashion: "But Nature has done greater Things and furnished nobler Materials there. The Oceans, Island, Rivers, Mountains, Valleys, are all laid out upon a larger Scale."[78]

Jefferson, all the while quantifying the monetary cost of the gardens he'd seen, had little to say about their value—just this judgment, apropos of a formal garden he saw in Germany: it "show[ed] how much money may be laid out to make an ugly thing."[79] He had no qualms about spending money for a *beautiful* thing, by his lights, or for living in a beautiful manner. While in France he repeatedly and embarrassingly had to request extra funds from the war-strapped American government to cover the costs of housing, food, and travel for himself and his entourage.[80] (This was a lifelong pattern, visible at least as early as 1774, when he ordered a fine, solid mahogany piano from England and had it shipped to Monticello in defiance of the Continental Congress's nonimportation resolution against Britain, a trick he repeated a few months later for some sash windows—self-indulgences worse than ironic in light of the painful embargo on trade with Britain that he later imposed during his second term as president, which almost split the country.)[81] By the same token, his love of gardens ignored their possible implications, political, social, or philosophical. That Blenheim required two hundred poorly paid servants to keep up bothered the defender of the common man not at all; the gardens' design was another matter. At some level, Jefferson saw the *jardin anglais* in the same light as he saw John Locke's theory of natural rights or Isaac Newton's laws of motion: as ideas, radical ones, fruit from the great tree of Enlightenment and weapons of liberation in the long battle to free the "sheep" from the depredations of the "wolves" of history, in his famous dichotomy. To him, the new English garden was a reaction against "autocracy" and the oppressive rule of the privileged few. It was a taste that implicitly criticized the politics of others, which is what attracted him to it, without requiring him to turn the mirror around and take a hard look at the politics of his own passions.

The same can be said about his taste in architecture: Palladian style to him wasn't classical in a simple sense; it was politically radical insofar as it was associated with the Whig tradition in England, and, since it looked to the ancient past for models of the future, it wasn't old in essence but *new*—modern. Jefferson, who read Greek and Latin, has been routinely described as among the greatest classicists of his time in America. Yet some have argued that he was, in fact, "anti-classical."[82] There is justification for this when we consider that he hated the dead weight of the past in ossified institutions, laws, and conventions; the inherited control of wealth and resources by the upper classes; the stupefying effect of established religion; and the corruption of illegitimate power. He believed that "the earth belongs in usufruct to the living"[83] and proposed that Americans vote on all their laws every nineteen years, which he reckoned one generation, to keep government refreshed. Later in life, he would write to his friend John Adams: "I like the dreams of the future better than the history of the past."[84]

In 1789, Jefferson returned from France to America, bringing with him forty pieces of luggage and having shipped many crates of wine and other luxuries beforehand.[85] George Washington had been elected president while he was away, and appointed Jefferson his secretary of state. In 1790, Jefferson again left Virginia, wearily, for the capital at Philadelphia. Washington's term was marked by partisan rancor between the emerging Republican Party and the Federalists behind Alexander Hamilton, and by bitter personal attacks that took an emotional toll on Jefferson.[86] In 1794, at the age of fifty-one, after eighteen years of near-continuous public service, he retired to Monticello.[87] He wanted "to be liberated from the hated occupations of politics, and to remain in the bosom of my family, my farm, and my books," he confided to a friend. And to another he gave this image: "living like an Antedeluvian patriarch among my children and grandchildren, and tilling my soil."[88]

Yet the reality on the plantation was not so tranquil. Already by the late 1780s, in France, Jefferson knew he might never dig himself out of his debt, half of it inherited from his father-in-law, John Wayles, along with his land and slaves.[89] Years of losses due to lax overseers and bad weather in his absence had added to the burden: he owed English creditors 4,500 pounds, and Scottish ones 2,000 pounds, all of it compounding viciously. He was not alone: Virginia planters after the Revolution owed the British 2.3 million pounds. Still, Jefferson owned almost eleven thousand acres, making him one of the largest landowners in the commonwealth.[90] He was determined to make it pay, applying the new theories of husbandry to return nutrients to his land, "as yet unreclaimed from the barbarous state" of depletion from decades of tobacco growing. He devised an ambitious seven-step crop rotation system and switched to wheat as a cash crop (following George Washington's lead).[91] But his holdings were spread among seven farms, in two counties, at points ninety miles apart, rendering oversight and economies of scale difficult. Further, just one thousand acres were cultivated, the rest left fallow or forest; these one thousand acres needed to grow food for the slaves, workers, the extended Jefferson family, and a constant stream of guests—leaving little room for wheat for cash flow. Bad clay soil, terrible weather, and voracious pests undermined Jefferson's efforts. In 1794 he started a nail factory, worked by teenage boy slaves, which he personally and assiduously oversaw. It did make money but presented a total contradiction of Jefferson's deepest-held and most fervently argued belief—that the United States should remain a nation of farmers. The nailery was a perfect if ugly example of that cliché of American history, the machine in the garden—a "satanic mill" clanking and smoking right on the mountaintop of Jefferson's agrarian Utopia.

But Jefferson's financial situation didn't temper his enthusiasm for house and garden. On his return in 1794, he began planning a major remodel of the house, influenced by the buildings he'd seen in Europe. He planned two major revisions: first, to take down the second story, leaving reconfigured attic rooms, and replace the double portico with a taller, single one to make the house appear as a single story—in line with Palladio's mature style. Second, he would add a dome, modeled on Palladio's Villa Rotunda, which Burlington had also copied at Chiswick, taking the particulars from Gibbs's plate 67.[92] It was an awesome undertaking—tearing half the building off to make it more aesthetically perfect. As in everything else, Jefferson's attention to detail was stunning: for years he had noted features of buildings in his travels that he wanted to re-create, and at Monticello he did, installing French three-part stacking windows, alcove beds, and a dumbwaiter sized specifically to lift wine bottles from the cellar to the parlor. His talented slave workers wrought exquisite moldings, furniture, and fittings. In his bedroom was a frieze of the skulls of oxen, a Roman motif for the blood sacrifice of a pagan fertility ritual—a little odd, but like everything in the house, perfectly executed. For decades Monticello was a construction site. This was Jefferson's real project as a statesman retired to his farm—not farming, but building and rebuilding his dream of perfect elegance. To the extent that he could pay for it, through credit, cost was no object.

It would have been useless to point out to him that what he was doing wasn't new, nor was it liberating anyone from the dead hand of tradition. Palladio wasn't the first architect to give his clients the aura of respectability and legitimacy that the past confers. His clients were rich Venetian families looking to invest their capital in mainland agriculture as wheat and land prices went up while Venice's historical merchant businesses in the Levant and elsewhere in the Mediterranean were being squeezed by the hostile Turks and competitors from Genoa. Some were old money, with, not coincidentally, connections to the slave trade: the Cornaro family had made a fortune growing sugarcane with Black Sea slaves on Cyprus, before the Turks took it; the Barbaro had been shippers of slaves from Africa and the Black Sea. Many were nouveaux riches: professional soldiers or merchants. Palladio built them villas that were really plantation headquarters, with outbuildings and yards for farm work and worker housing often attached, arrayed on each side of the house in measured, balanced symmetry. He used elements of classical Roman architecture to bestow on them "grandeur and magnificence," in his own words, namely porticos and occasionally a dome—originally used only for Roman civic and religious buildings.[93] What he did was give his clients houses that looked like temples and courthouses, ancient ones, with all the aura of power and tradition these radiated. The Palladian plantation campus worked, on two levels: as practical organization of the business of a large farm, and as signifier of the status of the owners—rich, powerful, cultivated, and ostensibly deeply rooted on the land, with the implied sanction of ancient civic and religious authority. Palladio purposefully used materials that quickly aged to imitate the patina of antiquity.

This combination not surprisingly found favor beyond Italy with similar entrepreneurs, especially English plantation owners, first in Ireland, England's first experiment in conquering a foreign island and reducing its population to slavery to grow cash crops. (One of the earliest meanings of the word *plantation* in English was the military colonization of Ireland by English landlords.) Lord Burlington's great-grandfather was one of these brutally efficient soldier-colonizers—the source of the family money that built the domed villa at Chiswick. From Ireland the planters moved to Barbados, then Jamaica and elsewhere in the West Indies, to grow sugarcane with black slave labor. From there they went to the Carolinas to grow indigo and rice and to Virginia to grow tobacco. They brought their taste and their slaves with them. In every one of these places one can see their legacy: in the descendants of enslaved people and in fine Palladian buildings, blindingly white like bleached bones in the bright, un-English sunlight of the New World. The most successful of them took their loot back to Britain and built their villas there; in the 17th and 18th centuries in London it was said of a particularly flush nouveau riche that he was "as rich as a West Indian." Who knows how many of the estates that Jefferson and the Adamses visited were paid for this way? It was a timeless dynamic, endlessly repeating, as Benjamin Disraeli understood in 1845 :

> *In a commercial country like England, every half century develops some new and vast source of public wealth, which brings into national notice a new and powerful class. A couple of centuries ago, a Turkey Merchant was the great creator of wealth; the West India Planter followed him. In the middle of the last century appeared the Nabob. These characters in their zenith in turn merged in the land, and became English aristocrats; while,*

the Levant decaying, the West Indies exhausted, and Hindoostan plundered, the breeds died away, and now exist only in our English comedies....[94]

Jefferson, who grew up in a wooden frontier house, was replaying the script. So was his friend George Washington, whose great-grandfather was a common Englishman shipwrecked on the Virginia sands, and who inherited a small wooden farmhouse at Mount Vernon from his brother and gradually remodeled it into a rather grand neo-Palladian villa, visible for miles up and down the regional main drag that was the Potomac River, with two stories, a high-columned central portico, and curving wings of porticoes leading to dependencies or outbuildings, all painted white and textured with sand to make it appear to be built of cut stone instead of shiplapped planks. Here is the timeless dynamic of real estate: keeping up with the Joneses, with a little stucco if need be. Washington faked a Palladio for curb appeal and to keep the tone of his home in line with his ever-rising celebrity. Jefferson built an exquisite one from scratch, twice, to keep his in line with his escalating estimation of perfection. In their self-consciously republican era, they risked criticism, and doubtless received it. On one hand, refinement in dress and possessions implied a superiority at once moral, spiritual, and worldly—George Washington was always decked out in fine clothes, a habit that added to his aura after the Revolution as a kind of living god. Most people then, as many do now, implicitly assumed that one's worth equaled one's worth—that is, that wealth conferred virtue and deserved higher status. On the other hand, Americans, having fought to free themselves from the oppression of English monarchs and aristocrats, were deeply ambivalent about displays of status, preferring in theory the idea of the simple yeoman farmer to any acknowledgment of worldly wealth. The clergy, with particular energy Puritans and Quakers, condemned refinement, and even avowedly elitist men like John Adams sniffed at the corruptions of urban life, where he found nothing but "Parade, Pomp, Nonsense, Frippery, Folly, Foppery, Luxury, Politicks, and the soul-Confounding Wrangles of the Law," as he delightfully wrote.[95]

How could a man like Jefferson reconcile his love of luxury with his profession of republican ideals? In concrete terms, he couldn't. His own status as a patriarch and landowner in a Virginia society that was profoundly pro-aristocratic disinclined him personally to renounce the refinement that advertised his status, just as the economic underpinnings of that status disinclined him from freeing his slaves. But it didn't stop him from denouncing the habits of luxury in others, or of warning young Americans traveling to Europe not to spend too much time looking at European art and architecture, because it distracted from the corruption of the rich and the poverty of the masses: "they are worth seeing, but not studying."[96] This seems like clear hypocrisy, but it also points to the deep ambivalence and tension in the American mind between our professed ideals and our economic imperatives. Our fear and distrust of luxury and urbanity has deep roots in the Christian, specifically Protestant, morality of self-abnegation and the elevation of rural simplicity in the British Whig tradition that fed the American republican one, but it has never overcome our devotion to a libertarian idolatry of the unrestrained economic individual, summed up by Jefferson as "the pursuit of happiness" and embodied in our national pursuit of inexcusably lavish real estate. This tension is clearly visible in the garden: the route from the formal to the natural garden is in part an effort to cover up this contradiction. From the beginning, the irresistible appeal of Italy, with its sensual aesthetic pleasures and indolent luxuries, clashed with their self-professed values of diligence, discipline, and the modesty of rural simplicity, real or feigned; at a deeper level, lolling about in sunny Italian idylls was more than faintly feminine, unbecoming to the northern sense of manliness. So English admirers of Italian style cloaked the aesthetics in ideas: political and intellectual virtues, borrowed from ancient Greece and Rome, as the Renaissance Italians themselves had. They proceeded further to inexorably cleanse them of the formal elements that reeked of royalist and French backsliding. Never mind that the house and gardens they built were equally monuments to the money and power of a new commercial class; they were laundered by their association with those earlier visions of Eden. The English Whigs cooked up the natural-style landscape garden because it made them look naturally virtuous, enlightened, and fit to govern, and it performed the miracle of hiding their money—in plain sight. For Jefferson, the beautiful ideas draped over the forms of his personal paradise bridged the moral chasm that yawned under it.

Jefferson savored his retirement. "No circumstance, my dear Sir," he wrote to a friend, "will ever more tempt me to engage in anything public."[97] But it was brief indeed: in 1796 he was elected vice president, under President John Adams. In 1801, he was elected third president of the United States, and reelected in 1804. As chief executive, he was, typically, the embodiment of the fundamental contradictions of his people. He fought bitterly with Congress to cut the national debt and limit government expenditures, and was famous for his dislike of pomp and circumstance; once, receiving a British ambassador who was dressed in full military regalia, the president appeared at the White House door wearing nothing but his dressing gown, causing an international incident. At the same time, he entertained "like a power hostess,"[98] inviting all sides to the same table, sparing no expense. The wine bill in his first term was ten thousand dollars.[99] Always, he was prodigally productive. In 1803 he bought Louisiana from France for $23 million, including interest, without congressional approval—notable in a man who warned ominously and often about the dangers of executive power.

The next year he wrote a memo to himself outlining a renewed campaign in the gardens at Monticello, titled "General ideas for the improvement of Monticello." It is startling in its ambition, and for the fact that his taste hadn't changed since 1771 but had only intensified in the picturesque, *jardin anglais* vein. He proposed "all the houses on the Mulberry walk to be taken away, except the stone house, and a ha! ha! instead of the paling along it for an enclosure." The vegetable garden was to be expanded by cutting into the slope and building a massive stone retaining wall below.[100] He would tap a spring on the hill of Montalto and pipe the water to Monticello, en route running it off a ledge to make a cascade that would be visible from the house.[101] He would build the Lantern of Demosthenes temple that he'd proposed in 1771, though in a different spot; then he changed his mind, deciding to copy Chambers's Chinese pavilion at Kew, which he'd seen in 1786. In another note he proposed to build four temples, in four different styles: "a specimen of gothic, model of the Pantheon, model of cubic architecture, a specimen of Chinese."[102] Later he decided on the Gothic, to be placed by the graveyard, and three scaled copies of classical buildings, their locations not stated. Along the south wall of the vegetable garden he proposed building alcoves to take refuge in from the hot sun. Then, in the next line, he decided against it, reasoning, "But after all, the kitchen garden is not the place for ornaments of this kind. Bowers and treillages suite that better, and these temples will be better disposed in the pleasure grounds."[103] None of these follies was ever constructed, but he did eventually build the one-room pavilion on the south wall of the vegetable garden that stands there today, reconstructed from archaeology and his notes: square, made of brick, in Palladio's Tuscan order, with white Chinese railings on the roof. It is a

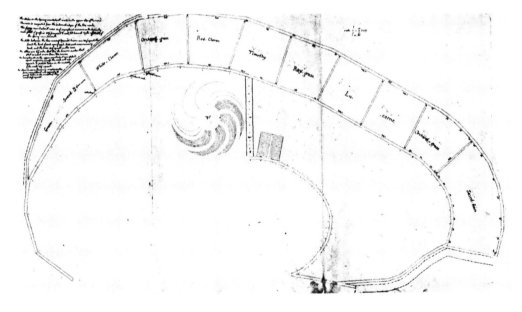

Thomas Jefferson, 1808 Monticello plan. (The Huntington Library, San Marino, California)

lovely building, unpretentious, filled with breeze and light on a hot day. From it a visitor can survey Montalto rising to the south and the green countryside stretching away to the east. It is just one satisfying moment of many that Jefferson carefully and brilliantly engineered in his garden by framing and editing views, opening some here and closing some there.

In 1809, his two terms of office up, Jefferson came back to Monticello for good. He wasted no time in rethinking the garden, putting into action a plan he'd drawn up the year before, incorporating the one from 1804, imagining the hilltop as a *ferme ornée:* with more vistas, more outbuildings moved away out of sight, a ha-ha replacing the wooden fence, a fish pond, long, swooping drives called "roundabouts" circling the mountain, a park and riding ground, a bridge, orchards planted in what were farm fields, and of course, more temples.[104] His vision hadn't been tempered a bit by age or maturity. That year, a Mrs. Margaret Bayard Smith, one of Washington, D.C.'s leading social climbers and a confidante of Dolley Madison, visited him at Monticello, where Jefferson told her of his plans. She later wrote in her diary: "little is as yet done." She went on: "I looked upon him with wonder as I heard him describe the improvements he designed in his grounds, they seemed to require a whole life to carry into effect, and a young man might doubt of ever completing or enjoying them."

But rare was the young man with the energy of the old Thomas Jefferson. Until the end of his life, he supervised the plantation almost daily by horse or telescope—ever the fan of gadgets.[105] His old friend Monsieur Thouin, director of the Jardin des Plantes in Paris, sent him the seeds of seven hundred species to experiment with.[106] Jefferson was less a farmer than a plant-obsessed gardener of scientific bent, experimenting over the years with 330 vegetable varieties, including twenty-three different English peas and thirty-seven types of peach tree.[107] He designed a better plow, but never manufactured it. He found the time to conceive, found, fund, design, and build the University of Virginia, then to establish its curriculum and recruit its professors. The campus he created, with its huge rotunda and carefully modulated pavilions housing classrooms and apartments stretched out along two lines of porticoes stepping down a graded series of broad terraces, is arguably the most beautiful, integrated, and humanistic example of the Palladian art form ever built. The gardens he laid out behind the buildings, framed by serpentine brick walls, are lovely and varied—and are notably geometric in places, evidence of the pragmatic flexibility he displayed when the situation merited straying from his dogmas. He designed houses for friends and another one for himself—his second home at Poplar Forest, a farm three days' ride and ninety-three miles to the west, using all octagonal forms, including a geometric if not formal garden based on the same figure.[108] Not to mention overseeing the planning for the District of Columbia, the new U.S. Capitol building, and the White House.

As busy as he was, Jefferson always took time for gardens. Once, when his friend the Comte de Volney (who had incidentally published a book called *Les Ruines; ou Méditation sur les Révolutions des Empires*, which expatiated on the lessons to be learned from ruined buildings about the cycles of history) was visiting from France, the two men returned late to dinner from a walk—unusual for the punctual Jefferson. It turned out "that the two philosophers had been detained by the labor of damming up a little stream in order that they might design a picturesque waterfall."[109] It is a touching scene, one that is at odds with another recalled by Monsieur Volney: that of Jefferson threatening some slaves with a whip while pontificating to his friend about democracy.[110]

THE SLAVERY QUESTION was not the only instance where his ideals were in conflict with reality, or where the ambiguities in his thinking had negative consequences. He was among the earliest Americans to show a deep interest in the culture and lives of the Indians, even affirming at one point that he saw theirs as the best way of life, but as president he gave license for their systematic removal or extermination and the expropriation of their lands.[111] Through his writing he laid the foundation of some Americans' distrust of government, but when he exercised power he did so forcefully and without hesitation. His attitude toward the American landscape prefigured the aesthetic appreciations of Romanticism and the conservation impulse of the later 19th century: he rhapsodized about the empty canvas of the West, boldly added it to the nation by outbargaining Napoleon, and sent Lewis and Clark to explore it; and he purchased Virginia's Natural Bridge rock arch, which he refused to sell, saying, "I view it in some degree as a public trust," and which he described like a breathless English poet: "It is impossible for the emotions, arising from the sublime, to be felt beyond what they are here: so beautiful an arch, so elevated, so light and springing, as it were, up to heaven, the rapture of the Spectator is really indescribable!"[112] He was beginning to see, in the picturesque landscape of the "virgin" wilderness, the outlines of a uniquely American identity. Yet he presided over the systematic destruction of that landscape as it was sold off and settled during his time in public office, including laying the groundwork for the Northwest Ordinance of 1784 and the machinelike surveying system that divided up and laid an unvarying rectangular grid over the continent.

A man of the 18th century who embodied its ideals of natural science, exploration, and enlightenment, Jefferson prefigured the momentous, wrenching changes of the 19th: slavery, which tore his own conscience, would very nearly tear the country apart; factories, of which he was one of the first owners, would transform the nation's economy and social structure and feed the explosive growth of crowded, industrial cities— anathema to him and to millions of others who would point to his articulation of the agrarian ideal as they fled those cities to suburbs modeled on the image of the vanishing wilderness, tamed into manicured private gardens, each a miniature, simplified version of his vaster, layered one at Monticello.

Two

A WALK IN THE PARK:
SUBURBIA AND THE SUBLIME (1820-1890)

Approaching New York City from the west on Interstate 80, aiming one's car at the tip of the Empire State
Building poking up in the distance, you drive across
the northern fringes of the Meadowlands, New Jersey's
enormous marshes through which the Hackensack River meanders southward for another sixteen miles before draining into
New York Harbor. Here we've constructed one of the ugliest,
saddest landscapes in America, a nadir rendered more depressing by the fact that its man-made character is generic, like many
more nowheres one might drive through on any interstate. The
lazy, sinuous creeks and tufted fields of reeds are still lovely in
persisting patches, but are mostly buried under stacked layers of
infrastructure and buildings, all done on the quick and cheap by
a civilization in a hurry to move on, so everything is in an equal
hurry to fall apart. Tangles of highways, roads, bridges, railroad
trestles, pipelines, and power lines knot through checkerboards
of unkempt lots littered with trailers, trucks, and decaying pieces
of obsolete warehouses, down-at-heel motels, and inexplicable
islands of houses, all of them surrounded by plastic-bag-strewn
chain-link fences and billboards. At highway speed it lasts for just
a few minutes, then the interstate rises suddenly out of the flat
marshes and digs itself into a slot blasted out of the gray diabase

of the Palisades ridge. The abrupt rock walls are astonishingly filthy, covered in graffiti and decades of greasy exhaust. Even at three-thirty in the afternoon, traffic shudders to a crawl in the chasm, then lurches, groaning, forward, filing into the lanes leading to the George Washington Bridge. Before the bridge I exit gratefully and head north on Palisades Parkway, which is quickly, miraculously swallowed by woods and fresh air. The cars thin out and pick up speed; between the trees I catch glimpses of the Hudson River stretching almost a mile to the cliffs on the New York side: Inwood Park, in Upper Manhattan, is crowned with buildings, but the cliffs below are green, thickly furred with hardwood forest.

In 1840, New York City, then occupying only the island of Manhattan, was North America's biggest city, with 300,000 people; a mere 34,000 of them lived north of Fourteenth Street, and the majority of them lived on farms.[1] Ninety percent of Americans lived in rural areas, most of them farmers.[2] The city clinging to the southern tip of the island then was bustling, bursting with commerce, immigrants, and epidemics. But the northern tip would have looked about as its riverside slopes do now, minus the roads and buildings: tangled forest and rocky outcrops looming above the slate-gray river. Every year, settlement pushed farther north and grew denser as farms invaded the woods and buildings invaded the farmland behind. The moving collision—and contrast—between the city and the wilderness gave 19th century America its basic economic and social energy, bent on transforming the wilderness into settled landscape. They also gave it its most distinctive artistic and philosophical preoccupation: contemplating the meaning of wilderness even as it was destroyed, capturing its essence in essays, fiction, and painting, bringing it paradoxically into the heart of the city in the form of parks, and, before the century's end, moving to shield portions of it from the tide of development by setting them aside as reserves. If the physical facts of canals, railroads, shipping, and buying and selling were largely bankrolled and coordinated in the financial center of New York, these latter, mental developments to a great extent were also worked out here and emanated from here—this landscape of the Hudson River, extending northward from Manhattan Island through the narrows of the Highlands, to the hills of the broad Hudson Valley and on to its sources in the Adirondack Mountains.

It was the collision between *this* city and *this* wilderness, resolving itself into a domesticated middle landscape of small towns and farms stretching along the banks of the Hudson, that more than any other landscape shaped the imagination and self-image of our young country and came to define America for the rest of the world. It was defined, represented, packaged, and sold by a small group of people, most of them New Yorkers by birth or adoption. Never mind that its intellectual roots weren't American at all but rather (once again) European, the romantic image of the Hudson reached across the continent to the Sierra Nevada of California and the shores of San Francisco Bay and ricocheted back again, in the process solidifying into a set of attitudes, assumptions, and aesthetic leanings in regard to nature that are quintessentially American. Never mind that the city got by far the best of the collision—witness the degraded Meadowlands. Bits of the vanquished wilderness, digested, transformed, and embedded in the particular mental landscape created along the 19th century Hudson, are still with us, everywhere: in our cities, towns, subdivisions, and "countryside," in the landscaped, seemingly wild parkway I drive on north toward the New York state line, in its twin parkway across the river, and right in my scrap of front lawn in Los Angeles—and in yours, if you have one.

In a couple of minutes I can see the spot across the river where, in 1852, the most prominent figure in the 19th century American garden met his untimely end, by drowning. Andrew Jackson Downing, a slight man with fashionably, one might say artistically, long hair and large, dewy brown eyes, was en route from Newburgh, New York, forty miles upriver, to Manhattan with his wife, mother-in-law, and a group of other family and friends. The steamer they boarded, the *Henry Clay*, was racing with a competitor for the title of fastest boat on the river when it burst into flames and ran aground a couple of miles below Yonkers. Seventy people were killed, including a former New York City mayor, Nathaniel Hawthorne's sister, Downing, and two others in his party. He was thirty-six.[3] Even for someone so young, his death was big news, as he ranked as a minor celebrity, the 19th century's Martha Stewart—or, I should say, Martha is our Downing, since it was he who wrote, directed, and starred in the role she would later reprise: the doyen of American house and garden style. Downing was the editor of the influential journal the *Horticulturalist* and author of a stream of books of landscaping advice and house patterns that told people where and how to live, and that played an outsize role in spreading the picturesque style across the country. In 1841, at the age of twenty-six, he published a book on gardens, *A Treatise on the Theory and Practice of Landscape Gardening*, which became the suburban homeowner's bible, so ubiquitous that, according to one contemporary writer, "nobody, whether he be rich or poor, builds a house or lays out a garden without consulting Downing's works. Every young couple who sets up housekeeping buys one."[4] News of his death brought nationwide encomiums. The *New York Tribune* called him a "man of genius and high culture . . . [T]here is none whom the country could so little afford to lose, or whose services to the community could so little be replaced, as Mr. DOWNING."[5] His publisher eulogized him: "He was the man best fitted to mould the architectural and rural taste of the country to a correct model, to guide public sentiment to whatever is highest in Nature and purest in Art, and to aid in making America what Heaven designed it should be, the garden of the whole earth."[6]

Downing is everywhere, to this day: he in effect designed the first hundred years of American suburbia; great swaths of the continent still bear his mark, since they were arranged according to his vision. He was one of the primary proponents of New York's Central Park and would likely have been its designer, in partnership with Calvert Vaux, the young architect Downing found in England and brought back to Newburgh to work with him. Instead Frederick Law Olmsted would step into Downing's shoes.

But who was this aesthetic giant? He was an unlikely candidate for the role: self-taught, the son of a wheelwright, born in and resident virtually all his life in Newburgh, population 2,370, a backwater town with dirt streets and wooden frame buildings on the west side of the Hudson at the feet of the Catskill Mountains. He was born October 13, 1815, and named in honor of the American general who had defeated a British army at the Battle of New Orleans, nine months earlier, in the last major battle of the War of 1812. Newburgh was part of the tide of westward migration that was reshaping the republic, a tide that his parents, descended from Puritans, joined around 1800, leaving Massachusetts for the Hudson Valley. Downing's father made wheels for horse-drawn wagons and carriages—a good profession among a mobile people following the frontier's relentless westward march—but he quickly recognized that there was greater opportunity in serving the increasing number who decided to stay put. So in 1810 he started a nursery and began investing in real estate. The westering wave of settlers rolled over the Hudson and kept going: the completion of the Erie Canal in 1825, the same year Andrew Jackson was elected the seventh president of the United States, connected western New York and Ohio Valley grain farmers to markets in seaboard cities and Europe.[7] Farmers in less fertile eastern areas suffered, and Newburgh foundered, then picked up its share of the prosperity as a middleman between farmers in the West and manufacturing in New England and New York. There was a building boom in town in the 1830s. Farmers in the neighborhood either moved to better soil to the west or turned to higher-value crops to sell to the growing cities: produce, and especially fruits, which thrive in the climate. The Downing nursery offered 150 varieties of apples and two hundred of pears.

Young Downing was educated at a nearby academy until the age of sixteen,[8] then worked in the family nursery, learning the trade. In his spare time he frequented the houses of local gentry landowners, including an English-born landscape painter and an elderly Austrian baron, the consul at New York who kept a summer retreat in the neighborhood. They discussed art, botany, nature, and evidently, houses and gardens, and took walks in the vicinity. Such fashionable friends helped him cultivate some very up-to-date tastes. In 1832, when he was just sixteen years old, he published an essay called "Rural Embellishments," in which he lamented that American landscape gardening was "completely in its infancy"—a familiar way of saying that the United States lagged behind

Great Britain—and urged the "many advantages of the picturesque style" on his compatriots. They were, of course, busy hacking down trees, but he urged Americans to plant them instead, to "begin to be as actively engaged in planting as our ancestors were in exterminating."[9]

At this time, the Hudson Valley was becoming a site of veneration for a generation of American intellectuals and artists excited by finding something that made their young country different from Europe, because in all other comparisons it was woefully deficient. That something was wilderness. The Hudson landscape was already mostly settled, but there were pockets of wildness that inspired and drew the city-bound for walks and reveries: the Highlands, and especially the Catskills, just hours by steamer from New York City. Washington Irving, who had become the United States' first literary success with his 1820 *The Legend of Sleepy Hollow*, and lived in fact along the Hudson in the town of Sleepy Hollow, wrote in 1819: "no, never, need an American look beyond his own country for the sublime and beautiful of natural scenery."[10] James Fenimore Cooper became the United States' second literary success when he abandoned the mannered, English-style stories he had been producing and published *The Pioneers* in 1823. It was the first of five Leatherstocking Tales, starring Natty Bumppo, the rustic hero who chose wilderness over civilization, and lamented, like Downing but in a far more colorful tongue, the destruction of the forests: "they scourge the very 'arth with their axes. Such hills and hunting grounds as I have seen stripped of the gifts of the Lord, without remorse or shame!"[11] The landscape painter Thomas Cole built a career on capturing romantic scenes of the New York forests (including a scene from Cooper's novel *Last of the Mohicans*, in 1826) and became a vocal defender of wildness: in 1835 he also railed against the "ravages of the axe" and America's "meager utilitarianism," and reminded Americans that "we are still in Eden; the wall that shuts us out of the garden is our own ignorance and folly."[12] Thinkers began to programmatically link nature to the divine, and so to limn its passing as the bitter price of civilization. In 1836, Ralph Waldo Emerson's essay "Nature" appeared, idealizing its subject as "the symbol of the spirit,"[13] an earthly manifestation of the divine force. These impassioned defenses of the vanishing wilderness didn't slow the continental bonfire a whit, but they did contribute to the national sense of self as thoughtful and ethical people, even if our national project of feverish settlement meant that we couldn't act on the insight.

IN 1835, WHEN Downing was nineteen, the *New-York Mirror* published some of his first essays describing the Hudson Valley—but he, in contrast, celebrated its pastoral, agrarian landscape of fields and villages: "a thousand cheerful homes gleaming in the sunshine." He was made uncomfortable by the constant movement he saw around him, the rootlessness, the "spirit of unrest," as he repeatedly put it, of Jacksonian America.

Thomas Cole, *Landscape*, 1825. (The Athenaeum, Minneapolis Institute of Arts/Wikimedia Commons)

Not alone among European observers, Alexis de Tocqueville diagnosed the malady in his *Democracy in America*, published the same year, as: "a restless spirit, immoderate desire for wealth, and an extreme love of independence."[14] "In the United States a man builds a house in which to spend his old age, and he sells it before the roof is on; he plants a garden and lets it just before the trees are coming into bearing; he brings a field into tillage and leaves other men to gather the crops; he embraces a profession and gives it up; he settles in a place, which he soon afterwards leaves to carry his changeable longings elsewhere," Tocqueville wrote.[15] Downing echoed him: the American was "unable to take root anywhere, he leads, socially and physically, the uncertain life of a tree transplanted from place to place, and shifted to a different soil every season."[16] And he prescribed as cure the "love of home," an "innate feeling, out of which grows a strong attachment to natal soil[;] we must look for a counterpoise to the great tendency towards constant change, and the restless spirit of emigration, which form part of our national character." Downing proposed a program of encouraging this love of home through cultivating taste: "Whatever, therefore, leads man to assemble the comforts and elegancies of life around his habitation, tends to increase local attachments, and render domestic life more delightful; thus not only augmenting his own enjoyment, but strengthening his patriotism, and making him a better citizen."

In the mid- and late 1830s, while still in his teens, Downing published a number of essays on horticulture, landscape gardening, and domestic architecture, retailing ideas drawn from the English press; they were unoriginal but well expressed and must have marked him as promising. He was embarked on an entrepreneurial career as an arbiter of taste, and so, in the time-honored tradition, he set out to make his first tasteful work himself. He married well, wedding Caroline DeWint, whose mother was the niece of John Quincy Adams (son of Jefferson's friend John Adams, and the republic's sixth president), and whose father had made a fortune in the Caribbean sugar trade and in real estate in the Hudson Valley and ranked as one of Newburgh's top burghers. The wedding was described as "a grand affair," with all the local nabobs present—Andrew Jackson

Downing now counted among them, with the designation "Esq." after his name on the invitation. (He never used his full name, signing everything "A. J. Downing," no doubt because his namesake was a bitter foe of Adams, having beaten him in the nasty presidential election of 1828, and therefore a foe of the interests of the wealthy Federalist social set Downing married into and intended as his clients.)[17] Immediately after, he began planning a new house near the cottage he'd grown up in. It wouldn't be classical, the dominant mode in Newburgh, which had mostly vernacular Georgian houses in the New England tradition plus some newer, more ostentatious Greek Revival buildings, including some churches and five town houses near the riverfront called Quality Row. Thomas Jefferson's Palladian idiom had evolved into Greek Revival in much of the North in the early 19th century, inspired by the discovery of the ruins of Herculaneum and the removal of the Parthenon marbles to London by Lord Elgin, as well as by Americans' sympathy for the Greeks' war of independence from the Ottoman Turks from 1821 to 1829. (It made the news in the United States in no small part because the English Romantic poet Lord Byron went to fight on the Greek side and died there of disease.) Ancient Greek architecture was glorified as simpler and purer than Roman and had the added advantage of not being associated with the English; it quickly became the standard style of westward settlement, a sign of American patriotism and a true national architecture. In the 1820s, Greek temples popped up like mushrooms in the forest after a rain, from Boston to Natchez to New Orleans.[18]

The Anglophile Downing decided his house would be in the latest English fashion, Gothic. The English architect Benjamin Latrobe (who later built the U.S. Capitol building) had designed America's first Gothic-style residence in 1799, near Philadelphia,[19] but the mode remained rare. The builder hired to draw the plans remembered that Downing had gotten his "ideas of such matters . . . from one or two English books." Like Jefferson, Downing turned to British books for examples: probably *Encyclopedia of Cottage, Farm, and Villa Architecture* (1833), by the Scotsman John Claudius Loudon, and almost certainly *Rural Architecture* (1835), by Francis Goodwin, which contains an engraving of "A Villa in the Elizabethan Style" that looks like the model of the house Downing had built in 1838–39, with its projecting central portico flanked by two narrow spires topped with cupolas. The house was big, with a view of the river to the east. The details were pretty much cribbed from the originals' ornamental moldings, shields, shaped chimneys, and tall and thin arched windows. But Downing added a veranda, a common American accommodation to the summer heat. And it was made of stucco made to look like cut stone, to save money. Nevertheless, Downing took out two mortgages, totaling five thousand dollars. The couple moved in in 1839, when he was twenty-four. He was making his play, and boldly. The house needed a garden, so Downing carved out of his half of the nine-acre nursery grounds (which had been split with his brother) a quasi-naturalistic garden, with a carriage walk winding around a large, irregular lawn studded with individual trees and flower beds arrayed next to the drive, some round and some

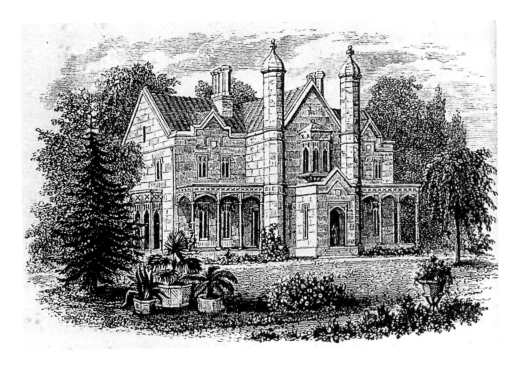

Andrew Jackson Downing residence. (From Downing, *A Treatise on the Theory and Practice of Landscape Gardening*, 1846 edition)

squiggle-shaped; several pots sat near the front door holding tender exotics: a palm, an agave, and perhaps a cycad, from the look of one engraving.

It was all in the latest Victorian fashion. It was also lifted straight out of J. C. Loudon's *Encyclopedia of Gardening* and *Suburban Gardener*, the latter the new bible of style in England, published in 1838 and bought by Downing in the fall of the same year. Just twelve years after the death of Thomas Jefferson, the leading edge of taste in America had changed in important ways—certainly in the house, with such cartoonishly Gothic effects and asymmetry. In the garden the changes were more subtle: the picturesque still reigned but had had its stays loosened enough to accommodate the return of parterres, bedding schemes, and formal geometries.

Presiding over this accommodation was Loudon. Born in Scotland in 1783, he had become the central figure in the Victorian English garden by making several improvements in the construction of heated greenhouses and by writing numerous articles and books, including the thousand-page *Encyclopedia*, and editing the *Gardener's Magazine*. Loudon championed what he termed the "gardenesque" style, built around the display of rare and exotic specimen plants and trees, in greenhouses, conservatories, and elaborate "rockeries," and in parlors stuffed with soft-leaved palms and ferns, the most extreme of the latter called "ferneries." He maintained an overall naturalistic style while enthusiastically welcoming back formal bed arrangements here and there, ranging from geometric parterres to his trademark squiggle or comma-shaped beds, planted with annuals arranged in elaborate color schemes, and the speckling of lawns with potted exotics and urns on pedestals dripping with flowers. What hadn't changed was that the most up-to-date Americans still took their cues from Britain. But the English garden had, in some senses, come full circle.

The discerning Englishman wanted more nature in his garden, no matter what. Horace Walpole, the writer and politician, famously wrote of William Kent, who had helped create Lord Burlington's Roman-temple-and-Gothic-ruin menagerie at Chiswick and the massively trendy landscape garden at Stowe for Lord Cobham: "He leaped the fence and saw that all nature was a garden." (Walpole also, to demonstrate the overlap of seemingly opposed aesthetic trends, built the first Gothic-style house, beginning in 1747, at Strawberry Hill, near Pope's place in Twickenham.)

After Kent's death in 1748, his former protégé at Stowe, Lancelot "Capability" Brown, so named because he spied out the "capabilities" of a site, seized the heights of clientele, including the richest aristocrats and King George III, and gave them nature, *improved*. The grottoes and temples fell away, replaced by blankets of undulating lawns—the smooth turf coming right up to the houses, clumps of trees, meandering lakes, tangles of wild-seeming flowering shrubs, and ha-has with deer and cattle grazing beyond. His landscapes were perfect imitations of pastoral pictures. And they were expensive: Brown routinely dammed rivers to make lakes, and employed hundreds of laborers to move dirt by hand, building hills here, taking them down there, and transplanting trees. He even moved entire villages to "improve" a view.[20] His art was subtle; to some it seemed godlike—especially in its presumption and cost. (Someone is supposed to have said to him that they wished to die before he did, to which Brown replied "Why so?" "Because I should like to see Heaven before you have improved it," came the answer.) Of course, before long there was a backlash, goaded by the real pain inflicted on the poor villagers of Britain by the enclosure of common lands by rich landowners; in the forty years between 1760 and 1800, more than 21 million acres were enclosed, their inhabitants forced off the land and into the "satanic" slums and factories of industrializing cities. Landowners became very interested in the gospel of "improvement" and "scientific" farming, like Jefferson, but just as interested as well in the aestheticization of the land, by making it into "landscape." As usual, the British press displayed its talent for inventive, highbrow ridicule *and* its obsession with gardening. All were on display in a William Cowper poem of 1786:

> *Improvement too, the idol of the age,*
> *Is fed with many a victim. Lo, he comes!*
> *Th'omnipotent magician, Brown appears! . . .*
> *He speaks. The lake in front becomes a lawn;*
> *Woods vanish, hills subside, and vallies rise:*

And streams, as if created for his use,
Pursue the track of his directing wand.

Brown, who died in 1783, was in turn replaced as top design dog by one Humphry Repton, who invented the phrase "landscape gardening" and kept up the pastoralizing tendency, feeding to a clientele that had expanded to include bankers, lawyers, and merchants as well as aristocrats a softer version of the picturesque, suitable for smaller properties and smaller budgets. Repton talked of the "feasibilities" rather than the capabilities of the place, and perhaps unspoken, of the client's wallet. Overseeing a team like a modern design office and traveling like a road salesman, his output was astonishing, reportedly four hundred jobs in a three-decade career lasting into the 19th century. Repton did Brownian picturesque but he was a pragmatist, allowing some formality to creep back in when the client wanted it, especially around the house, in kitchen gardens and flower parterres. Predictably, his ubiquity as much as his adaptability inspired attacks. Some critics called for a less pastoral naturalism, more Salvator Rosa than Nicolas Poussin, to take the two landscape painters who had inflamed the passions of the Italians in the 17th century and subsequently gained favor with the English. The popularity of this new tendency was given a big boost by the huge commercial success of Walter Scott, whose historical novels set in a heroic medieval past, such as *Ivanhoe, Rob Roy,* and *The Bride of Lammermoor,* played to British nationalism in the grim years of the Napoleonic Wars and featured Gothic architecture in the "sublime" scenery of windblown, ruin-flecked Scotland. The house Scott built there, Abbotsford, a fairytale "Tudor" Gothic-castle confection said to have cost twenty-five thousand pounds, was widely publicized—the Hearst Castle of its day. The medieval taste was in. People rummaged through their attics for old suits of armor to polish up and display in the hall. (Mark Twain joked in *Life on the Mississippi* that *Don Quixote* had destroyed the age of chivalry, but it was resurrected by *Ivanhoe.*)[21]

Not surprisingly, the picturesque garden came in for a thorough bashing by writers like Jane Austen, who delighted in skewering social climbing and gauche overreaching. Being herself a committed, and English, gardener, Austen had many opinions on the subject. In *Mansfield Park* she actually used his name derisively: "any Mr. Repton" for landscape "improvers."[22] In *Northanger Abbey,* Austen mocked picturesque pretensions by lampooning the actual folly built in 1766 to look like an ancient structure, at Blaise Castle, where Repton had worked. "'Blaise Castle!' cried Catherine [Morland], 'what is that?' 'The finest place in England; worth going fifty miles at any time to see.' 'What! is it really a castle—an old castle?' 'The oldest in the kingdom.'"[23] Austen was interested more in the pretension than in the hairsplitting specifics of the pretender's program; she tended to speak out for a simple, uncomplicated appreciation of garden pleasures, especially those that didn't need costly "improvement"—like the "nice old-fashioned place" of Colonel Brandon in *Sense and Sensibility,* or Donwell Abbey in *Emma.*[24] But of course her characters were all involved in the garden game, the rich and the aspiring alike. In the early 19th century, gardens were becoming a luxury object within reach for more and more British people, as the middle classes grew and looked to spend their time and discretionary income on gardens, whether on scraps of tillable earth behind the new terrace housing estates or on larger plots in the new villa park suburbs creeping out from the cities and larger towns. It was trickle-down suburbanization, with the amenity and status symbol of the garden as its emotional heart and economic engine drawing people and their money out of the city. Here is where Loudon came in.

John Claudius Loudon was Repton's successor as England's most visible garden designer, following the latter's death in 1818. Loudon enlarged on Repton's reinstatement of the formal, and the frankly practical, as his clientele skewed even more downmarket—or more accurately, "mass market," since this was the beginning of the era of mass production, mass media, and mass consumption. He found early success with writing, reaching a larger and growing audience, and soon stopped designing to write full-time. His output was prodigious: in addition to the journal, he published seven big books in a fifteen-year span, including the thousand-page *Encyclopedia of Cottage, Farm, and Villa Architecture* (1833) and a compendium of every tree and plant growing in Britain, the *Arboretum et Fruticetum Britannicum* (1838). He was a popularizer of elite ideas: interested in the idea of "utility," or the greatest good for the greatest number (he had met the famous philosopher Jeremy Bentham and approved of his Utilitarian philosophy), he tried to apply the picturesque garden to smaller gardens to extend their benefits to the working classes. In practice, this meant the expanding middle classes, who were helped in their quest by time-saving technology, such as the lawn mower invented by Edward Budding in 1831. Loudon added to the Brownian repertoire of lawn, trees, and water an eclectic set of elements that came to define Victorian garden style (Queen Victoria was crowned in 1837): hothouses, rockeries, and lawns densely inhabited by curving walks, pots, urns, and flower beds in whimsical shapes, all stuffed full of exotic plants. This was the golden age of horticulture: the 18th century Age of Discovery with its occasional hauls of new plants from voyages returning from the colonies yielded in the 19th to a frenzy of commercial plant hunting in far-flung zones, from the Himalayas to Africa, all transported back to Europe in the newly invented Wardian case, a sealed glass vessel used to maintain temperature and humidity on ocean passages, and cultivated in coal-heated greenhouses at an exploding number of arboreta and botanical gardens. New exotics, especially "annuals" (the name of convenience for any plant that couldn't survive a European winter and so had to be propagated and planted anew each year) were massed in garish, color-coordinated schemes in the new "bedding system," which became all the rage in the 1830s. In 1839, one writer complained that "scores of unmeaning flower beds in the shape of kidneys and tadpoles and sausages and leeches and commas now disfigure the lawn." But it was a craze, not to be slowed by one or two sniffing Sallies.[25]

In Loudon's gardenesque, the centuries of anxious disputation by landscape theorists were simply mixed up in a bowl, then ladled about the garden with a smile. One might have it all, in a sense, combining the picturesque and the formal, the beautiful and the sublime, the rusticated and the sophisticated as the mood suited. Loudon assembled a grab bag of windy quotes on the principles of landscape gardening from

Shenstone, Whately, Pope, and many others, including this list from Repton: "congruity, utility, order, symmetry, scape, proportion and appropriation." Far from justifying his jettisoning of rigor in categories—if there had ever really been any—he composed his own hierarchy of styles: he dismissed the formal, man-made mode as "mixed art," while design "guided by natural and universal beauty" he called "inventive art." The former was passé, of course, while the latter could be divided into three species: *picturesque gardening*, meaning imitating wild nature, with, as the old saw went, composition that could be "considered as particularly suitable for being represented by painting"; *rustic*, that is, what was "commonly found accompanying the rudest description of labourers' cottages in the country"; and finally *gardenesque*, the imitation of nature "subjected to a certain degree of cultivation or improvement, suitable to the wants and wishes of man."[26] It was a pretentious and hopelessly vague doctrine, full of idiotic rules like this one: local trees must be planted in lines, while exotic trees must be planted in irregular arrangements.[27] And this one: "the trees, shrubs and herbaceous plants must be separated" (in other words, they shouldn't touch one another). Always, Loudon warned, the garden maker must be attentive to "design, taste, and fitness of the means employed." When he wasn't writing about actual plants, about which he knew a lot, Loudon mostly produced pretty gibberish, like so much Victorian writing long on a kind of sibilant felicity of phrasing and short on meaning. But the people ate it up.

In Newburgh, Downing recognized a good idea when he saw one: Loudon's career. He set out to write a book, first to be about arboriculture, which is what his nursery training qualified him to write. But then it morphed into something bigger, more confident, a compendium of landscape gardening, horticulture, and theory—cribbed mostly from Loudon, who in his turn had glossed Humphry Repton. Downing's version was published in 1841: *A Treatise on the Theory and Practice of Landscape Gardening, Adapted to North America*, weighing in at nearly six hundred pages. As he acknowledged in the subtitle and admitted in the preface, "I have availed myself of the works of European authors, and especially those of Britain." Downing largely repackaged Loudon, whom he called

"The Beautiful and the Picturesque in Landscape Gardening." (From Downing, *A Treatise*)

"my valued correspondent" and "the most distinguished gardening author of the age." He included discussions of landscape theory, history, and principles of design, borrowing illustrations from Loudon, and added his own sections on trees, vines, and such practical matters as building fountains and transplanting trees—all topics he knew much about. He reduced Loudon's cake-mix rendition of landscape theory to two modes: the ancient (formal) and the modern (naturalistic), dismissing the former whenever it was mentioned as "the display of labored art" invariably "attained in a merely mechanical manner."[28] It might be acceptable in public squares, he allowed, or where "a taste for imitating an old and quaint style of residence exists . . . like old armor or furniture, as curious specimens of antique taste and custom."[29] The modern style he divided into the beautiful and the picturesque: "the Beautiful is nature or art obeying the universal laws of perfect existence easily, freely, harmoniously, and without the *display* of power. The Picturesque is nature or art obeying the same laws rudely, violently, irregularly, and often displaying power only."[30] (Curiously, he rested the distinction on the quality of *menace*— a novel garden category, to say the least.) Fortunately for the would-be landscape improver, in the backyard one could differentiate between the two modes without worrying about whether power was being displayed by simply planting "round-headed" trees to achieve a beautiful result and "spiry-topped" trees for a picturesque look.

Downing's styles occupied a hierarchy, corresponding to states of refinement and states of civilization—very typical of the 19th century, with its obsession with evolutionary paths and rankings, which served the rhetorical purpose of proving that one's proclivities were the most advanced while those of others were primitive and crude. Little escaped this: societies, art, language, politics, even people's skull shapes, the study of which was called phrenology and pretended to rank the races according to their tendency to be criminals or good citizens, idiots or geniuses, and so on. It all predated Darwin and mocked his methodology. Nevertheless, it was ubiquitous. For Downing, the "absurdities of the ancient style" appealed only to "the mass of uncultivated minds," because it was "a meagre taste, and a lower state of the art, or a lower perception for beauty in the individual."[31] Of course, "men of genius" preferred the natural style. His concept was the neo-Platonic one, common among Christians in this era, which imagined the moral order expressed in the surface aspects of things. The difference between the beautiful and the picturesque then was a manifestation of the "Struggle by spirit and matter."[32] (One might ask why, if the beautiful was perfection, did we, men of genius and refinement, bother with the picturesque? Downing explained that it was due to "the imperfection of our natures" and that we picturesque appreciators would have to accept our congenital inferiority.) He offered a series of

Wodenethe. (From Downing, *A Treatise*)

examples, mostly drawn from local estates, like beautiful Hyde Park, the seven-hundred-acre estate of Dr. David Hosack, designed by the Belgian émigré André Parmentier; picturesque Wodenethe, owned by Henry Winthrop Sargent, a wealthy Boston scion who had built a summer place along the Hudson in Beacon, directly across from Newburgh; and the writer Washington Irving's picturesque cottage in the Dutch style, Sunnyside, downriver near Tarrytown. The distinction was often very subtle and had to be taken on his authority.

The *Treatise* also contained an architecture section, really a collection of pseudo-historical building types illustrated with more local examples. To prepare the plans and views, Downing wrote to Alexander Jackson Davis, a New York architect and rising star who was also one of the most talented engravers in the country. They met at another Hudson estate, Robert Donaldson's Blithewood, a neo-Gothic wooden house designed by Davis and for which Downing landscaped the grounds. Davis agreed to do the drawings from Downing's sketches, and the engravings on woodblock. This technique was the reverse of metal intaglio engrav-

Blithewood. (From Downing, *A Treatise*)

ing, with the image raised like type, allowing one printing instead of two, rendering the printing process much cheaper.[33] Again Downing began with a style hierarchy, dismissing the popular "Grecian" as "unfit for American domestic life," based on the fact that residences are not temples.[34] (He was dismissing out of hand most structures built in his region in the previous twenty years.) He instead recommended any one of the following styles: Italian, castellated, Tudor, Elizabethan, and rural Gothic—unbothered by the fact that medieval castles weren't "homes" any more than temples were; in the second edition of 1849 he added Swiss and Bracketed,[35] the latter a style concocted by his new collaborator, Davis, and named by Downing.[36] He added a porch or veranda to each European type in deference to America's weather, and the assurance that following his advice conferred moral status, since the person who builds a beautiful house brings "benefit to the cause of morality, good order, and the improvement of society." Reviews for the book were positive; Loudon himself pronounced it a "landmark."[37]

The *Treatise* was successful in no small part due to nationalism, to the burning desire for American voices to measure up to Americans' sense of their own importance, promise, and uniqueness. Emerson, addressing a class of college graduates in 1837, promised: "Our day of dependence, our long apprenticeship to the learning of other lands, draws to a close."[38] Downing in some measure satisfied this need by bringing the exalted taste of England to American soil, in American terms. He himself saw his work as providing a public service: "While yet in the far west the pioneer constructs his rude hut of logs . . . in the older portions of the Union, bordering the Atlantic, we are surrounded by all the luxuries and refinements that belong to an old and long cultivated country. Within the last ten years . . . the evidences of the growing wealth and prosperity of our citizens have become apparent in the great increase in elegant cottages and villa residences." The problem was not a lack of money, but a lack of professional expertise: "it is not surprising that we witness much incongruity and great waste of time and money," which he would personally remedy. "I have ventured to prepare the present volume, in the hope of supplying, in some degree, the desideratum so much felt at present," he generously offered. Until then, architecture books had been written for builders, as pattern books, while garden books were written for hands-on gardeners; the *Treatise* was a new animal—a how-to book for those who would hire others to do the work for them, aimed at training their taste so they would know to request the right things. Thus the images of houses depicted the building surrounded by its gardens, their sum constituting the owner's "demesne," an image that would-be estate makers could grasp and communicate to their contractors, aided by easily followed diagrams for clumping or grouping trees, and sequences of different treatments for different acreages and intents. They were cartoonish but clear, and easily re-created. This practical ease of use made the *Treatise* popular with readers of varying economic "capabilities"; his theories may have been improbable but there was a certain simplicity in the recommendations: first, choose between the two allowable schools, beautiful or picturesque, then add "embellishments" such as arbors, vases, benches, summerhouses, and flower gardens, as space and purse would admit. Downing recommended an estate of fifty to five hundred acres, but allowed that adequate effects might be achieved with just ten or twenty.[39] He defined a villa as a coun-

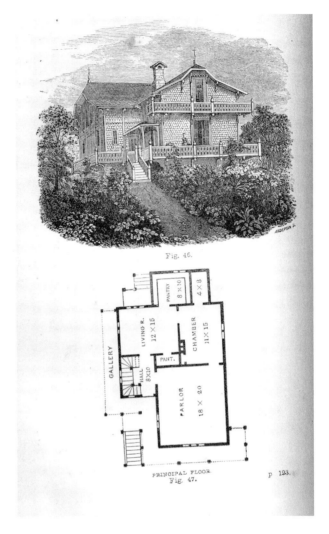

Fig. 46.

PRINCIPAL FLOOR
Fig. 47.

p 123.

Swiss Cottage. (From Downing, A Treatise)

try residence needing at least three servants—an unlikely prospect for most northern farmers.[40] But he assured the "many persons with small cottage places, of little decided character, who have neither room, time, nor income, to attempt the improvement of their grounds fully, after either of those two schools" that they might still have a garden, " . . . *by attempting only the simple and the natural*; and the unfailing way to secure this, is by employing as leading features only trees and grass" (emphasis in original).[41] Trees and grass were the bare minimum, flowers extra credit.[42]

Late in 1841, Downing wrote his friend Robert Donaldson that, since the book had come out, "Landscape Gardening bids fair to become a *profession* in this country," which was to say it had helped his design business. He began writing a second book, *Cottage Residences,* published in 1842, again with help from A. J. Davis. It was written ostensibly for the rural American of lesser means, for whom a Gothic mansion wasn't a fit "expression of purpose," besides being too expensive. Instead he offered an array of "cottages," all picturesque and asymmetrical, since "artistical irregularity" was better than regularity. Good taste was within everyone's reach. Simply pick a style for your site, family, and predilection. Or mix the styles up, as with "Villa in the Italian Style, Bracketed."[43] In the garden, all one needed to be tasteful were "the character of dignity and simplicity arising from extensive prospect, large and lofty trees, and considerable breadth of lawn." The two books were successful, running through many editions. Downing gained renown and influence. In 1842 he ran an ad in his journal advertising his services as a "professional" landscape gardener.[44] But with influence came critics, one of whom accused him of "corrupting the public taste, and infecting the parvenues with the mania for Gothic Castle-building."[45] Others ridiculed his proposal of a "cottage ornée," a "gingerbread, crocketed, turreted cottage,"[46] as completely unrealistic for real farmers. The agricultural reformer Solon Robinson complained that Downing's models worked for "the upper ten thousand," but "the wants of 'the lower ten thousand' are not satisfied."[47]

These comments revealed tensions in the larger national "rural arts" project under way—a seemingly universal call to return to America's agrarian roots. It found expression most often in worries about the exploding cities and factories of the eastern seaboard, as here in Emerson's "The Eye and the Ear" lecture of 1837: "We divorce ourselves from nature; we hide ourselves in cities and lose the affecting spectacle of Day and Night which she cheers and instructs her children withal."[48] Especially acute were anxieties about children in cities: Henry David Thoreau

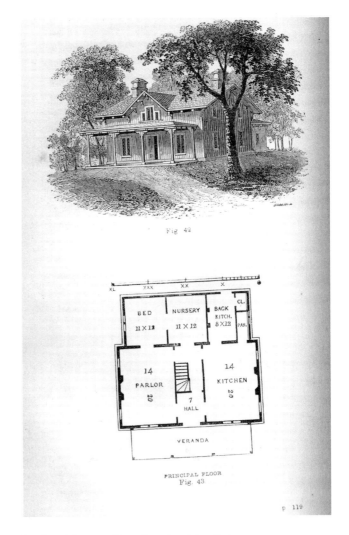

Bracketed Cottage. (From Downing, *A Treatise*)

was taken aback by the sight of several "ill-dressed and ill-mannered" twelve-year-old boys smoking cigars and loitering on a city street in 1851: "A true culture is more possible to the savage than to the boy of average intellect, born of average parents, in a great city. How can they be kept clean, physically or morally? It is folly to attempt to educate children within a city; the first step must be to remove them out of it."[49] Thoreau pulled a complete pole reversal, making cities out to be the real wilderness or jungle, where civilized people reverted to savagery. These worries took on the character of an all-out attack on urbanism by the American intelligentsia, with a moral dimension coming chiefly from clergymen and social reformers, and a philosophical and self-help bent articulated by Transcendentalists such as Emerson and Thoreau. It was an echo of the British response to the pollution, poverty, and vice of its Dickensian industrial cities—recall that Charles Dickens wrote his novels from the 1830s to 1860s. But in the United States, so self-conscious of the singular advantage of its vast lands, the reaction took the form of a programmatic idealization of rural life, with its clean air and experience of nature.

The rural Utopia was lauded in sermons, in lectures like Emerson's, in the popular press, and by popular writers like Thoreau and Susan Fenimore Cooper, whose *Rural Hours*, a journal celebrating country pleasures and the observation of birds and wild things, was published in 1850 and became a model for American nature writing (Thoreau read it four years before publishing *Walden*). Cooper, the daughter of James, who was educated in Europe and only took the name Fenimore as an adult launching a literary career, updated the Virgilian tone to a modern American idiom and described a rural world where the wilderness has long been vanquished, a tamed landscape where the birds every year diminished and the great trees were felled by the greedy. Its bucolic serenity demonstrated how much had changed: her grandfather, Judge William Cooper, had also written about the same Otsego Lake, New York country, after he purchased a large swath of land and founded Cooperstown. He published a series of letters about how to settle the virgin wilderness with axe and ox as *A Guide to the Wilderness; or, The History of the First Settlements in the Western Counties of New York with Useful Instructions to Future Settlers,* in 1810. Her father's books, too, had been centered on the raw confrontation between wilderness and civilization, between Indians and land-hungry settlers, mediated by the frontiersman Natty Bumppo. By 1850, when she wrote, the Indians and the wilderness were but romantic vestiges in an orderly agrarian landscape around Cooperstown.

But reality didn't always comply with the rural reformers' vision. Travelers in the countryside were appalled at the poor state of eastern farms, where they found not bucolic bliss but considerable poverty amid ugly, falling-down shacks, barns, and fences, with farm animals running loose in the mud and filth. There was no sign of the cottage ornée with its velvet lawn and exotic trees.[50] Many theorized, as Downing did, that the lack of attachment to place was the culprit and took the poor upkeep of houses and yards as signs of moral debasement.[51] To them beauty equaled virtue. Downing quoted Yale president Timothy Dwight's comment that "uncouth, mean, ragged, dirty houses . . . will regularly be accompanied by coarse, groveling manner. The dress, the furniture, the mode of living, and the manners will all correspond with the appearance of the buildings and will universally be in every such case of a vulgar and debased nature."[52] The solution was instruction: Downing wrote to his hero Loudon that American farmers were "deficient in knowledge" and "sadly in need of enlightening."[53] His calling to inculcate taste took on the character of a crusade of betterment echoing the "perfectibilist" campaigns of religious betterment that raged in New England in the first half of the century, but with the goal of spiritual salvation replaced with that of a beautiful home, to be reached through imitation of the wealthy and refined.[54] The first step would be to convince his countrymen to plant trees, as though in penance for all they had chopped down. He joined an explosion of horticultural and arboriculture groups, like the recently founded Ornamental Tree Society, and next published his *Fruits and Fruit Trees of America,* in 1845, probably modeled on Loudon's massive *Arboretum et Fruticetum Britannicum*, drawing on his Newburgh nursery expertise; it went through thirteen editions and sold close to fifteen thousand copies, an impressive number, by his death.[55] Downing became an acknowledged fruit expert, widely cited and lauded.

Horticulture was good for morals and no less good for business. The Erie Canal and the welter of other canals and railroads that followed it had electrified the movement west by providing frontier farmers with access to markets. In the 1840s, the advancing line of statehood extended beyond the Mississippi River to include Wisconsin, Iowa, Missouri, Arkansas, Louisiana, and Texas. Eastern farmers, with generally poorer soils, were unable to compete with the tides of wheat from the more fertile West and so turned to perishable crops that couldn't be shipped long distances to market: fruit, vegetables, and dairying. In 1847, total U.S. "garden" produce earned $459 million.[56] Most Americans were still farmers, and agricultural production was worth twice as much as all other business. Nevertheless, most farmers struggled with high debt loads to buy land, low commodity prices because of overproduction, and high transportation costs because of the distances involved and the freight rates of the proliferating railroads.[57] Farmers around cities added spiking land costs and severe pollution from coal burning to their woes. Fruit orchards near New York City were devastated by soot. Many farmers sold out; many of the others let most of their land revert to forest and switched to dairy cows on a small part, which afforded better cash flow than mixed farming. All of this sped up the conversion of mixed farms in the East to gentlemen's hobby farms that didn't have to earn their keep, such as Senator Daniel Webster's much-admired model farm south of Boston, and well-capitalized market farm operations owned by men of means, such as on Long Island, where high land costs drove small farmers to sell out to "retired, or half-retired merchants . . . a class of persons farming about as much for amusement as for profit," according to one contemporary journalist.[58] Perversely, the cult of fruit culture fed into the ancient Country ideology equation of economic position with moral character, and the cultivation of land with the virtuous cultivation of politics; rich men with urban fortunes, otherwise objects of natural suspicion in rural, egalitarian America, could claim patriotism by buying country estates and planting them with fruit.[59] This was model farming, but it wasn't a model for many.

The market revolution had an analogous effect on the lives of women. As they caused the demise of mixed farming, commercialization and industrialization led to the demise of the piecework system of manufacturing in the home, thereby taking many women out of the economy. Their sphere was then limited to, and defined as, the home, shorn of its responsibilities for production and income. The rise of the middle class created its own, circular incentives to accelerate this process: since a family would be eager to show off its arrival in the middle class, it became imperative for a man of means to have a "dependent lady" and a pleasure garden, rather than a working farm or working wife, at home.[60] Downing and others sought to enlist these newly idled ladies in their campaign for taste: he used his editorship of the *Horticulturalist*, from 1846 until his death, as a reformist pulpit, urging women to beautify their surroundings as a form of quasi-spiritual uplift—in effect, it gave these women a job to do to replace the status and responsibility they had lost. In one editorial, "On Feminine Taste in Rural Affairs," he advised ladies to tend flowers, but nothing more strenuous, no "rough toil," since it was "beyond their province." This view of gender roles aligned with his aesthetic categories, since Burke had conventionally equated the beautiful with the feminine and the picturesque with the masculine,[61] and his veneration of the home fit perfectly with the broad focus on and redefinition of the home as women's space in American (and British) culture. Downing's *Treatise* appeared the same year as Catharine Beecher's *Treatise on Domestic Economy*, which defined the household as women's exclusive world. In 1843, Downing edited the U.S. edition of Mrs. Jane Webb Loudon's *Gardening for Ladies*.[62]

The notion that there was a moral lesson to be found in flower gardening was widespread, supporting a minor publishing industry, including books such as Mrs. Loudon's and Joseph Breck's *Flower-Garden*, in which Breck compared women to flowers, as "they resemble them in their fragility, beauty, and perishable nature," and that of Catharine Beecher's brother, the hugely influential abolitionist preacher Henry Ward Beecher, who in his *Plain and Pleasant Talk about Fruits, Flowers, and Farming* asserted that flowers were "revelations of God's sense of beauty, as addressed to the taste, and to something finer and deeper than taste, that power within us which spiritualizes matter and communes with God through His work."[63] (Catharine and Henry's sister was Harriet Beecher Stowe, the author of the antislavery bestseller *Uncle Tom's Cabin* and the paragon of the sentimentalist literature of the era.) But the passive, feminine, and essentially nostalgic values the culture asserted were exactly the values it didn't possess. The historian Ann Douglas showed that the sentimentalism of Victorian culture and its obsessions with feminine purity and religious conformity served to cover up the ugly underlying reality of the nineteenth century as an agrarian society being transformed into an urban, industrial, and violently expansionist continental state: "Between 1820 and 1875, in the midst of the transformation of the American economy into the most powerfully aggressive capitalist system in the world, American culture seemed bent on establishing a perpetual Mother's Day."[64]

Henry Ward Beecher wrote: "Money is the one manure which the farm greedily covets."[65] He'd hit the nail on the head. Fruit culture demanded cash up front. It was one face of the wedge of a fast-moving capitalist transformation—of manufacturing, of domestic life, of the farm sector, and of cities, with the result the creation of a "Country" space surrounding the cities, hollowing out former farmlands, populated by gentlemen and beautified and improved with city money. Thoreau's Concord, Massachusetts, was already a country suburb of Boston when he wrote his masterpieces. When he encountered real wilderness, on a trip to Mount Katahdin in Maine, he was frightened by it—"vast, Titanic, inhuman nature," he shuddered, "savage and dreary"—and hurried home to his tamer fields.[66] Nathaniel Willis, who published a series of views called *American Scenery Illustrated* in 1840, remarked of the Hudson River houses, "There is a suburban look and character about all the villas on the Hudson which seem out of place among such scenery. They are suburbs; in fact, steam has destroyed the distance between them and the city." Away from navigable waters, the railroad served the same purpose. The first railroad in America began service in 1829, and by the 1840s commuter railroads were transforming rural areas around major cities into bedroom and second-home communities.[67]

The literary critic Leo Marx, in his landmark study *The Machine in the Garden*, published in 1964, dated this epochal transformation of the American landscape—physical and mental alike—to 1844, when Nathaniel Hawthorne, sitting in the fields near Concord, sketched a story in his notebook in which a quiet, bucolic farming village called Sleepy Hollow finds its peace shattered by the Iron Horse: "But, hark! there is the whistle of the locomotive—the long shriek, harsh, above all other harshness. . . . It tells a story of busy men, citizens, from the hot street, who have come to spend a day in a country village, men of business. . . ." The same year, the English poet William Wordsworth wrote a poem decrying the arrival of the railroad in his beloved Lake District, which began: "Is then no nook of English ground secure / From rash assault?" Even the aging Washington Irving complained when his "little nookery" at Sunnyside, in the actual Sleepy Hollow, New York, was rudely cut off from the river by the new railroad line roaring past. Ralph Waldo Emerson satirized Wordsworth's ineffectual resistance to the march of progress by noting that he had "attempted to exorcise" the railroad "with a sonnet."[68] But most to the point, now as much as then, is the journal entry Emerson made in 1842:

> *I hear the whistle of the locomotive in the woods. Wherever this*
> *music comes it has a sequel. It is the voice of the civility of the*
> *Nineteenth Century saying, "Here I am." It is interrogative: it*
> *is prophetic: and this Cassandra is believed: "Whew! Whew!*
> *Whew! How is real estate here in the swamp and wilderness? Ho*
> *for Boston! Whew! Whew! . . . I will plant a dozen houses on this*
> *pasture next moon, and a village anon. . . .*[69]

These same writers, city bashers all, had no love of farming, either. The attack on the city was mirrored by attacks on the unsightly realities of real agriculture, which they sought to replace with a sanitized, aestheticized, feminized version of pseudo-agriculture, subsidized by the commercial activity of men who commuted to, or retired from, cities. What they called this new construct was "horticulture." Susan Fenimore Cooper liked her cornfields "at a little distance, where one may note the changes in its coloring with the advancing season." Thoreau too, couldn't romanticize it: "I know the country is mean enough," yet he still preferred it to the city.[70] In practice, the value of suburbs for those who could afford them was as a refuge from the city, with its stresses, pollution, and masses of immigrant poor—and a refuge from work. No country villa

View from Wodenethe. (From Downing, *A Treatise*)

owner wanted to get off the steamer only to milk the cows in the early morning darkness.

Suburbanization is a dream of transcendence, and has been since Virgil discovered Arcadia in a pasture not far from Rome. Emerson understood this in his 1838 lecture "Home," where he made clear that a residence must have a garden to offer as a "balsam" to relieve the stress of "studies, handiworks, arts, trade, politics"—in short, work.[71] At the end of the day, Loudon and Downing were serving not the rural but the country-suburban classes, in their several gradations, according to whether they could afford a mansion, villa, or merely a cottage surrounded by trees and lawn, all equally concerned with showing good taste. What Loudon was doing, in his own words, was cataloging the "beauties and conveniences" that are the proper "objects to be desired for a wealthy man in his country residence."[72]

In July 1850 Downing boarded ship for Liverpool, bound on a tour of England and the Continent. He had several purposes: to see English houses and gardens for himself (many that he had previously written about); to buy woodcuts and engravings for the *Horticulturalist;* and to seek an English architect to partner with back home. The same year he published *The Architecture of Country Houses,* his most ambitious architecture book yet, still in collaboration with Alexander Jackson Davis—who received any building commissions that came their way. Downing needed to team with another, more junior architect, "so as to be enabled to put in practice on his return to America his aspirations with regard to that art," the man he partnered with would later recall. From Liverpool he toured for six weeks en route to London, visiting estates, botanical gardens, and arboreta, including Chatsworth, the estate of the Duke of Devonshire, where he saw the huge *Victoria regia* water lily, the tropical sensation du jour recently brought from Brazil. He was especially impressed by the public parks, including Regent's Park in London.

The park was a British craze, one of the quintessential inventions of the age, a new kind of landscape that was a reaction to and paradoxical product of the increasing density of urban life. The grime and poverty of the teeming, seething industrial cities had fueled a reform movement, beginning with the 1819 Factory Act meant to protect women and children from the abuses of the industrial system. An outgrowth of this concern was the demand that city dwellers, who had no access to the refreshment afforded to gentlefolk on their country estates, with their deer-stocked hunting parks, should have "parks" of their own, within a short distance of the city. In the 1830s, a series of royal properties in the fashionable West End of London were opened to the public, including St. James's Park, Green Park, Hyde Park, and Kensington Gardens. Reformers pushed for something similar in the crowded East End, and eventually saw the opening of Victoria Park in the early 1840s. Simultaneously, a fashion for living in what we would call inner-ring garden suburbs blossomed among the upper and middle classes: owners of land adjacent to cities found they could build fashionable housing and provide park amenities as a sales pitch. This was the business model for Regent's Park, a piece of crown land near Buckingham Palace, which the Prince Regent profitably subdivided into town houses surrounding a park designed by John Nash and paid for with the proceeds. Regent's Park opened to subscribers in 1820 and to the general public in 1835.[73] The model spread, including to Birkenhead Park, a new residential development across the Mersey River from Liverpool, and to a growing number of other private "villa parks," really just subdivisions, many gated, of fashionable houses with private gardens set down in a parklike, suburban setting. During the three years he spent in England as American consul, Nathaniel Hawthorne lived in two villa parks: Rock Park, Cheshire, a boat ride from shabby Birmingham, and which was gated and policed so that "no ragged or ill-looking person" could enter; and Blackheath Park, outside London: "one of those oases that have grown up (in comparatively recent years, I believe)," he wrote, describing it this way:

> *The scene is semi-rural. Ornamental trees overshadow the side-walks, and grassy margins border the wheeltracks. The houses . . . stand aloof from the street, and separated each from its neighbor by hedge or fence, in accordance with the careful exclusiveness of the English character, which impels the occupant, moreover, to cover the front of his dwelling with as much concealment of shrubbery as his limits will allow. Through the interstices, you catch glimpses of well-kept lawns, generally ornamented with flowers, and with what the English call rock-work, being heaps of ivy-grown stones and fossils, designed for romantic effect in a small way.*[74]

The park hadn't escaped notice in America: *New-York Evening Post* editor and poet William Cullen Bryant crusaded for a public park in the city throughout the 1840s; in 1844 he warned that time was short, as "commerce is devouring inch by inch the coast of the island, and if we would rescue any part of it for health and recreation it must be done now."[75] Downing also got on board, writing an editorial in his journal in 1848 praising the new German parks such as Munich's Englischer Garten—publicly funded pleasure grounds, open to all, which granted, he claimed (without ever having seen them), a "social freedom, and an easy and agreeable intercourse of all classes, that strikes an American with surprise and delight."[76] What he later saw in England awed him, with its level of taste and attainment, but he hewed to his American identity, reporting that, while standing on the ramparts of Warwick Castle, he had looked westward and thought: "to America has been reserved the greater blessing of solving for the world the true problem of humanity—that of the abolition of all castes, and the recognition of the divine rights of every human soul." This was high rhetoric indeed, but highly commonplace in his era, especially in the Northeast, where the tide of abolitionism was rising and infusing its urgent, exalted spirit and language into the general project of social reform. (The need for abolition alone proved that America was far from a classless society; if Downing was to be right, his country had a long way to go to fulfill its "reserved" mission.)

As to the practical reason for his trip, Downing hit the jackpot. After seeing an exhibit at the Architectural Association in London, he asked to meet the man responsible for several drawings he liked. Summoned, Calvert Vaux appeared. The two hit it off, and the charismatic Downing had Vaux convinced almost immediately to accompany him to New York; they left in less than a week. Vaux later recalled his unlikely seduction: he had no reason to leave London, "but," he said, "I liked him so much, his foresight and observation were so apparent in the conversations we had and above all his style was so calculated to win confidence that without a fear I relinquished all and accompanied him."[77] Back in Newburgh, the two added an office wing to Downing's house and began taking architectural as well as landscape commissions: a dozen or so houses in the first two years, including several near Newburgh, and Springside, an estate for the wealthy brewer Matthew Vassar upriver in Poughkeepsie, and, marking Downing's arrival as the leading designer in the country, the public grounds in Washington, D.C., between the Capitol building and the White House.

IN SEPTEMBER 1851, Downing drove his carriage into Brooklyn and through the Green-Wood Cemetery, which had been founded in 1838 as a landscaped park of two hundred acres and had become an instant favorite attraction for fashionable New Yorkers.[78] Green-Wood was modeled directly on the success of Mount Auburn Cemetery in Cambridge, Massachusetts, near the Charles River, just upstream from Harvard. Opened in 1831 to great acclaim, Mount Auburn had been proposed as a "suburban cemetery," designed along the lines of a picturesque pastoral landscape garden and intended specifically to avoid the unhealthful "graveyard exhalations"[79] that many people imagined emanating from the dank, crowded churchyard burial grounds supposedly common in British and American cities. After passing a massive, Egyptian-style gate and a Gothic chapel, a visitor would drive his carriage along paths named after trees and plants (Magnolia Avenue, Cowslip Path, etc.) while admiring the tasteful and grand mortuary monuments and enjoying the breeze and the views. There were views because Mount Auburn was intentionally set in a field of small hillocks, to guarantee well-drained soil. (Green-Wood in Brooklyn was also set on a hill, actually a glacial terminal moraine, a pile of loose till scraped up and left behind by a glacier, hilly and sandy, so no good to farm but perfect for landscaped cemeteries; Green-Wood would soon be joined on its moraine by Evergreens, Lutheran, Mount Carmel, and Cypress Hill cemeteries.)[80] Mount Auburn was funded by the Massachusetts Horticultural Society, both as a demonstration project of how a properly executed landscape might lift the spirits in the face of death, and as an investment; it was a success on both counts. It was one more entrepreneurial expression of the wave of public welfare reform coming out of Boston—the self-styled "American Athens"—along with calls for abolition, public education, child welfare, water and sanitation systems, prison reform, asylums for the indigent and insane, and greater freedoms for women.[81] Among those yearned-for freedoms was the liberty to be seen in public, social space—increasingly difficult as respectable "ladies" were confined to their homes by middle- and upper-class norms of refined domesticity. In Britain and the Continent, parks, squares, and promenades like London's Pall Mall served this function, but these were mostly lacking in the United States, making the new garden cemeteries magnets for carriage riding for the well-to-do.[82] Visiting the cemetery became so popular that in 1839, an illustrated guidebook was published: *The Picturesque Pocket Companion and Visitor's Guide Through Mt. Auburn.*[83] Other cities fell over themselves to construct copies: Laurel Hill Cemetery in Philadelphia followed in 1836, then Green-Wood two years later, and all across the country (today there are at least sixteen other "Greenwood" cemeteries in the United States).

To Downing, the cemetery was an advance guard, preparing the way for public parks. He wrote in an 1849 editorial:

> *The great attraction of these cemeteries is not in the fact that they are burial places. . . . The true secret of the attraction lies in the natural beauty of the sites, and in the tasteful and harmonious embellishment of these sites by art. . . . Hence to the inhabitant of the town a visit to one of these spots has the united charm of nature and art—the double wealth of rural and moral associations. . . . Indeed, in the absence of great public gardens, such as we must surely one day have in America, our rural cemeteries are doing a great deal to enlarge and educate the popular taste in rural embellishment.*[84]

Three years later he published another appeal: "The New York Park." His tone and diction had grown more impassioned, nationalist, and populist, aligning the need for a park with the current philanthropic conviction that the poor urban masses could be raised out of ignorance and vice with access to the finer things, through public libraries and painting exhibitions like those put on by the American Art Union in Manhattan.[85] He dismissed New York City as an "arid desert of business and dissipation"[86] and exhorted grandly: "Open wide, therefore, the doors of your libraries and picture galleries, all ye true republicans! Build halls where Knowledge shall be freely diffused among men, and not shut up within the narrow walls of narrower institutions. Plant spacious parks in your cities, and unloose their gates as wide as the gates of morning to the whole people."[87]

New York City was exploding, from 123,706 people in 1820 to 813,669 in 1860, a quarter of them Irish immigrants pushed out by the English and the potato famine.[88] In 1852, Downing's plan for the Washington, D.C., public grounds, a cross between a naturalistic English landscape garden and a Loudonesque arboretum, was approved by President Millard Fillmore. The next year, the New York state legislature voted funds to buy land for Central Park. Downing would almost certainly have been picked for the job if he hadn't stepped aboard the *Henry Clay* one year earlier.

––––––––––––

In the late spring of 1850, a month before Downing's departure, another young American, by the name of Frederick Law Olmsted, shipped out of New York Harbor for Liverpool. Along with his younger brother, John, and a friend, Charles Loring Brace, he was bound for a six-month walking trip through England, France, Belgium, Holland, Germany, Scotland, and Ireland, intending to see the great sights and study gardens, arboretums, and farms along the way, since he was a farmer.[89] Olmsted was twenty-eight years old, seven years Downing's junior. He had arrived at farming after trying his hand at a fair selection of the avenues open to a boy born in Hartford, Connecticut, in the early 19th century: surveyor, mercantile clerk, Yale student, and common seaman on a China trading ship.[90] Once he'd made his career choice, his father, a prosperous enough merchant, had staked him first with a farm on the Connecticut coast near Guilford, then, when it failed to make a profit, with another on the south shore of Staten Island, near New York City. Olmsted was a "scientific" farmer and an avid reader of journals such as the *Cultivator* and the *Horticulturalist*, both owned by the same man, Luther Tucker. In 1847 he wrote a letter to the latter (which Downing edited) inquiring about growing fruit trees on the windy shoreline, and later traveled to the Newburgh nursery and bought seventy-five apple and sixty quince trees from him. When he returned from Europe, Downing asked him to write about his experiences in Germany for the *Horticulturalist*. What he wrote about instead was Birkenhead Park. Built by Joseph Paxton (who would construct the glass and steel Crystal Palace for London's 1851 Great Exhibition) and opened in June 1844, the park featured 120 landscaped acres surrounded by private house lots sold by the city to cover costs. Olmsted and his companions had not heard of it (Downing apparently hadn't, either, and didn't see it while he was in Liverpool roughly a month later) but were advised by a local baker not to miss it. They shouldered their packs and took the ferry across the Mersey to have a look. Olmsted marveled at the "simple," naturalistic effect Paxton had created in an old clay field by digging ponds, raising hills with the spoils, and planting a faithful recreation of the English countryside, complete with meadows, brambles, and meandering footpaths. He was even more impressed by the fact that it was a "People's Park": "I was glad to observe that the privileges of the garden were enjoyed about equally by all classes. There were some who were attended by servants . . . but a large proportion were of the common ranks. . . ."[91] Olmsted's piece was well received and led to publication of his letters home while on the trip as a book, *Walks and Talks of an American Farmer in England*, the first volume of which appeared in 1852, its first review printed in the *Horticulturalist*.[92]

It might seem like a series of improbable convergences that the lives of Downing and Olmsted overlapped in just such a way that the baton of building New York's great park could have passed between them at so precise a historical juncture. But in their time American society was incomparably smaller and more intimate than in ours; people of Olmsted and Downing's social class knew one another, and people who shared the same interests found one another. What is more amazing is how much of the sequence of events happened entirely by chance.

Olmsted's book impressed the editor of the *New York Daily Times*, who sent him to the American South as a special correspondent to the paper, charged with reporting back on conditions in the slave states. Olmsted traveled extensively through the region during the years 1853–57, and his pieces, distinguished by their careful observation and reasoned argument that the emancipation of the slaves ought to be effected gradually, eventually were published in three volumes. None was a big financial success, but together they established his reputation as a knowledgeable and fair-minded man. Back in New York, he was asked to become a partner in a publishing venture, which ultimately failed, leaving him in considerable debt. In 1857 he was thirty-seven years old, still dependent on his father and without real prospects of a career. Then, by chance, the job of assistant to the superintendent of the new Central Park, then in the early planning stages, came open. His friends encouraged him to apply. He wrote to his brother: "What else can I do for a living?" Friends in high places wrote letters of recommendation, including William Cullen Bryant and Washington Irving.[93] With no direct experience in landscape gardening, Olmsted was hired. In the meantime, Calvert Vaux had moved his architecture practice to New York City after designing a dozen houses with Downing and more on his own. He had met Olmsted at Downing's nursery and asked him to collaborate with him on an entry to the newly announced competition for a comprehensive design for the park. Olmsted, somewhat doubtfully, agreed. Their plan, "Greensward," was chosen, and the rest is history.

Both Vaux and Olmsted later acknowledged their debt to Downing's ideas and influence. Olmsted dedicated the second volume of *Walks and Talks* to him, and Vaux dedicated his book *Villas and Cottages* to Mrs. Downing, who survived her husband. But there are fundamental differences in the vision of Downing and that of Central Park. The genius of the Greensward plan is in how it masked the crush of urbanity around the park: by putting the necessary crossing streets below grade, by using diagonals and the land's rocky terrain to create illusions of extension and isolation from the city. The plan was all about circulation, with its winding, separated carriage and walking paths, and the great promenade that sliced straight through the southern half of the space, providing the otherwise naturalistic park with a formal entrance and strong structure. But the rest of it seemed an outright re-creation of nature, certainly inspired by Paxton's work at Birkenhead and the English landscape tradition of the 18th century. Its essential elements were Capability Brown's: trees, grass, and water. Olmsted and Vaux had a single clear intent—to bring the country to the city. The park's "one great purpose," they wrote, is "to supply the hundreds of thousands of tired workers, who have no opportunity to spend their summers in the coun-

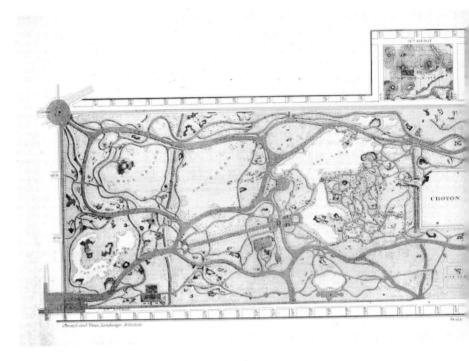

Central Park plan. (Courtesy National Park Service)

try, a specimen of God's handiwork that shall be to them, inexpensively, what a month or two in the White Mountains or the Adirondacks is, at great cost, to those in easier circumstances."[94] (The idea of the vacation was more pointed in these days; it wasn't for fun or recreation, but re-creation, literally the rest and repair of unhealthily stressed minds and bodies.) Elsewhere Olmsted would use a remarkably medical language to describe the park, casting it as therapy for the tired masses, a kind of gigantic public health measure. He listed the city's stresses: "vital exhaustion, nervous irritation and constitutional depression . . . tendencies, through excessive materialism, to loss of faith and lowness of spirit."[95] If the diagnosis was clear, equally clear was the medicine needed: since the vast majority of urbanites had been raised in the country, Olmsted reasoned, a dose of it would cure their urban ills. If Jefferson's garden was created in the service of enlightenment and Downing's in the service of domesticity, Olmsted and Vaux's was created in the

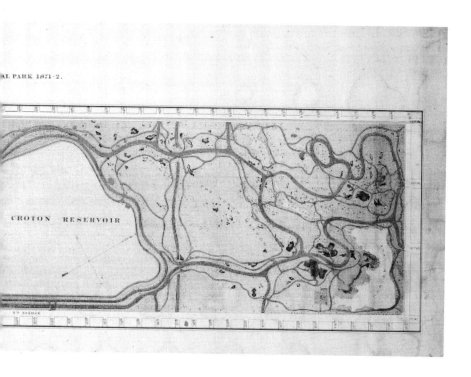

service of therapy. This was the distance traveled by American culture in its first independent hundred years.

Work on the park was interrupted by the outbreak of the Civil War in 1861, and Olmsted accepted an appointment to head the U.S. Sanitary Commission, a privately funded effort to send hospital ships, doctors, nurses, and supplies to the battlefront to care for wounded soldiers (and the forerunner of the American Red Cross). He performed brilliantly, demonstrating his exceptional talent for organizing vast numbers of people and flows of money and matériel. After two years the army was able to assume the work, and Olmsted took a job offered him managing a huge gold mine in California's Sierra Nevada, the Mariposa Estate, located just miles down the Merced River from Yosemite Valley. Yosemite in those years was just becoming nationally famous through the photos of Carleton Watkins and the paintings of Albert Bierstadt and others of the Rocky Mountain School, the legacy of the Hudson River School of

People in Central Park. (Courtesy National Park Service)

Thomas Cole. In 1864, the U.S. government granted the Yosemite region to California as a public reserve; Olmsted was appointed to the commission charged with writing a management plan for the area as a park. But after two years the mine syndicate went bankrupt and so Olmsted was again out of a job. He decided to try his hand at landscape design full-time, making plans for a cemetery and a college in the Bay Area and proposing a great city park for San Francisco (his ambitious plan never came to fruition).

In 1865, Olmsted was back in New York, working again with Calvert Vaux, this time on Prospect Park, the city of Brooklyn's answer to Central Park (which had opened in 1859 but wouldn't be fully completed until 1873). The partners believed that the new park could be even better, as they didn't have to contend with existing reservoirs, city streets, or a long, narrow site. Instead they had a broad diamond, more than a mile

Carriageway and rocks, Central Park. (Courtesy National Park Service)

across, divided into three natural terranes, which they capitalized on by reducing each to one pole of Brown's triad: *grass* in the Long Meadow, a big sweep of pasture bordered by trees; *trees* in the middle, hilly portion, a wooded glacial moraine the designers striated with paths, and *water* in the lake carved from a former farm field at the south end of the site. Vaux wrote Olmsted that their plan would enact "the translation of the republican art idea in its highest form into the acres we want to control."[96] But vague political philosophy aside, they intended the new park to have a primarily therapeutic function, as they explained in their preliminary report on the design: "the feeling of relief experienced by those entering . . . on escaping from the cramped, confined and controlling circumstances of the streets of the town; in other words, *a sense of enlarged freedom* is to all, at all times, the most certain and the most valuable gratification afforded by a park" (emphasis in original).[97]

What Olmsted, Vaux & Co, Landscape Architects (as their firm was now called, the first use of the title) were doing at the level of the individual park visitor was mood engineering. At the level of the city as a whole what they were doing was social engineering, since the park for them embodied a vision of community, and harmony with nature, descended straightforwardly from the ideal of the New England village and applied to the pathologies of the new megalopolis. The success of Olmsted and Vaux's parks was a sign of, and a perfect metaphor for, the urban transformation of America in the 19th century. Even more than the agrarian dreaming of the 18th century, they were art works in the pure pastoral mode. A simple definition of pastoral is that shepherds and sheep are depicted; this works for Virgil and Poussin, and it works well enough for the picturesque landscape garden if we allow the shepherds and sheep to be replaced by workers with scythes, cutting the grass. A secondary definition of the pastoral is an ideal, idealized world,

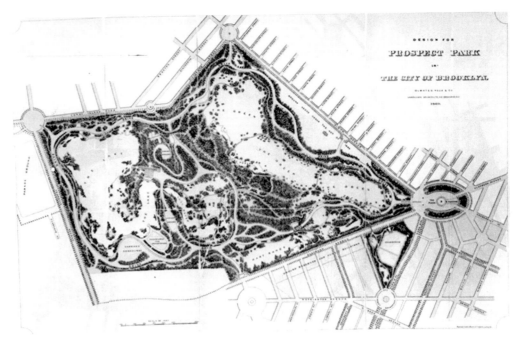

Prospect Park plan. (Courtesy National Park Service)

set against the fallen, corrupted, alienating world of the present. In any age, pastoral opposes nature to culture, simplicity to sophistication, order to disorder, the past against the present, and the country against the city; it is fundamentally anti-urban. Great irony, then, that the key art forms of the 19th century city were the wilderness landscape painting and the landscaped city park.

As cities spread and dominated their hinterlands, and the true agrarian countryside emptied of population as the small farm economy was replaced by factory farming, fear of the city had become a pervasive, basic element of the Victorian worldview. (In 1852, Herman Melville had a character in his novel *Pierre*, a country girl seeing New York City for the first time, ask: "Think'st thou Pierre, the time will ever come when all the earth shall be paved?") Once the city had decisively triumphed against the wilderness, modern pastoralism reclaimed the landscape, first in the form of the city park, bringing "country" into the city, then reexporting this aestheticized wilderness ideal to the areas around cities, as garden suburbs, which were linked to the city by parkways—city streets turned into linear parks, such as Olmsted and Vaux's 1868 Eastern and Ocean parkways connecting to Prospect Park, and later Riverside Park in Manhattan. (Olmsted in fact had a plan for a system of parkways that would allow a carriage to be driven from the ocean to the top of Manhattan in a day—in effect turning New York into one big scenic, mock-rural leisure attraction.)[98] In a few years the natural park idea was extended to the national park, with the establishment of Yellowstone National Park in 1872, New York's Adirondack Park in 1885, and Yosemite National Park, transferred back to the federal government in 1890. This last development can be best understood not as the preservation of wilderness, since this was not the goal, but the designation of large tracts of scenic lands, cleared with guns of Indians and wolves, as resorts for public recreation—in essence, city parks once removed from the city.[99] In other words, the advent of the national park marked the total triumph of the city over the wilderness.

Until his retirement near the dawn of the 20th century, Frederick Law

Llewellyn Park, view. (From Downing, *A Treatise*)

Olmsted spent his career systematically applying his therapy to the continent, hired to design an incredible list of parks, city plans, campuses, estates, and suburban subdivisions. His practice completed the translation of the vision of the 18th century English landscape garden into an all-purpose template for the making and remaking of the American built environment—the city dressed as the country. Garden suburbs have been called "habitable" parks,[100] transpositions of the picturesque ideal to planned housing developments on the outskirts of cities. The first was Llewellyn Park, laid out in a stretch of wooded hills in West Orange, New Jersey, in 1853, in part by the architect Alexander Jackson Davis, for a wealthy New York druggist whose interesting aim for the project was to provide "a retreat for a man to exercise his own rights and privileges." The key to its success with other wealthy businessmen lay in the fact that it was connected to Manhattan, thirteen miles away, by the new Delaware, Lackawanna, & Western Railroad. Its aesthetic appeal lay in its winding roads, big, wooded lots, views, and fifty-acre "Ramble" at the center, a park for residents left in a nearly wild state—and from the fact that it was private, gated, and guarded.[101] It would be the model for the

American villa park, the houses farther apart, the layout more naturalistic than its English forebear. It was the shape of things to come. Susan
Fenimore Cooper wrote, prophetically, in 1868:

> *The time may come, perhaps, when the cities—greatly diminished*
> *in size—shall be chiefly abandoned to the drudgeries of business,*
> *to commerce and manufactures during the hours of day, and*
> *deserted at night; then the families of the employers and laborers*
> *shall live alike in suburban village homes. In the present state*
> *of civilization, every hamlet within a hundred miles of a large*
> *city may be considered as one of its suburbs. In former centuries,*
> *he was a wise man who left the village for the city. To-day, he*
> *is wise who goes to the city as to a market, but has a home in the*
> *country.*[102]

Olmsted and Vaux together designed sixteen suburbs, including Riv-

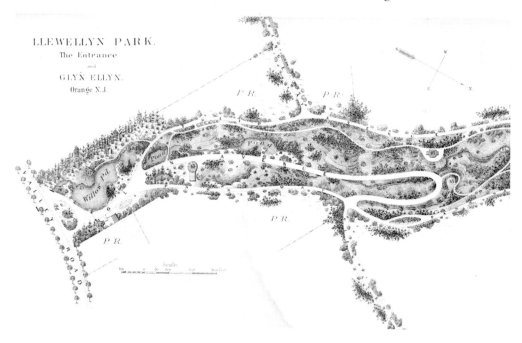

Llewellyn Park plans. (From Downing, *A Treatise*)

erside, Illinois; Brookline and Chestnut Hill, Massachusetts; Roland Park, Maryland; and Yonkers and Tarrytown Heights, New York. Normally dispassionate, Olmsted reveled in the garden suburb; they were, he wrote, "the most attractive, the most refined and the most soundly wholesome forms of domestic life, and the best application of the arts of civilization to which mankind has yet attained."[103] Olmsted himself left New York City in 1881 for Brookline, a leafy and wealthy suburb near Boston. It was a good dose of his own medicine, and he responded well to the treatment: "I enjoy this suburban country beyond expression," he rhapsodized.[104]

To begin to assess the legacy of Andrew Jackson Downing and the middle 19th century on our contemporary American landscape you don't have to look far: the nearest lawn will do, and it is most likely very near; whether you're in Poughkeepsie, Pocatello, or Phoenix, lawn literally carpets the country, about fifty thousand square miles, an area larger than Pennsylvania and larger than that occupied by any food crop.[105] Lawn is now the de facto national garden style. But when Downing wrote, lawn mowers were still uncommon and manicured turf was the exclusive province of well-off and well-informed gardeners. In the second edition of the *Treatise*, published in 1849, he wrote: "We can already, especially in the finer places on the Hudson, and about Boston, boast of many finely-kept lawns, and we hope every day, as the better class of country residences increases, to see this indispensable feature in tasteful grounds becoming better understood and more universal."[106] By 1870, grass had become the central issue in the American garden. It was de rigueur, as Frank J. Scott made clear in his book *The Art of Beautifying Suburban Home Grounds* (which he dedicated to Downing): "A smooth, closely shaven surface of grass is by far the most essential element of beauty on the grounds of a suburban home."[107] And it was *moral*, a sign of good citizenship, which must be made visible to the neighbors: "It is unchristian to hedge from the sight of others the beauties of nature which it has been our good fortune to

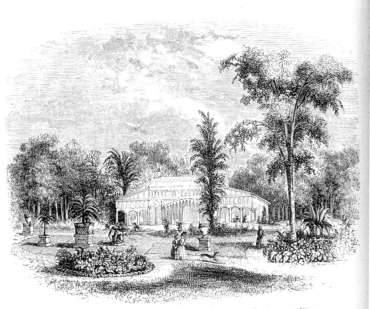

FIG. 73.—The Conservatory and Flower Garden at Montgomery Place.

Montgomery Place. (From Downing, *A Treatise*)

create or secure."[108] Downing had dismissed hedges as "an abomination," and English to boot. The "careful exclusiveness of the English character" that Hawthorne thought explained the hedges and vine-covered houses of England had evolved into, in small-town, democratic America, a compulsory inclusiveness that looked to a well-kept lawn as a bona fide of community membership and religious good standing.

The practical value of lawn for promoters like Downing was that it was a relatively inexpensive and quick way to spruce up a yard, and it had the added advantage of mimicking the vast greenswards of English estates, transforming the humble American rural dwelling into a miniature version of a baronial manor. On one hand, this toy castle was a testament to the American dream, as here the common man could hope to own land and build his own house to suit himself—even if that meant a castellated cottage in stucco on a small suburban lot. The results were often disconcerting. Instead of the vaunted American practicality, to which Downing gave lip service, what his clients were treated to were faintly ridiculous fantasies of gentility, delusions of grandeur in a self-consciously republican land: each householder with his own mini-Greek temple or Gothic castle, secure and independent in his own gentleman's deer park (even if the deer were made of cast iron; such ornaments proliferated in Victorian gardens). The contradictions are too obvious to miss, but nearly everyone did, and does: the idealization of wild land while liquidating the real thing as quickly as possible, of agrarian discipline and virtue while scorning actual farmers and actual work, of productive agriculture while producing little more than carpets of turf and annuals, of republican simplicity while aspiring to aristocratic pretension and display, of community harmony while fleeing the embrace of one's fellow (city-dwelling) citizens like the plague. To be fair, crime, filth, cholera epidemics, and other real hazards to health rendered 19th century cities like New York frequently unpleasant and occasionally dangerous. But the crusade to build city parks and garden suburbs did nothing to actually ameliorate any of this. The great 20th century architectural critic Lewis Mumford wrote of Olmsted, "By making nature urbane he naturalized the city."[109] But he did no such thing, merely bringing an artfully urbane simulacrum of nature into convenient reach and leaving the fundamental structure and reality of the city untouched. If the English liked the natural style because it hid their new money behind their progressive politics, Americans liked it because it hid their crimes against nature behind their vaunted veneration of it.

By ascribing the positive moral value of community responsibility to the lawn and the rest of the domestic enclosure and encouraging imitation of "the better class," tastemakers like Downing also ascribed its flip side: taste imitation as an arena of class competition. Downing encouraged Americans to view their gardens no less than their houses as emblems of virtue, and markers of upward mobility—in fact he constantly conflated the two things. So gardens and houses became articles of highly conscious conspicuous consumption, and, as the dynamic goes, places where the middle class imitated the rich and the rich struggled to stay one step ahead by grasping after the latest intellectual fashion. Downing is a classic American figure: from the middle ranks, self-made, doing well by preaching the good. He denounced envy while efficiently stoking it as his main line of business. This vector of taste toward aristocratic forms in the middle 19th century seems at odds with the main developments of the era: the technological progress of industrial capitalism and the steady march of egalitarian, reformist commitments, exemplified by the Civil War, emancipation, and the long list of public health and welfare programs that moved America from a basically backward 18th century to a 20th century position of world leadership. It was; and it was a rare, and rarely clear, surface sign of the emotional currents running beneath the march of progress: fear of rampant industry and cities, and anxieties about social change. As true progress moved in one direction, taste moved guilelessly in the other, retrograde direction, opening up an increasingly wide chasm between the two.

A big—perhaps the main—legacy of Downing and his protégés is our suburban sprawl—a complicated and ambivalent inheritance. In its worst aspects, the suburbs have signaled the displacement of agriculture, the despoliation of millions of acres of land, the withdrawal of vast swaths of the middle and upper classes from the common sphere, and the abject abandonment of the central cities to the poor, immigrant and native-born alike. But, at their best, the leafy garden suburbs are every bit as nice as Olmsted found them. Who wouldn't want to live there?

Mostly everybody does, even if it takes the form of a three-story condominium stacked against a long row of its clones like books on a shelf, such as those pushing into the woods that have grown up over Springside, the estate that Downing designed for Matthew Vassar in Poughkeepsie. The site exists today only as a remnant, a garden ruin, dotted by the rubble of eleven of the twelve whimsical "bracketed" cottage buildings Vaux designed for Vassar's *ferme ornée*, now sinking into the soil. Many times in the 20th century the house and its grounds came close to being subdivided as the adjacent fields have been, but were saved by the concerted effort of preservationists. Nevertheless, condos and houses loom close, and the roar of the adjacent Route 9 highway is loud. Next to the steep-roofed gatehouse, the only building still standing, a man pushes a shovel into a foot-high berm between his slightly yellowed, slightly ragged lawn and the asphalt of the road, and adds some bright, tall, new perennials he's bought from the garden center to a proud strip of color that delineates his private world from the pavement and hullabaloo beyond. This is gardening at its irreducible core—labor, money, vision, and optimism. Walking into what is left of Springside, now overgrown by weeds and forest growth barely beaten back by volunteer caretakers, you can glimpse the little Eden that Andrew Jackson Downing created for Matthew Vassar. The ground is dominated by a smattering of rocky outcrops, ten to fifteen feet high, dividing small, concave fields. It has the feel of a glacial landscape. Downing left the mini-hills forested and gave them names for their distinguishing features, like Maple Hill, Summer House Hill, Stone Henge, and Rock Roost, while in the hollows between he mostly prescribed mowed grass, with here and there a theme, such as Jet Vale, which featured a basin with a fountain spraying into the air. Trails and

[Fig. 78.]

Rustic Seat. (From Downing, *A Treatise*)

walks with occasional rustic twig benches and Italianate urns completed the picture of distributed interest. Upslope lay the kitchen garden, orchard, apiary, and the other farm buildings.

Vassar never built the mansion Vaux designed, living instead in the "cottage." He had spent eight thousand dollars for the property, and Downing managed to spend another hundred thousand dollars before his untimely demise. Apparently the *ferme ornée* that Vassar intended didn't pay—perhaps because the land is rocky and soggy (at least in the portion that now remains undeveloped). He originally bought it to build a landscaped cemetery à la Mount Auburn for the town, but the town council picked another spot, and so Vassar turned it over to Downing's vision. From surviving images, one can see that Springside was sweet and full-blown "Victorian" with its brightly colored dollhouse architecture and cheerfully contrived features; from these and walking the site one can see that it was also diminutive, even Lilliputian, the scale contracted and compressed like Walt Disney's three-fourth's-scale Main Street at Disneyland—designed to appeal to children. The gardenesque, with its fussy, random clutter and strange miniaturization, has not aged as well as the 18th century landscape garden, though it continues to dwell in our collective garden unconscious and is conjured in the form of brightly colored annual bedding schemes in civic and office parks, monotonous rose collections, and "Chinese dinner" assortments of single exotic plants arrayed in curved beds around a lawn.

In the middle of the 19th century an eerily dead-on riff on the aspiration of American gardens was published. Its author had for a time in 1826, the year of Thomas Jefferson's death, inhabited a dorm room on Jefferson's Range, as the terraced porticoes came to be called, at the University of Virginia. Edgar Allan Poe's story "The Domain of Arnheim," published in March 1846 in *Columbia* magazine, tells of a man named Ellison, an exemplary genius who inherits an unimaginably enormous fortune from a distant relative who has been dead for an interest-compounding century.

Ellison donates some of the fabulous sum, $450,000,000, to charity, but has "little faith" in man's ability to help himself, so he turns to his deep attraction to personal "poetry" or art, where he feels that the "sole legitimate field for the poetic exercise, lies in the creation of novel moods of purely physical loveliness." Upon further reflection, he decides on his preferred art form:

> . . . it seemed to [Ellison] that the creation of the landscape-garden offered to the proper Muse the most magnificent of opportunities. Here, indeed, was the fairest field for the display of imagination in the endless combining of forms of novel beauty. . . . In the multiform and multicolor of the flowers and the trees, he recognised the most direct and energetic efforts of Nature at physical loveliness. And in the direction or concentration of this effort—or, more properly, in its adaptation to the eyes which were to behold it on earth—he perceived that he should be employing the best means . . . in the fulfilment, not only of his own destiny as poet, but of the august purposes for which the Deity had implanted the poetic sentiment in man.

So Ellison deploys his fortune to create the garden of all gardens. Poe rehearses a hilarious parody of Downing's theories, pontificating about the Natural and the Artificial styles, while reversing their valence: "That the true result of the natural style of gardening is seen rather in the absence of all defects and incongruities than in the creation of any special wonders or miracles, is a proposition better suited to the grovelling apprehension of the herd than to the fervid dreams of the man of genius." Ellison the man of genius decides to bridge the poles of nature and art by creating a garden that would combine the two, and reach beyond to appeal to the angels loitering, bored, over Earth: he will be not quite man-the-garden-maker becoming God, but certainly becoming closer to God, akin in his power and vision to a supernatural being. After searching the globe for four years, Ellison settles on a plateau near an unnamed city. There he builds an improved version of nature, which Ellison considered to be always flawed. In his creation all is perfect: a "visiter" leaves the city in the morning and boards a boat traveling up a crystal-clear river, passing "in the forenoon" into a pastoral landscape of verdant hills and sheep, which "slowly became merged with a sense of retirement," à la Horace. Then the channel narrows and the canyon deepens, becoming a series of deep turns and twists of a gorge shaded by overhanging mosses. After many hours of sailing through deepening "gloom," the boat enters a circular basin with sloping walls "clothed from base to summit in a drapery of the most gorgeous flower-blossoms; scarcely a green leaf being visible among the sea of odorous and fluctuating color." Next, the "visiter" leaves the boat for an ivory canoe, of all conceivable incongruities, which nearly soundlessly propels him to a massive, golden "gate of the vista," under which it flows with the stream, to see, in the light of a sunset worthy of the painter Thomas Cole, an over-the-top Eden obtained by limitless money and perfectly refined conception:

> . . . *the whole Paradise of Arnheim bursts upon the view. There is a gush of entrancing melody; there is an oppressive sense of strange sweet odor—there is a dream—like intermingling to the eye of tall slender Eastern trees—bosky shrubberies'—flocks of golden and crimson birds—lily-fringed lakes—meadows of violets, tulips, poppies, hyacinths, and tuberoses—long intertangled lines of silver streamlets—and, upspringing confusedly from amid all, a mass of semi-Gothic, semi-Saracenic architecture sustaining itself by miracle in mid-air, glittering in the red sunlight with a hundred oriels, minarets, and pinnacles; and seeming the phantom handiwork, conjointly, of the Sylphs, of the Fairies, of the Genii and of the Gnomes.*

Poe's parody of the 19th century's garden obsessions was dead-on: of the fortunes required, of the rejection of the real world and the retreat into contrived and costly improvements on nature, of the vanity of the enterprise, and of the puerility of it (being the handiwork of fairies, genies, and gnomes). His rendering of the visual spectacular of the Victorian garden was equally accurate, with its unearthly colors and exuberant, overflowing foliage. Of course Ellison's project takes the form of a journey by boat up a river of American wilderness splendor into the deepest, most twisted, never-before-glimpsed canyon, and finally arriving at an approximation of the Golden Gate where California meets the Pacific Ocean, to bathe in the golden light of a continental sunset over the promised realm. While Arnheim was a construct of the unimaginable wealth attained by one lucky man, the irony was that not just the rich invested their fortunes in making their gardens into a private fantasy domain. Generally anybody who could get out of the city and put their money down on a piece of Eden did so, even among the working classes, according to their buying power and the inventiveness of land developers who marketed to them. Poe's unsettling insight was that, in the era of breakneck urbanization and industrialization, including the industrialization of agriculture, Americans' headlong flight away from their new reality wasn't just a flight away in physical space, but equally a flight away in imaginative time.

Three

THE GOLDEN AGE: MODERNITY AND ITS DISCONTENTS (1880-1915)

A bout one hour this side of Albany is the center of the world—I own it,"[1] the painter Frederic Edwin Church wrote to a friend describing his estate, Olana, which crowned a hill overlooking the Hudson River one hundred miles or so north of New York City. Edgar Allan Poe died three years after publishing his fantastical vision of the ultimate Victorian garden (and his ironic paean to the ambitions of Victorian garden makers), in 1849. But his vision was acute, and not so far-fetched—he might have been describing the real house and landscape Church constructed (though it was on a measurably smaller scale than the Domain of Arnheim). His character, Ellison, brings to mind (again, on a less literary scale than Poe's vision) Frederic Church: his skills were prodigious, his life an uninterrupted success, his paintings scintillating, vividly detailed depictions of scenes of exotic wonder glimpsed on journeys to far-off paradises. Church's career was the apotheosis of the Hudson River School of landscape painting: apprenticed to Thomas Cole at the age of eighteen, he quickly rose to prominence as a landscape painter of unusual skill in rendering light and natural detail. At the age of twenty-six he painted *Natural Bridge, Virginia* (1852), capturing the rock arch that Jefferson had owned. The picture was in the romantic vein of Church's mentor Cole but with more fine grain, yielding an American nature at once more realistic and more exalted, since in it was to be found the sanction for American uniqueness and American possession of the vast continent. The depiction of landscape and its subjugation went hand in hand. Influenced by the work of the renowned German geographer and explorer Alexander

Frederic Edwin Church, *Natural Bridge, Virginia.* (University of Virginia Art Museum)

von Humboldt (whom Jefferson had met and admired), Church went on to travel to South America, the American West, and the Arctic, sketching scenes of sublime natural beauty, and produced huge, panoramic canvases—including *The Heart of the Andes, The Icebergs, Cotopaxi,* and *Chimborazo*—of icy crags and smoking volcanoes glowing as if from within with a surging luminance. He unveiled his paintings in specially designed, paid-admission showings that drew thousands in New York and London, and sold them for astronomical sums.

In 1860 Church bought a farm in a small valley across the Hudson from the town of Catskill and hired the architect Richard Morris Hunt to design a "Cosy Cottage" there; seven years later he added eighteen adjacent acres including a hilltop with spectacular views of the river and mountains beyond, and planned to have Hunt build him a medieval French-style mansion. But on a trip with his wife to Europe and the Middle East he became smitten with Islamic styles and called in Calvert Vaux, the master of the Victorian eclectic, to design an Orientalist house for him. The result, finished in 1872, Church christened Olana after an ancient Persian fortress. It is an arresting sight, a cluster of brick battlements and towers crazy with pointed arches and red and gold tile flourishes, rearing incongruously from a New York forest. On a smaller scale than Ellison's castle, it nevertheless fits Poe's fictional description: "upspringing confusedly from amid all, a mass of semi-Gothic, semi-Saracenic architecture sustaining itself by miracle in mid-air, glittering in the red sunlight."[2] The landscape it surmounts, carefully choreographed by Church over several decades, is a perfect achievement of the Olmstedian picturesque: 250 acres, much of it a working farm, with a dammed stream filling a lake in the valley surrounded by fields, then meadows on the rising slopes flecked by stands of trees giving way to woods thickening toward the hilltop. A road climbs gently through open ground alternating with forest, revealing intimate seats and windows onto distant prospects, until, getting out of the car near the top and walking around the imposing house to the porch, the endless, breathtaking western panorama stops a visitor in his tracks. Alone on its mount, Olana recalls Monticello, lofty, isolated, and serene in the same way, with a similar grandeur—of intention and achievement—in its craftsmanship and perfect framing. It also possesses a similar dreamlike quality, of dissociation from the world below, partly achieved by the elevation, partly by the natural beauty of the spot, and partly by the fantasy role-playing of the architecture, imported by a cultivated, wealthy American traveler from thousands of miles and years away and erected on his private hill as the demonstration of one man's fulfillment of the American dream. It's an interesting dream that way—deeply artistic, completely solipsistic. Jefferson achieved it by way of erudition, inheritance, and credit; Church achieved it by way of talent, marketing moxie, and inherited wealth.

If Olana was a crowning achievement of high Victorian aesthetics and ambitions in the United States, it was hardly unique. Every American man of means, it seemed, longed for a castle of his own, Orientalist or Gothic, or both, mixed together. Down the river, in Tarrytown, New York City mayor William Paulding, Jr., had Alexander Jackson Davis design him a Greek Revival castle in 1838, to which Davis subsequently added a four-story Gothic tower for the succeeding owner, George Merritt, who sold it to railroad tycoon Jay Gould, who Gothicized the whole. The showman P. T. Barnum built his Iranistan, a wildly colored, scallop-arched, and onion-domed confection in Bridgeport, Connecticut, modeled on the Royal Pavilion at Brighton, England, a fine example of the "Indo-Saracenic" architecture the British inflicted on India in their imperial heyday: a pastiche of local Indian architecture and modish Gothic, intended to make the British rulers appear as the successors to the bygone Mughal emperors.[3]

The British had India, and we Americans had a newly acquired continental empire, wrested from Mexico by rifles and from Russia by dollars, still waiting to be cleared of its native inhabitants by the U.S. Army and settled and developed by a fast-moving and avaricious people. And some Americans at least had money to spend: after the Civil War, fortunes were made in banking, coal, railroads, lumber, meatpacking, cotton, wheat, shipping—and oil, after Yale professor Benjamin Silliman figured out how to fractionate petroleum in 1854 and Edwin Drake drilled for it in Pennsylvania in 1859. Newly wealthy and technologically adept Americans built to show it, whether Ogontz, the financier Jay Cooke's fifty-room house near Philadelphia, which boasted an Italian garden with a brand-new ruined castle,[4] or the Brooklyn Bridge (1857–83), the perfect expression and symbol of modern America's muscular ingenuity and originality—except for its architectural details, the castellated top and pointed arches, borrowed from far away and long ago.

All over the English-speaking world, high Victorian eclecticism was in full flower, with its swirl of imagery inspired by exotic locales, especially those of the British Empire as depicted by Alfred, Lord Tennyson and later Rudyard Kipling, and by a new surge of interest in the medieval period and the Gothic, accompanied by a renewed appetite for Sir Walter Scott's novels and given new expression in music by Richard Wagner's Arthurian *Tristan and Isolde* and mythic Norse *Ring* cycle. In houses, fashions ran to the extreme of mixed styles: borrowing from Byzantine, Moorish, and Persian from the East, Swiss Chalet or any of the other flavors of Alexander Jackson Davis's mythic-European kit of parts, plus a new French influence visible in mansard roofs. Its signature achievement of overkill in bricolage was the Queen Anne style, cooked up in the United Kingdom in the 1870s, a mix of fake half-timbering, clumped Tudor chimneys, and peaked gables.[5] Hindsight has narrowed its eyes at Victorian taste: in 1949, the art historian Oliver Larkin deemed it "visual torment"; in 1955, Lewis Mumford dismissed it: "with the little eddies of eclecticism . . . there is scarcely any need to deal; they represented only the dispersion of taste and the collapse of judgment which marked the Gilded Age."[6] But at the time the welter of styles provided a physical expression of the exuberance and confidence of a Western civilization that had reached out and taken hold of the entire globe, almost effortlessly it seemed, and then cherry-picked what it fancied from the world's cultural basket to decorate its triumph. Fashionable gardens did the same, hewing to variations on the picturesque landscape style of Olmsted and Vaux and Downing's gardenesque, with its mix of Capability Brown's trees and turf, ornamented with fanciful, garish carpet bedding, coleus-festooned mounds, and urns on pedestals, stuffed with novelty tropicals and clutches of dwarfed, bizarrely tinted conifers (really genetic freaks or "sports" taken from cuttings of oddball branches on otherwise normal trees) grouped on the lawn. Wealthy and ambitious gardeners grew bedding annuals by the hundreds of thousands; nursery catalogs included colored paper to help customers compose their designs before ordering.[7] With the eclectic at its crescendo, the time was ripe for a rebellion—and one was getting under way.

———

At the beginning of February 1892, Frederick Law Olmsted wrote a note to a young apprentice in his office, William Platt, who was planning to undertake a study trip to Italy with his older brother Charles, a noted landscape painter and etcher. Olmsted struck a cautionary, dour note: "I am afraid that I do not think much of the fine and costly gardening of Italy. . . ." He was plainly alarmed at the prospect that the older artist intended to indoctrinate William in the Italian influence—by which he meant the formal style. Olmsted had sent William to his friend Charles Eliot Norton, the famous professor of fine arts at Harvard, for advice on how to structure the trip, with a letter explaining: "His brother . . . is going to Italy with the intention of obtaining material by sketching and photography for a volume of . . . illustrations of gardens and garden furniture, seats, fountains, terraces, staircases, pergolas, rustic paths, and other amorettes of Italian outdoor life. That at least is my understanding of his project which I think is still lacking definition in a little partly because of hazy information as to what is practicable."[8] Olmsted had reason to be worried: Charles Platt was in fact intending to undermine Olmsted's teachings, leading his brother toward the formal Renaissance garden as a new model by exposing him to the siren song of the Italian villa.

Charles Platt had himself undergone such a conversion experience. Of old New England stock, he grew up in New York City amid the social and artistic elite; his merchant father was a founding member of the Century Club, along with Olmsted and many well-known painters of the time, including Stephen Parrish, a family friend. Described as inward, even taciturn,[9] from boyhood he was drawn to art and soon began painting, then taking study trips to Europe, hoping to emulate the American expatriate painter James McNeill Whistler, who had gone to Paris in 1855,[10] the English landscape painters Constable and Turner, and the French Barbizon School. In 1883 he began formal training in several ateliers in Paris, crowded with wealthy Americans, many from prominent New York families.[11] All of the pictures he submitted to the Salon that year were rejected; the next year those that were accepted weren't listed in the catalog.[12] He moved on to the Académie Julian and was gradually drawn into a stream diverging from the dominant taste, away from the Romantic and the picturesque and toward Renaissance and classical subjects, with a focus on architecture. An emerging classicism in painting drew inspiration from the neoclassical movement in architecture centered at the Ecole des Beaux-Arts in Paris, which preached symmetry, ornament, and fine construction, combining Greek, Roman, and Renaissance modes with later Italian and French versions, composed with systematic rigor and rendered with meticulous drafting. Both were part of a reaction, usually dubbed the "academic reaction" to artistic Romanticism, which had an additional motive as a conservative backlash against the social modernism of the French Revolution and an urgent political function in legitimizing the Second Empire, 1850–70, of Napoleon III through classical models. The three vectors coincided but they didn't need to be recognized as related by their partisans—such is the way the arts, culture, and politics play at the same game while each pretends to be minding its own, private pasture. Platt himself was drawn to the movement slowly, writing to his family that he was moving toward a greater appreciation for "the beautiful" than "the picturesque."[13]

From 1882 to 1887, he spent winters in Paris and summers on sketching trips around Europe. An odd duck, not always communicative, he struck many people as cold. When the young Platt went to visit the Stephen Parrishes at their expatriate home in France, the painter's wife wrote that Platt's visits upset Stephen, because Platt "criticizes faults but does not see or at least does not speak of virtues; his coming is always depressing as he seems to give so little, he is a queer fellow and we always have to get used to him over again, after an absence, the first impression is always chilling."[14] Nevertheless, he moved widely among the circle of American expats, many of them with family connections. He was invited on a trip to Italy over the winter of 1886–87 by a wealthy New Yorker, Colonel Richard Hoe, and his wife, Annie. Hoe's company made printing presses. He had an estate in the Bronx but had lived in Paris through the Civil War years and continued to travel on the Continent after.

Platt and the Hoes were part of a new wave of well-off Americans traveling to Europe in search of what they couldn't find at home. By the 1840s there were more than one hundred American sculptors in Rome, attracted by the cheap supply of good marble and stone carvers,[15] but also by the atmosphere, beauty, and cultural intensity wanting at home. Some were women—drawn as well by the comparative freedom allowed women (of means) in Europe, including Harriet Hosmer, who had built a studio with nine rooms just to house her workmen. Nathaniel Hawthorne spent time in 1858 in Florence and Rome among the expatriates, and set his 1860 novel, *The Marble Faun*, in an Italy clearly modeled on theirs, with one of his characters, "Kenyon," based on an actual American sculptor, and several important romantic scenes staged in the neglected gardens of the Villa Borghese.[16] The transatlantic telegraph cable had come into service in 1865, making European trips lasting months more manageable for businessmen and their families.

Europe, and especially Rome, was like a drug to culturally minded Americans. Henry James arrived in 1869 and gushed in a letter to his brother William: "At last—for the first time—I live! It beats everything; it leaves the Rome of your fancy—your education—nowhere. . . . I went reeling and moaning thro' the streets in a fever of enjoyment."[17] Henry Adams, great-grandson of the second president, called Italy "altogether the most violent vice in the world, and Rome before 1870 was seductive beyond resistance."[18] The decaying, picturesque Old World fed some hunger deep within Americans, who were upset by changes in the United States, with the explosion of economic and social competition, of cities, noise, filth, and flood tides of poor immigrants. Especially unhappy were members of the old patrician class, but the sentiment, and the ironic desire to retreat to Europe, wasn't limited to them—new money went too.

Garden of Stephen Parrish, Cornish, New Hampshire. Photo by Maxfield Parrish, ca. 1900. (Dartmouth College Library)

And there was a lot of new money, even though the American economy for half a century had weathered a rough ride. A post–Civil War expansion led by an onslaught of speculative investing in railroads, docks, and other transportation facilities ended in the Panic of 1873, the bursting of the bubble brought on by the bankruptcy of Jay Cooke's overleveraged firm when it couldn't sell a bond issue for its Northern Pacific Railway— a sequence not dissimilar to the financial crisis of 2008—and triggered a nearly decade-long depression. Before long, however, another bubble began to inflate, piling up fortunes for the owning class: wealth grew by $20 billion in the decade between 1883 and 1893.[19] European travel grew apace.

Beginning in February, Platt and the Hoe family together toured from the port at San Remo to Genoa, Pisa, Siena, and on to Rome. Charles sketched, but mostly was content to "rummage with mademoiselle," as he called Annie Hoe, the colonel's daughter. The two announced their engagement en route. In the spring, after continuing on to Naples, Platt came ill with typhoid fever, and the couple decided to get married in Italy while he convalesced. Then disasters struck: the colonel died in June, and all returned across the Atlantic. Late that summer, Platt's father also died. In October, Charles and Annie sailed back for France, where Annie died in childbirth with twins.[20] Platt was devastated. He returned to New York, where he began a slow recovery and reentry into painting. In 1889 he took a sketching trip with a friend to Cornish, New Hampshire, where an artist-writer summer colony had grown, populated with many New Yorkers among the wealthy and celebrated literati gathered around the sculptor Augustus Saint-Gaudens. Maxfield Parrish, the painter son of Stephen, headed a long list of artists, writers, singers, composers, and other luminaries that eventually would include Ethel Barrymore and Woodrow Wilson and his wife, Ellen.[21]

Life at Cornish consisted of a daily round of painting, in studios and plein air in the countryside, and socializing, often in the flower gardens and shaded terraces savored by the colonists. Cornish was relaxed, even slightly bohemian, in a patrician way, but it was also a hotbed of the new classicism, a locus of a self-conscious "American Renaissance" pursuing a revived interest in Greek and Roman precedents to define the United States. This movement drew on the contemporary European classicist revival, combined with a search for usable American precedents, generally from the colonial period and specifically from New England—where the young architect Charles Follen McKim had made sketching trips to study the colonial-Georgian style in 1876. What made Cornish fertile was the collaboration between different disciplines: the sculptor Saint-Gaudens worked with the young architect Stanford White, a rising New York star, on an acclaimed monument to Civil War admiral David Farragut in New York's Madison Park from 1876 to 1881:[22] Saint-Gaudens and the painter John La Farge would go on to collaborate with the firm of McKim, Mead, and White, formed in 1879, on a series of commissions, including the original Madison Square Garden (1890) and the Boston Public Library (1887–95).[23] McKim, Mead, and White's early residential

Charles Platt garden, Cornish, New Hampshire. (From Platt and Cortissoz, *Monograph of the Work of Charles A. Platt*)

work was at first disarmingly eclectic, drawing on the American colonial with some Queen Anne thrown in (a massive brown concoction that came to be called the Shingle style), but it soon took a strongly classicist tack, beginning with the 1883 Villard town houses in New York (built for Henry Villard, the German immigrant titan who had cleaned up on the stock of the Northern Pacific Railway after Jay Cooke's fall).

Charles Platt was a major contributor, not as a painter, but as an architect, a profession he fell into "through the garden gate," as a contemporary critic put it.[24] In the 1890s he began designing country houses for friends in and around Cornish, like the hilltop house, High Court, which he explicitly modeled on the Frascati villas outside Rome, and the colonial-classical house he designed for himself. He also designed their gardens, which were geometric in plan but simply organized and limited to a very human scale, often subordinated to distant views, and invariably full of flowers. After his 1892 trip to Italy with William, he pulled the material he'd gathered into a book, *Italian Gardens*, published in 1894, a series of photographs of old villas, many of them in a state of quasi-abandonment, with a few paragraphs of text for each. Platt was not given to writing, but he quickly and clearly set out a philosophy of design derived from these villas, which was foremost integrative, interlocking the spaces of the house opening outward with those of the garden:

> *The evident harmony of arrangement between the house and surrounding landscape is what first strikes one in Italian landscape architecture—the design as a whole, including gardens, terraces, groves, and their necessary surroundings and embellishments, it being clear that no one of these component parts was ever considered independently, the architect of the house being also the architect of the garden and the rest of the villa. With the problem being to take a piece of land and make it habitable, the architect proceeded with the idea that not only was the house to be lived in, but that one still wished to be at home while out of doors; so the garden was designed as another apartment, the terraces and groves still others, where one might walk about and find a place suitable to the hour of the day and feeling of the moment, and still be in that sacred portion of the globe dedicated to one's self.*[25]

It's hard to imagine a stronger statement of purpose for the home garden than Platt's last two phrases: for him it is to be above all personal, concretely utilitarian, and unencumbered with symbolic, religious, or other charges. Not surprisingly, *Italian Gardens* was reviewed by some, including leading practitioners of the dominant Olmsted school, with barely disguised scorn: "works of this kind only appeal to the aesthetic sense; they delight the eye and satisfy the cultivated taste as a beautiful piece of tapestry or pottery does. It is beauty for its own sake. It expresses no sentiment and carries no inner meaning; it does not address itself to the nobler part of our nature as simple natural scenery does."[26] Maybe so, but the simple pleasure of being at home while out-of-doors and enjoying the feeling of the moment, in Platt's words, was gaining appeal for many Americans, and the Italian model of "beauty for its own sake" was gaining adherents. Platt was in the vanguard of another Italian revival, but he wasn't the first: the Massachusetts finance magnate Horatio Hollis Hunnewell had planted a fanciful Italianate topiary garden at his estate, Wellesley, from 1851 on, inspired by Elvaston Castle in England,[27] and in 1884 the wealthy Boston art collector Isabella Stewart Gardner had begun laying out her Green Hill in Brookline, which included long vine-covered pergolas, formal walks, fountains, and statuary.[28] The Italian siren song had for a long, long time seduced sophisticated seekers—yet, because of its almost limitless depth, it proved a continuous fount of inspiration, becoming tradition, provoking backlash, only to come around again.

Ironically, in 1892 Olmsted himself was headed to Europe—in part to study formal gardens for a new estate job commissioned by William Henry Vanderbilt.[29] And he'd been tapped to lay out the grounds of the World's Columbian Exposition, awarded in 1890 by Congress to Chicago, to take place in 1893, the four hundredth anniversary of the Italian navigator's discovery of the New World. It would be the crowning achievement of Olmsted's career; yet it would also be in important ways a repudiation of his deepest convictions about aesthetics, principles he had stood for and built for more than three decades. Blustering Chicago, the nerve center of the booming Northwest, had rebuilt itself in muscular fashion after the Great Fire of 1871 and was eager to prove it had arrived in the first rank of world cities. The design of the fair was given to John Root and Daniel Burnham, two leading local architects, whose first conception for the buildings was a riot of color and styles: Romanesque, Spanish, Russian Kremlin, Orientalist, Islamic mosques, and Chinese pagodas, festooned with bright flags and pennants streaming in the wind off Lake Michigan.

Olmsted, then seventy, and his young associate Henry Codman were to choose from seven options and design the site. They chose Jackson Park on the lakeshore, because Olmsted maintained that the only thing interesting about Chicago's setting was the water. And, Columbus had, after all, arrived by ship. The "park" at that point amounted to a sandy, waterlogged plain of six hundred acres, mostly empty and treeless. Olmsted and Codman envisioned a transformed landscape of buildings and plazas with water the unifying theme: beginning with the lake, opening to a winding, naturalistic lagoon carved out of the sand, then a wide, formal basin modeled on Venice's Grand Canal and along which the major buildings would be arrayed, crossed by a canal that led to subsidiary areas of the fair, all also dotted with bodies of water. Visitors could arrive by boat, train, or on foot from opposite ends of the site and move in a circular procession around it.

It was immediately acknowledged as a brilliant scheme. Burnham & Root brought in national architects to design half the buildings, including Richard Morris Hunt, and Charles McKim of McKim, Mead, and White; Chicagoans, including Louis Sullivan, would design the other half. But at the time of their first meeting in early 1891, Root had died suddenly of pneumonia, and the group, joined by Augustus Saint-Gaudens as artistic advisor,[30] agreed to pattern the entire fair in the classical revival style. With the exception of Sullivan, whose Transportation Building tried to invent a new American form within the bounds set by the others, the designers created a unified neoclassical theme, beginning with a six-hundred-foot-long peristyle, or Roman columned court (with each column standing for a U.S. state) at the head of the basin, which was called the Court of Honor. The Court was plied by gondolas and lined with the gleaming façades of the main buildings, each of which was fronted by a forest of columns, most topped with a remarkably tall or wide dome. The buildings were in fact fakes: plaster and wood covering steel frames—a new technology that made it possible to throw them up cheaply and in under two years. The press dubbed it the White City, in part for the color of the architecture, in part because the fair was lit at night with electric light—the first large-scale demonstration of electricity ever seen.

Saint-Gaudens did his job many times over, assembling a vast corps of artists and sculptors to adorn the buildings. He gasped to Burnham that it was "the greatest meeting of artists since the 15th century." There were statues everywhere: at the head of the canal stood a towering, sixty-five-foot-tall[31] golden *Republic,* holding a spear in one hand and a globe with a dove perched on it in the other, set on a massive pedestal in the water, by Daniel Chester French. In front of it was the eighteen-foot *Diana,* by Saint-Gaudens, originally created for Stanford White's Madison Square Garden in New York and moved to Chicago for the occasion.[32] A massive circular fountain included allegorical sculptures of Fame, Father Time, and Columbia, as well as seahorses, cupids, and maidens, all washed by spray and jets of water. Figures of nymphs and heroes and the occasional elk were everywhere, on columns and posts, all over the grounds and buildings like gargoyles on a Gothic cathedral; composed of a mix of cement, fiber, and plaster, these were meant to last at least a few months before the Chicago winter reduced them to rubble. In the meantime, it was splendid. Saint-Gaudens crowed: "It seems impossible that such a vision can ever be recalled in its poetic grandeur and elevation."[33]

Not everyone bought into the bombast. Louis Sullivan stubbornly designed his contribution in his idiosyncratic and nonclassical idiom, with intricate decoration and gold-leaved arches that provided the only glint of color in the main buildings; later he wrote that the exposition had set architecture back by forty years. Olmsted worried about the pretension of the buildings: "I question if ours are not going to look too assuming of architectural stateliness and to be overbonded with sculptural and other efforts for grandeur and grandiloquent pomp." And he worried that they would be blinding: "I fear that against the clear blue sky and the blue lake, great towering masses of white, glistening in the clear hot, summer sunlight of Chicago, with the glare of the water that we are to have both within and without the Exposition grounds, will be overpowering." He designed an island for the middle of the lagoon to be thickly planted with woods to provide shade for visitors and a contrast of wild informality from the severity of the rest. He proposed many times bringing a lighter, more festive note to the proceedings: he actually brought in ducks, geese, swans, all carefully color-modulated; he wanted lots of boats but no steam launches, since they were too large, too fast, and too modern; instead a fleet of Venetian gondolas, a Norwegian Viking ship, a Japanese dragon boat, a New England whaleboat, and from Spain, replicas of the *Niña*, *Pinta*, and *Santa Maria* swarmed the lagoon. He proposed fleets of bark canoes paddled by Indians in buckskins to be rented out, and roving bands of banjo players, and costumed Indian performers brought over from the amusement park next door at the Midway Plaisance, in order to "give spice and variety to the scene, and a picturesque element."[34] But Burnham held fast: "The influence of the Exposition on architecture will be to inspire a reversion toward the pure ideal of the ancients," he wrote, spicelessly.

The claim that hurly-burly Chicago was the reincarnation of ancient Athens may or may not have completely convinced many visitors, but the

World's Columbian Exhibition, Chicago, 1893. (H. D. Nichols, artist. Color lithograph from Rare Book: Bancroft, *Book of the Fair*, 1893. Courtesy of the Field Museum Library.

Lagoon and Wooded Isle. (Smithsonian Institution Archives, Chicago World's Columbian Exposition, 1893. Record unit 95, Box 61, Folder 8, Negative #12181.)

exposition drew 27 million people in its six-month run (equal to half the U.S. population) and most reported themselves duly impressed. In all there were two hundred buildings housing the agricultural, cultural, and technological wonders of the world, not to mention a Ferris wheel (the first one, built by George Washington Ferris), displays of Nikola Tesla's phosphorescent and neon lamps and George Westinghouse's transformers, lectures by Eadweard Muybridge on locomotion along with his moving pictures, and by Frederick Jackson Turner on the end of the frontier. As if to prove Turner's thesis that the American frontier had closed and that a new epoch in the nation's life was beginning (which he based on data from the census of 1890), Buffalo Bill's Wild West Show, pointedly not invited by Burnham, set up next door at the Midway to great crowds and profits. A visitor to the exposition could see an enormous electrical dynamo, watch Hawaiian hula dancers or an Egyptian belly dancer, all the while eating newly invented Cracker Jack popcorn candy. Inside the California pavilion, an arched stucco Spanish colonial pastiche with a different Mission-style front on each of four entrances (topped by, of course, a dome), one could have lunch on a roof terrace studded with potted agaves and palms[35] or inside see a map of the United States drawn in pickles.[36] The fair was a huge success, even in the face of another financial meltdown, the Panic of 1893, set off by the bursting of yet another railroad-building bubble, which would inaugurate the deepest economic depression in the country's history.

Nevertheless, Olmsted wasn't the only doubter. After touring the exposition, Henry Adams sat down on the steps of Richard Morris Hunt's Administration Building to ruminate: he was impressed by the "self-assertion" of the generation that included Saint-Gaudens, McKim, and White;[37] he was impressed by the fair's "scenic display," which surpassed that put on by Paris in its Exposition of 1889, where Gustave Eiffel unveiled his tower—the inspiration in many ways for Chicago's effort, which was four times bigger.[38] But as an unreconstructed Boston Brahmin, he found that the sudden appearance of so much modern wizardry amid so much pseudo-ancient grandeur on a windswept midwestern lakeshore "defied philosophy": "the inconceivable scenic display consisted of its being there at all, more surprising than Niagara Falls, or the Yellowstone geysers . . . [S]ince Noah's Ark, no such Babel of loose and ill-joined, such vague and ill-defined and unrelated thoughts and half-thoughts and experimental outcries . . . had ever ruffled the surface of the Lakes."[39] It was, he thought, "a step in evolution to startle Darwin." But for all the White City's enormous incongruity, he appreciated that the hypothetical typical American "had the air of enjoying it as though it were all his own; he felt it was good; he was proud of it; for the most part, he acted as though he had passed his life in landscape gardening and architectural decoration." As to the appropriateness of the assorted neoclassical styles that it presented, Adams could only shrug that "all trading cities had always shown traders' taste. . . . All trader's taste smelt of bric-a-brac; Chicago tried at least to give her taste a look of unity."[40]

The return to the classical was motivated partly by fatigue with the excesses of the Victorian eclectic: as early as 1866 there were calls for returning to white and rectilinear in architecture[41] and the sentiment only gained currency as the eclectic became more florid. The Chicago architect John Root proposed new, farcical names for the most popular styles: the Victorian should become the "cathartic"; the Romanesque the "dropsical"; and Queen Anne the "tubercular."[42] But this reversion to the classical had deeper, social roots in a generalized nostalgia for a pre–Civil War nation supposedly simple, orderly, and agrarian. The Civil War had been totally destabilizing socially, emotionally, and spiritually, its aftermath a roller coaster of industrial expansion and urban growth, with often frightening surges of immigration, punctuated by economic panics and devastating depressions. The dominant culture—which remained essentially the established Protestant elite centered in the Northeast (peppered with arriviste millionaires trying their best to fit in)—had, despite deep misgivings, encouraged and benefited from the nation's turns to capitalist and territorial expansion. The most salient event of the period was the rise of what was universally referred to as "Eastern monopoly," as financiers and trusts consolidated local and regional businesses into huge, national enterprises controlled from New York, Boston, or not uncommonly, London. Leading members of that culture were acutely aware of the need to relegitimize the American narrative and their hegemony over it, especially since their new values were not those of Jeffersonian or Jacksonian America. With their distrust of democracy and affinity for aristocratic forms and pretensions, they were much closer to those of Jefferson's old antagonists, the Federalists. But far more than their 18th century forefathers, who were steeped in Calvinist mistrust of money and power alike, the new patricians had turned their religion into a softer thing, allowing them to get rich without too much thought of damnation and to turn firmly toward Europe and its aristocratic culture.[43] For many of them, classicism provided a sense of continuity in links to a past that was more comfortably and somewhat plausibly "American" than was America's chaotic present—to the architecture and iconography of the early republic, and to the Roman and Greek antecedents that had so inspired the founders.

Classicism accomplished at the same time something like the very opposite: it asserted a superior, aristocratic claim to rule, drawn from the appropriation of European cultural history. In this it shared the essential doubleness of Jefferson's classicism: both its cultural ambivalence and its cultural ambition. But this second classical revival was different from the first. Jefferson's was intensely nostalgic, and his agrarian Utopia was modeled on a past golden age. McKim, Mead, and White's was also obviously nostalgic, yet in a more diffuse way, as it mixed influences from hither and yon, ancient and recent; but it was strikingly modernist in its economic and social reality, since it was commissioned by a modernizing industrial elite that used its elegant forms to showcase enormous machines and engines. And it was imperial in its political reality, insofar as it aimed to provide symbolic ratification for a newly powerful, burgeoning nation that was swallowing territory as fast as it could. The stakes, and the reality, had changed in a century. Lewis Mumford described the comparative loss of innocence from Monticello to the White City somewhat acidly: "It would be foolish to quarrel with the style that was chosen . . . [the architects] divined that they were fated to serve Renaissance despots and emperors with more than Roman power, and unerringly they chose the proper form for their activities."[44]

To the west of the lagoon at the White City, laid out in a field beside the massive Horticultural Building, was an utter incongruity: a 2,500-square-foot garden, filled with a jumble of typically old-fashioned flowers, mostly shrubs and hardy perennials, such as might have grown in an old New England dooryard. They had been planted as an educational display by the state of New York. In the official brochure it was described in deliberately old-timey prose: "mignonette and marigolds nestled together; hollyhock and foxglove reared their rival spires of many colored blossoms over the monkshood and snapdragons, as they were wont to do against the old cottage door. Phloxes, larkspur and Jacob's ladder were there too with dusty miller, Joseph's coat and heartsease. The brilliant glow of zinnias, the old fuchsias and geraniums, the petunias, the verbenas, the sweet breath of heliotropes, reminded of many a gray-haired visitor of other days."[45] The contribution of the Empire State's powerful nursery industry, which ever since Downing's day had dominated the trade in the Northeast and the expanding Northwest by taking advantage of the new canal and railroad networks radiating from New York, was meant to be "a model of an old-fashioned New York garden." Like the similar display next door in the picket-fenced yard in front of the Massachusetts state building, a replica of the 18th century Hancock house in Boston,[46] what it demonstrated besides horticultural skill was the currency of a new idea about an old thing: "Grandmother's garden," a phrase coined sometime after the Civil War that had gradually assumed the status of a formula. Grandmother's garden was studiously unrefined, by design without design, consisting of some number of simple flower beds—at their most complex rectangles, traversed by one or more paths, and bounded by walls or fences as the case may be, the whole arranged tight against the house. The plants, a mishmash of brightly colored flowers and herbs, overflowed their confines, climbing every surface including one another, and reached ever upward—most perfectly the hollyhocks, the indispensable emblem of Grandmother's garden, almost a talisman, invoking a bygone colonial simplicity.

The form of Grandmother's garden had never gone away: before the Civil War it was called the cottage or dooryard garden, essentially a folk survival from the medieval period where herbs and flowers were grown within reach of the kitchen. It was more utilitarian than fashionable, more medicinal than agricultural, resolutely feminine, domestic, and commonplace. Interest in it began to ramp up as soon as people felt themselves squeezed uncomfortably in the grip of modernity, with its cities, factories, crowds, and relentless pressure of time. (American authors like Fenimore Cooper and Hawthorne had been attracted to the cottage gardens they saw in England, even though they recognized the crushing rural poverty that the cottagers endured.)[47] By 1848, Walter Elder could publish a history, *The Cottage Garden of America;* by the 1890s Grandmother's garden was the focus of a huge burst of cultural activity, whether the

sentimental tracts identifying flower culture with femininity and innocence, like those of Henry Ward Beecher and Harriet Beecher Stowe, or
acres of published poetry with flower themes (not least Emily Dicken-
son's), or the cascade of paintings with flowers and gardens as their subjects. Like the picturesque garden before it, the cottage garden on both
sides of the Atlantic drew inspiration and support from painting, which
tracked strongly toward gardens and flowers as the century wore on: beginning with the English Pre-Raphaelites, whose works were first seen in
the United States in an 1857 exhibit,[48] then the French Barbizon School of
the 1860s and '70s, followed by Impressionism in the 1880s. These translated into a flood of paintings of garden scenes, often featuring women
doting among the flowers; the genre was called "hollyhocking." Winslow
Homer made a career of depicting women outside in gardens and fields,
often wearing old-fashioned costumes. Many of the artists themselves
had cottage gardens at their homes, which appeared prominently on canvas.[49] From 1883, when he moved to Giverny, Claude Monet's paintings
were seen in the United States; the first American Monet acolyte arrived
in the village in 1887, followed by a torrent, many renting studios and
gardens to paint in (it continues unabated today). Though Monet didn't
start painting his own garden until 1900, he brought intense color to the
avant-garde vision of the outside.[50]

Even at the apogee of the Victorian gardenesque, the ubiquity of
cottage-style gardens revealed that they had remained the deeper current of the American garden stream even while submerged from time to
time by new fashions promoted by salesmen of the latest English fashions, like Downing. The revival only made the fact more pointed. Suddenly Grandmother's garden was everywhere, and it seemed as though it
had always been there. (Below the curving retaining wall of the driveway
at Olana, should a visitor peer over the edge, was [and is] a delightful,
billowing flower garden, tucked out of the way of the northerly winter
winds.) The cottage garden's resurgence or rediscovery shared the same
motive as the classicist urge: discomfort with modernity and a deep, nostalgic yearning for a simpler time—and an urgent need for a usable past
on which to remodel the present. But it came to the opposite conclusion:

Grandmother's garden was conservative and populist, with a strong identification with the middle class and, at least in theory, the working class. Grandmother herself actually took care of it; there was no need to hire "Pat O'Shovelem," as the Irish immigrant laborers of the wealthy were derided. It was a reaction against fashionability, sophistication, and opulence, and so sought to accentuate its simplicity and lack of "art." It sought to literally re-create the small-town past, an obsession it shared with wide swaths of American culture, including male literature, which was dominated in the late 19th century by two genres: medievalist fantasy (the revival of Walter Scott, especially in the South, where it anchored the myth of chivalry, is one example; Mark Twain's *A Connecticut Yankee in King Arthur's Court* [1889] is another); and the celebration of small-town boyhood (*Being a Boy*, by Charles Dudley Warner [1877], is one example; Twain's *Adventures of Huckleberry Finn* [1884] is another).

In a very real sense, Grandmother's garden was a political garden, an assertion of the common people in a time of increasing inequality and "conspicuous consumption" by the rich (the phrase was coined in 1899 by Thorstein Veblen, who taught at the University of Chicago, in his coruscating book *The Theory of the Leisure Class*). Walter Elder's complaint against tastemakers like Downing was that they only speak to "the inhabitants of the *mansion*." And while "some of them may say 'how do you do' to the cottager at a distance . . . they then pass on seemingly afraid to be thought associating with them." But Elder pointed out that the wealthy ought to encourage cottage gardens, as they had the almost magical power to raise property values for landlords, help in "reforming and moralizing the young," and "exalt the national character" as they were inherently "patriotic" and "christian."[51]

If Elder's language echoed Downing's, it is because they shared a conscious social objective; and yet the cottage garden one-upped Downing's prescriptions by encouraging a devotion—not religious, but still spiritual—in its identification with nature, and in a certain way managed to revive the lost Calvinist humility in its worship of simplicity. Celia Thaxter, an accomplished poet from the upper middle class whose family ran a summer hotel on one of the tiny Isles of Shoals, off the New Hampshire coast, kept a flower garden on a speck of rock evocatively dubbed Appledore (it was formerly called Hog Island), which was celebrated by the numerous artists and writers who came to stay. She captured this new creed in her 1893 book *An Island Garden* (which was sumptuously illustrated with watercolors by Childe Hassam):

> *He who is born with a silver spoon in his mouth is generally considered a fortunate person, but his good fortune is small compared to that of the happy mortal who enters this world with a passion for flowers in his soul. I use the word advisedly, though it seems a weighty one for the subject, for I do not mean a light or shallow affection, but a real love which is worthy of the name. . . .*[52]

The mood of veneration in Thaxter's prose dovetailed with a broad national reaching out to the colonial and prewar past. One expression of it was the movement to preserve old houses and gardens, driven in part by demographics and real estate patterns, as an ever-increasing stream of the middle and upper classes fled the city for the country, where they confronted the challenges of buying and rehabbing old farmhouses—just like today. And just like today, authors wrote books to help them, with titles such as *Adopting an Abandoned Farm* (1891).[53] Preservationists convinced governments to buy historic places, like the 18th century botanist John Bartram's home and grounds purchased by the city of Philadelphia in 1891. The grandmother of all restorations had been the rescue of George Washington's home by the Mount Vernon Ladies' Association, organized for the purpose in 1853, and the restoration of the gardens after the Civil War. Nearly a century after General Washington laid them out, what most Americans celebrated in his gardens were not the modern, picturesque aspects he had somewhat laboriously included, like the serpentine walks and the "wildernesses" along the carriage drive, but the traditional ones such as the knot gardens and box-edged flower beds in the walled gardens that sit to the north of the lawn, one trimmed into the form of a fleur-de-lis—which the English architect Benjamin Latrobe had decried in 1796 as "the expiring groans I hope of our Grandfathers' pedantry."[54] At the end of the 19th century, Washington's restored garden provided the perfect form for a new garden nationalism, in part an expression of pride in the growing economic and military power of the United States but also an expression of considerable anxiety over that identity in the face of immigration, which reached 11 million newcomers between 1870 and 1900,[55] most from southern and eastern Europe, who were culturally and linguistically alien to Americans. Gardeners and garden writers trained their trowels and pens on native plants and fretted over what an American garden ought to look like: the critic and New York society maven Mariana Griswold Van Rensselaer, in her book, *Art Out-of-Doors: Hints on Good Taste in Gardening* (1893), wrote: "We want American gardens, American landscapes, American parks and pleasure grounds, not the features of those of a dozen different countries huddled together." The allusion to huddled masses was probably unconscious, but her search for a stable calculus of place was common in the 1890s.[56]

Ironically, the cottage garden wasn't a truly grassroots enthusiasm, bubbling up from the poor or even the lower middle classes; instead it bubbled up from putative ancestors, the carefully selected progenitors of upper-middle and upper-class intellectuals, and was in turn directed by them *at* the lower classes and poor immigrants as a new version of the "Gardening-is-good-for-you" doctrines of Downing and other horticultural reformers. Garden making became a highly visible part of Americanization campaigns aimed at acculturating immigrants: the owners of mines, lumber camps, and factory towns sponsored contests with prizes for the best gardens; more often than not the cottage mode was all but required, as it was by George Washington Cable, founder of the Home Culture Club, a promoter of garden competitions for the working class, who wrote: "Gardening is a benevolent, gracious *naturalization* of nature to citizenship under the home's domain, and an American garden should remain American whatever it borrows from Japan, England, Italy, or Holland" (emphasis in original).[57] Garden making equaled improvement—of the soil, the home, the community, and nation, and simultaneously, in a classic conflation of doing and being, of the spirit, of taste—in short, oneself. Again, the trope was therapy, but the specific prescription differed according to social class. For the exhausted mind of the (wealthy) individual, it was in the sanctum of a private garden, as in Charles Platt's hymn to withdrawing to "that sacred portion of the globe dedicated to one's self." For the poor and the immigrants, whose degradation under industrial conditions risked "irreligion, vulgarity and bad morals widening like a flood," in Cable's ominous words, it was a measure of moral hygiene and public health, as it had been in Olmsted and Vaux's parks.

But gardening like Grandmother didn't succeed in bridging the gaping and growing divide between rich and poor: neither did it uplift the poor masses far enough, nor bring the elite sufficiently down to the level of the people to smooth over the differences. The events of 1893 created a spiraling crisis that quickly turned violent as labor battled management in cities and farmers were crushed by a combination of falling crop prices and rising railroad shipping rates that led to a wave of bank foreclosures. Near Chicago, at the factory town of Pullman, built by railroad car manufacturer George Pullman as a model community featuring houses with indoor plumbing and gas, free schools and a library, and extensive gardens and public landscaping (a scale model of it was included in Sullivan's Transportation Building at the World's Fair),[58] the workers struck in May 1894 to protest a 25 percent wage cut due to plummeting demand for Pullman cars. The strike spread to 125,000 sympathetic rail workers nationwide, paralyzed rail traffic west of Chicago, and culminated in a brutal battle between strikers and twelve thousand federal troops sent in by President Grover Cleveland. In the rioting, the White City, its gleaming façades already darkening from air pollution, mysteriously burned.[59] A federal commission pinned blame for the strike on Pullman's paternalism, which it denounced as "un-American"; the town was later forcibly annexed by swelling Chicago.

No one embodied the Gilded Age in America more fully than the writer Edith Wharton, peerless chronicler of her own elite northeastern society who nevertheless couldn't bear to stay long in her own country.

Born in 1862 into a comfortably well-off and pedigreed New York family, at age four Edith Jones left for Europe on what would turn out to be a six-year sojourn: first to Italy, three years later to Paris, then back to Florence for the last winter.[60] She would later remember soaking up the Italian magic as a small child, on "sunlit wanderings on the springy turf of great Roman villas," often the Villa Borghese, and the ruined gardens of the Palatine hill; all Rome, she wrote, "fed my rich world of dreams."[61] Back in the States, the family spent summers at Newport, Rhode Island, which had become the premier coastal resort of the rich. After eight years in the United States, in 1881 Edith's family went back to France, to Cannes, looking to alleviate her father's failing health. There she was taught by European governesses and learned to speak German, French, and Italian.[62] Even at such a tender age she devoured Ruskin and explored nearby villages and countryside with her father, revealing a voracious curiosity and energy that would become legendary. When her father died, her mother took her back to America.

In 1885, in Boston, Edith married Teddy Wharton, a volatile but weak man who did little to quench her thirst—she dragged him to Europe nearly every year, where she nurtured an obsession with 18th century Italy with intense peregrination and study, wandering in search of dilapidated splendor in old villas and gardens. "The very air is full of architecture," she wrote. "I never weary of driving—looking at doorways, windows, courtyards and walls. What an unerring sentiment of form!"[63] Henry James, with whom she became friends and took several tours, laughed at her manic "excursionism" and dubbed her "the pendulum woman" for her frantic to and fro across the Atlantic.[64] As Wharton would do later, James used European villas and their gardens, often owned by Americans, as models and settings in much of his fiction: Francis Boote's Roman Villa Castellani, for example, sat in for Gilbert Osmond's house in *Portrait of a Lady*, which was partly written in Florence.[65]

In the 1890s, Wharton struggled to find her voice as a writer; her stories were marked by loneliness and a kind of desperation rendered by scenes and metaphors of entrapment—her characters stuck in dark houses and suffocating rooms, bounded spaces that stood for stifling marriages, rigid social conventions, and anomie; she endured rounds of editorial rejections and depression. Not coincidentally, then, she found the subject for her first book in houses: 1897's *The Decoration of Houses*, written with her friend, the American architect Ogden Codman. Their advice was unapologetically elitist: "changes in manners and customs . . . usually originate with the wealthy or aristocratic minority, and are thence transmitted to the other classes. Thus the bourgeois of one generation lives more like the aristocrat of a previous generation than like his own predecessors. This rule naturally holds good of house-planning, and it is for this reason that the origin of modern house-planning should be sought rather in the prince's mezzanin than in the small middle-class dwelling."[66] The book was a success, and its happy reception freed her pen: her short fiction began to be published, then her first novel *The Valley of Decision*, set in 18th century Italy, with an overwrought plot à la Stendhal, but not so good. The book is suffused with images and scenes in Italian gardens of delight: it is populated by nymphs, fauns, goddesses, and statues come to life in penumbral darkness; vistas, allées, fountains, and glades lend it remarkably cinematic settings.

Edith's feel for Italian gardens led to a commission from an American magazine to write a series of articles about them, to be paired with paintings by Maxfield Parrish; beginning in January 1903 she toured the peninsula searching for villas and gardens, often way off the beaten track, steered to many prizes by tips and introductions from Vernon Lee, the English expatriate, lesbian writer of supernatural tales and expert in 18th century art history, whose intellect Wharton found as inspiringly formidable as her personality was famously abrasive. The collection of articles was published in 1904 as a book, *Italian Villas and Their Gardens*, with a dedication to Lee: "Who, better than any one else, has understood and interpreted the garden-magic of Italy," Wharton wrote. Hers was miles more erudite than Platt's book, the history of the villas researched in three languages; and where Platt's consisted of photos with minimal descriptions, hers offered in-depth analysis, focusing as much on her intellectual involvement with the spaces as the spaces themselves. The diffident Parrish did not come along, but since no plans were allowed by the publisher, his dreamy, not-too-specific paintings had to suffice to evoke the "garden-magic" Wharton described.

The Italian "garden-magic" that she felt, and contemporary visitors to Italy feel, of course has everything to do with dilapidation, the patina of age evoking the mysterious, "silent" presence of the past. Henry James captured it perfectly in his travel journal *Italian Hours*, in this remarkable passage about the Boboli Gardens in Florence:

> *. . . when the garden is in the Italian manner, with flowers rather remarkably omitted, as too flimsy and easy and cheap, and without lawns that are too smart, paths that are too often swept and shrubs that are too closely trimmed, though with a fanciful formalism giving style to its shabbiness, and here and there a dusky ilex-walk, and here and there a dried-up fountain, and everywhere a piece of mildewed sculpture staring at you from a green alcove, and just in the right place, above all, a grassy amphitheatre curtained behind with black cypresses and sloping downward in mossy marble steps—when, I say, the place possesses these attractions, and you lounge there of a soft Sunday afternoon, the racier spectacle of the streets having made your fellow-loungers few and left you to the deep stillness and the shady vistas that lead you wonder where, left you to the insidious irresistible mixture of nature and art, nothing too much of either, only a supreme happy resultant, a divine tertium quid: under these conditions, it need scarce be said, the revelation invoked descends upon you.*[67]

Back in the United States, Wharton had bought an estate in Lenox, Massachusetts, in the folds of the Berkshire Mountains, where she had built an English-Palladian house (after a house in Lincolnshire by Christopher Wren, originator of the first generation of the style) that stands out sharply against the surrounding pine woods with its imposing blocks of white masonry and stern eyelashes of black shutters. Completed in 1902, she christened it (apparently without irony) the Mount. Then she began building a terraced and balustraded garden *àl'Italienne*, which she designed herself (though she commissioned her young niece, Beatrix Jones, to design the kitchen garden). From a broad, raised plaza off the rear of the house, a series of turf terraces descends southward, spindled on a white balustraded staircase, before T-ing at a central gravel walk extending between rows of squat, pleached trees. To the west the walk steps down and terminates in a walled "giardino segreto" partly sunk at the bottom of the slope; to the east, on a higher clearing, is a rectangular flower garden surrounding a rectangular pool, called the red garden, which she kept bright in season with masses of mixed hot-colored stocks and pinks "in every shade of rose, salmon, cherry and crimson," according to one account.[68] Evidently this rash-inducing color scheme agreed with her: she looked down on it from her third-floor corner room, where she wrote in bed each morning, producing, in the years 1902–11, *Italian Villas*, *Ethan Frome*, and her 1905 masterpiece, *The House of Mirth*. Besides the loudly Victorian touch of the red garden, there are overwhelming amounts of green: the grass terraces, each one bounded by low arbor vitae hedges and clipped, pointed cones that resemble nothing more than eight-foot-tall artillery shells. It's an odd color palette: black and white, and red and green. For all Wharton's study of the Italian garden, this one seems more French Renaissance; the connection between house and garden is stiff and indirect—though the house opens through wide doors to an elevated, balustraded stone terrace, to reach the garden one has to trundle down a lot of stairs, and once there, one finds a lot of structure without a lot of variety, more straight walks than enclosed rooms, with little feeling of arrival or recompense of repose. Henry James said of the Mount that it was a "monument to the almost too impeccable taste of its mistress."[69] A visitor might wonder that its surfeit of structure and trajectory over lingering spaces enacted her taste for staying in motion, never settling down in one place. And oddly, for someone who maintained that "the American landscape has no foreground and the American mind has no background,"[70] the garden never quite achieves a poetic dialogue with the site. While the house enjoys a view of a curve of water and distant

Historic postcard of the Mount. (Courtesy of the Mount)

woods to the south, the terraces are parallel to it, that is, crossways to the main axis, so the view from most of the garden isn't framed but diverted, where it isn't blocked by a rank of shaggy white pines on an intermediate hillock that seem to be marching down on the estate like a horde of Vikings. Opposite the red garden, the main axis steps down a slope and terminates in the secret garden's walled enclosure with a fountain at its center, the space too big to feel intimate but not big enough to escape feeling low and inert. All around, tall, dark pine woods glower down.

The garden inspires an admiration of good geometry touched with a note of claustrophobia—feelings not unlike those Wharton was so good at conjuring in her fiction. As her biographer, R. W. B. Lewis, asserts matter-of-factly, it is "evident that Edith Wharton had a profound addiction, sometimes amounting to an obsession, with enclosed as against unbounded spaces: with houses themselves (her own and those of others), the arrangement of rooms within houses, the make-up of properly designed gardens. . . . Elements like these were habitual sources of metaphor in her fiction."[71] On one hand, they represented attainment of worldly place and security, especially crucial for women seeking a hold in a tumultuous and unforgiving society—women like Lily Bart, Wharton's magnificently ambivalent heroine in *The House of Mirth*, who exclaims on entering a man's New York apartment, "How delicious to have a place like this all to one's self! What a miserable thing it is to be a woman." On another, they represent the Faustian bargain of trading away one's freedom for the real estate and everything it signifies—entrapment, the gilded cage of wealthy women in the Gilded Age.

On yet another hand, to Wharton houses and gardens represented Americans' often-tortured relationship with history, the past, and questions of cultural inheritance in a society modernizing and moving at breakneck speed. Her now justly overlooked but interestingly moody novel *Hudson River Bracketed* relates the story of Vance Weston, a young man from the small town of Euphoria, Illinois, who seeks his fortune in New York, eventually to become a writer, but first sojourning with downwardly mobile cousins in a Hudson Valley backwater. En route he gets caught in the tension between his soaring aspiration and the family ties that bind and drag down, symbolized by one older girl cousin, nicknamed Halo, a soaring free spirit, brightly aristocratic in temperament and breeding, who leads him toward the salvation of literature and sensibility but is herself beyond his reach, and another, younger cousin, Laura Lou, dull, uneducated, and childlike, whom Vance Weston marries only to find himself trapped. The cousins' family is charged with keeping up an old house, empty after the death of an ancient grandmother, which is a surviving architectural example of Andrew Jackson Downing's signature style of the novel's title. Vance represents the newness and tradition-blindness of America, particularly the West: "He had been born into a world in which everything had been, or was being, renovated," and "could not dissociate stability from stagnation." The old pile, called the Willows, lies down an overgrown drive, hiding behind overgrown willow trees, surrounded by slopes of unmowed grass and swathed in rank lilacs, the scent of which, Wharton rhapsodizes, "is so like the sound of bees on a thundery day." Its old, crotcheted porch, supported on ornate brackets, is gripped tightly by a gigantic wisteria vine:

> *with huge distorted branches like rheumatic arms lifted itself to the eaves, festooning, as it mounted, every projecting point with long lilac fringes—as if, Vance thought, a flock of very old monkeys had been ordered to climb up and decorate the house front in celebration of some august arrival. He had never seen so prodigal a flowering, or a plant so crippled and ancient; and for a while it took his attention from the house. But not for long. To bear so old a climber on its front, the house must be still older; and its age, its mystery, its reserve, laid a weight on his heart.*

Like most Wharton characters, Vance never (or if ever, only in the last few paragraphs) achieves enlightenment, catharsis, or release from this weight on his heart, but the mood of ambivalence is poignant. And the Willows, like most houses and gardens in Wharton's work and life, is the scene of emotion, often melancholy, a drawing backward into a past that pulls at her characters and readers like quicksand, without us necessarily knowing why or what lesson to draw from it. (It is worth noting that Edith Wharton never returned to America after 1911, when she divorced Teddy, sold the Mount, and moved to France,[72] where she had two gardens over the decades, both looser and more "country" or cottagey than anything she'd lauded in Italy.)

ELSEWHERE IN THE Northeast, a renaissance of Renaissance gardens was in full swing, with Charles Platt in the vanguard: in 1897, he built an Italian fantasy world modeled on the Villa Gamberaia and the Villa Lante for Charles F. Sprague, said to be the richest man in the U.S. Congress, at his Faulkner Farm, in Brookline, Massachusetts.[73] It was one of several such commissions that garnered Platt much press, and he was in demand: in the period 1901–17 his office averaged five houses a year, each scru-

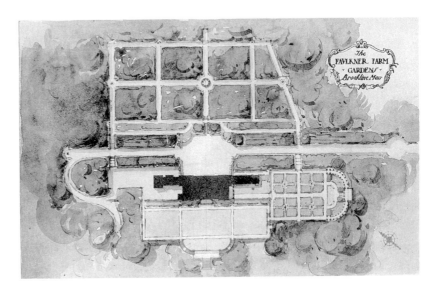

Charles Platt, Faulkner Farm. (From Platt and Cortissoz, *Monograph*)

pulously Italian and carefully meshed with its garden, with axial vistas, terraces, and pergolas. Over time, Platt's villas and gardens became more elaborate and expensive, some rivaling the Roman originals in splendor, but he always managed to strike a balance between opulence and clarity. Frank Lloyd Wright is reported to have said of him that he was "a very dangerous man—he did the wrong thing so well."[74] McKim, Mead, and White in the same era were laying down a swath of fine classical buildings across the country; Oliver Larkin wisecracked that "McKim, Mead and White . . . had no peers in the art of the polished quotation. Having conquered the Chicago Exposition, the McKim idea proceeded to conquer the country."[75] Most were commercial and public, but the firm produced some notable residences, foremost among them Stanford White's Box Hill, an old farmhouse along the North Shore of Long Island, New York. White serially remodeled the place in ever-more classical accretions, which he complemented with a lovely, fairly unpretentious garden of box-edged parterres around a central pool that featured giant clamshells shooting jets of water over a crouching nude.

The neoclassical wave was brought to America by people steeped in the best of Europe to a wealthy clientele eager for instruction—both parties conscious of their mission to rise above the flood tide of Victorian bad taste enthusiastically embraced by a burgeoning middle class. Every time she returned to her native land, Wharton recoiled: "My first weeks in America are always miserable, because the tastes I am cursed with are all of a kind that cannot be gratified here." Once, forced by car trouble to stay the night in a summer hotel on the Connecticut shore, she was appalled by her compatriots: "I despair of the Republic! Such dreariness, such whining callow women, such utter absence of the amenities, such crass food, crass manners, crass landscape!! And, mind you, it is a new and fashionable hotel. What a horror it is for a whole nation to be developing without a sense of beauty, and eating bananas for breakfast."[76] Like Wharton, what most took her friend Henry James aback when he returned from abroad for a tour— as a foreign tourist essentially—wasn't the sight of the upper middle class eating bananas for breakfast but the greater crassness and misbegotten aesthetics of the newly rich. In the book that resulted in 1904, *The American Scene*, James described the endless lines of new mansions sprouting up in Long Branch, on the New Jersey shore, as: "a chain of big villas . . . stretched tight, or at least kept straight, almost as for the close stringing of more or less monstrous pearls." He watched swarthy southern Italian immigrants building a garden for a "a large new rural residence, where groups of ditchers and diggers were working, on those lines of breathless haste which seem always, in the United States, of the essence of any question, toward an expensive effect of landscape gardening." The houses were being built, it appeared, mostly for upwardly mobile German Jews, as he pointed out in descriptions redolent with his habitual anti-Semitism:

> *There was gold dust in the air, no doubt—which would have been again an element of glamour if it had not rather lighted the scene with too crude a confidence. . . . The huge new houses, up and down, looked over their smart, short lawns as with a certain*

familiar prominence in the profiles, which was borne out by the accent, loud, assertive, yet benevolent withal, with which they confessed to their extreme expensiveness. . . .

The ostentation of minor arrivistes, especially Jews, James could easily wave off, but the sheer spending and speed of it spreading outward from the city had no European analogue. And, more to the core of his complaint was his response to the villeggiatura being perpetrated at the highest socioeconomic levels, particularly Newport, where James made his famous appraisal of the massive houses of the multimillionaires: "The white elephants, as one may best call them, all cry and no wool, all house and no garden, make now, for three or four miles, a barely interrupted chain, and I dare say I think of them best, and of the distressful, inevitable waste they represent. . . . "[77] There was incredible wealth in the 1890s—one Astor is said to have sniffed that a millionaire was "almost as well off as if he were rich."[78] Not all of it was new, but all of it aspired to the imprimatur of taste—the only potentially acceptable substitution for bloodline, achievable one way and one way only: by copying European models. What Henry James was dismissing was, at the high end, actually the scrupulous re-creation of the most elaborate European finery, designed by architects trained in Europe and built by the best European craftsmen imported for the purpose. Richard Morris Hunt, the first American trained at the Ecole des Beaux-Arts in Paris, had become the Vanderbilt family architect, building a couple of French châteaux-inspired houses on Fifth Avenue in New York for two of the sons, then remodeling Cornelius II's Newport "cottage," the Breakers, as an Italian villa for an unimaginable $3 million.[79] McKim, Mead, and White knocked down the mansion at Hyde Park along the Hudson that Frederick William Vanderbilt's father, William Henry Vanderbilt, had bought from a grandson of Jacob Astor in 1895, and replaced it with a fifty-room, fifty-thousand-square-foot Roman palace in a mere two years, for a cool $2.5 million. The majority of its sixty servants were employed in the six hundred acres of gardens: a vast desert of lawn dotted with specimen trees around which a drive circled in a huge arc, so that a visitor had no

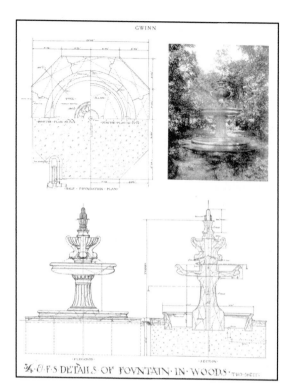

Charles Platt, fountain at Gwinn. (From Platt and Cortissoz, *Monograph*)

choice but to view the mansion from each one of 180 degrees before finally arriving, as if carefully appraising a big diamond on a sheet of velvet. Off to the sides were a greenhouse, the largest in the United States at the time, and a walled formal garden as big as any on the eighty-plus significant estates that swarmed the Hudson from New York City to Albany. Men like the Vanderbilts and J. P. Morgan were compared to the Medici and built like them—but were no better loved than their predecessors; Charles Francis Adams, Jr. (Henry's brother), said of the "New Medici": "Not one that I have ever known would I care to meet again in this world or the next."

IN THE GARDENS of the average superrich, Platt and Wharton's Italian strict constructionism had less appeal than the tried-and-true gardenesque bedding out, which reached alarming levels in Newport, where in some society gardens the flowers were changed two to three times per week over an eight-week season.[80] Mariana Van Rensselaer dismissed Newport's gardens as tasteless displays of "a greedy love for conspicuous plants as such. They are huddled little conglomerations of trees and showy shrubs, and of bits of grass splashed with chromo-like flowerbeds, and speckled with exotic plants which have recently been brought from the greenhouse and loudly confess their homesickness for tropical surroundings. . . . Nowhere better than at Newport can we understand what a French artist meant when he said that most people's idea of gardening is 'the cleaning up of spontaneous vegetation' followed by 'the accumulation of strange and dissimilar objects.'"[81] Still others leaned toward baroque French parterre confections iced with delicate knots and squiggles amid expanses of raked gravel. (The Hunt-trained architects Carrère & Hastings, designers of the New York Public Library and the Frick Mansion, went all out in this direction with the *trop-grandiose* Nemours for Alfred I. duPont, in Wilmington, Delaware, a copy of André Le Nôtre's Petit Trianon at Versailles and as astonishing a sight in the supposedly egalitarian, democratic United States of America as can be imagined.)

The "distressful, inevitable waste" that Henry James bemoaned didn't, as one might expect, refer to the conspicuous consumption, but to the fact that the expenditure was nevertheless useless to secure the aristocratic permanence it sought. James instinctively understood the physical facts of cultural life as manifestations of the inner life of the protagonists: their aspirations, intentions, anxieties, and illusions. He called the whole business he observed among the wealthy "this interesting struggle in the void . . . the upper social organism floundering there all helplessly, more or less floated by its immense good-will and the splendour of its immediate environment, but betrayed by its paucity of real resource."

WHAT WAS MISSING from this rehearsal of aristocracy was the reality of aristocracy. In commercial America, where without title, primogeniture, or landed estates, status is based almost solely on money, the only thing that is permanent is the coming and going of said money, the only thing sure the endless arrival of new arrivistes. It galled James, stumped

him, and nearly spoiled his enjoyment of the luxury around him. But he
clearly read it as a "void," an emptiness at the heart of the American social
enterprise that drained that spectacle of wealth of the glow and promise
it wanted to hold. This was the milieu captured so brilliantly by Wharton in *House of Mirth*, and the deep tragedy of Lily Bart, a young woman
raised and trained to scale the social heights, who strikes the character
Lawrence Selden as though "she must have cost a great deal to make, that
a great many dull and ugly people must, in some mysterious way, have
been sacrificed to produce her."[82] She was built to be a bauble, but in the
end it is her humanity, her fragmented, semiconscious inner nobility that
puts an end to her climbing and sets off her fall. Wharton described her
as "a captured dryad subdued to the conventions of the drawing-room,"
but who still had a "streak of sylvan freedom in her nature that lent such
savour to her artificiality." She has spirit and morals, but is sacrificed to
a society without any: bottled up like the dryad, she suffocates and dies.
That money can't buy happiness was the basic trope by which the Gilded
Age knew itself, but this realization didn't stop those with money from
trying: and society watched raptly, especially horrified and transfixed
by the shaky ascents of outsiders, notably Jews like Simon Rosedale in
Mirth, whom Wharton, as James had, painted with an ugly brush of racial
clichés, and who inexorably nears the center of possibility as he gets ever
richer, while economic depression squeezes the WASP gentry.

Even insiders had trouble fitting through the eye of the most exclusive
social needle. Isabella Stewart Gardner, a New Yorker who married the
scion of Boston's wealthy Peabody family, never quite lived down the little scandals her eccentric public behavior stirred among the Beacon Hill
smart set. She achieved another kind of fame as a collector of European
and Asian art and bric-a-brac, with help from the scholar and art con-
sultant Bernard Berenson—a classic outsider-made-good, born a Lithu-
anian Jew, who immigrated to America, married a WASP, was educated
at Harvard, wrote numerous books that built his reputation as a connois-
seur, and enriched himself through agent commissions from clients like
Gardner. She filled Fenway Court—a replica Venetian palazzo near the
Back Bay Fens that she cobbled together from bits of Venetian build-

ings shipped home and crowned with a four-story, glass-roofed central court—with treasures vacuumed up on her trips abroad or suggested by Berenson: paintings by Titian, Botticelli, and Raphael, as well as every conceivable kind of drawing, tapestry, carving, and sculpture, the majority of which had originally served a religious function.

Gardner's trove exemplified the paradoxical attraction that premodern Catholic art held for the Protestant upper class in America and Britain in the period: the rich could buy anything save meaning in the commercial world their class had made and dominated ruthlessly, and so they sought out a deeper vein of experience and sense of purpose through collecting old things, created by real human hands in the long sleep before the industrial revolution. Collecting was the passion of the age: paintings and assorted art filled the houses of the new classicists, and urns, statuary, friezes, bits of architectural ornament, wells, and fountains, not to mention exotic plants from the four corners of the world, filled their gardens. American tastemakers like Berenson and Platt also made their living from supplying these desires with an endless stream of objets plucked from the recesses of a European countryside impoverished by the same forces that made the collectors wealthy: factories, finance, railroads, mining, and the overproduction of farm products in the American heartland. But collecting, no matter how assiduous or scholarly, was also irretrievably associated with outsiders trying to buy legitimacy, tradition, and a share in the sanctioning past, trying to launder their new money. Fenway Court is magnificent but it is also shocking in its cupidity: it is a trophy case, stuffed to near bursting with anything that wasn't nailed down in the ruined, open-air museum of Europe. And for Isabella Gardner, in spite of the triumph of Fenway Court, a small cloud remained—the fact that she bought her way into the sealed insularity of Boston society.

Even in the United Kingdom, the ancient social order was breaking down in the onslaught of the capitalist world economy: competition from American farmers and bad weather set up a vicious cycle of British wheat crop busts, followed by floods of cheaper U.S. imports, undercutting the market and driving property rents on landed estates to collapse in the

1880s and '90s.[83] With plummeting income, many owners were forced to sell out. To whom? To new money: often Jewish bankers with names like Sassoon and Rothschild, more often American plutocrats who had come to England as to a finishing school, to learn to act like aristocrats. For real European aristocrats, one way to avoid selling land was to sell titles: one of the first American girls to land a noble was Jennie Jerome, the daughter of a New York financier, who married Lord Randolph Churchill in 1874 and gave birth to a son, Winston, eight months later; by 1910 more than five hundred Americans had married European titles, with thousands more marrying Europeans without titles but with some other negotiable asset, whether genealogical, financial, or real estate, such as a castle—castles, as always, being irresistible to Americans with money to burn. In 1903, William Waldorf Astor, one of the richest heirs in America, famously bought Hever Castle in Edenbridge, Kent, the childhood home of Anne Boleyn; became a British subject; and restored it for a mere $10 million. It took a thousand men over four years to hand-dig a thirty-five-acre lake and construct an Italian garden for his sculpture collection, a rockery, grottoes, pergolas, herbaceous borders, rhododendron walks, and an impressive lakeside "ruin" of an Italianate pavilion with a scaled-down version of the Trevi Fountain in Rome fronting the water.[84]

IN AMERICA, THE most ambitious and celebrated castle of the Gilded Age, with no rival before and few since, was built in the steep, wooded mountains of western North Carolina, for George Washington Vanderbilt, the youngest son of William Henry Vanderbilt, who had left a fabulous $200 million estate to be divided among his eight children. G. W. Vanderbilt had come to the new mountain resort at Asheville, high in the Smoky Mountains, prized by southerners for its cool summers and by northerners for its mild spring and fall, before beginning to amass land for a fantasy domain to rival Arnheim.[85] He hired Richard Morris Hunt, who had built his brother William Kissam Vanderbilt a French Renaissance mini-château at 660 Fifth Avenue in New York, to design him a full-sized castle, also in the overblown, wedding-cake style of the huge châteaux erected by the ultrarich in the 15th century Loire Valley. Client and architect traveled to France to visit examples, including those at Chantilly, Chambord, and Fontainebleu, and set their sights on more or less copying choice bits of each, plus the 15th century façade added by King François I to the more ancient Château de Blois. They had also gone to England to see examples of estates built in the style in the previous few decades, such as Waddesdon Manor, Buckinghamshire, designed by the French architect Destailleur for Baron Ferdinand de Rothschild in the early 1870s. Never mind that it had been the architectural craze among the British nouveaux riches in the 1860s and '70s, sparking the construction of a rash of gaudy London hotels which were imitated all over the United Kingdom.[86] To Vanderbilt, French Renaissance was neither gauche nor a ludicrous transposition to modern, industrial America, but a testament to the continuity between men like him and Rothschild and the commercial princes of the Renaissance, and made the incipient claim, as merchant castles always have, that their control of money rendered them the peers of the kings they served. But hubris can sink the ship: one recalls the cautionary tale of King Louis XIV's finance minister, Nicolas Fouquet, who built what was then the finest château and garden in France, Vaux-le-Vicomte, designed by the architect Louis Le Vau, the painter-decorator Charles Le Brun, and the landscape architect André Le Nôtre. When it was finished in 1661, Fouquet threw so lavish a party—the Molière play *Les Fâcheux* was performed, and dinner for hundreds was accompanied by an extraordinary fireworks display—that the king, who had not yet built his palace at Versailles, suspected him of embezzlement on a vast scale (how else could he have afforded such buildings and gardens?) and had him summarily arrested and jailed for life. He then hired Le Nôtre to lay out Versailles. (Voltaire later quipped: "On 17 August, at six in the evening Fouquet was the King of France: at two in the morning he was nobody.")

At Biltmore, the role of Le Nôtre was played by Frederick Law Olmsted, whom Vanderbilt had called in at the beginning to help him assess the best siting and approach for the house. Olmsted worked at Asheville in the same years as the Chicago Fair, and split a trip to Europe to study watercourses for his lagoons at Grant Park and French formal gardens to dress out Hunt's stone confection. The task was nearly as immense as the site, situated inside a 125,000-acre fiefdom of forested land descending the slopes around Mount Pisgah down to the banks of the French Broad River. Olmsted carefully planned the drives, entrance sequences, and locations of each piece of the self-contained world Biltmore would become: railroad, brick factory, woodshop, quarry, dam and waterworks, indoor swimming pool, nursery, church, and workers' village to house, among others, the skilled French craftsmen brought over to build the exquisite interior woodwork and carve the exterior stone details as perfectly as their 12th century confreres had carved the cathedrals.[87] The house itself included 225 rooms, a massive banquet hall hung with medieval tapestries, and a pipe organ. If the Chicago Fair was a repudiation of the democratic and romantic principles Olmsted stood for, with the exception of the wooded island, Biltmore was their death by drowning in champagne: in the gardens around the house, he laid out tennis courts, lawns, an esplanade, a bowling green, and a walled garden of curlicue knots and parterres, elaborate enough to have pleased Louis XIV. Away from the house he was able to loosen up the lines, threading a ramble and a wandering approach drive through the trees. For the forest acreage, much of it badly cut through and eroded by prior misuse, he recommended a program of "scientific forestry," a newly popular discipline in continental Europe, and convinced his client to hire Gifford Pinchot, a young American educated in France in the latest forestry techniques (he went on to serve as the first director of the U.S. Forest Service), to oversee replanting the forests with an eye to profit. (Olmsted, acknowledging finally that the gentleman farming he had tried and failed at earlier in his life wouldn't pay, insisted that managed timber harvesting would.)

The one part of the scheme that most preoccupied Olmsted was his vision for a nine-mile road lined with a carefully arranged collection of thousands of trees, native and imported—in effect a drive-through arboretum. The idea of trees possessed him, and no doubt consoled him somewhat, as success had taken him away from his passion, building parks for the people. "If man is not to live by bread alone, what is better worth doing well than the planting of trees?" he asked himself.[88] As the work proved itself more arduous and complicated than anticipated and schedules were delayed, Olmsted, by then in his eighties and feeling exhausted by his constant travel and long days in the field, was diverted away from the arboretum, and Vanderbilt showed little enthusiasm for it.

Over the years, Olmsted slid into senility, and his son, Frederick Jr., and his nephew and adopted stepson John Charles, took over the firm's projects. In 1898 the family placed him in a sanitarium in Brookline, where years earlier he had designed the grounds.[89] The arboretum was never built, the only piece of Olmsted's plan not executed. In 1903, Frederick Law Olmsted was dead.

The two younger Olmsteds renamed the firm Olmsted Brothers and remained busy for the next four decades, designing elegant city park systems for Portland, Maine, Portland, Oregon, Charleston, Dayton, Seattle, and Spokane, as well as a cavalcade of individual city parks, settlement houses, schools, universities, asylums, libraries, hospitals, state capitols, expositions, and private gardens—many of them in the neoclassical, Beaux-Arts style. Even in the forests of the Pacific Northwest— where the firm had forty private commissions in Seattle in the decades after 1903, thirty or so in Portland, and nineteen in Spokane[90]—the natural aesthetic of their father suffered near-total defeat: for parvenu timber millionaires and Jewish department store owners alike, Olmsted Brothers designed enormous, fussy French gardens, almost completely flat compositions, incongruously surrounded by towering trees, as though a meteorite or a jet had crash-landed and cleared a swath. By the turn of the century, the success of Charles Platt's program at the apex of American garden design had been the undoing of Andrew Jackson Downing's, and Downing's houses and gardens had all but disappeared by the turn of the century—hence Edith Wharton's eulogy for them in *Hudson River Bracketed*.

Beginning in 1900, Daniel Burnham, Augustus Saint-Gaudens, and Frederick Law Olmsted, Jr., reworked the master plan for the Capitol and Mall in Washington, D.C., replacing Downing's vision with a rectilinear Beaux-Arts style considered more in keeping with the neoclassical architecture of the government buildings and more evocative of the grandeur they thought the site demanded. The Burnham plan was part of what had come to be called the City Beautiful movement, a coinage and personal crusade of Charles Mulford Robinson, a journalist from Rochester, New York, who had visited the 1893 Chicago Exposition and come away a zealous convert to the idea that well-designed cities and beautiful surroundings could alleviate urban ills. Neither he nor many others who believed in the City Beautiful's promise found the juxtaposition of pristine white buildings and urban filth incongruous, but the perfect architectonic order of the White City couldn't quite mask the disorder and squalor that most of Chicago's citizens lived in. Violence was just behind the curtain in the Windy City: the Haymarket riot had rocked it in 1886, followed by the Pullman strike in 1893. These events helped bring to the attention of the better-off residents of small towns and garden suburbs the shocking poverty in American cities, exacerbated by waves of poor immigrants to inner cities. The U.S. population grew between 1860 and 1910 from 31.4 million to 91.9 million; and where in 1860 most Americans were rural, by 1910, 46 percent of them lived in communities of more than 2,500 people. Reformers like the photographer and journalist Jacob Riis shone light on urban conditions, sending a shudder through polite society. The depression of 1893–97 saw more labor violence from coast to coast, stoking a real fear of disorder among the elites, who were suddenly motivated to begin to extend some social services to the immigrant ghettoes, chiefly in the form of private settlement houses like Jane Addams's Hull House, opened in Chicago in 1889 (modeled on Toynbee Hall, which opened in London's squalid East End in 1885, and which Addams had visited).

Guided by the City Beautiful principles, there was a tidal wave of classicist construction from coast to coast, civic and private alike. Landscape and gardens were central to all of it, and the key practitioners, Olmsted Brothers and their colleagues, enthusiastically put their shoulders to the wheel. Robinson spread the gospel in magazine articles, books, and lecture tours and was hired by local City Beautiful committees and cities themselves to prepare reports on how to remake American cities as Renaissance Utopias: he prepared twenty-five reports from New York to Honolulu, the latter just after its forcible annexation by the United

States.[91] The visions he and others set out were grand, with long diagonal boulevards, parks, monuments, and tree-lined boulevards inspired by Baron Haussmann's Paris—and sometimes even provisions for improved housing for the working class. The plans were rarely executed beyond a park or courthouse here or a monument there to war dead from one of America's growing list of armed conflicts. Lewis Mumford wrote that "the evil of the World's Fair triumph was that it . . . introduced the notion of the City Beautiful as a sort of municipal cosmetic, and reduced the work of the architect to that of putting a pleasing front upon the scrappy building, upon the monotonous streets and the mean houses, that characterized vast areas in the newer and larger cities."[92]

Even at its apogee, the classical rule never pushed the eclectic urge out of the Anglo-American mind; as at the White City, it provided a grand shell inside which to display one's collections, gathered from the farthest crevices of the world. Collecting was more than a hobby: accumulation and cataloging of natural objects and economic goods was the scientific-practical buttress of the imperial enterprise. Economically important species had to be sought out, propagated, spread around the empire, cultivated, and exported; this traffic was at the heart of the mercantile theory and structure of imperialism's grip on the globe. Rival European empires sent out spies to filch seeds and stalks from one another's tropical possessions; this horticultural intrigue fed a mad florescence of exotica in gardens, which, to be interesting, had to have one of everything, both at the botanical gardens established in the 18th century like Great Britain's Kew, and in private arboreta, where collecting signified erudition, resources, and taste all at once. So-called anthology gardens were a fad among people with those three possessions, or at least resources and ambition for the other two, and they popped up everywhere. One of the earliest and best in the United States was Sonnenberg, at Canandaigua, New York, twenty-five miles south of Rochester. Over several decades, a wealthy couple transformed a fifty-acre spread into a Victorian fantasyland to rival Queen Victoria's Kew. It boasted a so-called Italian garden, with parterres of fleur-de-lis in garish bedded-out annuals; a rose garden in the shape of a flower with five thousand specimens; a colonial garden with a vine-covered arbor amid walks lined with Grandmother's billowing flowers; four color gardens, including a blue-and-white garden, a pansy garden, a "Sub Rosa" (secret) garden, and a Moonlight garden, with all white, fragrant flowers; a three-and-a-half-acre rock garden; a deer park; an aviary; and a trio of the sports facilities newly fashionable in the Gilded Age—a swimming pool, a tennis court, and the indispensable nine-hole golf course. (Playing golf was the latest expression of fervent across-the-pond Anglophilia: Henry James called it "a clear American felicity; a *complete* product of the social soil and air which alone have made it possible.")[93] Sonnenberg's most exotic feature was the Japanese garden, complete with standing rocks and stone lanterns, miniature conifers, and bonsai in pots, set around a replica of a Kyoto teahouse, all built by a K. Wadamori, brought over especially from Japan. A photograph reveals a party of stolid couples arranged around the teahouse, the women in boot-length white dresses, bustles, and ridiculous hats piled high with fake flowers; to the right of the frame stands a Japanese gentleman in an ill-fitting suit, evidently the gardener.[94]

Japan was the second great influence and sensation of the Gilded Age—the polar opposite of Italy, working counter to it in form: asymmetrical, flowing, and allegorical instead of symmetrical, geometric, and rational; and in affect feminine, mysterious, and colorful instead of masculine, assertive, and monochrome. In practice the two were often deployed in close association: many an estate included an Italianate house set in formal gardens but with its Japanese garden tucked in a semi-secret spot, shielded by trees. If the botanical and anthology gardens were reflections of the progress of imperial reach, a new flavor and collection of treasures installed as each new part of the world came under Western dominion, it is appropriate that Japan was the last major culture to be incorporated, in the second half of the 19th century. Prior to then, Japan had remained militantly unknown, a sealed island kingdom that had closed itself in the early 17th century after a tentative opening to the Portuguese, then the

Spanish, curtailed with deadly force when the Iberian missionaries over-stayed their welcome with aggressive proselytizing. In 1853–54, a U.S. naval fleet under Commodore Matthew Perry opened trade and diplomatic relations with the kingdom Melville called, in *Moby-Dick*, "impenetrable Japans."[95] Thereafter, a slowly increasing traffic in Japanese objects, mostly decorative arts pieces, fueled interest in the country's imagery and mystery. Plants too, made their way abroad: Japanese honeysuckle (*Lonicera japonica*) was growing in America by 1861.[96] In 1860, actual Japanese people could be viewed up close in the form of the first Japanese diplomatic mission to the United States, which paraded down New York City's Broadway. Poet Walt Whitman witnessed the spectacle of mass gawking and published his response as three stanzas of verse in a New York paper. The poem was an open expression of the West's fascination with the East, a laundry list of Orientalist tropes and rather lurid fantasies of the Asian Other, all nationalities somehow conjured for Whitman by the appearance of a few Japanese officials in a carriage. "Lithe and silent the Hindoo appears, the Asiatic continent itself / appears, the past, the dead . . . / The north, the sweltering south, eastern Assyria, the Hebrews, the / ancient of ancients, / Vast desolated cities, the gliding present, all of these and more / are in the pageant-procession."

Japanese culture seeped into the West in the form of books, pictures, and bric-a-brac. Japanese graphic art and calligraphy exerted an enormous influence on the first really unique artistic style the 19th century produced, the Arts & Crafts movement, and its daughter, Art Nouveau. *Japonisme* was seen in painting, with Whistler, in all manner of decorative objects made by Arts & Crafts acolytes, and in interior decoration, where rooms decorated with Japanesque wallpapers and furniture—sometimes real imports, more often Western copies, depicting whimsical architecture and gardens, flowers, birds, and patterns—were common among the cognoscenti. The Japanese imagery was an update of the 18th century Chinese taste that Jefferson shared with the English and French—a new variant on the Eastern idyll, complete with lotus blossoms. A Japanese room was installed in the mansion McKim, Mead, and White built for William Henry Vanderbilt at Fifth Avenue and Fifty-first Street. Before long, Harvard began offering lectures on Buddhism. Bohemian travel journals stoked curiosity among the leisured classes, and the more adventurous added Japan to their Grand Tour, alternating it with Europe in odd years. Rudyard Kipling was there in 1889, and again in 1892, and his dispatches were widely read and admired.[97] Images of Japanese visual opulence combined with a unique kind of literary exoticism appealed to the artistic avant-garde, Hokusai's manga prints pervasive among them. In 1886, Henry James visited the American expat painter John Singer Sargent's garden in Broadway, England, with its lilies and tree peonies and paper lanterns from Japan—details that worked their way into his fiction—and visited Whistler's English garden, which, with its many Japanese notes, including the ubiquitous paper lanterns, provided the model for the garden in his 1903 novel *The Ambassadors*.[98] Whistler collected Japanese prints and often put Japanese themes and objects in his paintings: *Caprice in Purple and Gold* is but one example.[99] Monet's Japanism was central to Impressionism's own exotic feel, and much imitated: Degas, Van Gogh, Rouault, and Toulouse-Lautrec all revealed it. Japanese imagery quickly invaded pop culture: Gilbert & Sullivan wrote *The Mikado* in 1885—Gilbert was said to have fixed on the theme for the opera when a samurai sword fell from the wall in his study. While the story may be apocryphal, they were clearly good readers of the zeitgeist. The cultural sensation of the age was *Madame Butterfly*, first an 1895 novel, then a 1900 New York and London play, then a 1903 Puccini opera, and finally a 1915 movie starring Mary Pickford as Cho-Cho-San ("Butterfly"), the fifteen-year-old geisha of the title, and shot on location in a Japanese garden in New Jersey.[100]

Outside, in gardens, Japanism spread, materially aided by the Japanese government's effort to woo the Western powers that controlled the seas around its islands, by sending mock-ups of its historical buildings and gardens to expositions around the world. Japanese contributions were on view in London in 1862, Paris in 1867, and Vienna in 1873. The first Japanese garden in America was built at the 1876 Philadelphia Centennial International Exhibition in Fairmount Park, complete with a house, teahouse, and garden.[101] The Chicago Fair had the "Phoenix Villa" or

Japan Building, Chicago Fair, 1893. (Field Museum, Chicago)

Ho'oden in what came to be called the Imperial Japanese garden, built on Olmsted's wooded isle by Japanese craftsmen with the contents of forty freight cars shipped via California. The effort bore fruit: the Phoenix Villa influenced Louis Sullivan afterward and sent Frank Lloyd Wright on a lifelong mission to plumb the lessons of Japanese architecture. The Japanese government paid for additional installations: at the 1894 California Midwinter International Exposition in San Francisco's Golden Gate Park, and at the St. Louis Louisiana Purchase Exposition of 1903–1904.[102] The exposure resulted in a vogue for private Japanese-style gardens; magazines published articles on the theory and practice of the mode, including one 1908 *House & Garden* issue entirely devoted to the subject.[103]

Japanese village, Golden Gate Park, 1894. (By Clark B. Waterhouse)

George Turner Marsh, an Australian immigrant who had spent five years in Japan before landing in San Francisco and opening a Japanese art boutique in the city's opulent Palace Hotel, saw the business possibilities and, after the 1894 Midwinter Expo, bought and operated the one-acre "Japanese Village" in Golden Gate Park as a commercial Japanese tea garden. It was a hit, and he expanded to a site in San Diego near the grand Hotel del Coronado, and to Pasadena. The concept quickly spread across the country.[104] (On April 25, 1906, in one Japanese-inflected garden on the rooftop of Stanford White's own Madison Square Garden in New York, the famous red-haired architect was shot in the face by the millionaire husband of Evelyn Nesbit, the actress and It-Girl with whom White had slept when she was sixteen and he forty-seven. The subsequent murder trial riveted New York; Nesbit, reputation ruined, became a real-life Lily Bart.)

Having a Japanese garden, preferably built by designers and craftsmen imported for the purpose, became de rigueur for the rich: John D. Rockefeller had a fine example at Pocantico Hills, New York; a roster of tycoons soon owned one—Gould, McCormick, Armour, Seiberling (founder of Goodyear Tire and Rubber), Mellon, Mayo, Gardner, and Crocker, and slightly lesser business nobility also built Japanese gardens, from Boston to Honolulu. Most of them were of the "hill-and-water" type, which the Japanese call *tsukiyama-sansui*, like the stunning one built in 1913 for the California railroad king Henry Huntington in the exclusive enclave of San Marino, near Pasadena, which featured a bright red lacquered drum bridge and a Japanese house complete with a Japanese family in residence who were expected to appear in kimono costume for guests. Even Daniel Burnham, pitiless enforcer of the neoclassical rule, designed a Japanese-style house, in 1907, in Chevy Chase, Maryland, near Washington, D.C.

Why the appeal, in an era otherwise marked by an almost slavish imitation of European models? On both sides of the Atlantic, people looking for new inspiration in creating beauty found in Japan a rich source; in trying to grasp how to use it, they searched for an essence of Japan that was antipodal to Western culture.[105] What they focused on were its apparent mystery, its alternate spiritual and imaginative realms, and its perceived femininity. Of course, most of the details were taken completely out of context. At Chicago in 1893, the Phoenix Villa was modeled on a "Hoodo" Buddhist temple type from the 11th century but was set in a stroll garden typical of 19th century Japanese restaurants. That the combination was ahistorical was beside the point; what was important was that the cultural transaction continue between the two sides, each of which was trying to woo, and fool, the other. This is because there was genuine, mutual attraction and admiration for each side's cultural forms, and genuine fear: dreams of empire were in the air on both sides, and clear comprehension that the two nations might be on a collision course in the Pacific Basin. A few lines down in his 1860 poem, Whitman captured America's longing and determination to reach into the ocean and seize it: "I chant America the mistress, I chant a greater supremacy, / I chant projected a thousand blooming cities yet in time on those / groups of sea-islands, / My sail-ships and steam-ships threading the archipelagoes, / My stars and stripes fluttering in the wind, . . ."

AMERICAN DREAMS, WRAPPED up in the pull of a western empire since Jefferson, had by the second half of the 19th century given way to an explicitly racialized program of armed conquest, grandiosely appointed Manifest Destiny, which accompanied the American spread across the continent and sanctioned its appalling cruelty and bloodshed. When the Americans arrived on the Pacific shore, they didn't pause, but looked farther, south to Mexico and into the Caribbean Sea, and west across the Pacific to a seemingly limitless world of islands ripe for trade, Christianization, and possession. In 1898 the dream was wrenched into reality with the sound of the unexplained explosion that sent the U.S. battleship *Maine* to the bottom of Havana harbor, launching the United States into war with Spain over that frail dowager empress's remaining overseas colonies. Swift victories resulted in Cuba and the Philippines, where U.S. admiral George Dewey sank the superannuated Spanish fleet in Manila Bay with a half day's shelling. It was a "splendid little war,"[106] in the view of the bellicose American press. The United States was suddenly an imperial power with colonies flung halfway across the globe; it found itself bogged down in a brutal war against Filipino insurgents that would last almost ten years. Just as suddenly, America looked at Japan from its new Asian doorstep, and each took nervous note of their newfound proximity. Culturally the two maintained their mutual surface attraction, but the ingrained distrust only deepened.

Nowhere were the push and pull in greater relief than in California, where Americans and Japanese actually mingled: Japanese immigrants, many having served out terms as laborers on Hawaiian sugar plantations like those owned by superrich San Franciscan Klaus Spreckels, moved to the mainland in growing numbers. Tensions rose in step as the Japanese were branded with the same worries previously aimed at the Chinese population over labor competition and the corrosions of opium, prostitution, and gambling that had led to attacks, burnings of Chinatowns, and systematic efforts to ban immigration, beginning with the first Asiatic exclusion law in 1882.[107] San Francisco, born in the Gold Rush that kicked off in 1849, was probably the fastest-birthed major city in history, an instant cosmopolis, flush with money and filled with people from all over the globe who, encountering no established Protestant, American hegemony, made it one of the most diverse and culturally freewheeling places in North America. Building on California's Spanish and Mexican Catholic base, a huge influx of Irish saw many of their number rise to wealth and power and civic leadership, part of what the historian Kevin Starr termed San Francisco's "Irish ascendancy"—the very opposite of Boston, where the Irish were held almost beneath contempt.

But San Franciscans of all stripes shared with the Bostonians of the "American Renaissance" a sense of their city as being fated to repeat the glories of Rome and the Italian Renaissance: dreams of a new Rome on the Pacific, a Florence of the Pacific, were constantly invoked. In California the claim seemed effortless, even natural, because of its inherited Mediterraneanism. San Francisco, born rough and corrupt as a feverish miner's supply station, had by its infancy anointed itself as the future commercial, industrial, and military colossus of the Pacific Basin, controlling it from its incredible harbor through the Golden Gate—named after the Golden Horn in Constantinople by John Charles Frémont, the military adventurer and ardent expansionist who seized California from Mexico and became one of its first two senators. San Franciscans foresaw the inevitable construction of an isthmus canal, either in Nicaragua or Panama, which would inexorably extend American and therefore San Francisco's dominance, throughout the hemisphere. The city's businessmen prepared the way and profited from it, lobbying Washington for military bases and military contracts, none greater than those won by the Union Iron Works, south of Market Street, to build a new generation of battleships. Several of these were sold to the frantically modernizing and militarizing Japanese government. The rhetoric of the time was suffused with strident militarism and imperial visions: in the words of a local paper, San Francisco was "the new city by the western sea, the home of the strongest, bravest, and sturdiest people of their race."[108]

Gilded Age San Francisco's story is encapsulated in the person and life of James Duval Phelan, the son of an Irish gold seeker who had made it big. Elected mayor in 1897 on a reformist platform of taking on corruption, Phelan was a banker and deal maker who was also well traveled, with cultivated tastes—he wrote poetry and was president of the Bohemian Club. A fervent convert to the City Beautiful ideals, he dreamed of world-class status for his city and paid for grand sculptural monuments all over town to demonstrate it.[109] In April 1906, as the city lay in ruins from the earthquake and three days of firestorm that consumed its wooden buildings, Phelan dedicated the California Volunteers monument he had commissioned to honor the state's dead in the still-raging Philippine war, featuring Bellona, Roman goddess of battle, mounted on a winged Pegasus, brandishing a sword and a flag, with two Californian soldiers, one standing with a pistol, the other with his rifle, fallen to the ground in his last agony.[110] Phelan exhorted the crowd that Admiral Dewey's naval success had reawakened "the warlike spirit of the race."[111]

Phelan's enthusiasm for such neoclassical pomp was shared by the city's new oligarchy, which had set aside a thousand acres in 1870[112] for a Golden Gate Park to rival New York's Central Park. Frederick Law Olmsted was naturally asked to design it, and after studying the situation, proposed a wild landscape of native plantings adapted to the harsh, dry, windy dune site. The oligarchs would have none of it and instead hired a young mining engineer, William Hammond Hall, to create an English-style park. Hammond did so, ingeniously and expensively, by hauling in hundreds of tons of manure and inventing a plant-succession scheme in which grasses gave way to mosses, then shrubs, then trees, brought from every continent to form the largest such collection on the planet (subsequently called Strybing Arboretum). Hammond's scheme required huge quantities of imported water, contributing to San Francisco's justifications for its (still) controversial damming of Hetch Hetchy Valley in Yosemite National Park.

In predictable succession, the city's Merchant Exchange in 1904 commissioned Daniel Burnham to prepare a plan "for the improvement and adornment of San Francisco." Burnham's finished plan featured a series of diagonal boulevards shot through the city's rigid grid, meeting at the grand plazas and squares sprinkled throughout.[113] A perspective rendering from the documents depicts the new city seen from a Nob Hill made over into Rome's Capitoline Hill, surmounted by a statue of a mounted centurion rather threateningly looming over a garden scene complete with ornate urns, stone stairways and balustrades, potted citrus trees, and flowers and vines tumbling over the lot.[114] Phelan was a true believer in this vision: monuments and buildings like those of Athens under Pericles, he opined, "render the citizens cheerful, content, yielding, self-sacrificing [and] capable of enthusiasm."[115] Burnham delivered his report on April 17, 1906—the day before the earthquake. It might have seemed a God-given opportunity, but in the disaster's aftermath the plan was shelved while San Francisco rebuilt on its old, unenlightened lines. Years later, the by-then U.S. senator Phelan explained that San Franciscans "dropped the ideal plan in order to house themselves and rehabilitate their affairs. It was the worst time to talk of beautification."[116] (Burnham also prepared plans, at the request of then secretary of war, later president, William Howard Taft, for Manila and the Philippine summer capitol at Baguio—notable for its crude imposition of a grid and monumental Government and National districts on the hilly contours of the existing city.)[117]

Wealthy San Franciscans escaped the wind and fog of the city to the peninsula to the south, shielded from the Pacific weather by oak-shrouded mountains and watered by trout-filled streams, which they diverted to water lavish gardens. Phelan's own, on his 175-acre estate, Villa Montalvo, in Saratoga, near San Jose, was Italianate, with four statues of Roman emperors and an obelisk he had brought home from a nine-month world tour. His spread was flanked on the south by his neighbor Max Cohn's Japanese-inspired Kotani'an and on the north by Hakone, the Japanese garden of Isabel Stine, a socialite and founder of the San Francisco Opera, who had *Madame Butterfly* staged there in costume in her Japanese-style tea pavilion.[118]

Who built and maintained these gardens? In large measure, immigrants from Japan. In addition to his civic improvement efforts, James Duval Phelan was a founder of the Japanese Exclusion League and coiner of the slogan "Keep America White." He campaigned tirelessly for Japanese exclusion, segregation, and U.S. military armament against the "Yellow Peril." Phelan formed one pole of America's Janus-faced attitude toward Japan. While he excoriated its immigrants and urged federal funding of a massive naval buildup in the Pacific—ships to be built at the Union Iron Works—the business oligarchy of San Francisco and the federal government itself, led by President Theodore Roosevelt (who admired the Japanese martial spirit) made strenuous efforts to tone him down and to placate and court the Japanese. Phelan's own niece dedicated a shiny new battleship for Japan as it rolled off the Union Iron Works yard, and he was doubtless present for the grand occasion, since he was a great friend of the United States Navy.[119] There is a surviving image of a party in his garden, with an Orientalist fantasy tent set up on a lawn against the backdrop of the San Mateo hills, in front of which pose a group of naval officers in dress uniform and their white-shrouded and flower-hatted wives.

James Phelan's Villa Montalvo, Santa Clara Valley, California. (By Gabriel Moulin)

In 1905, the Japanese fleet, much of it built in San Francisco, destroyed the Russian Pacific navy and opened eyes wide from Berlin to London to Washington, D.C., to the truth that Japan was a force to be reckoned with.[120] Anti-Japanese sentiment in California was whipped to a frenzy by Phelan, who claimed the perfidious Japanese bred like vermin and aimed to take over the West Coast by sheer numbers. Ugly images spewed from the Hearst press in New York and San Francisco—the same papers that had howled for war with Spain in 1898.[121] Under pressure from Phelan, San Francisco segregated its schools in 1906, shunting Japanese pupils to a separate school. Japan talked openly of war. Only the intercession of President Roosevelt calmed the waters. So the relationship went, back and forth, the United States and Japan several times to the point of conflagration, with James Phelan fanning the flames. But the cultural attraction remained there too, for Americans less bellicose than Phelan: in 1912, first lady Mrs. William Howard Taft planted the first cherry trees sent from Japan along the Tidal Basin in Washington. (At her husband's inauguration in 1909 she had worn an embroidered gown from Japan made especially for her.)[122] Yet Phelan blustered on, successfully bullying the California legislature to pass a spate of anti-Japanese laws, including prohibiting them from owning land in 1913. The next year, he was elected to the U.S. Senate, bringing the Yellow Peril hysteria to the national stage.[123]

Winds of change were blowing that would end the long reign of the Gilded Age and push the showdown in the Pacific to a later date. In 1913 the federal income tax was instituted, putting a damper on the building of huge mansions and estate gardens. In 1914, Europe fell to savage war, and the United States looked back to the East. At the White City in Chicago, twenty-one years earlier, Henry Adams had seen the enormous power of Westinghouse's electrical dynamos and wondered at the capacity of machines and energy to drive the world toward a new paradise, or to a new form of war too cataclysmic to be imagined.[124] He well understood the danger posed by the possession of such power by an elite that proclaimed itself the inheritor of Rome and was intoxicated by the advent of its own imperial destiny. Looking back at the White City after the Great War had drawn America even further into global conflicts and temptations, Lewis Mumford warned that in the buildings of the fair were bad portents:

> *Architecture, like government, is about as good as a community deserves. The shell that we create for ourselves marks our spiritual development as plainly as that of a snail denotes its species. If sometimes architecture becomes frozen music, we have ourselves to thank when it is a pompous blare of meaningless sounds.*
>
> —Lewis Mumford, *Sticks and Stones*, 1924[125]

Four
_____

FORWARD TO THE PAST: THE LONG ROMANCE OF THE ARTS & CRAFTS GARDEN (1850–1945)

*As for the actual remains, these palaces now become con-
vents, condominiums, and asylums, surrounded by copies
of Western European and Far Eastern landscapes grown
up in briar and poison ivy, what is their ultimate value?
They were built on the crassest piles of American loot,
and the cultural history they reveal is one of frantic
borrowing and adaptation of every available garden
model. Yet running through their owners' lives, and
implied by every casino, pagoda, and tumbling rambler
rose, is a more wistful sense of appropriation: a desire to
re-enter the old garden of delight.*

—MAC GRISWOLD AND ELEANOR WELLER,
THE GOLDEN AGE OF AMERICAN GARDENS, 1991

As a kid growing up in Santa Barbara in the 1970s, I remember life being a kind of endless ramble through
one big garden. In part I enjoyed the usual green pleasures that childhood afforded in what seems now a
simpler, less paranoid time: climbing in giant avocado trees in
old orchards not yet subdivided for houses, their fat limbs coated

with a seaweed-green, dusty-smelling powder that mingled with the sharp chemical smell of ants; or standing still, arms extended, tickled by the thousand tiny feet of dribbling gobs of mating monarch butterflies in the dappled shade of the hundred-year-old Blue Gum grove on Eucalyptus Hill, one of their winter roosts along the California coast; or skateboarding down Middle Road past stark white Andalusian houses spangled with aloes blooming coral red at Christmastime. But in part it was a more mysterious, hidden adventure, roaming through neighbors' lots (today it would be called trespassing) discovering secrets behind old stone walls and towering pittosporum hedges: sagging pergolas draped in wisteria, ancient, untended bowers, benches covered in ivy, bits of colored tile glinting on old pavings, a reflecting pool seemingly forgotten in a bright clearing in a dark grove of araucarias and cedars. I especially remember exploring, with my sixth-grade best friend, the gardens at El Mirador, the old Armour family (of Chicago meatpacking fortune) estate up Cold Springs Road, with its lake, Japanese garden, five-hundred-foot-long Italian formal garden lined with cypresses along a staircase set with water rills, and subterranean grotto complete with glued-on stalactites and stalagmites.

Such a mélange of wonders was transporting, and let our imaginations and feet run; it was no doubt made more thrilling by the knowledge that we were probably not welcome there, that we were trespassing through another's domain. But such scenes didn't yet seem to me to come from another world, since they were of a piece with the rest of my own. Santa Barbara and its satellite, Montecito, were thoroughly American places below a surface patterned on Spain in the 15th to 18th centuries. The emulation began with the mission, founded in 1786 by Franciscan friars, with its delightful fountain, courtyard gardens, and high, thick, whitewashed adobe walls. Elsewhere in town a similar vein of architecture and gardens was ever present: white stucco walls decorated with recessed windows guarded by ornate wrought-iron grilles and rough, nailed wooden doors, topped by sloping red tile roofs and protruding wooden beams. Palms and oaks shaded courtyards and birds of paradise and agaves cast their spiky shadows against hand-plastered walls. Someone without perfect vision could be excused for thinking they were in fact in southern Spain, so pervasive was the effect of stylistic continuity, at least in the older, central parts of town.

I didn't realize that apart from the mission, more than once damaged by earthquakes and neglect and since painstakingly restored, and a handful of other historic buildings, all of it was essentially new, built by Americans adopting Spanish and Mexican styles. This adoption was even mandated: after an earthquake in 1925 destroyed much of the downtown business district's masonry buildings, the city government adopted an architectural code requiring structures in that area to be designed in a Spanish-Moorish style. Santa Barbara's civic elite, while the most determined, was not alone: there was a concerted effort in several parts of California to literally construct the appearance of a vanished civilization, though American California shared nothing of its religion, society, economic or governing systems, nor language. It didn't strike me as odd that this should have coexisted, even coincided, with other styles wildly different from it: brightly painted Victorian wedding cakes; harsh white neo-Roman palazzi; dark-shingled wooden bungalows, and umpteen variants of modernism. Around them were juxtapositions of diverse gardens butting into one another: here a strict Italianate hedge composition, here a rose collection to make Grandma proud, there a topiary funhouse, elbowing an untamed collection of cacti and other succulents.

Completely typical was the house my parents built on Eucalyptus Hill, a late 1970s-era modernist prism by architect Bob Easton, with redwood cladding, an atrium, floor-to-ceiling panels of plate glass, and skylights, the whole an homage to the style of Charles Moore, an influential progenitor of postmodernism in architecture. It was built on the subdivided grounds of Solana, the old Peabody estate, a 1917 neoclassical temple built for an heir to the Arrow shirt fortune. When new, before the landscape grew in around it and softened it, the Peabody house was blindingly white and naked and surely must have seemed garish in its ostentation, like the McMansions of today, but it had long since become classic, seemingly ancient and a natural part of our cultural inheritance. Once our house was complete, my parents dug down under the rank vinca that covered the uneven yard to find an elaborate series of stone-walled terraces cascading down the hill in consummate Italianate style. And we amalgamated our wooden decks and naturalistic sweeps of planting with them, forming a new corner of the hybrid tapestry that was the "one big garden" that covered the town, which I and my friends roamed through, happy and oblivious to its collective provenance, much less significance.

But over time I came to wonder, not simply at the coexistence of historical types and "modern" ones—after all, I understood historical layering, as I'd seen in Washington, D.C., where it's common to see tiny 19th century town houses, vaguely Queen Anne with crockets and turrets glinting with colored bricks and terra cotta, sandwiched between looming concrete monoliths from the 1980s and faceless glass towers from the 1990s and 2000s. In such a situation the old pieces are just leftovers, for the time being left out of the financial logic of constant redevelopment. Like old foundations sticking out of the dirt below a new wall, they are just fragments for archaeologists to catalog and date. The Santa Barbara mission was such a vestige. But what about the brand-new buildings being built in the Mission style, to house banks, brokerages, car dealerships, and fancy residences? And what of their neighbors, in a hundred styles, all built roughly at the same time, and more confusingly, still being built? It was not melting pot but mixed salad, with at least one example of every conceivable variety thrown in, heterogeneity the only commonality.

In my travels I've come to see that Santa Barbara isn't unique: everywhere in America one finds that many of the streets are museums of the country houses of history, lined up like old locomotives in the kind of railroad park one takes kids to, each a period piece, festooned with ornament and bric-a-brac, all the detail that once set it loudly apart to advertise the intentions or pretensions of its builders and owners now mute, useless, pointless. Drive down any street in Beverly Hills, for example, and marvel at the parade of miniature Roman villas, "Tara" southern plantation mansions, half-timbered Tudor keeps, Queen Anne confections, Gothic castles, and French baroque châteaux. And strangely peppered among them are modernist statements of various kinds, shapes, sizes, and colors according to the era of their conception—all vaguely of the same modern school yet each one as different from the next as the historicist styles are to one another. Around the houses spread gardens, occasionally in keeping with the style of the house, as often as not themselves eclectic grab bags and layerings in miniature, each one blending into its neighbor, to form the polyglot patchwork quilt of the urban garden-forest. It's not just the extreme examples of the posh backwaters of the rich, the streets of the Beverly Hills, Palm Beaches, Chevy Chases, and Scarsdales. Such a mess is typical of most of the American-built environment, given a wide enough angle; it is often true of modest working-class districts as well as tony ones, first-ring suburbs as well as new gated communities on the exurban fringes.

And I increasingly came to wonder: what does this heterogeneity—the commingling, proximity, and coexistence of these forms, old and new— say about us Americans? What were the builders trying to communicate about themselves, or their community? Were they trying to express an ideology or vision of the world, or a vision of self? Each house and garden is a book of symbols, a volume in the library of the history of the world, and potentially—if we can read it—a guide to the lesser-known reaches of the minds of its builders and occupants. The problem is that for most of us the forms have lost their meanings, their ability to speak—since most of us have forgotten the languages that they spoke; they are either completely mute or now just project vague connotations—about the wealth, status, age, race, religion, and other characteristics of their makers and occupants. Yet we still confidently build in these well-rehearsed idioms. Indeed, in spite of the ubiquity of modernism in the mix-up of our towns and cities, it is mostly confined to places of business: banks, office buildings, or infrastructure. It is ubiquitous but somehow irrelevant, below the radar, invisible in plain sight. Where the vast majority of us choose to live are in nonmodern forms, even antimodern ones, re-creations of ancient pasts, generally unrelated to the pasts of the inhabitants. Why this persistent allure? What explains why the exotic, amazing, faraway historicist landscape strikes us as more correct for us, more satisfying, more expressive of what we want, deep down? Why would the Armour family, which had grown rich by bringing modern, industrial methods into the meatpacking business, choose to build a baroque Spanish fantasyland, with exotic notes from all over the world, as its private retreat? An armchair psychologist might reply that they chose a fantasy past to hide the sometimes unsavory facts of their position in the modern, industrial present. Surrounding oneself with the trappings of ancient history also encourages the illusion that one has descended in lineal succession from ancient rank and glory, thereby making one's present-day wealth appear to be "natural." And above all, we Americans want things to seem natural.

Interestingly, our modern mishmash is in many ways a continuation of the Victorian eclectic, with, from the 1920s onward, an increasing salting of modernist forms. Modernism in some places succeeded the historicist styles, but generally by adding to them, rarely by taking their place entirely. And yet, perhaps these seeming opposites are not so unalterably opposed. Their juxtaposition, once jarring, is now old hat. Perhaps their coexistence—their very proximity—suggests deeper commonalities, both in the genealogy of their physical forms and surface styles and in their psychological fit to the needs of their builders. Although it advertised itself as a radical break from the eclecticism that came before it, modernism shares with its nemesis, historicism, roots in a single, complex, paradoxical aesthetic and philosophical movement. The Arts & Crafts movement was born in the mid-19th century as a resolutely backward-looking reaction to modern, industrial, urban conditions, yet it also contained within itself forward-looking impulses, ready to engage with those conditions, if not to fully adapt to them— and so reached deep into the 20th century in forms that are not always easy to identify as related to their common root. The movement was self-contradictory but not self-canceling; it led to diametrically opposed manifestations—medievalism and modernism—that each borrowed from the other, and in certain illuminating cases, hybridized. It was fertile, seeding nearly every aesthetic realm in a century-long period, but was also diffuse and so could appear ineffective or indecisive. Its influence is everywhere but is rarely noticed, because it came to branch and flower in so many seemingly contradictory ways that it is hard to recall that they emanated from the same root.

IN HIS 1853 book *The Stones of Venice*, the English art critic John Ruskin gave voice to the fundamental sensibilities and anxieties of the Romantic worldview: the Age of Reason's obsession with the rational mind had obscured human feeling and imagination; its inventions, machines and industry had robbed us of the ancient dignities of work and art made by the human hand. Ruskin had a gift of clarifying the world by antitheses: hand versus machine, heart versus mind, art versus industry, nature versus artificial, and assigning each a distinct historical era and aesthetics, one good, one bad: medieval versus modern, Gothic versus Greek. He pronounced the English Gothic that had peaked in the 15th century the best style because of its reverence for natural forms, since "organic" beauty resides in nature and behaves according to clear laws of function and fitness—keywords in any justification of aesthetic preferences. He saw in the building of the Gothic cathedrals a model not just of how to build, but of a moral order: between the workers and God, nature, and community—all connected, seamlessly, in a quasi-egalitarian Christian Eden. The Renaissance had broken the bonds of that moral order, replacing its organic unity with the harsh disciplines of a foreign and, not incidentally, pagan empire. What the commercial princes of the Renaissance labeled the Dark Ages had in fact been a golden age, to which we must struggle to return. The making of art, then, was the key and kernel of an earthly Utopia: if it was made the right way and expressed the full range of human capacity, feeling, memory, and meaning, it would return to the worker the dignity, satisfaction, and spiritual connections to his work that the modern industrial system had robbed him of. Ruskin's artistic worker was the Whole Man, and through him and his labor would grow a right society.

Ruskin was a writer of unimaginable productivity and unflagging vitriol; his attack on neoclassical architecture was lyrical and slashing, and a convincing call to arms to many: "Pagan in its origin, proud and unholy in its revival, paralysed in its old age . . . an architecture invented, as it seems, to make plagiarists of its architects, slaves of its workmen, and sybarites of its inhabitants; an architecture in which intellect is idle, invention impossible, but in which all luxury is gratified and all insolence fortified."[1]

His manifesto became an inspiration and template for a generation of artists and intellectuals and found its paradigmatic expression in the work of William Morris, a poet, architect, and textile and furniture designer who in 1861 started a design firm with the pre-Raphaelite Brotherhood artists Edward Burne-Jones and Dante Gabriel Rossetti, based on ideas similar to Ruskin's, summed up by his conviction that art must be "the expression of man's pleasure in labour."[2] The multitalented Morris worked in almost every medium in an effort to lift decorative art from a mainly commercial sphere to a fine art, creating an all-consuming model that other workshops followed, producing hand-printed books, architecture, printed textiles, furniture, jewelry, stained glass, metalwork, and ceramics. The Arts & Crafts movement, as it came to call itself in the 1880s, believed in close attention to nature, in step with 19th century naturalism, which was more rigorous and less idealistic than the empiricism of the 17th and 18th centuries. But it also shared the ambition of other 19th century movements to produce a "total work of art" or *Gesamtkunstwerk*, as the German Romantics called it, by sweeping up vast swaths of human knowledge and experience and refashioning them in a single, encyclopedic effort (this urge found its apotheosis in the music of Richard Wagner, who first used the term in his 1849 essay "Art and Revolution"). Morris and others were obsessed with nature and the past, as was all the romantic 19th century, and labored to give their work at least an implied patina of the traditional, but the actual forms they designed were startlingly new, and beautiful: sensuously rendered details of tendrils and leaves, flowers, and birds woven into careful, knotted patterns as intricate as anything produced by medieval monks illuminating their Bibles.

This was a world of strange bedfellows: utopian social critique couched in a backward-looking medievalism, and resolute antimodernism enthusiastically at the forefront of the avant-garde for over half a century. The Arts & Crafts movement was a loose and promiscuous one, moving in tandem with and overlapping the 1860s Gothic Revival in architecture and the Aesthetic movement in painting and literature of the 1870s. It was deeply involved with British socialism with its critique of industrialism—the term "industrial revolution" was popularized in the early 1880s by the economic historian Arnold Toynbee; Morris was a founder of the Socialist League in 1884. (At its center were quite literally strange bedfellows: Morris's wife, Jane, who posed as a model for many of the painter Rossetti's canvases, over time took up with the painter, while the two of them lived with Morris.) Taken as a whole, the movement had inherent tensions and contradictions: it professed love of simplicity, churning out heavy wooden furniture with simple, hand-wrought hinges, but also reveled in intricate, richly ornamented forms, becoming equally known for its delicate jewelry and glasswork—the progenitors of Art Nouveau's luxuriant celebration of organic form in the 1880s and '90s. It had an ambivalent relationship with machines: on the face it was a rejection of them in favor of handcraft, yet part of the movement wanted to find a means to accommodate the possibilities that machine production offered. Morris wrote that it wasn't the machine per se the movement wanted to abolish, but its negative effects: "we want to get rid of the great intangible machine of commercial tyranny, which oppresses the lives of all of us."[3]

Morris and others worked to make handcraft affordable, but under modern conditions of industrial competition it couldn't be, except for the rich. So, ironically, it flourished commercially in larger cities where a suitably wealthy clientele, enriched by industrialization but nevertheless sympathetic to the movement's critique of it, bought its wares. This was money laundering, even if for a noble cause. Over the door of an Arts & Crafts hall in industrial Manchester, England, was inscribed: "By the gains of industry, we promote art."[4] It didn't take the movement's leading lights long to be frustrated by this need to effectively sell out. C. R. Ashbee, who had started a workshop and art colony in Chipping Campden, in the bucolic Cotswold Hills,[5] lamented: "That is what we in England have been doing—we of the A&C—and have thus made of a great social movement a narrow and tiresome aristocracy working with high skill for the very rich." Ashbee was an enthusiastic part of a back-to-land movement, which built workshops and colonies in the countryside, often with semicommunal living arrangements, with the goal of reforming art, work, and society by example in one fell swoop. But the mission was launched on some fundamental mistakes. The first was trying to use the past as prescription for the problems of the complex present without coming to grips with the roots of the social problem, which lay in unequal access to land, capital, education, and power. Instead the movement focused its critique on industrialization's obvious social effects—cities, mass production, and labor specialization—and focused its efforts on its aesthetic effects—mass-produced decorative objects—in hopes of crafting a solution to the deeper problems by lovingly making lovely things.[6]

Morris listed the two most beautiful works of art he could think of as houses and books: "To enjoy good houses and good books in self respect and decent comfort seems to me to be the most pleasurable end towards which all human beings ought now to struggle."[7] This was so far from a revolutionary battle cry as to be an outright parody of the workingman's plight and shows how totally cut off from real social issues the Arts & Crafts leadership quickly became. By focusing on the domestic ideal of the well-equipped home, the movement not only supported but made itself dependent on the market economy that it sought to undermine. Going back to the past and to the land, it was in the same fix as the agrarian revivalism of Loudon and Downing: while promoting the ideal of national revitalization through rural rehabilitation, it was at base no more than hobby farming, dependent on the subsidy of city money, and so was a failure on its face at its own program. This bind of dependency on the economic system it sought to escape was the 19th century reformer's stumbling block (it was equally Jefferson's) and remains a problem for would-be aesthetic reformers today. It explains why, while it produced much powerfully beautiful art, its political program was doomed to failure. Lewis Mumford expressed the contradictions well in his 1924 book *Sticks and Stones:*

> *Such a retreat is the equivalent of surrender. To hold to Gothic precedent in the hope of re-creating the medieval community is to hope that an ancient bottle will turn potassium permanganate into claret. The romanticists have never fully faced the social and economic problems that attend their architectural solutions: the re-*

sult is that they have been dependent upon assistance from the very forces and institutions which, fundamentally, they aim to combat.[8]

In the garden, the movement traveled the same road, from populist intention to a collision with a more complicated and rarefied economic reality. William Morris made what must be called the first Arts & Crafts garden at his 1859 Red House, near Bexleyheath, on the edge of Kent, then amid miles of apple orchards; now the area is a suburb of London.[9] It was a redbrick, medievalish L-shaped affair with steeply pitched roofs and a fairy-book well house with an exaggerated conical top augered into the backyard. The house was set in an old orchard, the garden marked off from it by brick walls. Rambling vines climbed the walls and old-fashioned plants ranged in strips of bed against the house; the rest was lawn and trees. The Red House garden was simple and unaffected, meant to look like a well-kept farmstead. Morris had no shortage of strident opinions: he shared a dislike of the Victorian gardenesque with most of the aesthetic avant-garde and memorably called carpet bedding "an aberration of the human mind." He said of the Victorian obsession with plants, "Many a good house both old and new is marred by the vulgarity and stupidity of its garden, so that one is tormented by having to abstract in one's mind the good building from the nightmare of 'horticulture' that surrounds it."[10] The early A&C garden, as interpreted by a collection of people and projects not always tightly bound to a common program, was clear in its dislike of Victorian style and displayed a natural affinity with the old-fashioned or Grandmother's garden, but not an explicit commitment to it as American garden reformers had. In its search for authenticity and a usable past that predated industrialization, the English Arts & Crafts movement found itself drawn backward, finding first the typical British cottage and its garden, which appealed in its simplicity, closeness to nature, and singularity as a national type (Dutch, French, or German cottages were surely not the same). Then it located earlier examples of Old English houses with Old English gardens, each more grand than the last, such as Penshurst, Kent, and Levens Hall, Cumbria, ancient houses with 17th century formal gardens. Then there were the even older and

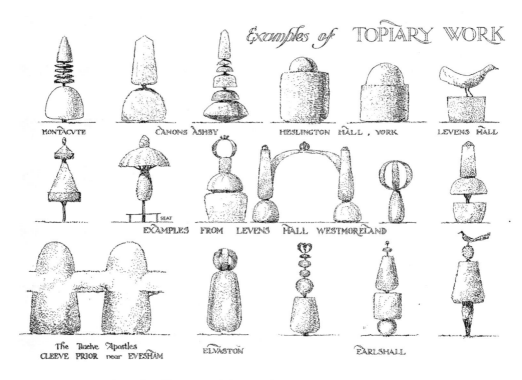

Examples of Topiary Work. (Drawing by H. Inigo Triggs, 1902)

grander Tudor places, surviving in some altered form. That these places seemed to offer a bridge over the mire of modern classicism back to a past that was distinctively English and had visible links to the Gothic period, though they were not appreciably Gothic themselves, proved utterly beguiling. A new project of revitalizing the corrupt present with the purity of the past gripped architects in particular, a number of whom embraced the newly discovered old formal gardens. One was the prominent Gothic Revival architect John Dando Sedding, who wrote in his 1890 book, *Garden-Craft Old and New*, "The old-fashioned garden represents one of the pleasures of England, one of the charms of that quiet beautiful life of bygone times." It was, he wrote, "beautiful yesterday, beautiful to-day, and beautiful always . . . [W]e do well to turn to them, not to copy their exact lines, nor to limit ourselves to the range of their ornament and effects, but to glean hints for our garden-enterprise to-day, to drink of their spirit, to gain impulsion from them." But what he was talking about wasn't Grandmother's garden, but big, formal gardens bristling with masonry and topiary, such as at Levens Hall. And so, just like that, the old Italian formal garden slipped back into the loving arms of the avant-garde, since the Elizabethan gardens they embraced were not expressions of anything especially English, just the first, somewhat clumsy English imitations of the Italian Renaissance gardens seen on the earliest grand tours. If the Italian influence had to be smuggled in again through the back door in Shakespearean garb, before long it was back out of the closet and wearing its Italian suit: designers like Harry Inigo Triggs renewed interest in the originals and designed a new raft of straight Italianate formal gardens, like his 1890 Barrow Court, in Somer-set, with yew hedges and balustraded walls, gardens that got wide public-ity in his books *Formal Gardens of England and Scotland* (1902) and *The Art of Garden Design in Italy* (1906).

Simultaneously, another, seemingly contrary strain swirled in the mix, a naturalism that also grew out of the twin trunks of the 18th century landscape garden and the 19th century "old-fashioned" cottage garden, but took new energy from the surge of interest in natural science and the natural world, combined with a nationalistic interest in native plants and landscapes. A strain of naturalism comes from way back in the Brit-ish mind, from at least Bacon and Shakespeare, reaching an exquisite elaboration in the picturesque English landscape garden of the 18th cen-tury. In the 19th, reverence for nature had become deeply and program-matically scientific—this was the golden age of British natural science of the outdoor variety, of Charles Lyell, the father of modern geology, and Charles Darwin, the father of modern biology—first and foremost care-ful observers of nature. One of the first examples of ecological thinking in the appreciation of British wild landscapes cropped up in 1789, when Gilbert White, a country parson in Selbourne, Hampshire, published *The Natural History and Antiquities of Selbourne*, a collection of his letters carefully cataloging the detailed interrelationships of the natural world in his district. A hundred years later, this voice found its garden reincarnation in William Robinson, an Irish-born horticulturalist who found his true calling in writing, first with his 1870 book, *The Wild Garden*, illustrated by Alfred Parsons, which advocated improving the woodlands and meadows of estates via "the naturalization and natural grouping of hardy exotic plants" (the book's subtitle), with one chapter devoted to the uses of native British plants as well. Like everyone else writing on the topic, it seemed (except the silent majority of garden makers who annually defied the intellectuals in planting their gardenesque mounds with brightly variegated coleus and impatiens) Robinson abhorred carpet bedding: "And so we may cease the dreadful practice of tearing up the flower-beds and leaving them like new-dug graves twice a year."[11] Instead he proposed seeking plants that might thrive and spread on their own over the years and setting them up in tasteful "natural" situations—a meadow of spring bulbs, a woodland path, a fernery, a grouping of shrubs on a woodland margin, a rocky outcrop, a bog. He urged the appreciation of just the kind of floral beauty that Morris captured in his intricate textiles. In the book's many editions over several decades, he was at pains to explain that his prescriptions were first of all practical, as they would save on money and maintenance, and applied only to areas away from the immediate house. In 1871 Robinson started the magazine the *Garden*, for which he commissioned engravings by famous artists; together with his books, which included 1883's *The English Flower Garden*, it made him hugely influential as a garden style maven, like Loudon and Downing before him, even advising Frederick Law Olmsted on a visit to Central Park.

Robinson's success stoked a very public confrontation with champions of the formal, led by architect Reginald Blomfield, who published *The Formal Garden in England* in 1892 as a riposte to *The Wild Garden*. Blomfield's main charge was that horticulturalists like Robinson weren't competent to design gardens, but only to fill them with plants. Architects stood in the hierarchy over plantspersons, just as they did over building contractors; as such blue-collar workers, it came as no surprise that the horticulturalists "ignored" the house and the finer requirements of design. According to "a witty Frenchman" (tellingly, Blomfield frequently turned to French texts for authority and comic effect), "nothing is easier than designing an English park; one only has to get the gardener drunk, and follow his trail."[12] Naturalistic gardening as practiced by "the landscape gardener" was all about deception, staging nature in the artificial confines of the garden: "his aim is not to show things as they are, but as they are not. His first ambition is to make his interference with nature look 'nature-like'; his second, to produce a false impression on the spectator and make him think the grounds to be twice as big as they are."[13] His retort to the charge that formal gardens are "unnatural" was that "it is no more unnatural to clip a yew-tree than to cut the grass."[14] A paper storm of spirited writing flew back and forth between the factions, though most of it was beside the point, aimed backward at 18th century battles long since fought to a draw. Mostly it reflected a territorial, professional hassle between architects and garden designers for the right to claim unique expertise. Blomfield accused: "it is the object of the landscape gardener to exclude the architect from the garden, for he feels, like Demetrius, the silversmith, that his craft is in danger to be set at naught."[15] This bitter little tussle persists in the business of gardens to this day and is one of its most lamentable features, since neither side is right.

At Robinson's own Gravetye Manor, in West Sussex, where he lived from 1885 to 1935, there were axial gardens, pergolas, and lawns close to the house; only away from it did his wild gardening begin. In later editions of his books he repeatedly affirmed that there was no real argument, and that furthermore all parties shared a loathing of the beastly gardenesque bedding out: "Some have mistaken the idea of the wild garden as a plan to get rid of all formality near the house," he wrote, "whereas it will restore to its true use the flower-garden, now subjected to two tearings-up a year . . . new patterns every autumn and every spring—no rest or peace anywhere."[16] Blomfield, for his part, in regaining his breath at the end of his polemic, acknowledged that the formal garden had become overblown after an initial simplicity, when "the paths were straight and ample, the garden-house solidly-built and comfortable; everything was reasonable and unaffected. But this simple genuine delight in nature and art became enfeebled as the seventeenth century grew older. Gardening became a fashionable art, and this was the golden age for professional gardeners."[17]

And they deserved the blame for everything, especially tacky statues imported from France and bedding out. In a miracle of argument worthy of O. J. Simpson defense lawyer Johnnie Cochran, he accused the professional gardeners, in their zeal for exotic plants, of treason against the floral kingdom they were meant to serve: "meanwhile the flowers were forgotten." In the next passage is a remarkable convergence with Robinson and his other enemies, as Blomfield waxed like a Grandmother himself: "there is delight in the associations of the sweet old-fashioned flowers. There is music in their very names. . . . Gillflowers and columbines, sweet-williams, sweet-johns, hollyhocks and marigolds, ladies' slipper, London pride, bergamot and dittany" and on for a paragraph!

In the smoke of the skirmish the distinctions broke down and coexistence continued between lofty design ideals and grubby horticultural reality, always the native habitat of gardeners. The genius of the Arts & Crafts garden, as it gained its mature, full-bosomed form in the late 1890s, wasn't just shambling or awkward coexistence, but the seamless yoking of naturalism, Grandmother's flowers, and Italian-derived formal rigor into an unusually coherent and satisfying unity of house and garden. The main figure in this synthesis was Gertrude Jekyll, an untrained plantswoman who paradoxically did more than anyone else to revive formal gardening in Britain and America. Born in 1843 in London, she moved at the age of five to Surrey, where she enjoyed "childish primrose-picking rambles" in her cultivated upper-middle-class family's big garden and park. At eighteen she returned to London to study painting; she knew Ruskin and Burne-Jones and met Morris, and naturally started training in the decorative arts, especially embroidery, woodwork, and silverwork—in which she excelled. But the strain of close handwork saw her eyes deteriorate to the point where she was forced to stop, in her late thirties. In 1878, after her father died, she went back to Surrey, moving into the house at Munstead Heath with her mother and brother. Soon she bought fifteen acres across the road called Munstead Wood, and began in 1883 laying out a woodland garden, very much in the mold of William Robinson, whom she'd met when he visited in 1880. She began writing for his magazine, spreading the gospel. But the decisive event came in 1889, when she met the twenty-year-old architect Edwin Lutyens, whom she commissioned to design a house for her. Trained in architecture at the South Kensington School of Art (the Royal College of Art), Lutyens extended his pen into the garden, laying out an axial plan with much stonework and balustraded stairs, whose main feature was a big border along the central walk, two hundred feet by fourteen feet. Jekyll filled it to overflowing with flowers, muscularly arranged in sweeps and clots according to color and bloom sequence, achieving an arresting combination of classicist geometric rigor and horticultural vigor. It was a pumped-up version of Grandmother's garden, with artistic pretensions. Jekyll, as many good garden makers do, compared her work to painting and to nature, from which she said she'd learned: she described "the importance of moderation and reserve, of simplicity of intention, and directness of purpose, and the inestimable value of the quality called 'breadth' in painting. For planting ground is painting a landscape with living things; and as I hold that good gardening takes rank within the bounds of the fine arts, so I hold that to plant well needs an artist of no mean capacity."[18]

Propelled by a knack for publicity, the duo of Jekyll the planter and Lutyens the designer saw their gardens and often his houses alongside become status symbols for the Edwardian country house elite. Their formula was a nicely calibrated and easily repeatable marriage of Italianate garden rooms made by hedges and stone walls and linked in series, lushed up with bold, colorful plant groupings; the main move was generally a big, straight walk lined with herbaceous borders backed by walls. All in all it was a limited typology, but it satisfied just about everyone's urges and was frequently beautiful to boot. It had the advantage of seeming at once reassuringly old and English—as its formal bone structure wedded it to the classical, laundered through Tudor examples and rough stonework, and new—as its color palette and textural massing echoed fashionable European painting: first Turner, then Monet. Yet a Jekyll garden was very labor-intensive. She had replaced the Victorian obsession with exotic horticulture with an ambitious art of painting with plants, and in so doing replaced the simplicity of Grandmother's garden (which Grandmother might even have maintained herself) with the perennial border—a high-maintenance proposition even in England's climate, and a near impossibility in most of the United States outside the wet, warm, coastal Pacific Northwest. And Lutyens's fine country houses were not designed to house the egalitarian workers' revolution that William Morris heralded. The path the Arts & Crafts movement chose, back into the past, was in the end a return to the old British Whig cult of rustic gentility and fine gardening; it didn't lend itself to the fruition of its reform agenda.

The failure of its political program aside, the Arts & Crafts garden in the hands of Jekyll and Lutyens was a smash. It perfectly suited a new generation of country partisans who were upper middle class and frequently part of the intelligentsia: the A&C mixed formal and natural, ancient and modern, in precisely the right measure for it to be refined and progressive at the same time—no mean feat. The pair collaborated frequently from 1900 to 1910, doing their best work and reaching a huge audience through Jekyll's writing, first for a new magazine, *Country Life Illustrated*,[19] then in more than a dozen books,[19] including *Colour Schemes for the Flower Garden*, in 1908, and *Gardens for Small Country Houses*, with Lawrence Weaver, in 1912. Both were big sellers in the United States, where her assertive compositions satisfied a desire for fashionability as well as a reassuring resemblance to the cottage garden. A Jekyll border in full summer regalia—and, as she herself acknowledged, her gardens were only at their best during the fleeting months of summer—is a wondrous thing, a doorway to that "imponderable something" that Edith Wharton called "garden-magic." Jekyll well understood that this has always been a prime purpose of gardens, as she wrote in the July 1896 *Edinburgh Review:*

> *After all what is a garden for? It is for* delight, *for* sweet solace, *for the* purest of all human pleasures, the greatest refreshment of the spirits of men, *it is to promote* jacundite of minde; *it is to call home over-wearied spirits. So say the old writers, and we cannot amend their words, which will stand as long as there are gardens on earth and people to love them. (Emphasis in original.)*[20]

FROM THE BEGINNING, the Arts & Crafts movement traveled easily to the United States through magazines, books, and major practitioners visiting and trading ideas. British pattern books did particularly well, and Ruskin and Morris were bestsellers. Jane Addams visited London's Toynbee Hall in 1889 and imported the concept to Chicago as Hull House the same year. Americans had the same interest in place, local materials, traditions, and the romantic past as their British counterparts. The Gothic Revival architect Ralph Adams Cram and his young partner, Bertram Grosvenor Goodhue, helped found the Society of Arts and Crafts in Boston in 1897, and Goodhue, who had prodigious drawing skill, produced *The Altar Book of the Episcopal Church*, a hand-lettered and illustrated book to rival William Morris's best, the *Works of Geoffrey Chaucer*, which his Kelmscott Press published in 1896. In Chicago, Louis Sullivan pioneered a new American architecture through the simplification of form and mass and by reinventing ornament using plants as a model, the better to capture and resonate with the spirit of America's agrarian heartland.[21] C. R. Ashbee came to America and met two of the leading A&C architects, Charles Greene in California and Frank Lloyd Wright (one of the founders of the Chicago Arts & Crafts Society, in 1897) in Wisconsin, and Wright returned the visit in England. Greene also traveled in England and came away energized. Gustav Stickley, born in Wisconsin, just as Wright was, published his *Craftsman* magazine from 1901 to 1915, popularizing British Arts & Crafts ideas adapted to American regional circumstances. Art colonies and workshops began to be set up, such as Roycroft, in East Aurora, New York, near Buffalo, and Byrdcliffe, in 1902, in Woodstock, New York.

In the garden, the aesthetic appealed to a new generation eager to move beyond the old paradigm of the classical-Italianate versus the picturesque-romantic. In the beginning, as in the United Kingdom, the American Arts & Crafts garden was indistinguishable from Grandmother's cottage garden; in fact the American colonial cottage garden influenced Gertrude Jekyll, who read Alice Morse Earle's *Home Life in Colonial Days* (1898), which was in turn indebted to Celia Thaxter's color experiments on Appledore Island.[22] One side of the Arts & Crafts movement in gardens remained true to this approach, of simplicity and reverence for "hardy" plants, well into the 20th century. In a 1911 *Craftsman* piece, Stickley cautioned against succumbing to the temptations of "the rich man's garden, ostentatious, spectacular, sumptuous." Instead, he exhorted, à la William Robinson: "A garden must be spontaneous—allowed to spring from the ground in a natural way. . . ." The movement as a whole took pointed inspiration from Emerson, Thoreau, and the Transcendentalist cult of nature; *organic* was a key word, from Sullivan to Wright and well beyond. "Nature" offered a symbolic system and a belief system ready-made, providing both the vegetal forms as leitmotifs to repetitively adorn stained glass, metal, tile, wood, and almost any surface or object, inside and out of the house. It also provided a self-justifying narrative of Americanness and rightness in context that fueled the movement's ardor in the face of machine-made mass production on one hand and the continuing grip of bad styles, whether Victorian or classical, on the minds of the people on the other. Local materials became primary sources for textures, colors, and symbols of "fitness," that old word for right taste. This regionalism meshed well with the ecological thinking ascendant among both the scientific and artistic communities, helping to underpin the movement as a philosophy in the United States, a country where the British reliance on its own deep medieval history couldn't provide a convincing foundation for a critique of the existing moral and social order. But regionalism was natural, and closeness to nature won the argument. (It's worth noting that Downing's version of a reformed moral and social order never got past being a sentiment, because his ideas about nature were sentimental; whereas Jefferson's had also constituted a philosophy, a complete, coherent worldview rooted in a deeper understanding of change over time in nature; Jefferson's was a user's manual for the life of the nation, not just a set of piecemeal instructions for designing one's country house.) This appeal to a kind of natural law translated in the garden into a predilection for "natural" or unshaped forms, which meant cottage garden exuberance, big flowers like hollyhocks and climbing roses, and often also the regionally specific native woodland plants, like the azaleas, rhododendrons, magnolias, dogwoods, sweet pepperbush, and asters that Stickley promoted in the *Craftsman*.[23]

But, as in the United Kingdom, by the 1890s another strain was emerging in the center of the Arts & Crafts garden, splitting open its grandmotherly flower beds like a fissure in shifting ground. As with Jekyll and Lutyens, the American old-fashioned garden had a fatal attraction to the sophisticated European accents of formal geometry and found itself quickly at the altar, merged with its opposite to form a mature, strong, adept syntax combining exuberant color and texture with axial discipline. The postmarriage version became unmistakably the form of the Arts & Crafts garden that we recognize now, although in the United States these gardens are less identified with the label Arts & Crafts than they are in Britain, since from the beginning the American version was more comfortable with a range of different architectural styles and achieved a continuity over different historical types. It's impossible to imagine a British Arts & Crafts garden next to a neoclassical house, but such pairings have been commonplace in the United States. This is of course because American nationalism depends less on choosing one iconography and sticking to it. Here Georgian colonial can stand in, or Greek Revival, or the straight-up Italianate, Prairie style, or even proto-modernist—all can be called quintessentially American and few will protest—because Americans have tended to acquiesce in Walt Whitman's proposal that "I contain multitudes"; hierarchies of architectural style are not durable here. And, as in Britain, the key figures in the development of this Arts & Crafts garden and its best practitioners were women, rare leaders in a field dominated by men. Only one of them was formally trained; one took her formative education as an apprentice and later collaborator with Charles Platt, and one was essentially self-taught—though self-taught in an uncommonly erudite and fertile milieu.

BEATRIX JONES WAS born June 19, 1872, in New York City. Her dad, Frederic Rhinelander Jones, was Edith Wharton's oldest brother. Her parents, both from wealthy Philadelphia families, were divorced before Beatrix was twelve. Henceforth she grew up in her mother Mary Jones's Eleventh Street brownstone. Minnie, as she was called by her friends, acted as Wharton's literary agent, and hosted a well-known, ongoing salon that drew from the most rarefied artistic circles. Brooks and Henry Adams and John La Farge were familiar faces, and Henry James was a longtime correspondent of Minnie and frequently stayed with the family on visits to New York. James called Beatrix "the Earthshaker" in 1905, not only because she was professionally designing gardens by then but because he was impressed by the force of her personality. Her rich uncle John Lambert Cadwalader admired her "indomitable will" and took her with him to Scotland on shooting excursions; he said, prophetically, "Let her be a gardener, or, for that matter, anything she wants to be. What she wishes to do will get well done."[24] Young Beatrix grew up around gardens: her grandmother's in Newport, her parents' at Reef Point on the elite summer colony of Bar Harbor, Maine. She also grew up in a world where few women went to college, and of those who did, half went on to live single lives, so great was the social discomfort if not opprobrium of women staking out a place for themselves in male professions and domains. Beatrix had models: at minimum her mom, and her aunt. Though she never went to college, she traveled many times to Europe, spending considerable time in Berlin, France, and Scotland, and learned to speak French well. In 1892, in view of her evident interests, she was invited to study with family friend Charles Sprague Sargent at the Arnold Arboretum in Boston. It was a sort of private apprenticeship while she lived with the Sargent family at their estate, Holm Lea, in Brookline. Her education would have been wide: besides imbibing the botanical and horticultural minutiae of Sargent's world, she visited Frederick Law Olmsted's Brookline office, and would have seen umpteen examples of both Olmstedian picturesque gardens as well as various types of formal gardens in the area. At Sargent's urging she visited Italy in 1895, and she recrossed the Atlantic the same year to visit England, where she met Gertrude Jekyll and saw Penshurst, Kent, an old Tudor garden influential among the A&C brain trust. Back in New York in September 1895, she opened her first office in Minnie Jones's house. She had little choice: at that time, male landscape designers would not hire women, nor were women encouraged to go it alone. But Beatrix Jones did. Olmsted is said to have remarked of her, condescendingly, that she was "supposed to be in some way inclined to dabble in landscape architecture."[25] But she garnered good commissions and enough respect that, a few years later, in January 1899, she was a cofounder of the American Society of Landscape Architects with John Charles Olmsted, Samuel Parsons, and eight others. Needless to say, she was the only woman in the bunch. The next year, Harvard began its landscape architecture program, the first in the nation, as an adjunct to its architecture program. No women were admitted. The year after that, in 1901, the Lowthorpe School of Landscape Gardening for Women was founded, also in Cambridge, Massachusetts—but it was too late for Beatrix to benefit from it. She was out the gate, on her own.

While she had gotten a broad exposure in her travels and study to the gamut of garden modes and traditions, her earliest drawings show that she was a fashionable member of her generation and was taken with the new Arts & Crafts iconography—an 1897 sketch of a garden gate festooned with Celtic crosses and topped by an overscale, pitched roof supported by massive, intricately carved and curved beams revealed the English Arts & Crafts influence. She allowed that she followed the "naturalesque" precepts of Englishman Thomas Mawson's 1900 book, *The Art and Craft of Garden Making*, and her earliest gardens were distinguished by a power of planting clearly influenced by Jekyll. In a 1906 article she echoed Jekyll's painterly language: "The garden large or small must be treated in the impressionist manner. . . . The planting must be done on a big scale. The artist must try to keep step with the great stride of Nature and copy as far as may be her breadth and simplicity."[26] And she followed Jekyll in considering herself an artist foremost: "It is work—hard work and at the same time it is perpetual pleasure. With this grand art of mine I do not envy the greatest painter, or sculptor or poet that lived. It seems to me that all arts are combined in this."[27]

But from the beginning, she demonstrated that she, unlike Jekyll, was as strong a formal designer as she was a plantswoman—her gardens have well-balanced, often fine geometric plans, with concentric squarings, central crossings, repeated cruciforms providing them bone structure, and judiciously placed stairs and pools livening them up. She was adept at knitting the straight lines at the center of her compositions to the rest of

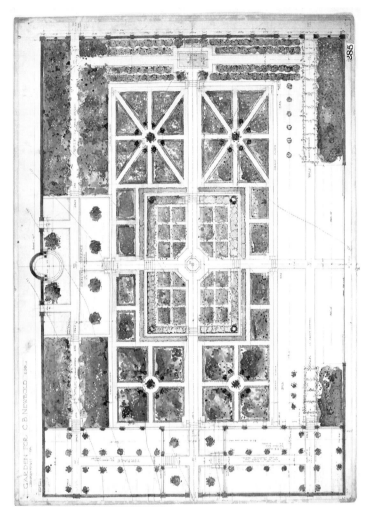

Beatrix Farrand, Newbold garden plan. (University of California, Berkeley, Design Archives)

the property with perimeter pergolas and walks, which eased the transition to looser, "wild" gardens or woodlands. A Beatrix Jones—or Beatrix Farrand, after she married Yale historian Max Farrand in 1913[28]—garden was a balanced one, partly because of her innate skill and eye, but also because her attitude to the squabbles of her profession was catholic: "The arts of architecture and landscape gardening are sisters . . . not antagonists," she wrote. "The work of the architect and landscape gardener should be done together from the beginning . . . not, as too often happens, one crowding the other out." In embracing the synthesis of opposites that was the mature Arts & Crafts garden, she also demonstrated a measure of the pragmatism that marked American attitudes toward theory in general, over which they were far less inclined than the British to battle. The American critic Mariana Griswold Van Rensselaer captured this commonsense posture in her 1893 book, *Art Out-of-Doors:* "In truth, if we use our own minds and eyes, we find no reason to think that formal gardening and naturalistic gardening are deadly rivals, each of which must put the knife to the other's throat if it wishes to survive. No garden can be absolutely artificial, and none can be absolutely natural." And: "The only right theory is that no theory is always right." Design must be pragmatic, echoing Henry's brother William James, the enormously influential psychologist and philosopher and author of *Pragmatism:* "each and every problem needs new consideration."[29]

THE SECOND IMPORTANT woman designer of the era was Ellen Biddle Shipman, the daughter of an army colonel. She had grown up on the western frontier, playing as a small girl with Indians and once being evacuated due to a tribal uprising. She first visited the Cornish, New Hampshire, colony in 1894 and was taken with the gardens she saw there: Stephen Parrish's Northcote, Saint-Gaudens's Aspet, and the garden of Rose Standish Nichols, Saint-Gaudens's niece, who was a respected designer in her own right. These Cornish gardens were cottagey color gardens, almost always set in a somewhat formal frame, often enough sitting unconcerned beside a classical house designed by Charles Platt.[30] A few years later she moved to Cornish with her new husband, Louis Shipman, a promising playwright; for the first two years the couple shared a farmhouse with Herbert Croly, the editor of *Architectural Record* and later founder of the *New Republic*, and his wife (Platt later did a house for the Crolys).[31] In Cornish gardens, and in the work of Cornishites for others, flowers were everywhere, even, conspicuously, in Platt's most formal concoctions, such as Weld, the Brookline estate he built in 1900 for one Lars Anderson; the garden was noted by contemporaries for its uncharacteristic liberality of bloom in an Italianate framing. As early as 1899, Platt recognized talent in Ellen Biddle Shipman, who was described as regal, tall, and commanding but also down-to-earth, and encouraged her to draw. As her skills progressed, he asked her to help him with planting plans and brought her into his office as an informal apprentice. Not having had the advantages of family money, college, or trips to Europe, she took advantage of Platt's library and knowledge to educate herself. By 1910, at the age of forty-one, she had her own practice in addition to collaborating with Platt on his commissions; one of the first she largely managed herself was Fynmere for Fenimore Cooper II (the writer's grandson) in Cooperstown, in 1913. Her work with Platt was a collaboration akin to that of Jekyll and Lutyens, with Platt doing the architecture and Shipman the planting plans. By the late teens she was confidently deploying Jekyllesque drifts of color, using plants, as she put it, "as a painter uses the colors from his palette." In these years she cleaved to a cottage garden sensibility, writing: "eschew all outlandish plants" and "remember that the design of your place is its skeleton upon which you will later plant to make your picture. Keep that skeleton as simple as possible." Simplicity and forthrightness suited her sense of democratic ethics and aesthetics, as her credo made clear: "Gardening opens a wider door than any other of the arts—all mankind can walk through, rich or poor, high or low, talented and untalented. It has no distinctions, all are welcome."

In 1920, separated from the erratic Louis and raising three kids, she moved to New York City for access to a larger client pool and hung out her shingle. Through the decade her designs showed more complexity, embracing the full Arts & Crafts repertoire of axial plans with walks in Celtic crosses (a cruciform with a central circle), often with another concentric square or rectangle, creating gridded fields, peppered with statues, armillary sphere sundials, stone posts, columns, and stairs, benches, fountains, and pergolas. Big flower borders iced the cakes, and her client list grew. In 1919, she secured the first of what would become forty-four jobs in Grosse Pointe, Michigan, a summer bastion of the midwestern industrial elite. Several of these were wild gardens, which Shipman handled with equal aplomb. Like Beatrix Jones Farrand, she embraced the Arts & Crafts garden's synthesis of formal and informal, structured to wild, understanding it as a progression from one to another: "Each part should lure you on and should become less and less formal until you reach the wild walk leading to the wild garden."[32] This course was a return to the ancient Italian model of formality near the house giving way to a wild or agricultural landscape at a certain remove. Each part was necessary for the whole to be right; Edith Wharton wrote that the woods, or "bosco," was "the indispensable adjunct of the Italian house."[33] It is in the management of the sequence, the transitions, that the success of the venture lies—a precondition perhaps of a visitor finding garden-magic in it.

The three decades after 1900 saw a proliferation of country houses in the United States—more, but smaller, than the estates of the 1880s and '90s. By 1910, more than fifteen thousand families made at least fifty thousand dollars a year, enough to buy and keep up a substantial second house and garden.[34] Land and construction costs were relatively low, and skilled European immigrants to build and maintain things were easy to come by. This combination of available resources and the aesthetic vision of the best designers of the age enabled some of the biggest, most impressive American gardens ever made. Two of the best are still very much around, where one can see and experience in person the subtlety, craftsmanship, and astonishing scale of what money and taste could achieve.

Henry Francis duPont, born in 1880, grew up at Winterthur, the farm-turned-estate of his father, Henry Algernon duPont, near Wilmington, Delaware. He would make it his life's work. He matriculated at Harvard in 1899, where he was reintroduced (he had met her once previously) two years later to a young woman named Marian Coffin, whose mother had been a bridesmaid at Henry's parents' wedding.[35] Coffin was a "special student" in landscape architecture at the Massachusetts Institute of Technology's brand-new program—special because women were not admitted, though she was allowed to take the same courses as the men. Neighbors in Cambridge, Henry and Marian began visiting gardens in the area together, including Arnold Arboretum, and exchanging letters.

Henry went on to the Bussey Institute, Harvard's college of agriculture and horticulture, which sat adjacent to the Arnold Arboretum. He was devoted to the books of Jekyll and Robinson and began working at Winterthur planting out bulbs on the hillsides by the tens of thousands. The two continued to exchange books and letters as Coffin launched her career. She was well prepared, having followed the Beaux-Arts-inspired curriculum at MIT under landscape architecture director Guy Lowell and taken the same math, history, and structures courses as the architecture students for three of four years. And she was well connected, coming from a prominent, if not rich, family. In 1905 she set out her own shingle in New York and got her first commission in 1906, from Edward Sprague, followed by jobs for two duPont cousins, followed by gardens for several of their friends; soon she was working from Kentucky to New York, with a cluster of projects in Wilmington, the home turf of the duPont clan and company. A notable example was Gibraltar, a six-acre garden she began in 1919 for Hugh Rodney Sharp, who had had the good fortune to marry a duPont cousin. Coffin used the full-dress Arts & Crafts vocabulary of statuary, armillary sphere sundial, reflecting pool, fountains, masonry walls, balustraded steps, a statue-lined walk through the woods to a colonnaded Roman-style teahouse, and big, bold flower borders throughout to create a series of linked garden rooms that have as much delight and mystery as any garden from the period. Today the name Gibraltar seems an irony, since the house stands empty, a caving wreck sitting on a rock outcrop, but the garden has been beautifully restored and maintained by the group Preservation Delaware.

Over the years, Henry duPont continued his assiduous experimentation and planting at Winterthur, gradually transforming its two hundred acres from woods and farm fields to a procession of horticultural flights of fancy that would have bowled over William Robinson with their ambition. He tended to take a genus of plants and throw it at one portion of ground until it deserved the genus name: there is the azalea woods, the magnolia bend, the winter hazels, the pinetum, the peony garden, the quince walk, and oak hill; there is also the sundial garden, the quarry garden, and the march bank, and other whimsies besides. He carefully calibrated each zone by color and time of bloom, so that walking through Winterthur, which is exhaustively maintained and open to the public, should be done every week in spring and summer to fully appreciate the tour de force of Henry's vision. Marian Coffin worked with Henry on various parts of the Winterthur gardens from 1910 onward, and in 1924 did his Southampton, New York, summerhouse. In between she designed many estates on Long Island. In 1927, after Henry inherited Winterthur and planned a large expansion of the house, he commissioned Coffin to design a swimming pool and gardens linking the existing house with the addition. What she came up with for the steep slopes of the ravine between the buildings was a masterful series of stone stairs, walls, and landings leading to the pool (now a reflecting pool full of frogs) and from it to several terraces and a lawn on different levels. The insertion of a formal stone matrix linking the house to the Winterthur woods gave duPont's horticultural wonderland a heart, and a kind of gravity that radiates outward on the many meandering paths that lead into the wild gardens—just the necessary balancing effect that Wharton and Blomfield had insisted on.

The greatest of all Arts & Crafts–derived gardens in this period was Beatrix Farrand's Dumbarton Oaks, in the Georgetown district of Washington, D.C. Farrand worked there from 1921 to 1947 in close collaboration with the owner, Mildred Bliss, the wife of diplomat Robert Woods Bliss. The Georgian house sits on a hill, its entrance facing south across big, gently sloping lawns, but its important rooms look north and east over uneven slopes descending down to a creek bed cutting diagonally through the property. It would have been a very tricky design problem to knit together a conventional garden, which was to include a swimming pool, pool house, and tennis court, without bulldozing some greater order and flatness into the chaotic grades. But, Mildred Bliss later wrote, "Never did Beatrix Farrand impose on the land an arbitrary concept"; instead she "listened to the light and wind and grade of each area." Her solution was to follow the quirky level changes in a descending series of rooms threaded along the contour lines of the topography, linked by walks and stairs, long or short, steep or gentle as circumstances required. From the beech terrace you descend to the rose garden, then turn left down the boxwood walk, emerging at the ellipse, from which you meander along the meadow edge of the cherry hill and the forsythia dell, listening to the gurgle of the stream in the draw below before coming upon the fenced nursery, guarded by two Lutyensesque buildings. You continue on this way in a kind of spiral procession, each turn revealing surprises, changes in texture, flavor, and rhythm of walking depending on the footing. Dumbarton Oaks has been called "the chambered nautilus of gardens," which is a poetic but accurate way to describe the dense, involute way it fits together, at once orderly and asymmetric, and how it pulls the visitor through the garden from room to room, experience to experience, with a carefully measured flow. All the elements are here: formal planning, even to the point of baroque flourishes, strict geometries, floral exuberance to put a smile on Miss Jekyll's face (Farrand designed the plantings for spring and fall, since the Blisses weren't in residence in the summers), plus meadows filled with bulbs, hillsides swathed in unkempt shrub masses, and woodland stretching away up the hills opposite the house. Even in winter the garden has impressive power to dazzle and surprise. Here "the Earthshaker" was at the top of her game, master of what she called "this grand art of mine." She described the effect she intended to achieve in one corner of the garden, a bit of woodland outside the music room, as wanting "to keep it as poetic . . . as possible," that is, "the sort of place in which thrushes sing and . . . dreams are dreamt."[36] The entire garden fulfills her intent; the garden-magic is undeniable: it is fitting that the clockwise course described earlier ends by ascending "lover's lane," a fieldstone path through an oak-studded meadow rife with crocuses and bluebells in earliest spring, which ends at the lover's lane pool, a shallow oval that sits before an amphitheater of curving stone seats with a wall of bamboo to one side, the mirror-smooth water forming the stage for what might be a midsummer night's dream.

BEATRIX JONES FARRAND, Ellen Biddle Shipman, and Marian Coffin ranked high—if not highest—among the most accomplished, artistic, and successful garden makers of their era. (They were joined on the West Coast by Florence Yoch and her partner, Lucile Council.) That they were

Dumbarton Oaks site plan. (Library of Congress online collection, Historic American Building Survey, Survey number HABS DC-825. Drawn by Paul Dolinski, National Park Service, U.S. Department of the Interior.)

as successful as they were is astonishing in view of the barriers placed in their way by a male-dominated society skeptical of women's abilities and ungenerous with its support, and a male-dominated profession often outwardly hostile to their prospects. Nevertheless, Shipman, who by her death in 1950 had logged over six hundred projects, regarded the role of women as the critical factor in the achievements of American gardens in the first half of the 20th century: "Until women took up landscaping, gardening in this country was at its lowest ebb,"[37] she wrote; "the renaissance of the art was due largely to the fact that women, instead of working over their boards, used plants as if they were painting pictures and as an artist would."[38] Yet for all their evident success, these women continued to face skepticism and denigration. Even Farrand, whose curriculum vitae went on to list an impressive string of plum public commissions, including work on the campuses of Princeton, Yale, the California Institute of Technology, and Occidental College, the rose garden at the New York Botanical Garden, and the plan of the Santa Barbara Botanic Garden, among others, wasn't above it. The author of a 1938 *New York Times* article mused: "people . . . who admire the scope of work done at Princeton and Yale will find it difficult to realize that these huge undertakings are directed by a woman."[39]

Among the striking paradoxes of early 20th century America is the fact that, just as the adolescent country tasted the urban modernity its upper class had long envied in Europe and flexed an industrial might that increasingly challenged European supremacy, American culture in important ways dug deeper into the past-gazing of the late Romantic era, epitomized by the Arts & Crafts movement. This active nostalgia had its greatest pull precisely on the members of the urban, industrial elite, who were busy putting into practice the progressive rationalism advocated by liberal reformers like Herbert Croly in his book *The Promise of American Life*, which foresaw an elite corps of managers overseeing the transition from an agrarian to an industrial society. Members of that same elite were equally busy funding the construction of elaborate Gothic churches and campuses—the new University Gothic style—such as Ralph Adams Cram's buildings at Princeton University, the University of Notre Dame, and Phillips Exeter Academy, and his partner Bertram Goodhue's spectacular Rockefeller Memorial Chapel at the neo-Gothic University of Chicago. That millions of dollars made in the oil business paid for monuments to the era of tallow candles and serfdom, in places of higher education, would seem the opposite of the Renaissance spirit of enlightenment—but such were the bizarre paradoxes of American life in this period. (Another measure of irony is the fact that, for his managerial elite, Croly had in mind men like his Cornish friend Charles Platt, who efficiently designed and built replicas of ancient pagan temples.)

Similarly, just as the continental nation was drawing itself territorially, physically, and culturally together (one marker of this, widely discussed at the time, was Frederick Jackson Turner's lecture at the 1893 Chicago Fair announcing the closing of the American frontier three years before), many people in disparate parts of the country began to express a strong urge to define themselves by their region, each of which, they proposed, boasted a distinctive architectural and landscape context and tradition. The ascendancy of a regional style was most pervasive, though maybe least noticeable, in the Northeast, where by the 1920s, the Arts & Crafts synthesis of formal and informal in the garden had almost completely replaced the Olmstedian picturesque as the default style of the upper-middle and upper classes. It was able to do so because of its flexibility: it could embrace nearly any other mode, including the picturesque, within its broad boundaries, and was as happy gracing English colonial revival or Georgian buildings as it was Victorian eclectic or Arts & Crafts–inspired medieval ones.

In the same years, the South found its own regionalism, which came, as garden fashions so often seem to do, by way of revisiting the past. The early decades of the century saw the region painfully and slowly emerging from the dark years of post–Civil War Reconstruction, occupation by the North, economic devastation, social upheaval, migration, and violence. One way southerners responded to the pervasive stress and tension in their midst was to return to a sense of beauty and repose they located in the antebellum years, and specifically, in neoclassical plantation houses, which offered a ready image of gentility and roots in a simpler time. Considerable effort was put into rehabilitating surviving houses and landscapes, beginning with George Washington's Mount Vernon, bought in 1858 by the Mount Vernon Ladies' Association, which managed to raise two hundred thousand dollars for its reconstruction.[40] In 1923, Monticello was purchased by the Thomas Jefferson Memorial Foundation, which, with the Garden Club of Virginia, spent fifteen years restoring the estate.[41] In 1926, John D. Rockefeller, Jr., the son of the founder of

Standard Oil, began to buy up the town of Williamsburg, eventually knocking down 720 buildings that dated from after 1790 to create Colonial Williamsburg. Parts of the South's finest cities, particularly those that had escaped destruction in the war—Charleston, Savannah, and New Orleans—began to be restored, property by property, often enough by northerners who bought in, bringing their ideas of garden and house style along with the cash to achieve it.

In the garden, a southern "plantation revival" gathered steam, taking its cues largely from Mount Vernon—what was in essence a very coherent, English-derived tradition essentially unchanged from the colonial period. The South had mostly been left out of the industrial and urban changes that had transformed the rest of the nation, changes that had seen their ripple effects in the garden beginning with Downing and Olmsted. In many respects the region remained a backwater eddy from the stream of American life, but as such it retained its direct contact with its antebellum architecture, exemplified by the Greek Revival of the 1840s on display in Natchez, Mississippi, and the plantations of Louisiana, and with its antebellum garden: comprised of brick paths and boxwood hedges laid out in simple rectangular geometries, often around a central circle, and adorned with signature "southern" plants: camellias, azaleas, wisteria, dogwoods, holly bushes, and lawns. It is a lovely fit for the generally flat terrain, the climate, the small scale of southern houses, towns, and cities, and for the region's need for a historically rooted sense of self that reached back to—or over, in a psychological sense—the traumas of the Civil War and its protracted aftermath. This, in good portion, is what one sees there today.

———

The urge to create a national identity through regionalism manifested itself most strongly in the upper Midwest, with emphasis on Chicago, which had emerged as the nation's second-most dynamic city, the self-styled City of Big Shoulders, an industrial powerhouse of stockyards, meatpacking plants, foundries, and vast immigrant-filled districts, sitting astride a tentacular railroad network that tied its huge, booming agricultural hinterland to the city like a spider at the center of her web. Agro-industrial money fueled a building boom in the city and its suburbs, quickly expanding into the adjacent prairies and up and down the shores of Lake Michigan. What it paid for was an increasingly assertive and self-conscious architecture to show that Chicago had arrived. In the wake of the 1893 World's Fair, much was neoclassical, but the Arts & Crafts spirit also reached in, working against its nemesis on the same ground, in good part by inspiring efforts to seize and define some singular essence of the place, to celebrate itself by making a new image of itself—not the self-portrait as a rising dynamo to be reckoned with on the world's stage that the fair had presented, but a more nuanced one of a community of individuals rooted and thriving in a particular, unique place. The Midwest had long gripped the American imagination as a new kind of space, naturally fitted for the perfection of yeoman democracy: flat, agrarian, boundless; like a continental sea, the prairie represented unlimited horizons and the chance to achieve Jefferson's dream of the unity of the people and the land. This Midwest-as-Promised-Land theory was expressed in architecture by the Chicago partners Louis Sullivan and Dankmar Adler, who battled against the neoclassical that they so hated at the World's Fair with new building forms, such as taller skyscrapers than had ever been built, made possible by the steel beams being mass-produced for the first time. These were utterly modern yet still resolutely, richly ornamented with a symbolic vocabulary taken from the organic forms of the surrounding fields and forests—wheat, corn, and writhing masses of vines and tendrils. Sullivan's operating word was *organic,* which expressed for him an ideal harmony between building, place, and function. It was Sullivan who coined "Form ever follows function"—which in its abbreviated version, "form follows function," became the modernist mantra less than a generation later.

This ideal would find its avatar in Sullivan's young apprentice, Frank Lloyd Wright, who had grown up in Wisconsin farm country, groomed by his Welsh mother from a young age to be a builder, with pictures of medieval cathedrals hung above his crib and later a kindergarten play table set with maple block squares, circles, and triangles—"the basic forms lying hidden behind appearances. Cosmic, geometric elements," he called these learning toys: "All are in my fingers to this day."[42] Wright dropped out of a degree program in engineering at the last moment in order to pursue architecture, finding his way in 1887 at the age of eighteen to Sullivan's office to work as a draftsman. With Whitman, larger-than-life poet of *Song of Myself*, and Sullivan he shared an "arrogant self-consciousness," in the words of one historian,[43] a conviction in his own and his country's limitless creativity and power to transform the world through art. He was deeply imbued with the Arts & Crafts movement's veneration of the medieval past, drawn from Ruskin, and in his case, his mother; he wholeheartedly agreed with Victor Hugo's assessment that the Renaissance had been not a step forward but a step back: "the setting sun all Europe mistook for dawn."[44] Having worked with Sullivan on his Transportation Building at the Chicago Fair, he too hated the retreading represented by the White City, calling it a "disaster . . . more than ever tragic—travesty: florid countenance of theoretical Beaux-Arts formalisms; perversion of what modern building we then had achieved by negation; already a blight upon our progress. A senseless reversion."[45] He shared the movement's critique of industrial modernity: he would dismiss "this poetry-crushing, transitory era of the Machine,"[46] yet he also shared the ambition of a part of the Arts & Crafts intelligentsia to adapt machine methods to the cause. In 1901 he gave a lecture at Hull House on "The Art and Craft of the Machine," and throughout his career he maintained that embracing new materials and methods was the only path forward, since one must acknowledge the "Inexorable Law of Change" and accept that "art can be no restatement." In his book *A Testament*, written two years before his death in 1959, he would write, "any true cultural significance our American free society could know lay in the proper use of the machine as a tool and used only as a tool."[47] He found mentors in a seemingly diverse group of architects, from the medievalist Arts & Crafts to the determinedly modern: William Morris, Charles Rennie Macintosh, Adolf Loos, and Otto Wagner. What he sought was neither pole, but rather a middle path, which he described with Sullivan's "organic" metaphor and sought to achieve in the conscious unity between building and landscape, all tied to the larger place and region. He spoke of this unity in naturalistic terms: "I came to feel that in the nature of Nature—if from within outward—I would come upon nothing not sacred. Nature had become my Bible."[48] And he explicitly linked the veneration of nature with the democratic, individualistic American project as he saw it: "All buildings . . . should serve the liberation of mankind, liberating the lives of individuals. What amazing beauty would be ours if man's spirit, thus organic, should learn to characterize this new free life of ours in America as natural!"

By the 1890s, Wright already knew that whatever was distinctive in the midwestern prairie landscape must be distilled and injected into his architecture if it was to be unique and serve as symbol of this political creed and quest. In his Chauncey Williams House, of 1895, he had boulders collected from the nearby Des Plaines River and cemented to the visible foundation as a symbol of place and interconnection. He began to speak of the prairie landscape's flatness, its "quiet, intuitional, horizontal line," as the key to an organic architecture.[49] His adoption of Sullivan's vegetal metaphor of the organic and natural versus the horticultural and artificial—a version of the same complaint about the Victorian hothouse ethos advanced by critics on all sides—was echoed by commentators, such as Robert Spencer writing about him in *Architectural Review* in 1900: "If we are to have a real basis for a great national architecture, our beautiful buildings must not be the forced fruits of an artificial civilization, but must be the bloom of a hardy native growth with its roots deep in the soil."

Wright almost always designed the landscapes for his buildings. He knew the Arts & Crafts idiom, to the point of advising that Jekyll's *Home and Garden* "should be in every library."[50] And the Arts & Crafts influence remained strong throughout his career, notably in his fondness for sculpture and urns—often oversize dishes overflowing with dripping foliage, placed at the corners and intersections of planters and low walls. Yet from early on he was headed in a very different direction. At the 1893 fair he had seen the Phoenix or Ho'oden pavilion, built by the Japanese government on Olmsted's Wooded Isle. It stunned him. In it he saw for the first time "the true human scale"[51] of architecture, not seeking verticality for its own sake but instead a determined horizontality: "Japanese art had a truly organic character, that it was closer to the earth," he would later write about his epiphany.[52] The low roofs, deep overhangs, and horizontal lines of the pavilion were a direct influence on his Winslow House, of 1893, and the influence grew over time. In 1900 he began collecting Japanese prints. In 1904 he traveled to the Louisiana Purchase Exposition in St. Louis, where Japan had erected another model building and garden. In 1905 he spent six months in Japan, studying architecture and landscapes, which he thought achieved, seemingly effortlessly, the organic unity he sought:[53] "Japanese buildings, like rocks and trees, grew in their places."[54] Above Yokohama Bay, he admired the terraced mountain slopes with their sinuous, man-made yet natural-seeming patterns. "For pleasure in all this human affair," he wrote, "you couldn't tell where the architecture leaves off and the garden begins."[55] And: "Japan is garden-land."[56] He would have learned the subtle riddle that landscape painting, *sansui*, and landscape gardening, *sensui*, shared the same written character, with different pronunciation. He would have become familiar with the use of *shakkei*, or borrowed scenery. In his own work, he used low privacy walls and planters to delineate and extend the base of the house into the landscape. Instead of foundation plantings, trees and grass came right up to the buildings, which Wright carefully blended with the background using brown and beige exterior materials. Vines cascaded from planters all over the façades, like the proverbial hanging gardens of Babylon. He began designing "hide and reveal" indirect approaches to the entrance, a Japanese subtlety.[57]

At his Coonley House, 1907–08, in Olmsted's Riverside, Illinois, subdivision, foundation plantings flanked the house for the first time and the landscaping included a raised garden and a sunken one, with gridded plans like a Beatrix Farrand formal garden, though these were planted with loose massings of perennials that overflowed the frames. Here Wright worked for the first time with Jens Jensen, a rising Chicago landscape designer who moved in the same milieu and was Wright's counterpart in the garden in many ways, being the person most often associated with a "Prairie" school of landscape design. Jensen had collaborated with Sullivan on his Babson House, in 1907, and would work with Wright again on his Sherman Booth House in Glencoe, Illinois, in the years 1910–12.

Jensen was born in 1860, in Slesvig, Denmark, a contested border region that Germany occupied during his childhood. He was raised in country schools set up to inculcate Danishness, which succeeded in giving him an acute sense of regional identity rooted in local nature as well as cultural differences—a feeling only reinforced by time served as a conscript in the Prussian military. Though born into a prosperous farming family, Jensen didn't want to be a rural burgher, and so rather impetuously emigrated to America, arriving in Chicago in 1886. He found work as a laborer in the city parks, quickly rising to supervisor and designer. In 1888 he planted what he called an "American" garden in a corner of Union Park, using native plants he'd come to know on walks in the surrounding countryside. His early design work was conventional, in the sweeping Olmstedian mode, guided by his—equally conventional at the time—identification of the "natural" with American democratic ideals and an association of formality with Old World oppression, for him embodied no doubt in German militarism. The "natural garden," he wrote, fit "in place everywhere" and was "the garden for the poor and rich alike." His instinctive egalitarianism would find expression throughout his career in building into his parks physical enactments of social reform: playgrounds (it was then a novel concept that children needed exercise), allotment vegetable gardens to encourage city dwellers to grow and eat healthy food, and what he called "council" or "story" rings for gathering groups, often children, around for talks and performances. Before long he was head of the West Parks District. In the course of his career he would design Columbus Park; redo Humboldt, Garfield, and Douglas parks; and work on fifteen smaller parks.[58] Demonstrating a hardheadedness that would become legendary, in 1900 he quit over demands that he engage in the usual city government corruption, and went into private practice.

Slowly Jensen developed a distinctive style, inspired by the Illinois landscape: at the Rubens House, in 1903, he had a lagoon dredged and striated rockwork built along the water's margin to mimic the local rivers he admired on his rambles. Echoing Wright's language, which was

Jens Jensen, Prairie River, Humboldt Park. (Chicago Park District Special Collections)

common to more than a few other architects and writers and was in the Chicago air, so to speak, he began talking about the horizontality of the midwestern horizon. In a 1908 article, he wrote: "Here on the western plains we admire horizontal lines so much; lines that are characteristic of the plains themselves." What that meant in the garden and park was not replicating the prairie sea of grass, but planting hawthorns, with their horizontally oriented branches, between swaths of dense woods and open meadows. With help from men like Jensen, the open prairie was quickly becoming an ornamental forest as suburban development encroached on it and homeowners planted shrubs and trees. The same year, in Humboldt Park, he designed a "prairie river," which was no more than a long, meandering lagoon lined with rocks stacked up in horizontally striated beds. He opened an office in Steinway Hall, where many of the architects associated with the so-called Chicago School (a name coined by one of their number, Thomas Tallmadge, that same year) kept studios: at various times the tenants included Tallmadge, Robert Spencer, and Walter Burley Griffin (who would go on to design Canberra, the capital district of Australia). In addition to Sullivan and Wright, Jensen worked with Tallmadge, Spencer, and George Maher, a Sullivan protégé who well expressed the midwesterners' determination to be different in a 1906 essay titled "The Western Spirit": "Does nature around us ape that of the Greek or Goth? Is not our landscape beautiful, grand beyond expression?"[59] Jens Jensen used similar language whenever he got the chance, as in a 1912 lecture to the Illinois chapter of the American Institute of Architects, whose members he urged: "Let nature be your teacher," as it was "as ideal and as beautiful as anything else in the world, including the vegetation and stratified rock."

The celebration of local nature served two gods. The first was a genuine love of the natural world and concern for its conservation in the face of a rampant despoiling civilization. Jensen was a pioneer in the use of native plant associations and ecological concepts in landscape design and would go on to spearhead successful conservation campaigns in the Indiana Dunes on the Lake Michigan shore. In his way he was comparable to John Muir, the Scottish-born immigrant and prophet of the conservation movement. The second was tied up in questions of identity, with regionalism as a celebration of the distinctiveness of place; but it often was enlisted in the exhortations of a surging nationalism, which too often took the form of militaristic, imperialistic, and stridently racist calls to arms. Odd as it sounds today, appreciating the natural forms of the prairie was then easily yoked to other, uglier agendas, as is hinted at by the language used by Wilhelm Miller, a professor of landscape horticulture at the University of Illinois and influential editor of *Country Life in America* magazine, to describe what he called the "new" "virile" school of design in the Midwest and the great social effects it would help achieve: "the greatest race the world shall ever know will be cradled in the Middle West."⁶⁰

Wright wrote of Jensen in his essay "Chicago Culture" that he was the city's "native nature poet" and "a true interpreter of the peculiar charm of our prairie landscape."⁶¹ Wright shared with him a preference for naturalism in the landscape, with trees and grass doing the lion's share of the work, and, even after coming into conflict over the siting of trees on a job (Wright believed Jensen planted them so as to obscure his building), the two remained friends into old age, with Jensen visiting the architect at both Taliesin in Wisconsin and Taliesin West in Arizona. Wright clearly learned from Jensen: he made council rings at both Taliesins and at the house he designed at Kentuck Knob, Pennsylvania. Yet Wright had his own vision for the outside, every bit as programmatic as his architectural vision, because he believed that landscape and architecture "are one" and "become as one in organic architecture."⁶² Especially in his later work, the garden and the building seem to have mated, with vines and tendrils dripping from planters placed high and low on the building, from the parapets to the foundations, making them look very much like the overgrown Mayan temples that had been discovered moldering in the jungles of Central America in his youth and had impressed him greatly— he would also likely have seen the dramatic re-creation of a Mayan ruin outside the Anthropological Building at the 1893 Chicago Fair. One can see Wright's urge to festoon architecture with drapings of plants in his Midway Gardens in Chicago, Millard House in Pasadena, and preeminently in his Imperial Hotel, built in Tokyo for the Japanese emperor and opened in 1922. In it the Mayan influence met the Japanese and the English Arts & Crafts in an extraordinary tour de force of garden amalgamated with architecture. Wright wrote: "The Imperial Hotel is designed as a system of gardens and sunken gardens and terraced gardens—of balconies that are gardens and loggias that are also gardens—and roofs that are gardens—until the whole arrangement becomes an arrangement of gardens."⁶³

But Wright's greatest landscape project was his home and workshop at Taliesin, in Spring Green, Wisconsin, near where he had spent summers

Ruins of Yucatan, display outside of Anthropological Building, Chicago Fair. (Field Museum, Chicago)

as a boy working on his uncle's farm. Begun in 1911, it was named after a Welsh poet whose name translates as "Shining Brow," presumably to describe how the compound of buildings Wright designed crowned a low ridgeline overlooking a broad farming valley and the slow, sinuous curve of the Wisconsin River flowing by to the north.[64] Wright bought nearly everything within his gaze—essentially the whole valley—and treated it as part of a carefully designed and controlled landscape, planting trees, terracing slopes as he had seen in Italy and Japan, contour plowing, and scheduling crops for color and texture in the farm fields. He bought and razed a total of thirty-two existing buildings, including a tavern and a gas station, by burning them to the ground, and even got the local power company to relocate some of its lines, which had offended his eye for scenic composition. He even designed the visual effect of cattle grazing in the distance, keeping his herd of Guernsey cows in spite of his dairy manager's recommendation that Holsteins would make more cream and hence more butter (which Wright liked to eat for breakfast), on the grounds of harmonizing their hides with the backdrop; he reportedly said: "coffee and cream, which are the color of my Guernseys, on green, are the three most restful colors you can find." He decorated the building interiors with arrangements of dried field plants that he called "weed-scapes," in "earth tones" of brown and beige. The courtyards between the structures showed a strong Japanese influence, even before he filled them with some of his collection of Asian art, on which he spent his entire Imperial Hotel fee of three hundred thousand dollars. And here and there the hand of the cottage garden aesthetic showed its touch, prescribed by Wright in detailed planting plans, often garishly, with beds filled with perennials in clashing hot colors, sometimes spectacularly so, as with the half-acre triangular petunia beds he had set out at the entrance to the property to welcome visitors.[65]

Taliesin was Wright's own, very personal temple, dedicated to his ideas and vision, a community that revolved around him, maintained by a "fellowship" of apprentices who paid to work, garden, cook, and learn architecture at the master's feet. It was similar to earlier Arts & Crafts colonies in Britain and the United States, but Taliesin had a distinctly patriarchal, near-cultish character: every detail was carefully managed by him, every moment scripted; he gave talks to the gathered apprentices every day at tea, and at Sunday breakfasts.[66] Aesthetically Taliesin was a fruitful synthesis, with contributions from America, Britain, Japan, and Italy; it showed a modernist sensibility in massing and plan, and an Arts & Crafts exuberance in ornament, rusticity of materials, and hand-craft. It looked forward to the series of houses he would design in Los Angeles in the years 1919–22, especially Hollyhock House, the complex atop Olive Hill in Hollywood that he, with help from his young associate

Rudolf Schindler, designed for the Chicago theater heiress Aline Barnsdall. Hollyhock House is a crenellated Mayan fantasy made of patterned, incised concrete blocks, baroquely proud with ornament, especially repeating images of a stylized hollyhock, Barnsdall's favorite flower. The architecture is unique yet clearly came from the Arts & Crafts tradition, channeling Charles Rennie Mackintosh in particular, and just as clearly shared in the emerging modernist lexicon, with its simplicity of basic forms, open plan, and horizontality. Most important, it shared with both idioms a dedication to the idea of uniting inside and outside: "half house and half garden," Barnsdall confirmed, what Wright "believes that a California house should be."[67] This doubleness is what is distinctive not only in Wright's work but in the inheritance of the Arts & Crafts movement: its ambivalence, at once backward-looking and forward-looking. This is what gives it the complexity and instability that generations of people have found simultaneously captivating and maddeningly difficult to categorize.

Wright's acknowledged residential masterpiece was Fallingwater, begun in 1935, when he was nearly seventy, in a remote, forested canyon in western Pennsylvania, for Pittsburgh department store magnate Edgar J. Kaufmann. (Kaufmann's son Edgar J. Kaufmann, Jr., was briefly an apprentice in Wright's Taliesin fellowship, in 1934, and helped mediate between the client and the architect.)[68] The site, centered on the channel of Bear Run Creek, which flows through the property before joining the Youghiogheny River in a deep ravine below, had been used since the 1910s as a vacation camp for company employees, before a small cottage was built for the Kaufmanns in 1921 and it became the favorite family getaway.[69] Wright sited the house provocatively right over the creek where it pours over a dramatic, rocky ledge. The scene is not unlike the one depicted in Hokusai's *Ono Falls,* of a Japanese cottage next to a vertically plunging fall; the architect had once owned the print.[70] Wright used stone quarried on site for much of the exposed structure of the building, the remainder being a series of smooth reinforced concrete "trays" daringly cantilevered over the creek bed. The whole is an arresting composition: of materials and alignments,

Fallingwater. (GNU Free Documentation License)

the smooth, horizontal concrete alternating with vertical masses of rough stonework; and of levels, the series seeming to cascade down the slope before pausing to hover over the waterfall. The house embodies the claim that architecture is frozen music, so fluid-seeming is the arrangement of rectilinear forms.

Fallingwater is a deeply Arts & Crafts–inspired house, with its elaborate, hand-hewn stonework, built-in furniture, woodwork, and leaded glass; yet is at the same time confidently modernist: the massive concrete sections jutting into space are clearly made possible by modern engineering and building techniques. In many ways it is the ultimate expression of both idioms—side by side, not mixed together, as though two contrary impulses were glued together. It expresses either unresolved ambivalence on Wright's part or, more likely, his embrace of the possibility of coexistence of two ideas, the naturalistic and the machinic, in one composition.

Another way to think of it is as the expression of two intentions: the Arts & Crafts program of recapturing the materials, forms, and values of an imagined past wedded to local particularities, and the modernist thrust to fashion a better future through using new materials and techniques and by stripping forms down to their universal essences. Wright, and presumably his client, wanted to achieve both ends, and the result is this extraordinary performance.

FALLINGWATER WAS NOT by any stretch of the imagination a minimalist intervention: it is big, complex, and entirely handmade, almost in the medieval mode, at enormous expense. Wright wanted the concrete to be gold-leafed—to mimic the color of the autumn leaves, of course—but the very idea reveals his disregard for cost.[71] If Fallingwater is emblematic of the contradictions of the Arts & Crafts movement in its structure, it is equally so in its sociopolitical assumptions: it, and Wright's work in general, was radical in form but deeply conservative as a social phenomenon—a deployment of new forms to protect the traditional patriarchal social order, present as a kind of totem in the massive hearth at the center of this and every Wright house.[72] It is studiously isolated and guarded in its green forest container, with no communication with the outside. In this the Arts & Crafts movement and the modern movement were perfectly, if ironically, aligned: both were founded as efforts to reform the living and working conditions of people in industrial, urban society; both ended by largely ignoring that mission, instead paying the bills by building expensive retreats for the industrial elite, tucked away in dramatic—and emphatically private—landscape settings. So against cities was Wright that he heralded the car and the dispersal it allowed as the liberator of Americans:

> *My suggestion would be to go just as far as you can go—and go soon and go fast. . . . We all have the means to live free and independent, far apart—as we choose—still retaining all the social relationships and advantages we ever had. . . . You would enjoy all that you used to enjoy when you were ten to a block and think*

of the immense advantages for your children and for yourself:
freedom to use the ground, relationship with all kinds of living
growth.[73]

It is often said that Fallingwater is "in dialogue with" the site: the colors and materials echo the forest outside; rooms open to the broad terraces, seamlessly integrating inside and outside; the building is visibly anchored to the rock, as though rising from it; a huge boulder surfacing in front of the living room hearth drives the point home. The native forest, with its rhododendron understory, was essentially unaltered; still it was an intentional landscape: nature as naturalistic garden. It represented an idealization of landscape, no less designed than a knot garden in that its owner and designer bought and paid for it, and their choice not to alter it was as much an expression of wealth and mastery over terrain as was Versailles' endless allées and intricate parterres. It was, to be sure, the return of the picturesque, sublime nature framed as a series of views. The landscape of Fallingwater pointed clearly away from the historicist roots of the Arts & Crafts movement and toward its paradoxical modernist flowering, but it was no less romantic for that.

America gained its most distinctive region in 1848, when the Southwest, which had until then been an utterly foreign land, became U.S. territory at the end of the brief Mexican-American War. New Mexico, Utah, Nevada, Arizona, and California had been parts of Spain for as long as four hundred years; they had been Mexican since that country's independence in 1810. At mid-century four-fifths of their inhabitants were members of Indian tribes, many of them still powerful and unconquered. The region had a radically different climate, terrain, and set of cultures than anything seen yet by Americans. And while mountainous, much of it is arid and warm, giving it the age-old allure of the South for northern people. Nowhere was this allure more pronounced than in California, with its dramatic coastline backed by precipitous slopes clothed in chaparral, a setting that instantly evoked visions of an American Mediterranean.

The first few decades of American control saw the ruthless dispersal, often accompanied by massacres, of the native peoples. By the 1880s, when the flow of American settlers into the state picked up, the Indians were mostly a memory and the Mexicans found themselves outnumbered, relieved of their ranchos by taxes and legal chicanery and reduced to second-class status and de facto invisibility. The newcomers were permitted, by the efficient brutality of their fellow, earlier pioneers, to engage in guilt-free, romantic nostalgia. While they imported their cultural and economic life along with themselves, many of them simultaneously wanted to flavor it with the exoticism of the new place: they eagerly adopted Spanish and Indian place-names as well as the iconography and forms of its architecture, agriculture, and landscape. The blueprint for building this new, locally colored American society in the Southwest was provided, appropriately enough, by a romantic novel.

Helen Hunt Jackson, a classmate and correspondent of Emily Dickinson's from Amherst, Massachusetts, passed through Southern California in 1883, looking for traces of its Indian and Spanish-Mexican past. For a day she visited Rancho Camulos, a homestead established in 1853 by Ygnacio del Valle, a soldier and politician, near present-day Santa Paula, amid citrus orchards north of Los Angeles. The rancho remained a good example of the old Californio way of life, a compound of low adobe buildings with deep tile-roofed overhangs shading the edges of dirt courtyards. The writer from New England borrowed the scene as a setting for a romance novel, *Ramona*, published the next year. Ramona is an orphaned girl born of Scottish and California Indian parents who runs away with Alessandro, an Indian, to his village, where chaos suddenly erupts as murderous Americans descend on it. Jackson set out to write a California frontier version of Harriet Beecher Stowe's *Uncle Tom's Cabin* (1852), about the injustices inflicted on Native Americans by her invading countrymen. When it was published, she had doubts that the intended lesson would be learned, acknowledging that she "had sugared my pill, and it remains to be seen if it will go down."

It did indeed go down—it was chewed right up by American readers who responded most to the romantic, exotic vision of the easy, bucolic California life. The rancho, she wrote, "was one of the best specimens to be found in California of the representative house of the half-barbaric, half-elegant, wholly generous and free-handed life led there by Mexican men and women of degree in the early part of this century" (the 19th). "It was a picturesque life, with more of sentiment and gayety in it, more also that was truly dramatic, more romance, than will ever be seen again on those sunny shores." Jackson's elegiac tone was just what Americans wanted to help them picture and enjoy their newly gotten paradise, their own Mediterranean. The novel was a sensation and helped pull a tide of people to the state looking for the romance of Ramona; many stayed.[74] While the book was about persecuted Mission Indians, the missions themselves, abandoned and crumbling since the Mexican government seized them from the Church in the 1830s, were its backdrop and provided the model for what became the Mission Revival style, and a ready-made iconography that allowed American California to set itself apart as an exotic, beguiling idyll. People from less salubrious climes the world over bought the myth greedily and flocked to the promised land by the Pacific.

One of them was Charles Fletcher Lummis, a newspaper writer who walked from Cincinnati to Los Angeles in 1885 to take a job at the *Los Angeles Times*. Once there he sojourned awhile at Rancho Camulos and was smitten by its charms, by indolent hours spent on its veranda overlooking the garden, and by Susana, Señor del Valle's seventeen-year-old granddaughter. Lummis proposed to her (though he already had a wife back in Cincinnati). His offer was not accepted, but he held on to his love affair with the family and its home by publishing *The Home of Ramona* in 1888, illustrated with blue cyanotypes: photographs showing the house and the gardens of dirt paths, orchards, hedges, round, clipped shrubs, and a huge black walnut tree that had been planted in 1860. One picture captures Lummis dancing exuberantly on a wide veranda with a young lady—possibly "Susanita," as he called her. He built a career as a tireless promoter of the uniqueness of the Southwest and its people as editor of *Out West* magazine, and in many books, including *Some Strange Corners of*

Our Country, in 1892, and was an outspoken advocate of Native Americans and of restoring the dilapidating missions. On the banks of the Arroyo Seco creek between Pasadena and Los Angeles he built a house for himself out of granite boulders washed down from the San Gabriel Mountains, and filled the inside with furniture and woodwork handmade in the Arts & Crafts fashion. El Alisal, as he christened the house after the Spanish name for the sycamore trees that grew around it, was his own fantasy castle, complete with a tower and a well, where he enshrined and enacted the rituals of a romantic Indian and Mexican past, hosting raucous parties attended by artists, writers, and musicians. Helped by Lummis's proselytizing, the image of the casually exotic California lifestyle began to gain traction in the American consciousness. It was given architectural form by the Mission Revival, a pastiche of bell towers, thick masonry, arched arcades, and courtyards filled with palms and tropical plants, exemplified by the California Building at the 1893 Chicago Fair.

As the state gained population, the Mission Revival shared space with other Arts & Crafts variants. In the San Francisco Bay area the architect Bernard Maybeck was doing unique and increasingly adventurous riffs on classical and medieval styles, including Nordic and Gothic, combined with Japanese influence, Shingle style, and wooden Arts & Crafts modes. (Maybeck had incidentally played an early role in both Mission Revival and Spanish Colonial Revivals, supervising construction of the California Building at the Chicago Fair for his employer at the time, A. Page Brown, and before that helping design and oversee the ornate Spanish-style Ponce de Leon Hotel in St. Augustine, Florida, which opened in 1888 and had been designed for Henry Flagler by the firm of Carrère & Hastings, the McKim, Mead, and White offshoot.) In Pasadena, the brothers Charles and Henry Greene were wedding the simple wooden bungalow with Japanese architecture (which they had seen only on paper, never having traveled there) and an exuberant Arts & Crafts vocabulary of intricate woodwork and stained glass in rounded, segmented, and plant-patterned forms. Their work looked as though trees had grown into houses. These sat side by side with an effusion of Victorian eclectic styles, such as Queen Anne, brought by eastern U.S. immigrants who rev-

California Building, Chicago Fair, 1893. (Field Museum, Chicago)

eled in the California climate, which allowed what were hothouse exotics back east to thrive outside year round: a typical California garden had a lush green lawn adorned with palm trees and gardenesque beds filled with cannas and birds of paradise.

But the most regionally specific expression of the Arts & Crafts movement, as well as the most subtle and often the most spectacular, followed a different genius. Bertram Grosvenor Goodhue was born in 1868, in Pomfret, Connecticut, into an old line New England family. He counted five ancestors on the *Mayflower* and six who had fought in the Revolutionary War. Self-taught, Goodhue showed prodigious skill as an illustrator at a young age. Unable because of family circumstances to afford college, instead he sought out the Boston architectural firm of Ralph Adams Cram and Charles Wentworth in 1891 and obtained a position as a draftsman. Cram, five years his senior, was at the beginning of an illustrious career: guided by his conversion to Anglicanism after experiencing an epiphanic mass as a young student in Rome and espousing medievalism as the answer for modern life, Cram brought us the Collegiate Gothic of Princeton, Notre Dame, and countless other crocketed and gargoyled college campuses. One year after joining the firm, Goodhue was made a partner. He worked on a series of residences in various eclectic styles, including Tudor Revival, with much half-timbering and classical modes. Soon he moved into designing churches, which Cram and other theorists had determined must be built only in Gothic styles, since the other available medieval option, Romanesque, was considered too pagan, too classical, or too Roman. Cram was a consummate historian, researching the English Gothic by touring the ruined abbeys of Britain. Goodhue, who did most of the finished drawings, provided the fine detail. The results were stunning buildings. Cram would later laud his partner: "As a master of decorative detail of every sort he had no rival then nor had had for some centuries before; his pen and ink renderings were the wonder and the admiration of the whole profession, while he had a creative imagination, exquisite in the beauty of its manifestations, sometimes elflike in its fantasy, that actually left one breathless."

Goodhue's associates recalled him as mercurial: manic-depressive, alternately fierce and charming, a self-described neurasthenic—a character type not uncommon among artists. And he was an artist, possessing a range of talents that far exceeded that of most architects or illustrators. His skills and his unconventional and unconstrained vision were on full display when he produced, in 1896, three travelogues he wrote, illustrated, and published in magazines: one about the Villa Fosca on an Adriatic island, one on the Italian town of Monteventoso, with its massive church of Santa Catarina, and one on the village of Traumberg, in German Bohemia. In each location he recorded the architecture in detailed plans and sketches, for example of St. Kavin's church and monastery in Traumberg, and made beautiful pen and ink drawings of public spaces filled with people in scenes of daily life, with incredible realism and movement, and he kept notes on his conversations with the inhabitants as well as on observations on each place's history, texture, and culture. The accounts are wonderfully precise and exquisitely detailed. All were fantasies; the young Goodhue had never been to Europe. They were dream cities—Traumberg translates as "dream village" in German. Complete, vibrant, and beautiful—medievalist Utopias of the mind.

Goodhue had traveled to Mexico in 1891; he made a second, longer trip in December 1898 in order to recover from a bout of pneumonia, spending four months accompanying architectural writer Sylvester Baxter and photographer Henry Peabody gathering material for their massive study *Spanish Colonial Architecture in Mexico*, to which Goodhue contributed the drawings and some of the text. He soaked up the detail. In 1901 he got the opportunity for his first trip to Europe, en route to the Middle East, the guest of his friend and client James Waldron Gillespie, a New York bachelor who had inherited money and become a notable collector of art, entertainer, and bon vivant. The two traveled through Italy, then made their way through the Levant to Persia, where they rode eight hundred miles on horseback from the Caspian Sea to the Persian Gulf, on the way visiting Isfahan, Shiraz, and Tehran. On their journey through the desert, Goodhue was amazed by the oasis cities they encountered, marveling at the way the Persians used their scarce water: "a rare and precious thing to be carefully cherished and used . . . over and over again." He admired the simplicity and spareness of how water structured the gardens: in shallow rectangles, with tiles, lined with trees, and connected by rills of water flowing down the gently terraced levels. He contrasted these scenes with the "torturous sinuosities of late Italian work" that he had seen in Renaissance villas there.[75]

When they returned, Gillespie, who also had houses in New York City, upstate New York, and near Mariel, Cuba, asked his traveling companion to design a Roman villa on 30 acres he had bought in Montecito. What Goodhue designed was Roman in its use of classical columns, though embedded in a simplified façade, the major detail of which was a series of bas reliefs of the medieval British Arthurian legends. The house enclosed a four-sided courtyard. Inside and adjacent to the house, he placed shallow, sunken pools, in the Islamic manner. After the house was finished in 1906, one guest complained: "it has too many pools in the floors, hazards for the unwary guest."[76] Outside was a stone terrace facing the view to Pacific Ocean, then descending stairs flanking a rectangular pool on another terrace, then more stairs down to a rectangular pool divided in four sections by walks to a central, circular fountain. Another, longer and grander staircase continued down to a series of three long, rectangular pools, pouring into one another and terminating in a colonnaded pavilion that stood over a boulder-lined creek bed that curved around the property. The gardens and drives were punctuated by cypresses, like what they had seen in Italy and Persia, and by some of Gillespie's eventual collection of 125 palm species. Gillespie added his own touches, such as a pair of twisted pink marble columns he'd bought in Italy. Like the house, the garden was a mix of elements: Persian, Italian, and Spanish. It was arguably the first "Mediterranean" house in California, a synthesis adapted to the 20th century lifestyle and imagination from ancient pieces, faithfully reproduced but whimsically and unhesitatingly combined to make a new design idiom. Gillespie christened it "El Fureidis," an Arabic word for paradise or haven. The whole had a freedom, a startling newness, yet was steeped in a romance of the past—a fantasy past, to be sure, taken as much from the Persian desert as from the late Victorian Orientalist fascination with Saracens and Moguls, sheiks and pharaohs. Goodhue had found America's Gothic, its own romantic past with which to replace the Roman-Renaissance hegemony of the classicists. It was made of what Californians have long called "movie magic," but was no less magic for that.

The historian Kevin Starr wrote of California in that era: "In a very real sense the entire society was a stage set, a visualization of dream and illusion which was, like film, at once true and not true." A silent costume drama was in fact shot at El Fureidis in 1915, just as director D. W. Griffith filmed an adaptation of *Ramona*, starring Mary Pickford, shot at Rancho Camulos, in 1910. Goodhue and Gillespie's creation at El Fu-

Bertram Goodhue, El Fureidis, Montecito, California. (By Clark B. Waterhouse)

reidis was a crowning achievement of a design philosophy of romantic historicism and exemplary of a powerful urge in American and European society in the period before World War I to retreat into interiority, nostalgia, and fantasy in the face of often dark industrial and urban reality. Not coincidentally, the same period, especially in Britain, was a golden age of children's stories—inventive, witty tales about blurring the lines between fantasy and everyday life, often in garden and outdoor settings: Kenneth Grahame's 1908 *The Wind in the Willows* and Frances Hodgson Burnett's 1910 *The Secret Garden* typified this flowering of Edwardian literature. The historian Seth Lehrer has written that "our default mode of childhood . . . remains that decade or so before the First World War: the time between the death of Queen Victoria in 1901 and the assassination at Sarajevo in 1914."[77] Both the United Kingdom and the United States were ruled by men "widely perceived to have never grown up"—King Edward VII and Theodore Roosevelt, both men who loved adventurous ex-

El Fureidis,
water staircase.
(By Clark B. Waterhouse)

ploits and dressing up in costumes. Anglo-American culture was caught between an imagined, simpler past and a day-to-day experience of break-neck social and economic change and continued military conflict in its imperial borderlands; its response to that uncertainty was frequently an embrace of "cartographies of nostalgia," in Lehrer's phrase,[78] most often taking the narrative form of a journey back in time. The medieval period was cast as the childhood of European civilization, so children's literature was often set in medieval milieux—as were the major aesthetic movements of the late 19th century. In Europe, the Great War would disillusion many of the appeal of traditional ideas of all stripes, and modernism would try to sweep those ideas away. But in America, itself unscathed by fighting, the effect of the trauma was to reinforce them.

In 1911, Goodhue was hired to design the buildings for the Panama-California Exposition, in San Diego, planned to begin in 1915, in time for the opening of the Panama Canal and intended to lure business and immigrants to the town, then with just thirty-five thousand inhabitants. Goodhue drew on his knowledge of the Mexican buildings he had studied and made a townscape of startling beauty, which visitors reached after crossing a long, arched bridge over a ravine, arriving at its end in an incarnation of one of his dream cities. Dripping with ornament from the Mexican baroque style of the 16th century called "Churrigueresque," the façades of the buildings are mesmerizing in their detail. Gardens with fountains and pools shaded by palms and lush, tropical vegetation tie the spaces together. It was a fantasy world, spun from an imaginary past, but somehow also evoked the promise of 20th century California—an intentional paradox Goodhue had mastered of turning to ancient, foreign forms to give shape to modern dreams and aspirations.

Goodhue's work, at both El Fureidis and the San Diego exposition, was hugely influential. He showed what heights were achievable in Mediterranean-derived architecture just at the moment that the Mission Revival grew tiresome: it was too bulky, low, thick, and plebeian for the aspirations of a new set of immigrants, patrician easterners rich from banking and midwesterners rich from meatpacking, who came in increasing numbers to winter in the sun. They sought a more exalted version of Mediterraneanism: the notion that California, similar in climate, terrain, ecology, and Latin history to the original, was America's Riviera and had to be made to look like it. So a new generation of architects, landscape architects, and clients mounted a concerted, deliberate, and lavish effort to bring not just crude Mexican copies but refined versions of the Spanish and Italian originals to Southern California—nowhere more so than in Santa Barbara. The New York stockbroker turned gentleman architect George Washington Smith traveled to Europe with his client George F. Steedman, carefully documenting Spanish models, then came home and built Casa del Herrero, "house of the blacksmith," with gardens by Lockwood de Forest, Jr., another genteel New York transplant, made up of a sequence of garden rooms linked by exquisitely tiled fountains and rills and lushed up with subtropical plantings. From the Santa Barbara enclave of Hope Ranch to Montecito, astonishingly well-executed versions of Mediterranean villas and gardens popped up, some spectacular in their scale, like Las Tejas, by Mrs. Oakleigh (Helen) Thorne, El Mirador, or La Toscana, an endless Roman fantasy villa, also by Smith and the Los Angeles landscape architect A. E. Hanson.

Santa Barbara wasn't unique—a few sister cities had embarked on the same project of making themselves Mediterranean paradises for the well-to-do at about the same time: Pasadena, Carmel-by-the-Sea near Monterey, Holmby Hills in Los Angeles, and La Jolla in San Diego. Yet they followed her lead and didn't go all the way to adopting a Spanish Colonial Revival architectural code as Santa Barbara did, at George Washington Smith's urging, before and after the 1925 earthquake, guaranteeing that Smith's austere, Andalusian-derived, unornamented version now stamps the city and sets it apart from the others.

But at the end of the day, Smith, Hanson, and the other talented historicists could with some justice be accused of being no more than skilled copyists. What they made was beautiful, it often reeked of money—an occupational hazard when your clients are would-be modern Medici—but it might or might not be magic. A signal moment of innovation in one key place, again provided by Bertram Goodhue, brought the Arts & Crafts garden to its last and greatest chapter. Gillespie had sold a piece of land next to El Fureidis to his cousin Henry Dater, a businessman, who hired Goodhue to design a house, called Dias Felicitas ("Happy Days"), in 1915. For Dater, he made another mixed-Mediterranean house, with long terraces descending a hillside to a reflecting pool at the bottom, on a bench above Montecito Creek. In 1924 it was sold to Charles Ludington, another wealthy New York art collector, who died two years later, leaving it to his son, Wright, who happened to be a cousin of "Lock" de Forest, with whom he had done a European Grand Tour, studying buildings and gardens. The two immediately set about remaking the estate, which Wright renamed Val Verde ("Green Valley").

De Forest came from an artistic New York lineage: his father, Lockwood de Forest, Sr., had studied art in Rome and, under Frederic Church at Olana, had designed furniture in partnership with Louis Comfort Tiffany, and began wintering in Santa Barbara in 1902 before moving his family there permanently in 1913. At Val Verde, the younger de Forest added outbuildings and a parking court and slowly began transforming the gardens: running low-walled paths through woods that he thickened with oaks, leading to "keyhole" rooms—round, walled enclosures where two paths met at angles. He replaced the lawns that flanked the house with shallow pools framed by lemon and olive trees and dominated by classical statues. Statuary was everywhere, and pieces of bas-relief, all from Wright's serious and expanding collection of antiquities. On the top terrace, de Forest built a massive colonnade, antiqued with different colors of paint and made simultaneously grand and eerie by the fact that the columns supported nothing. He complicated Goodhue's staid grass terraces with hedges of box and black acacia, and balanced dark oaks with silvery olive trees to give a play of chiaroscuro to the whole. He turned an unused water tower into a study and built a colonnaded courtyard for more Roman art, and turned the old reservoirs outside into pools. Paths and allées knit it all together into a stage set for Ludington's lifestyle, which bears describing: Hollywood actors, set designers and musicians mingled with the odd European royal at lavish, louche parties. Ludington liked the idea of himself as a Roman emperor holding court—Hadrian in his villa: there can be no doubt that he threw toga parties, with young men in the baths (there are pictures to prove it) and liaisons in the garden, one can only assume. The garden seems quite clearly made to induce romance: the keyhole rooms beckon through traceries of oak branches; hedges and columns offer tentative sight lines and privacy for moonlit walks down the garden path. The garden is perfectly of its place and time, based in traditional forms but modern in its eccentricity, and perfectly fit to the mind of its owner.

AT ABOUT THE same time, just up the road from Val Verde, de Forest was engaged with another client, Madame Ganna Walska at Lotusland, remaking an estate ground originally settled by nurseryman Kinton Stevens in the 1890s, who had peppered it with stands of palms, araucarias, and dragon trees that provided de Forest and Walska a dense, other-worldly frame in which to paint their pictures. Ganna, a Polish-born ingénue and sometime opera singer with great beauty and apparently seductive force as well, had lived a novelistic life, moving between St. Petersburg, Russia, Paris, New York, Chicago, and eventually Montecito, first collecting men—six husbands, most of them rich—before settling down and collecting plants and making gardens. To the existing formal gardens (laid out by Paul Thiene) around the Spanish Colonial Revival house (by Reginald Johnson), Madame Walska added unique, themed gardens over several decades, some organized around collections of exotic plants like cycads or bromeliads, some around a quality, like the color blue. She brought to her work a true passion—likely more than she ever allowed her husbands—amassing rare things and staging them in

Ganna Walska, Lotusland. (Ganna Walska Lotusland Archives)

whimsical, theatrical, often bizarre ways, such as the hedge theater populated by garden gnomes. Along the way she collaborated with a series of men to help her with parts of the garden: enlisting one to bring her rare cycads, one cacti and succulents, one ferns, one anything she fancied, one to make a Japanese garden, and another to work in stone and masonry.[79] With several of them she had to ask, cajole, or demand participation, and her working relationships with them were often fraught with dramas of resistance and acquiescence; each garden space had its own partnership, which ended when the project was done.

Walking through Lotusland is remarkably like walking through the inside of someone's head, each garden room resembling a fantasy or a dream, each one corresponding to a mental space. Unlike most Santa Barbara gardens, which fetishize the views of distant peaks, Walska's look down or in, not up, as she carefully framed not mountains but intricate, surreal compositions of light and color and textures of plants and stones. Many of the constituent pieces come from the Victorian bag of obsessions: the genera collections and the moments of Orientalism, such as the Japanese garden around the lake. Others are Arts & Crafts in the strict sense: the topiary, the hedge maze, and the Spanish Colonial Revival elements such as the olive allée and the Alhambra-derived patios, formal axes and tiled fountains near the house. Others are more personal expressions of Arts & Crafts romanticism, such as the sublime fern garden and the moon garden with its blue- and silver-gray foliage. Others are "clear felicities," as Henry James would have had it, of the California postwar imagination: the glowing sky blue of the shallow pools, surrounded by giant clams and coral encrustations seemingly plucked from a South Seas reef, surrounded by a forest of aloes and threaded by paths edged in bizarre, blue slag glass. Although well within the A&C trajectory, if not totally within its tradition, the sum is beyond category, in the sense that it is not interested in direct quotation and lineage with history but instead borrows from many sources and recombines them into something new, passionate, and personal. While certainly a collection, Lotusland is not an anthology garden of the imperialist 19th century type but a cabinet of curiosities for its time and place. The result is garden-

Lotusland. (Ganna Walska Lotusland Archives)

magic. Here, in a garden made by a Polish immigrant in a long-running opera of self-creation, is a fully formed, completely American style: free, individuated, intelligent, relentless in its gathering of bits of everything in the world, botanical and cultural, immersed in history but ultimately unconcerned with it.

Madame Walska's house and garden project recalls Frank Lloyd Wright's idea of house and garden as personal domain and a carefully controlled, creatively uninhibited world. At this point "style" as category or historical construct becomes irrelevant, because it is irreducibly individual. This might explain the persistence of the Arts & Crafts modes, in all their variety and contradiction, alongside and within modernism and its splinters; even more, it might explain the determined eclecticism of the American landscape and our blithe sense of comfort in it. For most of us, the primary job of design is to satisfy its user, inhabitant, or owner. The eclectic, unstable, and unconstrained is the "house" style of a society in which individualism is raised to a civic religion, and in which the persistent, probably unconscious response to the stresses of modernity is a retreat into interiority, fantasy, and the elaborate, sumptuous, and strangely satisfying forms of an imaginary past. This is why the sometimes deafening variety of our built environment doesn't strike most Americans as discord. At its best, the Arts & Crafts–derived romantic mode moves beyond a frantic ransacking of the forms of other people's pasts to become an enlightened borrowing, a bricolage, with results that are new and old, inspiring in their paradoxes, and occasionally magic.

Five

CALIFORNIA AND THE
MODERN GARDEN (1920-1960s)

n 1967, a month after I was born, my parents moved into a house in the hills above Goleta, California, an expanding suburb of Santa Barbara then mostly made up of cheap housing tracts lunging into citrus and avocado groves and stubble-grass ranchland lined with old eucalyptus windbreaks. The house was one of ten or twelve of wildly differing styles on a short spur road called Twinridge, a mile or so up the old San Marcos Pass road, which climbs up the Santa Ynez mountains. Ours was the "modern" one, what might be called a developer's Case Study house (after the famous program of experimental houses built in Southern California from the late 1940s to the 1960s): one-story, flat-roofed, post-and-beam, E-shape, open-plan, with floor-to-ceiling glass walls opening to the south and a wide view of the Santa Barbara Channel. My mother set about remodeling it, opening up walls inside and packing it with white deep-shag carpets, Danish teak modular furniture, hip art, and a freestanding black steel Scandinavian fireplace in the glassed-in corner of the living room, overlooking the garden. The Douglas fir planking on the ceiling continued beyond the glass to form deep, overhanging eaves that framed two outside patios. A handful of the four-by-sixteen-inch roof beams extended ten and twenty feet farther to support a four-by-six-inch trellis that shaded pebble-aggregate concrete

Twinridge house, Goleta,
California, 1967.
(Courtesy of the author)

Twinridge house, Goleta,
California, 1973.
(Courtesy of the author)

walkways, and, below it, a built-in redwood table and bench, of the by-
then-classic modernist type: backless, with a seat of three planks. The
lot was a shelf bulldozed into the natural grade—the standard rape-and-
pillage mode of postwar California tract builders, and still the preferred
one—but they had skirted a natural pile of rounded sandstone boulders,
each the size of a bathtub or larger, clumped on a hillet crowned by a
huge, gnarled coast live oak probably sixty feet across. On this "wild" side

of the patio, my mother had planted pointy junipers, aloes, jade, grap-topetalum, and other succulents in profusion. In beds along the house were massed lines of fortnight lilies, podocarpus, natal plum, star jasmine, and the bright red pompoms of the bottlebrush bush, *Calliandra haematocephala*, espaliered on one wall.

To the left, where the patio and planting ended, a lawn curved away toward an embankment and a small, detached studio with a wooden deck wrapped around it on three sides. Embedded in this was a hot tub, one of the first in the state. It was made from an old redwood water tank that my parents had salvaged from a Napa County cattle ranch with the help of an eccentric hippie birdhouse maker named Fred Carr, who lived in the same canyon west of town, called Refugio ("refuge"), as the newly inaugurated governor of California, Ronald Reagan. We had brought it home in a U-Haul truck, each board numbered with white chalk to aid watertight reassembly. It was heated, almost imperceptibly, by a crude solar hot water heater built of mats of black rubber tubing mounted at an angle on the ceiling of the studio roof. Beyond the lawn, where the bulldozer driver's scrape into the hill ended, the slope resumed, first clothed in a sward of annual grasses that burst out green in winter followed in the early summer by the loud yellow of black mustard (a lovely Mediterranean weed spread around by the Spanish padres back in the 18th century) that gave way to the crispy brown of late summer and fall. Below the point where my dad was willing to clear it (sometimes with the help of borrowed goats), clumps of chaparral formed a rough barrier between our suburban outpost and the former, agricultural world; a flowing grid of avocado orchards draped over the curving canyon slopes and soft ridges below us, down to the Goleta flats. The ocean gleamed in the distance like a wide blue-silver stripe on a Rothko canvas, dotted with oil drilling platforms that lit up at twilight as if a procession of Spanish galleons were returning from Manila. On the horizon, the dark shapes of the Channel Islands studded the blue band like the molars in a dog's jaw. Fog banks plied the miles in between, advancing and retreating in a slow dance of cool, wet, cotton gauze. Some weeks, especially in spring and summer, the fog filled the view like a thick white blanket, nearly to

Author and
grandmother.
(Courtesy of the
author)

the lawn's edge, then evaporated without a trace in crisp north winds and a frosting of whitecaps on the sea.

As a little boy, I remember living outside: eating, playing, climbing the trees, even occasionally camping in a tent. The glass sliding doors were always open, with no distinction between inside and out except when the Siamese cat sitting on the kitchen floor became too whiny for my dad and he threw it out and closed the door behind it. I remember, or at least see in my head from old color photographs, parties on the patio and the lawn, with my mother in a fabulous, flowing long dress, hair piled on her head, my dad in a tight, gray suit, with sideburns, holding forth animatedly, smooth and assured. Jazz played on an LP through the open glass doors. Guests sporting leather vests and mustaches enjoyed tumblers of wine and trays of hors d'oeuvres that we've since forgotten: roasted water chestnuts or chicken livers wrapped in bacon, smoked oysters, cream-puffs, and crab dip. They mingled amid modern ceramic sculptures set in the boulder garden or sat in the egg-shaped wicker swing that dangled from the oak. After dinner, trays of drinks and cordials were passed: Bailey's, Benedictine, brandy, Drambuie, and White Russians.

My parents had come to California by way of Oahu, where they'd met in 1958, each enjoying an unlikely, dreamy idyll, my dad a Marine lieutenant from Tennessee doing soft duty as a peacetime artillery spotter and

Rear façade of Monticello, Charlottesville, Virginia. *(Courtesy of the author)*

Monticello vegetable garden and pavilion. *(Courtesy of the author)*

ABOVE: Thomas Cole, *The Course of Empire: The Arcadian or Pastoral State.* *(Oil on canvas. Courtesy of New-York Historical Society)*

OPPOSITE PAGE, TOP: Governor's Palace garden, Williamsburg, Virginia. *(Courtesy of the author)*

OPPOSITE PAGE, BOTTOM LEFT: Falls and canal, Governor's Palace. *(Courtesy of the author)*

OPPOSITE PAGE, BOTTOM RIGHT: Sunnyside, Washington Irving's residence, Tarrytown, New York. *(Courtesy of the author)*

THIS PAGE, TOP: Mount Auburn Cemetery, Cambridge, Massachusetts. *(Wikimedia Commons/GNU Free Documentation License)*

THIS PAGE, SECOND PHOTO FROM TOP: Olana, Hudson, New York. *(Courtesy of the author)*

THIS PAGE, THIRD PHOTO FROM TOP: Olana flower garden. *(Courtesy of the author)*

ABOVE: Looking north from the Mount's walled garden, Lenox, Massachusetts. *(By David Dashiell, courtesy of the Mount)*

OPPOSITE PAGE, BOTTOM: P. T. Barnum's Iranistan, Bridgeport, Connecticut. *(From Orcutt,* A History of the Old Town of Stratford and City of Bridgeport, Connecticut, *1886)*

Flower garden, Dumbarton Oaks, Washington, D.C. *(Courtesy of the author)*

The Ellipse, Dumbarton Oaks.
(Courtesy of the author)

Winterthur, Wilmington, Delaware. *(Courtesy of the author)*

LEFT: Aloe Garden, Lotusland, Montecito, California. *(Courtesy of the author)*

RIGHT: Box Walk, Dumbarton Oaks. *(Courtesy of the author)*

LEFT: Author and sister in hot tub, Twinridge house, Goleta, California. *(Courtesy of the author)*

RIGHT: Twinridge house, 1967. *(Courtesy of the author)*

Thomas Church, Donnell garden, Sonoma, California.
(Photo by Charles Birnbaum, courtesy of The Cultural Landscape Foundation)

TOP: Schindler House, West Hollywood, California. *(Courtesy of the author)*

LEFT: Lawrence Halprin, Ira Keller Foundation, Portland, Oregon. *(Office of Lawrence Halprin)*

TOP: Richard Neutra, Kaufman House, Palm Springs, California. *(Barbara Alfors/Wikimedia Commons/GNU Free Documentation License)*

MIDDLE: Dan Kiley, Miller House, Columbus, Indiana. *(Photo by Charles Birnbaum, courtesy of The Cultural Landscape Foundation)*

BELOW: Schindler House. *(Courtesy of the author)*

ABOVE: Isamu Noguchi, UNESCO Garden, Paris. *(Isamu Noguchi Foundation)*

OPPOSITE PAGE, TOP: Robert Irwin, Getty Garden, Los Angeles, California. *(Courtesy of the author)*

OPPOSITE PAGE, BOTTOM: Getty Garden Maze. *(Courtesy of the author)*

ABOVE: Lurie Garden, Millennium Park, Chicago, Illinois. *(By Juan Rois)*

OPPOSITE PAGE, TOP: Jack Nicklaus, PGA West course, La Quinta, California. *(By John and Jeannine Henebry)*

OPPOSITE PAGE, BOTTOM: Oehme, van Sweden, the Gardens of the Great Basin, Chicago Botanic Garden, Glencoe, Illinois. *(By Lisa Delplace, Oehme, van Sweden & Associates, Inc.)*

Nancy Goslee Power, Norton Simon Museum garden, Pasadena, California. *(Courtesy of the author)*

The High Line, New York, New York. *(Photo by Iwan Baan)*

my mom a college girl from Michigan who had rather cleverly transferred to the University of Hawaii to "chaperone" her younger sister there. After marriage, grad school, and my sister's birth in 1964, my dad landed a job teaching American history at the new University of California at Santa Barbara campus, and this little house was the couple's starter home. They were part of just one of many waves of Americans that broke on the Golden State's shores after the war, the biggest being the World War II generation itself, which passed through on the way to and from the Pacific Theater and often stayed. California held 7 million people in 1940, and 10.5 million in 1950. The number would double again in twenty years.

The Twinridge house was a statistical bull's-eye of the new life: a nuclear two-plus-two family with no servants, living in a detached house in the suburbs, far from work, hence with two cars in the carport. It was a new kind of house, modern in plan and styling, but the most notable things about it were functional: the kitchen was in front, while the living and dining rooms opened to the backyard, where an historically unprecedented number of "household" activities went on, except in the

Twinridge yard, 1973. (Courtesy of the author)

rare event of precipitation. This was a complete reversal from traditional norms, and only recently had mortgage lenders accepted it. Glass sliding doors opened to several patios, tying inside and outside together in a tight knot. The postwar California garden didn't just offer the "outdoor room" of the Mediterranean-inspired gardens of the previous fifty years, but true outdoor living: a lawn for leisure, a barbeque for cooking, a patio for eating, drinking, and playing, a pool for the sheer delight of it (we had a "slip-n-slide" on the lawn—more in line with an assistant professor's salary). Its shapes were different: no primary axis, but several smaller ones tied to specific rooms; no overt symmetry; lots of curves; flowing lines; few "fine" materials, but instead concrete, wood, and gravel; less emphasis on flowers and plants, and more on the "plan"—the shapes of each piece and the relationships between parts of the garden and adjacent rooms of the house. There was a new relationship to work in the garden (the goal being as little as possible), with simplified planting plans, few flowers, and the selection of low-maintenance plants meant to look the same all year and not to require a skilled gardener (all this garden needed was someone to mow the lawn). Here is where Mow, Blow, and Go was invented: no bedding, mulching, trimming, deadheading. No agriculture, no seasons, no work, really: the new garden was all about play. Each man (or, increasingly, inescapably, woman) at leisure in his and her own happy home.

The New Garden's asymmetric geometries were intended to reflect a new world: of changing configurations of family, work, and community, and equally of the dreams and plans that the owners and designers of these gardens, people like my mother, had for it. But the evolutionary path of the modern garden's development was not—though it is invariably told as though it were—a series of artistic milestones by avant-garde landscape architects advancing the cause of innovation. It was driven instead by harder things: war, depression, and wrenching economic, social, and geographic shifts remaking the country and the world. And its innovators were not initially landscape architects at all, but a small group of visionary—if sometimes bizarre—architects designing responses to the voracious suburban space that was taking over America in the 20th century. The beachhead of the new wave was California, where these new

Author's mom, 1973.
(Courtesy of the author)

big-picture conditions met new ideas and new influences. Fashions and fads gathered there from all over America, Europe, and Japan. Though the modern California garden began as a distinctively regional style, it quickly spread, inexorably it seemed, back to those places and beyond, becoming in our own era a global style.

From 1967 into the mid-1970s, the house my mom made was *it*, as cool as it got in that time and place, full of artists who made ceramics and weavings chatting with progressive academics and intellectuals at end-less parties, traipsing through the empty threshold of the glass sliding doors that joined the shag to the succulent jade plants outside. The mode was the apex of hip, but it wasn't unique; it had been formulated over the course of a few decades—fully crystallizing in the late 1960s—and documented in the pages of *Sunset* magazine, the DIY bible of an entire culture taking root all over the American West, but preeminently in heavily populated coastal California. Our garden and the hot tub were featured, with me and my sister in it, splashing each other with very cold water, from the looks on our faces, in *Better Homes & Gardens* magazine's annual "Garden Ideas and Outdoor Living" issue in 1976. We were living in Utopia.

If this Utopia had a blueprint, an original paradise where transcendence had first been reached, it was for practical purposes the Donnell garden, built in 1948 in Sonoma County by San Francisco landscape architect Thomas Church. The garden, and the house that it has always overshadowed, occupy a corner of a vast ranch in south Sonoma overlooking the sunlit mirror of San Pablo Bay in the distance and a nearer expanse of wetlands and farmland where the Sonoma River enters the bay. Photographs inevitably depict the view toward the south, over the bold, boomerang-shaped swimming pool, at the center of which floats a stark white biomorphic-surrealist sculpture that looks like a blow-up recliner with a headrest and a drink holder. The pool is set in a grid of concrete paving that meets the lawn in a curve; then the lawn curves out again to meet a sweep of low, mounding shrubs at the base of the horizon, framed on either side by tall, dark green oaks.

The Jean Arpesque geometries boldly defined the garden's style, but this is a water garden as much as the garden at the Taj Mahal is: a composition of shimmering reflections where the Hockney blue of the pool mirrors that of a sky streaked with wispy horsetail clouds, which are in turn repeated in the creeks and grasses of the salt marshes and the open bay beyond. Off to the left, one cluster of large oaks embraces a wooden deck of plank squares set in alternating directions, pierced by tree trunks, with a built-in wood bench around the perimeter. The less common reverse photo shot always revealed the poolhouse by architect George Rockrise, a little rectangle that was cheerfully called a "lanai," the Hawaiian word for porch. Facing outward, from the inland side, it was executed in the by then already canonical modernist style, with a long, low-angled roof overhanging four panels of floor-to-ceiling glass, three of which could slide away to expose a single, open room. The building nestled into a mass of oaks. Some large boulders were set into the grass in front of it, along with a few, sparse, ovalish planting beds, and a single burst of tropical-looking birds-of-paradise at the base of the glass. Otherwise there were few other flowers in the garden, just anonymous, massed plants meant to weigh the other elements down.

The whole composition is simple, and now seems unassuming, involving just a few rather unglamorous materials: concrete, grass, wood, trees, lawn, and shrubbery. But it also remains assertive and dynamic, expertly balanced between the centrifugal—everywhere are curves swooping in different directions, drawing the eye out to the splendors of the view— and the centripetal, as the curves draw back from the corners, ballasted by the dark, heavy oaks, and return to the anchor of the icon-sculpture at the hub of the wheel. In spite of this centering object, there is no central axis, no front or back. The garden was clearly meant for people to inhabit it, move through it, or play in it, rather than gaze at it.

Thomas Church was at the time in mid-career, a successful, progressive Bay Area designer known for wearing gardener's khakis and carrying his pruning loppers confidently propped against a shoulder, and for reportedly trimming his clients' shrubs, unbidden, while having meetings. He and his collaborators (the clients, the architect, and a young associate in his office, Lawrence Halprin, who guided the project) had understood the context and the site perfectly: they kept the entire area level and set it back from the edge of the slope. The pool, lanai, and another accessory building were constructed first, because of material shortages in the years after the war, but the house was carefully sited well back from the slope, swathed in trees, out of view. Church understood that the garden would be secondary to the main event: *the view*. He also understood that the view wasn't a single event, but something that could lend energy and form to every part of the garden—the lanai, the pool, the lawn, or the deck. He made very conscious use of the Japanese theory of *shakkei* (borrowed scenery). In his 1955 book *Gardens Are for People*, Church would title one section "How to enjoy land you don't own" and included a diagram of an English ha-ha fence for do-it-yourselfers to copy.

As a garden, the Donnell project made a clear statement: the design was not a function of the plants, but of the form. This emphasis was no different from the 17th century classicists', though it was fairly ironic that the modernists, in spite of their revolutionary claims, had made it central to their program. In an article for *House Beautiful* that year, Church wrote: "A good garden is like a really beautiful woman. It is the distinction of her bone structure beneath her fresh, delicate skin that sets her

Donnell pool from house. (University of California, Berkeley, Design Archives)

apart. Architectural pattern is the bone structure of the garden . . . [If] a garden has a bold and basic pattern, it will have a beauty that neither snow nor sleet nor gloom of winter can ravage." This was another way of saying what the designer is not fully interested in: weather, seasons, time, change—in short, nature.

Nevertheless, the naturalistic bent of much California design in the 1920s and '30s persisted in the Donnell garden, especially in the treatment of the oaks, which Church took great care to weave into the built structure of the deck. And, in stark contrast to International Style precedents then also being imported from Europe and the East Coast, the formalism of the Donnell garden was in the service of an uncomplicated functionalism: everything unequivocally revolves around the swimming pool. And while modernist "art" stakes a loud claim at the pool's center, the sculpture appearing to float in the middle of the pool, by Bay Area artist Adeline Kent, was designed to be climbed on and sunbathed on and slid down (underwater there was a hole meant for swimmers to swim

Donnell pool from deck. (University of California, Berkeley, Design Archives)

through). The sculpture said: this is modernity, this is art, this is sophisticated and new. But it was a newly friendly, even whimsical art, art as the basis for a newly liberated, leisure lifestyle. After the privations, stress, and sacrifice of the Depression and war years, by 1948 there was an outpouring of youthful exuberance in American culture, of which the Donnell pool was a uniquely beckoning example. Church aptly captured what the evolution of social mores meant for gardens in *Gardens Are for People*: "The change from tea in the parlor to drinks in the garden gives us the terrace or outside room, which increases in importance as the house gets smaller. The change from high-neck ruffles and bloomers to the Bikini gives us the sun-bathing terrace."[1]

The Donnell garden was an important milestone in the movement toward transforming the garden into the singular site of family and social life, a kind of one-stop shop, a perfect domestic universe. Church's second book was aptly titled *Your Private World*. The question by then was, had he and other designers created a cut-off universe, one's own private Idaho, at the cost of community? In the Sonoma garden, the designers' attention to and near communion with the site provided for exquisitely sensitive sighting and ample privacy, but had taken the latter to an austere point. There is no "outside": one can't see the house, which was intentional; neither can one see cars, driveways, power lines, trash, or infrastructure—well and good; neither can one see any trace of neighbors, town, or city. The only sign of other people is many miles away—an exquisite sense of isolation it shares with Monticello, Olana, and Naumkeag, to name just three predecessors. The garden is ruled by a cleanness and self-sufficiency that erases context, society, history, politics, and nature. Practically the only clue we have to when it was made is the astonishing white sculpture in the pool. This result was, of course, the whole point of the exercise, the fulfillment of the modernist dream of liberation from all of the horrors of war and the dysfunctional baggage of bourgeois civilization, the creation of a clean slate on which to inscribe a new order of rationality, functionality, new materials, techniques, and attitudes. It was also, in some sense, what so many Americans and immigrants moved to California for: a fresh start, without the sticky encumbrances of the places they had left. In 1948 it remained to be seen what the price of this disassociation would be.

Could the Donnell project be a template for the New American Garden? The million-dollar view had cost real money: the owner, Otto Dewey Donnell, Jr., handpicked this spot out of the 5,500 acres—over eight and a half square miles—of ranchlands he'd purchased in South Sonoma. Donnell was originally from Ohio, where his father had been a lieutenant of John D. Rockefeller at Standard Oil. He'd gotten a business degree at Stanford in 1941 and decided to stay in the area and become a gentleman cattle rancher and landscape architecture patron. Many if not most people who moved to California during the period probably had similar ambitions, which they realized at a far more modest scale on small lots in cookie-cutter subdivisions. Nonetheless, they wanted to secure their separate domain to look out upon and contemplate. For many, the Donnell garden would become a template, and an exaltation of the new postwar cool.

The Donnell garden garnered lots of press, much of it breathless and admiring. It was the amoeba that launched tens of thousands of kidney pools. Thomas Church, already well-known in California, became a nationally recognized figure. The Church office, by his retirement in 1977, had completed two thousand or so gardens over the course of forty-eight years. Halprin, who oversaw and probably designed much of the work on the Donnell project, left Church's firm and would become one of the most important American landscape architects of the second half of the 20th century. Another associate, Robert Royston, went on to be a partner of Garrett Eckbo, Church's younger, more radical counterpart in Southern California. Yet another, Douglas Baylis, collaborated with *Sunset* magazine for several decades, beginning in 1951, designing and building innumerable gardens, often featuring barbeques, pools, shade structures, benches, and carports, which explored the possible permutations of the new aesthetic and the new lifestyle and showed ordinary homeowners how to do it. They were disciples, spreading the gospel far and wide.

Thomas Dolliver Church was an unlikely candidate for modernist master. Born in Boston in 1902, he grew up in Ojai and Berkeley, California, where he was surrounded by the architecture and gardens of California's Mediterranean tradition. He went to the University of California to study law, but graduated in 1922 with a degree in landscape architecture.[2] The University of California program offered a full Beaux-Arts education, which Church extended into graduate work at Harvard and a six-month fellowship to travel in Italy and Spain, where he toured the garden masterpieces that had inspired builders in California for two centuries. In 1927 he handed in his thesis comparing Renaissance Italian gardens to contemporary Californian ones, with explicit comparisons between the plans of Santa Barbara gardens with those he had seen in Tuscany. He identified similar ecological and cultural conditions that proved the comparison fruitful: "As in Italy and Spain, the pleasure of living out-of-doors, the need of shade, and the conservation of water are all problems which the California gardener must meet and answer." He asserted also that the gardens of both places were "delightful and livable because of scale and imagination—not magnificence."[3] This was an odd observation, since gardens in both places were notable for magnificence. But it was an early indication of Church's concern with the pragmatic and with function, as well as of his instinctive modesty, which would serve him well during the difficult transition from the estate garden making for which he trained in the 1920s and the tighter circumstances that were to come during the Great Depression and World War II.

He returned to the Bay Area in the fateful year 1929.[4] Through William Wurster, an architect with whom he'd worked on a project in Berkeley (and who would also go on to be an important modernist), he was hired as the house landscape architect for Pasatiempo, a new golf-course-focused residential community near Santa Cruz being developed by a team that included the famous golfer Marion Hollins.[5] Church's main job was siting houses amid the sand hills and groves of trees, but he also designed gardens for several of Wurster's modest rancho-style houses. The landscapes were decidedly traditional, with brick paving, symmetrical panels of lawn, and trimmed shrubs, yet they were spare and economical in a

1930s-modern way. He demonstrated an evolved sense of how to use the native flora to advantage, carefully preserving and pruning native trees both as garden centerpieces and backdrops. Economic conditions stalled the project, and Church and his wife went back to San Francisco in 1932.

Even in the midst of the Depression, Church managed to make a go of it, while some of his contemporaries, such as Paul Thiene, went out of business as the market for big estate gardens dried up. As demonstrated at Pasatiempo, his tendencies were more restrained than many of his flashier colleagues, and he turned this to his advantage, finding new ways to gain clientele by responding to changes either brought about or deepened by the economic crisis. Houses and lots got smaller, as did families, and the employment of servants all but vanished, diminished at first by the adoption of the first federal income tax in 1913, and then eliminated for all but a tiny elite by the Depression. Church designed smaller gardens using cheaper materials and fewer labor-intensive techniques, gardens geared to outdoor living with less need for maintenance.

The downsizing of houses, gardens, and families—forced by the Depression as well as the accelerating movement to suburbia—contributed to basic changes in the gardens Church designed, but by themselves these changes didn't produce modernist gardens, in the sense of gardens that were different from traditional modes and styles. Throughout the 1930s, Church's design was still wholly conventional, though sensitive and balanced, taking off from Florence Yoch, Bernard Maybeck, and Lockwood and Elizabeth de Forest. Toward the end of the decade, Church was increasingly adding curves to his plans, in the vein of Fletcher Steele, an accomplished Beaux-Arts landscape architect who was also dabbling with the French curve and whom Church had met in Boston, but that was the extent of his stylistic innovation at the time. It was not until the 1940s that Thomas Church evolved a truly "modern" garden style. More than ever before, gardens followed innovations in buildings, often at considerable remove. The fully modern garden had to wait for the modern house to arrive.

EVEN BEFORE WORLD War I, the tide of suburbanization sweeping the United States had become so profound and systematic as to transform every corner of the country, distinguishing it from everywhere else in the world. The average American was middle class, lived in a suburb far removed from his job, and owned a home. In the words of Columbia University historian Kenneth Jackson, in his book *Crabgrass Frontier*, "In 1920, when the Census Bureau announced that more than half the American population lived in urban areas, what was really unique about the United States was not the size of its huge cities, but the extent of their suburban sprawl; not the number of its workers, but the number of its commuters; not the height of its skyscrapers, but the proportion of its homeowners."[6] The United States had always posted high rates of home ownership, but this indicator shot up in the first decades of the century, driven by a concatenation of trends: skyrocketing marriage and birth rates, and migration away from the countryside as mechanization eliminated farm jobs. But the flow of people was not, as it had been previously, exclusively into cities (though cities grew enormously); this time there was unprecedented migration into the suburbs of eastern, southern, and midwestern cities, and into new western cities that were made up of little but suburbs—"centerless cities," best exemplified by the country's fastest-growing region, Southern California.

This centrifugal flight was abetted by the automobile—though the initial pattern of dispersal in many regions had already been established by light rail systems—and its full flower would not have been possible without it. Car ownership was not enough; a perfect alignment of forces was needed: roads, petroleum, land, and public policy all had to move in the same direction for the American landscape and lifestyle to be transformed. Nearly everyone moved to oblige. Over the first half of the century, the ratio of cars to people rose almost geometrically: in 1905 there was one car for every 1,078 Americans; in 1920 there was one for every thirteen; in 1930, one for every five; in 1950, one for every four. Between 1920 and 1930, car ownership rose 150 percent; in the same period suburbs grew twice as fast as central cores.[7] In the early years of the century, the car was imagined to be a way to clean cities of the filth and congestion of horses and streetcars and to revive both central cities and the farming countryside. The actual effect was to weaken them both and to loose the suburban monster on both of their interests. From the 1920s onward, a phalanx of newly organized economic agents—ranging from carmakers, car dealers, and road builders; rubber, oil, and asphalt companies; parking lot operators, truckers, and labor unions; to bankers and advertisers—joined forces to lobby for the public financing of roads.[8] They pitched highway construction as the means to the American dream of free movement and as a cure for the nation's social and economic problems.[9] Energy went from cheap to cheaper as oil was discovered and refined in more and more parts of the United States. The cost of operating a car—the sum of the price of cars, gas, parking, and maintenance—had fallen consistently from 1900 to World War II.[10] Land also remained cheap and plentiful as policies and market conditions making farming near cities less profitable than suburban development guaranteed a limitless supply of low-priced lots. The Fordist revolution in manufacturing, which had brought automobile ownership within the reach of the masses, likewise transformed the building business, bringing inexpensive, standardized, quality-controlled construction techniques to bear on a larger and larger share of housing starts, in places like Westchester, California, and Levittown, New York, driving the price of new homes way down and pushing their availability way up. For millions of Americans, it became cheaper to buy a house in the suburbs than to rent in the city. And buy they did.

In the winter of 1937 the San Francisco Museum of Art held an exhibition titled "Contemporary Landscape Architecture and Its Sources." Included were works by Thomas Church, Geraldine (Knight) Scott, Lockwood de Forest, Fletcher Steele, and the architects William Wurster, Rudolf Schindler, and Richard Neutra (all except for Steele were Californians).[11] From today's perspective, only the work of the latter two architects at that moment would qualify as modern in the modernist sense, yet even in the staid world of gardens, the outlines of change were visible. That same year, Church embarked on his second trip to Europe, this one organized around seeing firsthand the new modernism that was getting so much press in the United States. In France, he looked at work by the architect Le Corbusier and many modern painters and sculptors. He then traveled to Finland to meet Alvar Aalto.[12] The Continent was in ferment. In architecture and design, a progression that had grown from the Vienna Secession of the early 20th century and had been elaborated by the Dutch de Stijl movement and the German Bauhaus churned out challenging work and took its cues from recent developments in painting and sculpture. European architects and artists had translated these forms into a handful of experiments in modernist gardens. Most shared a decided formalism and minimalism, but not in the postwar American sense of the term, which amounted simply to a lack of clutter; rather, they were dominated by patterned structure, built, if possible, with blocks of primary colors à la Piet Mondrian and abstract shapes and gestures à la Wassily Kandinsky, Joan Miró, and Paul Klee (who taught on the Bauhaus faculty, and whose 1922 painting *Plan for a Garden* heralded the interest in and templating of gardens by modernist visual artists). Church must have seen or been aware of the few, widely hyped European examples of a "modern" garden, among them the French Cubist Gabriel Guevrekian's strange, colored invention at the Villa Noailles, with its triangular form set with square beds, schizophrenically walled off from the surrounding naturalistic English grounds.[13] The tropes of the day were abstraction and the extension of geometric and curving forms onto the ground plane, with little or no concern for plants or function. But they looked "modern."

On his return, Church began incorporating into his work some of the new forms he had seen. For the 1939 Golden Gate Exhibition in San Francisco, he designed two gardens featuring curved paving, a serpentine wall, and massed shrub plantings—modern touches (though Jefferson had built serpentine walls at the University of Virginia) but hardly a design revolution. Church's work manifested a gradual evolution in the 1940s toward replacing axial symmetry with compositions of paving, lawns, planting beds, walls, and projections that adopted the Cubist shape vocabulary of curves, swoops, and amoebas—labeled by enthusiastic critics as "untethered geometries"—and that combined nontraditional materials like wood and concrete. These gardens were plan-driven, dependent on the two-dimensional ordering of elements by the designer, rather than, for example, the growth, flowering, or form of plants, or the play of seasons or light. In this they harked back to the French royal garden, a comparison Church and many of his colleagues would have bristled at. And while it is often argued that the modernist landscape architects liberated the garden from the merely decorative, or even from the tyranny of plan designs on paper, many of their gardens really do resemble student exercises, transcriptions of newfangled European paintings. In working out how avant-garde art could transform the garden, their transformations seemed to take place precisely on paper: Church's 1938 Raoul-Duval garden is a gathering of curves taken directly from the French Curve drawing template.[14] An early experiment, perhaps, but the Donnell garden, an acknowledged masterpiece of 20th century garden art, is no less an exercise in tracing painters' forms on the ground.

In 1949, the San Francisco Museum of Art held another show dedicated to the modern garden. This one included Church's Donnell and Aptos gardens of 1948, undeniable éclats of the new regime, as well as Garrett Eckbo's more stylized work. In the ten-year interregnum between the two shows, the transition from an immature modernizing impulse to a mature modernism had been achieved. Church contributed an essay to the catalog titled, appropriately, *Transition*. But, where to locate its first achievement? The answer is not in Northern California at all, nor even with the garden designers who were its subjects and objects. Instead it took place a few hundred miles to the south, in Hollywood, a generation before—and the garden wasn't the star of the picture, only a secondary love interest who lucked into a speaking role.

The modern garden, for all the gesturing and talk about it in Europe, especially in the 1930s, was born in Southern California, in 1921–22, of a somewhat tangled European and American parentage. Like a human infant, it emerged fully formed. But like many of us, it would need a few decades to reach its potential, to develop more articulate phrasing, self-confidence, and self-consciousness. What is important is that its birth and the early phases of its development were accomplished by the architects who conceived it, built it, defined its terms, space, vocabulary, shape, and function. Architecture provided its DNA, and the rest was nurture: its education, care, feeding, stylish wardrobe, regional accent, and affectations were bestowed upon it by more architects and, eventually—and belatedly—by garden architects.

Before Le Corbusier's 1926 Villa Stein and 1928–29 Villa Savoye, and before Ludwig Mies van der Rohe's 1929 Barcelona Pavilion (all three early modernist houses that have been celebrated for helping redefine the relationship between architectural and garden space), Rudolf Schindler, a Viennese architect recently transplanted to Hollywood, all but invented the modern garden. Schindler found himself standing at the nexus of the Spanish courtyard tradition and the orthodox modernist avant-garde in architecture, and he engineered their marriage.

Born in 1887 in Vienna, Schindler was an elite product of this new school, having studied with Otto Wagner at the Vienna Academy of Fine Arts, and been influenced by Adolf Loos, Charles Rennie Mackintosh, Louis Sullivan, and, through the 1910 "Wasmuth" folios (produced in Europe at Loos's urging), Frank Lloyd Wright. He came to Chicago to take an apprenticeship at a commercial firm in the inauspicious year of 1914, only to find his return blocked by war in Europe. Both of his American masters, Sullivan and Wright, were at low ebbs in their careers, and in 1915 Schindler set off by train for a tour of the American Southwest. In New Mexico he admired the Pueblo style, in Arizona he was impressed by the landforms of the desert, and in California he saw the full flowering of the Mission Revival at the Panama-Pacific Exposition in San Francisco and the Panama-California Exhibition in San Diego, including the work of Bertram Goodhue and Irving Gill, a San Diego architect then pioneering a combination of the Spanish courtyard tradition and Bauhausesque unornamented white volumes. Back in Chicago he worked in Wright's office, beginning in 1917. In 1920 he was sent to Los Angeles to supervise the construction of the Olive Hill estate in Hollywood for Aline Barnsdall. Schindler worked on the project for two years, collaborating with the architect's son Lloyd Wright on Hollyhock House, codesigning with the elder Wright the Oleander House, and designing, mostly by himself, the Director's House. He also had a hand in the Ennis-Brown House, a Maya-inspired cliff dwelling on a steep hillside north of Olive Hill.

Los Angeles in those decades was full of new ideas and interests: in the outdoors, in hiking, fishing, and other robust sports; in the body and health, muscle building, calisthenics, gymnastics, yoga, vegetarianism, naturopathy, and nudism; and in spiritualism and the occult. The Theosophical Society, originally founded in New York in 1875 by Madame Blavatsky, was reconstituted in Pasadena in 1895, and Aleister Crowley and Georges Gurdjieff enjoyed repeating vogues among the literati. These tended to be pursuits of the liberal fringe and coexisted with and coincided with, to varying degrees, more populist religious enthusiasms such as Pentacostalism's Azusa Street Revival, founded in Los Angeles in 1906 by the black preacher William J. Seymour, and Aimee Semple McPherson's Foursquare Gospel Church, whose giant Angelus Temple was built in the Echo Park neighborhood of Los Angeles in 1923, just a few miles east of where Wright's temple complex was being finished on Olive Hill. It was as good a place as any to be an architect with a vision, since people were famously open-minded, interested in innovation, and readily accepted the self-imposed/self-described mission of modernist architects to change the world through buildings. Schindler was one such missionary, a visionary architect.

In 1921 he began work on a house on King's Road in Hollywood, just north of Melrose Avenue, intended to house him and his wife and another couple, the engineer Clyde Chace and his wife. In an old photo of it, you can see a treeless backdrop extending all the way to the sea, and the undeveloped Hollywood Hills a mile or two away. Hollywood was still semirural, its proverbial bean fields stretching across the gently tilted outwash plains that fanned out below the hills, here and there interspersed with orchards and ranchettes and clusters of houses and businesses around the central intersections of the growing town. In 1920, Hollywood held only 36,000 souls; all of Los Angeles held just 580,000.[15]

Across the street was Irving Gill's Dodge House. The proximity may or may not have been serendipitous, but the historical convergence was decidedly not. From his former mentor, Louis Sullivan,[16] who stressed the need to integrate man and nature, Gill had gained an awareness of the dialogue between buildings and the outside, through the media of light and air, structured by courtyards, terraces, pergolas, trees, vines, and plantings. In the Mediterranean idiom that he adopted in California, Gill found a subtle and varied vocabulary for expressing that conversation, taken from the missions and the revived practices of Spain and Italy and applied to the modern, suburban house. Gill's building stood at an intersection of influences: Lloyd Wright had worked for Gill, the Olmsted Brothers, and Paul Thiene before working for his father on Olive Hill. All of these experiences made Gill acutely aware of the role of landscape in the formation of architecture.

Schindler, unlike most of his European peers, was clearly open to regional suggestions—he had already adopted stucco from the Mission Revival, and his King's Road house, with its thick, angled, tilt-slab concrete walls and lightweight, open wooden clerestory, seemed drawn from the pueblos he had seen in New Mexico and the Pueblo Revival elements of Wright's practice. From the beginning of his career on the West Coast he was interested in new materials, partly due to the shortages of the war years and partly to his engineer's obsession with new building techniques. At the King's Road house the materials are rough, raw, and textured, with an organic feel clearly reminiscent of Wright's Hollywood buildings of the early 1920s, all of which had Schindler's hand in them, as well as a hint of the expressionism of Otto Wagner and Schindler's student work in Vienna. But in the King's Road house the materials are used with a spareness and straightforward simplicity that set the tone for later modernist work.

Walking around the house even now (it is open to the public) one seems to be walking through the blueprint for the entire cascade of modernist housing that would follow in Southern California, in its two extremes: the formalist style of Richard Neutra and his successors, and the organicist style of John Lautner and others. All of it is here: the flowing, interlocking volumes; the extension of horizontal planes past one another and into the garden spaces. The house is fundamentally asymmetrical, a sort of three-legged pinwheel, with no central axes, either in the interior or exterior, but instead a cluster of semi-self-contained living units, each one separate yet connected, like a series of suites, and each with its own garden space open to the inside yet clearly delineated and separated from adjacent spaces.

What was most radical about the house when it was built was the total, unreserved integration with the outside: sliding fiberboard panels open the common and sleeping rooms partially or completely to rectilinear garden spaces set at alternating grades; those facing direct exits from the house are patios or lawns at floor grade centered on an outdoor fireplace and bounded by hedges, and those opposite nonopening walls are sunken gardens with a private and mysterious feel. Above, two roofed but open-air sleeping porches accessible from interior staircases overlook the wider garden, the whole of which replicates and extends the variations of the house plan into the open air. There are no curves, as Schindler's world in the early 1920s was still a de Stijl world of interlocking rectangles and squares. Today the plantings are more mature than Schindler would have seen, with a huge jacaranda tree shading half the house, towering thickets of timber bamboo partially blocking the ugly stucco apartments that have grown up around it, and impossibly lush skeins of coral trumpet vine draped over the sleeping porches, the six-inch long red blooms lending an unlikely equatorial flavor to this unique hothouse flower of Austro-Californian genius.

Schindler was an exuberant, charismatic man, with a mane of hair and a flair for new ideas. He had a tendency to quarrel with clients, often because he dismissed their input in his zeal to push the envelope of building techniques or radical design concepts. More than once he pushed too far: projects went way over budget, or concrete walls cracked and let in the rain. But the architect's idealism was undiminished. In 1926 he guest-wrote six articles on the theme of architecture and health for Dr. Philip Lovell's *Los Angeles Times* column "Care of the Body." (Lovell was known as Doctor Health, and he proselytized for physical exercise, natural diet, and a progressive, unstructured education regimen for children, and even encouraged his own children to play in the nude.) In one, Schindler wrote: "Our rooms will descend close to the ground and the garden will become an integral part of the house. The distinction between indoors and outdoors will disappear. Our house will lose its front-and-back-door aspect. It will cease being a group of dens. Some larger ones for social effect, and a few smaller ones (bedrooms) in which to herd the family. Each individual will want a private room to gain a background for his life. He will sleep in the open. A work-and-play-room, together with the garden, will satisfy the group needs."[17]

Erasing the distinction between inside and out had already been and would continue to be a key talking point in the modernist program, but Schindler achieved it more fully than anyone up to that time. Much of his success was doubtless due to the mild Los Angeles climate—though he seems to have woefully underestimated the chill and wet that can prevail in coastal Southern California in winter and even in summer, when, as the sun sinks below the horizon, cool ocean air and fogs can roll in and lower temperatures twenty degrees in a matter of minutes. The house had no heating and no air-conditioning. Its embrace of the elements was the exact reversal of Le Corbusier's ultracontrolling dream of a "respiration exacte"—where fully sealed glass curtain walls would continuously maintain interior temperature and humidity through heating and cooling—in any climate, anywhere in the world.[18] Architectural historian Reyner Banham called the King's Road house "a model exercise in the interpenetration of indoor and outdoor spaces, a brilliant adaptation of simple constructional technology to local environmental needs and possibilities, and perhaps the most unobtrusively enjoyable domestic habitat ever created in Los Angeles."[19]

The King's Road house and garden were different from European and later American "International Style" modernism in one basic sense: they were of the earth, embracing the ground, like Wright's work, not isolated like a "pavilion in the landscape," à la Philip Johnson and Mies van der Rohe, peering panoptically at a distant, denatured green estate; nor a white "machine for living" à la Corbusier, divorced from the earth, literally lifted off of it, levitating in the air, gazing coldly off into the sky. Instead the Schindler house was designed with a complex interrelationship with nature at its heart. It was, granted, a Wrightean nature, complete with lawns, foundation plantings, draped vines, and built-in planters. Schindler's drawings from the period are much like Wright's drawings. The King's Road house was a high point for his garden architecture. Schindler had a long career, but as he progressed, the Wrightean urge to tightly link the building with the ground, and inside space with outside, gradually weakened in the face of the Corbusian urge to lift and separate the building from the ground. Dr. Lovell became a patron of Schindler's most important building to date, an elevated beach house in Newport designed and built from 1922 to 1926, which made the architect's reputation. But the beach house is uninteresting from the point of view of landscape, since the ground floor is given over to parking, structural supports, and stairs. Henceforth Schindler's houses would reach higher and higher off the ground and retreat into ever-boxier rectangular ramparts. Landscape was reduced to what could be seen within a rectangular, Corbusian frame—the view through the plate glass window, canonically a view from above, of unpeopled nature, or, if marked by human habitation or industry, then distant enough to be picturesque. This was landskip again, the picturesque, bringing modernist architecture, which had started out with such a stridently revolutionary mission, back squarely to the obsessions of the 17th and 18th centuries of the natural and pastoral, with their attendant exclusivity and anti-urbanism.

From the point of view of a history of gardens, in many ways the most important contribution of Rudolf Schindler was his friend, Richard Neutra, another Austrian and another architect immigrant to Los Angeles, who, like Schindler, didn't really make gardens per se but nevertheless exerted (and continues to exert) a controlling influence on how the modern garden would evolve. Neutra, though younger, had an architectural background similar to Schindler's. Born in Austria in 1892, he studied architecture and engineering in Vienna (where he knew the young Schindler), went to war in 1914, worked for a Swiss nurseryman and landscape gardener for a stint in 1917,[20] and in Berlin for the great expressionist architect Erich Mendelsohn in 1921.[21] In 1923 he came to the United States to make a pilgrimage to an aging, destitute, and forgotten Sullivan in Chicago. Poetically, he met Frank Lloyd Wright at Sullivan's funeral. He worked with Wright for just three months (it's reported that he couldn't bear the master's use of heavy, "unnecessary" masonry), then moved on to California in 1925, where he and his wife, Dione, moved in with the Schindlers and the two men formed a loose partnership.[22] Neutra designed landscapes for two of Schindler's residential commissions, the Howe and Lovell beach houses (these seem to have consisted mainly of potted plants), and collaborated on a competition plan for the League of Nations. Shortly thereafter, he picked up Schindler's main client, Lovell, after the two had a dispute, and designed for him a downtown Los Angeles office and a large house near Griffith Park called Health House. The house, with a novel prefabricated steel and concrete frame, was an international sensation. Neutra was off and running, displaying from the start a talent for self-promotion in the media, publishing his first book—of nine—in 1927.

Like his compatriot Schindler, Neutra was on the lookout for new ideas and new materials, partly for practical reasons—because of shortages through the Depression and World War II—and partly for philosophical ones—he felt no allegiance to the old ones: "because we don't have a tradition!" he wrote gleefully, dismissing out of hand California's highly distinct regional architectural tradition, as well as America's generally. "Here in our lovely country we may often enjoy a lack of local cultural encumbrance and should not artificially burden ourselves with the pasts of others."[23] His interest in new materials was also part of his lifelong search for liberation from heavy, traditional building techniques, which he had so disliked in Wright's work. What he craved was lightness. He used thin boards and beams, whether of wood or steel;

thin concrete layers for floors, walls, and roofs; and glass wherever possible, in larger and larger expanses. Before long he began to doctor his materials to give them the illusion of immateriality: wooden fascias and sills were painted silver, not to make them look like aluminum but to make them disappear against the sky; reflecting pools, at times just an inch or so deep, were spread out on terraces and rooftops to bring the sky down to the ground plane.

In 1937, Neutra built a house for Grace Miller in Palm Springs that employed all of these elements, plus a wall of mirrors facing a wall of glass windows and sliding panels, which had the effect of bringing the surrounding Mojave Desert inside the house. The house was customized for Miller, an American woman who taught wealthy clients a German body movement technique that involved practicing dance-type moves while watching oneself naked in the mirror. Building such an evanescent structure in such a harsh environment was considered quite a trick. Neutra—bearded, kinetic, and slightly wild-eyed, looking like a cross between an artist and a professor—had first arrived at the bare site in a Packard car towing a trailer customized with a drawing board and shade awning, under which his wife played cello while he studied the angles of wind and sun in order to align the house so that its stucco "front" backed into the sandblasting wind, to shelter its open, glass rear. He believed in good design as a kind of therapeutic prescription for physical well-being, and believed that the key to achieving it lay in careful assessment of the site. Neutra was famous for visiting sites at all hours, even walking about at night with a flashlight, noting microclimates, views, sight lines, and topography—the "physiognomy" of the site, as he called it.

As his technique developed, the interplay between materials and forms became a deft choreography of surfaces sliding past one another, traversing and blurring the boundary between outside and inside: ceilings extended beyond walls, interior floors continued outside to form terraces, reflecting ponds passed under panes of glass and wound into the kitchen. Only sheets of glass separated the two, and these frequently, magically, disappeared. Neutra perfected the butted glass corner using huge floor-to-ceiling panes. By making certain corners transparent, he shifted the gravitational center of the house from the central axis to the oblique. This became his signature move, and he almost always had his houses photographed, often by Julius Shulman, from carefully rehearsed oblique angles, with the camera as often looking out from the glass corner as back in. Increasingly, the house's structural members continued out into the garden to form outriggers or "spider legs"—"tentacles of structure in surrounding nature," he wrote in *Mystery and Realities of the Site*.[24] The technique also worked in reverse: "Just as the building may root itself in Nature by outward reaching tentacles, so the site may be tied into the building by pleasant infiltrations."[25] In the case of a pond slipping under the glass into the kitchen, one wonders if such infiltrations included mosquitoes.

All of his techniques were aimed at creating illusions of spaciousness in small houses on constricted lots. Like Thomas Church, he was a student

Richard Neutra, Miller House, Palm Springs, California. (IK/Creative Commons Attribution 2.0 Generic License)

of *shakkei:* "Even little benefits to be drawn from outside the property lines, like a neighboring garden, or an askew glimpse of a tree between two structures across the street, are often very precious. Anything that may serve the satisfying illusion of expanse is important."[26] Here is how he described the architectural importance of a distant view at one Montecito house: "The living space sweeps on through and reaches out for miles until finally it is closed off by the mountain. The mountain is, indeed, the 'back wall' of this stupendous living room."[27]

The potential downside of living in such a stupendous room was exposure, a feeling more than one Neutra client admitted to. But, unlike Philip Johnson's or Mies' glass houses, Neutra neither intended nor ignored the problem. In fact, he was very committed to privacy: he often "buried" bedrooms in the back (street front) of the house, making them small, with small windows, and comparatively dark, like a womb (the analogy is his). In the open, glassed part of the house (the functional front, though facing the backyard), he proffered a theory of "planting out" neighbors and "screening your little visual empire."[28] Nevertheless, the perception of many people was that his was a brave new world that they weren't quite ready for. An oft-quoted comment: "it was possible to sit inside a Neutra living room and still wish that one could get indoors."[29]

NEUTRA WAS FAMOUS for giving his potential clients a long, detailed, and very personal questionnaire, called a "Client Interrogation," covering their childhood experiences, family life, and current likes, dislikes, and aspirations with regard to the house. In analyzing the results, he filled out two columns, one labeled "client needs," the other "architectural response," which was to be rendered in drawing form, variously plan, section, or elevation, as the case required. His was a new paradigm: architecture equaled space equaled the optimal expression of the psyche. Space became environment, designed for and tailored to each person.

There is no way to understand Neutra outside the context of psychoanalysis, which suffused postwar urban America, especially in California. Psychoanalysis and psychology had been welcomed in the United States since their successes in treating shell-shocked soldiers after World

War II. The technique was not initially tied to Freud, as it later would be in the popular mind, but to a broad range of theories and techniques associated with other analysts. By the 1950s it had been "domesticated," playing roles in every field of public policy and private enterprise, broadly depicted in popular culture, with psychological therapy a widely consumed commodity and psychoanalysts ensconced in home offices in suburban neighborhoods as a matter of course.[30]

Neutra had been born and raised in the epicenter of the revolution, fin de siècle Vienna, where as a boy he was a close friend of Freud's son and for years frequented the Freud household. He met many other prominent psychoanalytic theorists, such as Otto Rank and Wilhelm Wundt, and as an architecture student would have been aware of the progress of his master Otto Wagner's Steinhof, a sprawling psychiatric hospital complex being constructed outside the city. Neutra wrote constantly of psychoanalytic theory, and in a psychoanalytic vein, yet he was more practically influenced by the gestalt theories of perception of Wilhelm Wundt than the ideas of Freud. Wundt believed that mankind's physical, sensory processes were tied to psychic ones, in a kind of two-way street: for example, feelings could be projected onto objects and imbue them, and space could become a receptacle for feelings projected onto or into it. For Neutra this meant that the tenor and quality of those feelings—both elicited from a person by the house or space, and projected into it by them—had to be carefully planned and managed. Throughout his career he fervently maintained that a well-designed house could and should provide a form of therapy for its occupants, helping defuse the ills and alienation of modern life. His concern with making people feel better through their environment was a thoroughly modern update on Olmsted and Vaux's earlier therapeutic program. Neutra explicitly cast himself in the role of the analyst, listening to the client-as-patient in order to learn who they were and what their needs were in order to prescribe the correct house. Where his prewar houses had offered prescriptions for physical well-being, his postwar houses offered prescriptions for mental well-being: an architecture of mood management, with careful attention paid to modulations of the domestic environment, using techniques for manipulating and directing air, such as louver systems and clerestories; using screens and deep overhanging eaves to determine light; water, deployed in thin, flat films, both as reflecting pools and for evaporative cooling; temperature, most dramatically in the form of the radiant heating in the floor extending from the hearth out into the garden; and of course, *space*, made to seem both infinite and domestic, cosmic and comforting. If Le Corbusier's modern house was to be "a machine for living," Neutra's was to be a machine for feeling.

Today we're accustomed to architecture and other forms of "environmental" design taking these issues into account, but for Neutra there was an additional, fundamental, and more radical substance to be choreographed with wood and glass: energy. He believed space "is vibrating life itself."[31] All flows—air, light, water, temperature—were infused with energy, and our bodies were highly tuned instruments for receiving it: "Our skin is a membrane, not a barricade," he wrote. "The most remote contours of the cosmos are not just 'out there somewhere' but causally interlaced with the nearest and deepest folds of our interior landscape."[32]

Neutra's ideas weren't far from those of Wilhelm Reich, one of Freud's early protégés, who broke ranks to pursue a theory of cosmic and bodily energy, called "orgone" energy, which he believed permeated everything in the universe. If orgone energy was blocked by neuroses and "body armoring," typically resulting from bourgeois sexual repression, illness ensued; his cure involved the physical release of blockages, preferably through orgasm. Reich built boxes called "orgone accumulators" composed of layers of different materials, organic and inorganic, in which patients would sit to absorb the cosmic rays. His methods, which also included measuring men's ejaculations with electrodes and subjecting his patients to therapy while dressed only in their bras and underpants, provoked angry denunciations by mainstream psychoanalysis. The Food and Drug Administration investigated his claims and banned the interstate sale of his boxes. In 1956 he was convicted of violating the injunction, and the FDA seized and then burned six tons of his books and other work. Reich died a year later in prison.

Neutra's houses were constructed much like Reich's orgone boxes:

with layers of sheet metal, wood, fabric, stone, and glass; and they were conceived with a somewhat similar aim, to rationalize and purify the interaction between the client's body and the environment. Indeed, their revolutions catered to some of the same personnel: the Clueys, clients for whom Neutra built a dramatic house high in the Hollywood Hills in 1955, owned an orgone box, and were friends of Timothy Leary, the LSD guru. Neutra went to parties with many of these protagonists, and frequented the commune of Krishnamurti, in the Ojai Valley north of Los Angeles.

FROM THE POINT of view of the garden, Richard Neutra brought about two major changes—one by conscious design, the other probably not. First, very deliberately, he categorically reordered the relationship between the inside and outside of the house by making openings at certain corners and by making other corners see-through. Earlier modernist designers had opened up the house and broken down the hierarchy between front and back, but Neutra's glass corners completely unhinged it. This change decentered garden geometry, far more than did copying avant-garde paintings onto lawns and pool decks, and decentered nature by reducing everything to the visual—to a constant, inescapable connection between inside and outside (not unlike surveillance). Second, it is what Neutra *didn't* do in the garden that most disturbed the traditional form of the garden: he didn't *garden*. He brought the foreground out and the background in until they touched, where the polished, heated terrazzo terrace reaches out to virtually touch the distant mountain peaks, and the "outward reaching tentacles" of the stretching house combined with nature's "pleasant infiltrations," as he poetically termed plants, water, air, and light—the materials of gardens.

Neutra blurred the distinction just as his disappearing glass walls blurred the entry threshold, transforming it into what he called a "membrane, not a barricade." In the process, the middle ground, what traditionally makes up the garden—the space between the house and the wild—all but disappeared. Where he could, Neutra eliminated it altogether by bringing the view directly to the end of the terrace and calling it a day—note that his terraces almost never have railings, even on precipitous slopes or on the roof of a house, so that the terrace edge functions just like a ha-ha, causing the distance to appear continuous with the house owner's more modest property. It was the return of the 18th century picturesque, lending a touch of transcendence to the suburban tract lot. But this 20th century suburban nature was no longer sublime in the sense of being untamed, wild, and symbolic of deeper metaphysical beauty; instead it was an abstracted, thoroughly tamed, denatured nature, reduced to a reassuring, soothing aesthetic—nature as *anaesthetic*. Where the circumstances didn't allow for this pure use of *shakkei,* he reduced the garden to strips of lawn circling the buildings, by reflex peppered with a few boulders and vaguely exotic-looking plants. With few exceptions, the gardens in photographs of Neutra's houses are indifferently planted. This isn't because he was a bad plantsman—he had had nursery training—but because he was ambivalent about the role of the garden, since it hadn't been assigned a role in his psychological and aesthetic reorderings of the universe. And Neutra's ambivalence about gardens has translated into a general, troubling, and unfortunate quality of much modernist design. Modernist buildings are often hard to design gardens for because it is unclear what function the garden should have in mediating between the building and the larger world—so much so that the designer's effort to speak the building's language often makes the garden seem pointless or pretentious.

The two outstanding exceptions to these charges against Neutra's gardens were each planted by independent nurserymen and designers. At his 1946 Kaufmann House in Palm Springs, built for the same client who had commissioned Fallingwater from Wright, Neutra had intended to plant a segmented, traditional garden of camellias and roses, and other things he and Mrs. Kaufmann fancied (as laid out in a ten-page plant list he prepared). Fortunately, the two were dissuaded when a local friend, Patricia Moorten, introduced them to her husband, who went by the *nom de plante* Cactus Slim. He took them to the nearby Joshua Tree reserve (now a national park) to see the desert's own, much better adapted architectural flora. Cactus Slim was then invited to plant a garden of succulents such as cactus, agaves, Joshua trees, and ocotillos that perfectly bridged the divide between the obligatory lawns that surrounded the house and the stark, rugged desert beyond, heightening the visual tension between the smooth machine aesthetic of the architect's object and the rough, organic forms of the wider landscape. Like the Kaufmann House, the 1948 Tremaine House in Montecito is a big pinwheel featuring long glass sections opening out to a heated terrace (an unbelievable fifty-six feet long here), a pool, and breathtaking views of distant mountains. Ralph Stevens, who had contributed much horticultural creativity to Ganna Walska's Lotusland, performed a similar feat at this far smaller site, creating a miniature version of that great estate garden, complete with an assortment of surreal aloes and other succulents densely crowded into an irregular bed between the terrace and a bit of lawn that terminated at the surrounding oak forest. What was striking was the effect that such a small area of planting achieved, joining together the two faces of Neutra's world with a demonstration of nature's own architecture of texture, form, and color. Each man in his own way introduced plants to the modern garden as architectural objects in their own right—the garden designer sharing credit for their genius with nature. After these two gardens, the best in modernist garden design would come from deep plantsmanship (as a love and facility for plant materials is called by garden makers) and from delight in exuberant natural forms, not simply from the formalist's brio with spatial and geometric effects.

The person who would take up what Thomas Church had pioneered in the Bay Area and carry it forward into the exploding suburban supernova of Los Angeles County was Garrett Eckbo. Born in Cooperstown, New York, of Norwegian heritage, Eckbo moved as a child to Alameda, across the bay from San Francisco. A few years younger than Church, Eckbo also studied at Berkeley, graduating in landscape architecture in 1935 and continuing at Harvard from 1936 to 1938. He matriculated a few months before Walter Gropius, the head of Germany's legendary Bauhaus, arrived as director of the Graduate School of Design with the aim of re-making American architecture in the Bauhaus's image. Eckbo drank in the excitement, intense idealism, and concern with transforming society that characterized the early 20th century avant-gardes (along with their fervent faith in science and technology). Eckbo wanted landscape architecture to become a "humanistic science"[33] and he wrote a series of articles with fellow students James Rose and Dan Kiley (each of whom would become important designers), outlining an important global landscape practice divided into a hierarchy of "urban, rural, and primeval" typologies. The language was turgid and pretentious, yet committed to a more analytical and structured garden making than had come before. Eckbo's penchant for words was unleashed: text began to appear on his student drawings, describing functions, layers, and intentions. So too did

Garrett Eckbo, Small Gardens in the City. (University of California, Berkeley, Design Archives)

Cubist lines and shapes and clear nods to Gropius's austere style. He experimented with tropes from modern painting and wrestled with how to inject "non-perspectival space" into the garden. He was exercised by what he considered the false dichotomy between formal and informal, and the tyranny of the "planar" view, with the paper plan view dominating composition. Above all, his work was extremely systematic. In one 1937 project, "Small Gardens in the City," he drew eighteen identical rectangular lots, then proceeded to design eighteen different treatments. Incorporating a three-foot level change, each one involved a unique geometry of steps, walls, gravel, concrete, lawns, beds, shrubs, trees, and fountains. The series demonstrated flat-out formal virtuosity—and was not a bad series of small city gardens, either.

On graduating in 1938 he went back to California, where he worked for Church for two weeks before decamping for a better-paying offer from the Farm Security Administration, a New Deal agency dedicated to planning and building housing for the rural displaced. Until the end of World War II, Eckbo designed migrant worker camps, nearly fifty of them, and defense housing all over the West, projects that included parks, sports fields, and community buildings. In 1945, with the end of hostilities, he opened up shop in San Francisco with two partners. Two years later he came to Los Angeles to open a branch office for the firm.[34] In Los Angeles, Eckbo hit paydirt, as breakneck suburban expansion—California's population tripled from 1930 to 1960, with most of the growth in the south—opened up a huge market niche for landscape designers. Much of the new housing in the western part of Los Angeles was modernist or partly inspired by it, and even that which wasn't was explicitly intended for "outdoor living"—the great mantra of postwar California life. No matter the style, the new California house had outdoor living space and needed someone to design it. Eckbo, a trim, tanned, and handsome figure in slacks and a white buttoned shirt, was the man for the job. For the next two decades he and a changing cast of partners kept up an astonishing level of production, designing hundreds, perhaps thousands of gardens, for every conceivable kind of house, all scrupulously modernist. Eckbo took Church's innovating concepts and scaled them up, multiplied

Garrett Eckbo, ALCOA Forecast Garden. (University of California, Berkeley, Design Archives)

them, and pushed them to their limits. He spun endless variations from the vocabulary of shapes and elements that Church and Halprin had first imported from painting, while adding his own, and tested endless permutations of the new "materials kit" of concrete, aggregate, metal, wood, plastic, and more. He wrote about mass production, industrial production, and how the use of modern manufactured materials would transform the garden art.

From the outset he was a fan of benches, walls, fences, screens, trellises, scrims, and accretions of several of these elements into quirky garden buildings. In 1959, funded by the Aluminum Company of America, which had been looking for new consumer markets for its defense materials, Eckbo got the chance to make a signature landscape at his own house in Laurel Canyon in the Hollywood Hills, part of a development he helped format, Wonderland Park. Called the ALCOA Forecast Garden, it was a wonderland—a futuristic stage set of shade scrims, screening walls, pergolas, and a huge faceted fountain in the shape of a flower, all constructed of bars, rods, panels, and meshes of aluminum in several colored finishes, arranged around a small lawn. In spite of the amount of metal, the garden is colorful and whimsical, with bits of varied materials set into the paving and lush, exotic plantings framing a circular procession of carefully modulated, unique garden rooms.

Even without such a level of building activity, Eckbo's gardens were often remarkably three-dimensional, yet always also essentially dependent on planar forms: usually concrete paving—patterned, angled, and curved—alternating with panels of lawn, often also with a swimming pool at the center, befitting their suburban settings. Eckbo designed every imaginable kind of pool, in a dizzying variety of shapes: amoebas, zigzags, arcs, semicircles, rhomboids, angular kidneys, and free-form Cubist doodles complete with islands. "The garden must shape the pool, rather than being forced to conform to it," he wrote in 1950.[35] Superficially, the pools might look like the pool at the center of Church's Donnell garden, but they were rarely ever balanced by the expanse of a distant view. Eckbo's gardens tended to be inward-looking and centripetal, often with terminal curves of hedges or tall walls literally closing them in on themselves. Eckbo liked enclosure and invented it where it didn't exist.

For all his mannerism, Eckbo did succeed in humanizing landscape architecture: his gardens really were for people, as this deceptively simple definition from his student days makes clear: "Gardens are places where people live out of doors."[36] He thought about how his clients would use

Garrett Eckbo, swimming pool from above. (University of California, Berkeley, Design Archives)

the gardens, and, no matter how stylized the shapes or materials he used, they all derive from a clear assessment of function. His drawing style was unique in favoring neat 3-D views: axonometric or isometric perspectives, done in clean ink, frequently with human figures inserted into the diagrams to give them scale and dynamism. On the other hand, a downside of his attention to European art invited the charge of simple-minded copying: many garden plans looked exactly like avant-garde paintings of an earlier generation. He proudly published one alongside a Kandinsky drawing he had used as a model.

Like Neutra, Eckbo wrote often and long, publishing his first book,

Landscape for Living, in 1950, the first modernist garden book to appear in English since the British designer Christopher Tunnard's 1938 *Gardens in the Modern Landscape*. It made his reputation nationally, and even internationally; the freshness of the design, a signature of the California style, made it visually irresistible. But it is a strange document, consisting of endless platitudinous classifications and typologies, sermons on theory and history, lacking narrative organization and wrought in a jargon-filled, ponderous pseudo-scientific mode common at mid-century. An impatient reader's carping aside, Eckbo did bury a few nuggets of wisdom in the sands, particularly about the importance of thinking carefully about site.

At his book's core lay the insistence that landscape architecture be considered a keystone art, modeled on science and the scientific method, which "takes nothing for granted, accepts no precedents without examination, and recognizes a dynamic world in which nothing is permanent but change itself."[37] He made big claims for the profession, arguing that it had an interdisciplinary reach and humanist latitude that ought to place it above merely decorative arts in the hierarchy; yet the terms he used betray delusions of grandeur: he repeatedly wrote of a "unified landscape" and a "total landscape" shaped by the all-seeing landscape architect. There is a strong undercurrent of defensiveness in his writing, a status anxiety about the field carried forward from his student days, when, enrolled in an architecture and design program, it was made clear to him that landscape occupied the basement. Walter Gropius was not interested in landscape; and it was not included in Alfred Barr's much-fetishized 1949 Museum of Modern Art show in New York on modernism in the arts. Eckbo is not alone among landscape architects of his era who trained at Harvard and seemed to come away with a bad case of "slide-rule envy." To accomplish this, he and others first tried to make it more like painting—and architecture, and "science" as Eckbo conceived it. His own "humanistic science" would ultimately become enveloped in a single, highly codified style that ignored architectural context completely, despite his habitually railing against "style."

It is tempting to frame this attitude as a gender problem: in an age of ascendant technocracy, the Harvard men (they were all men) tried to professionalize garden making, which had historically been the province of women, gay men, the self-taught, the unlicensed, artists, and trespassers from other realms like Thomas Jefferson, and had focused on flowers, horticulture, and seasons (a feminist view would translate these to procreation, generation, and dirt). These were effectively banished, and men—straight men—wearing white shirts and ties, drawing at well-lit desks with engineering tools, pouring concrete and welding steel, remade the garden into a place of expertise, technique, "science," and function, totally divorced from the garden's earthy origins but instead defined by modern use values as a place of consumption, leisure, and recreation—the three sisters of postwar American aspiration.

In his defense, Eckbo had a real concern for democracy and social justice. Like Neutra, whose designs for schools in the Los Angeles area and health clinics in rural Puerto Rico rank among his most important—and overlooked—contributions to opening modern institutional buildings to the outdoors, Eckbo's New Deal landscape work and his later collaboration on a series of cooperative suburban housing schemes demonstrated this. But the Eckbo firm increasingly turned to large public and commercial development work, designing campuses, parks, subdivisions, and, unavoidably, tacky desert resorts.

In the end, Garrett Eckbo succeeded. He designed, he estimated, 1,100 gardens.[38] Along with his cohorts—Church, Halprin, Baylis, Royston, and others—he literally remade the California garden and in turn much of the nation's garden. Through sheer volume and prolific media, including the *Sunset* magazine program, they wielded a huge influence over the weltanschauung of landscape, design, and, presumably, how people used outdoor space, all over the world. Eckbo helped define the physical contours of our suburban lives these past few decades, no matter where we live or in what style of house. In Wonderland Park today, as in so many similar neighborhoods, the houses have migrated away, via serial remodeling and creeping mansionization, from the original 1960s one-story pseudo-Mod boxes, but the gardens around them seem to retain something of his flavor with every revamping. One can't help but marvel at this small, surprising bit of cultural continuity in a society intent on tearing everything down and rebuilding it over and over again.

In 1963, Eckbo returned to the University of California at Berkeley, this time as chairman of the department of landscape architecture. He enjoyed stature and influence, but the modernist program he'd championed hadn't panned out as envisioned. Good design had not made the world a better place. There was no revolution, no social transformation, no outbreak of justice for those who needed it. Indeed, the beginning of the 1960s was marked by growing income stratification, continued residential segregation, building anomie, anxiety, and anger at society's direction. Even among modernist design stalwarts, there was a spreading realization that the suburban model had sold out nearly all of the movement's revolutionary commitments and had in fact encouraged, abetted, and worked for the bourgeois counterrevolution, if there was such a thing. Architects and landscape designers had been complicit. They had a suburb problem.

Suburbanization didn't just happen magically, nor was it simply chosen by consumers or ordained by free-market forces. The conversion of rural land to suburban housing development has always been a process stoked, shaped, and sustained by government policies—not a single, coherent, or necessarily intentional one, but many overlapping ones, promulgated by different parts of government at many levels, local, state, and national. It is a Kafkaesque, bureaucratic morass of crossed purposes that is singularly American and to which we owe a good part of our built environment. The first rule is that local governments nearly always encourage sprawl development because they stand to gain from property and sales taxes, even though it will cause them and their neighbors trouble down the road. Much of the time, local governments are in the pocket of business interests that benefit from public spending on infrastructure. The case of Los Angeles's bringing water from the distant Owens River in 1913 to fuel the development of farmland in the San Fernando Valley, which was owned by a cabal of well-connected businessmen, set the standard that others would follow. Los Angeles, already a dispersed city, was locked into a suburban model to the perpetual benefit of land developers reaping subsidies. By 1930, 94 percent of Los Angeles consisted of detached houses. By 1950 the proportion had fallen to one-third, but the City of Angels would always look different from Chicago (28 percent detached homes), New York City (20 percent), or Philadelphia (15 percent).[39] The Los Angeles model was adopted nationwide, and the gravy train for speculators feeding at the public trough has been rolling ever since.

The second rule is that state governments tend to behave just like local governments, especially in large states, since no one can see what they are doing behind the screen. Just one example is the California tax code provision that allowed local authorities to recalculate rural property taxes based on *potential* land value, rather than its real, assessed value, forcing farmers to sell out before development even came close to them. In Los Angeles County, which up until the 1940s was the single highest-earning agricultural county in America (in good measure because it specialized in high-value crops such as grapes, citrus, and vegetables), this rule helped crush the citrus industry and see it replaced by housing tracts: in 1947, citrus orchards covered 135,000 acres; in 1960 there were fewer than 50,000. A 1965 state law stopped the practice, but too late; today the number of acres in commercial fruit trees is negligible.[40]

At the federal level, the list of inducements to decentralization in the postwar period is long: a redirection of defense spending from the North to the Sunbelt; massive spending on roads extending from the Federal Highway Act of 1916 to the Interstate Highway Act of 1956, which by itself opened millions of acres to subdivision; the deduction of mortgage interest and real estate taxes from gross income; reimbursement for state and local government building of new water, sewer, and other infrastructure; and massive government spending on housing after the Depression, in the form of the Federal Housing Administration (FHA) and the Veterans Administration (VA) insuring mortgages. The federal government made it often literally cheaper to buy in new suburbs than to rent in cities, and millions did.[41]

In combination, these policies formed a big, tangled ball, which, once rolling, was unstoppable. There was a huge burst in housing starts,[42] but the majority was in suburbs, speeding the demise of inner-city areas by vacuuming up middle-class buyers.[43] The twinned stories of the American postwar landscape are the growth of affluent white suburbia and the decline of poor black cities—processes that were intimately intertwined. The historian Kenneth Jackson pointed out that it was not the racist exclusion of the postwar period that was new, "but the thoroughness of the physical separation"—the sheer distance that highways helped put between different parts of the American population.[44]

In an even deeper sense this process of withdrawal from the mixed public space of the city was at the core of the postwar American zeitgeist, especially in the 1950s. It was an age of paranoia: fear of the Soviet Menace, fear of racial miscegenation, and fear of infection, particularly in light of the polio epidemics of the period. Multiple, sometimes contrary threats of surveillance weighed on the public mind: fear of communist infiltrators and spies, but also of U.S. government wiretapping, aired in the congressional wiretapping hearings of 1953; fear of subliminal suggestion, hypnosis, and miniature spy cameras; and fear of UFOs. All of these reinforced a desire for privacy that was also a key selling point for the flight to suburbia, away from the noise and lack of privacy of city tenements, streets, and public transportation. This had an explicitly racial component: between restricted covenants and racist government lending criteria, suburbia was built only for white people. But it also spoke to a practical urgency: from the point of view of architects, builders, and landscape designers, the need for privacy was a consumer obsession that had to be factored into day-to-day business. The old rule of the house facing the street, with living room and dining room in the front and kitchen behind, was reversed. These family areas now opened onto the rear yard, with ever-increasing amounts of glass, making the achievement of privacy in the garden critical.

This was true of "traditional" house types as well as aggressively modernist ones, but the latter were caught in a self-generated paradox: the more modern the house, the more transparent, the more perfect its erasure of the distinction between inside and outside—and the more its occupants worried about "living in a goldfish bowl." House styles other than modernist, whether tract or traditional, borrowed this problem by building "picture windows" into inopportune parts of the structure, namely the center-front, visible from the street. As a consequence the modern garden increasingly turned in on itself, brilliantly fulfilling the movement's holy grail of linking house and garden into a seamless whole, yet shutting off the outside from the outside-of-outside. Eckbo's walls, screens, and fences are perfect embodiments of this. And he was a favorite of modernist architects such as A. Quincy Jones, who literally built glass houses and lived in one himself. In a 1957 magazine article on his own house, Jones said: "*Inside* the house you're always with your family or your friends—*outside* is where you want privacy. That's why we tried to provide as much privacy as we could, with screens, walls, fences and plantings." (Emphasis in original.)[45]

The postwar decades were also an age of anxiety about conformity, which generated another, weirder paradox for designers: anyone with the means *had* to live in suburbia but also had to guard against appearing the same as anyone else. Though it rose from the counterculture, Malvina Reynolds's 1962 song "Little Boxes," deriding the identical "ticky-tacky" houses of suburbia as unbearably conformist, expressed a broad spectrum of white Americans' fear of being "look-alikes," or drones—organization men. Yet difference had to be achieved within tight limits: too much originality was perhaps more suspect than too little. An astonishing how-to literature developed in magazine articles and books, advising Americans where the lines lay in their politics, dress, speech, vacations, and houses and gardens. Living in cookie-cutter suburbs was no more acceptable than living in a trailer park, but adding a bit of customization to your tract home could establish the right note of distinction. Building from stock house plans was smart, but buying a prefab house, which sounded too much like a trailer, was not. The architect-designed modern house and garden promised the perfect quantum of individuality and were celebrated in the shelter magazines from coast to coast. The editor of *House Beautiful* from 1945 to 1965, Elizabeth Gordon, waged a tireless campaign for individuality and privacy through "everyday modernism" (a squishy amalgam of post and beam, small windows, mild hip roofs, and softened traditional details) as the path to defending the ideals of American democracy threatened by conformity and lack of privacy. "The challenge of our time is individualism versus totalitarianism," she declaimed in a 1953 speech at the Chicago Furniture Mart, "democracy or dictatorship—and this struggle is on many fronts. Our front, yours and mine, happens to be on the home front."[46] Privacy was the primary battleground. The magazine's garden editor wrote this in a typical diatribe from 1950:

> We Americans give much lip service to the idea of privacy. We consider it one of the cherished privileges we fought a war to preserve. Freedom to live our own lives, the way we want to live them, without being spied upon or snooped around, is as American as pancakes and molasses. . . . The very raison d'etre of the separate house is to get away from the living habits and cooking smells and inquisitive eyes of other people. . . . [I]f your neighbors can observe what you are serving on your terrace, your home is not really your castle.

So the backyard had to be made private, unique, and distinctive, designed to showcase the owners' individuality—hence the endless variation of forms and geometries of the modernist California garden, with its proliferating new materials: corrugated plastic, Plexiglas, fiberglass, aluminum, and patterned concrete blocks, to name a few. Like Garrett Eckbo's eighteen "Small Gardens in the City," all of it was a variation in one style—like a General Motors product line, offering a model for every taste, one in every color—but every one had tail fins. Customization and satisfying each and every consumer whim was the order of the day, in the service of an attempt to turn the suburban American backyard into a private country club complete with barbeque grill for cooking, a table for dining, a lawn and swimming pool full of toys for recreation, outdoor stereo speakers, lounge chairs, and a fire pit for adult entertaining. In fact it needed to be even *better* than the country club: design magazines exhorted architects, landscapers, and homeowners to make the garden "more exciting than anywhere else, canceling the need for seeking family pleasures in private clubs or public beaches," as *House Beautiful* did in 1958.[47] In this age of total automotive mobility, garden designers challenged people to leave the car in the garage. When Thomas Church titled his second book *Your Private World*, he perfectly reflected the aesthetic of nuclear family atomization.

Though modern garden makers didn't invent these centrifugal forces in American life—Monticello is a testament to the deep English roots of American attitudes toward city and countryside—they surely did their part to reinforce them, by flacking, in effect, an anti-urban point of view. The preference for rural or wilderness sites, the glorification of unspoiled views, and the rhetoric of "planting out" all trace of the neighbors helped shape and drive suburban development, encouraging sprawl farther and farther away, especially into hilly or mountainous areas poorly suited to traditional development. Even while some designers, such as Eckbo, continued to talk of the need for remaking the city, the imagery and the actual plans they peddled were solidly, iconically suburban—like Wonderland Park.

Modernism never did become the housing choice of the masses. Some large developers, among them Eichler Homes, hired modernist celebrity architects like A. Quincy Jones and Craig Ellwood to design affordable tracts. Our house on Twinridge was an example of this sort of modest modernism for the middle class. But in general, the modernist house and garden, in spite of the publicity they garnered, remained objects of desire for a very limited slice of the middle class, and increasingly over the years, the wealthy. So total was this identification that by the late 1950s Alfred Hitchcock "cast" a Frank Lloyd Wright house as an emblem of utmost, unattainable luxury in his film *North by Northwest*—the residence of the evil villain, the spy Vandamm. Wright, the most famous architect in the world, defined modernism for most people, and his Fallingwater was nearly as well-known as the White House. The Master himself was too expensive even for MGM, but no matter—the set designers in 1958 pretty convincingly aped a Wright house, complete with dressed lime-stone walls, endless glass, and a massive cantilever (supported in very un-Wrightean but very L.A. style by steel beams), perched by itself, a million miles from anywhere, on a forested, rocky slope below Mount Rush-more, where the film's thrilling denouement is staged. It was instantly recognizable as *a* Frank Lloyd Wright to most Americans who could read (or who at least read magazines like *House Beautiful*, which devoted two issues to Wright in the 1950s). It was also the perfect "country home" complement to the Plaza Hotel, where the hero, Cary Grant as a Madi-son Avenue ad man, is mistakenly abducted as a spy and is then marched through a parade of luxe locales, cars, and Van Cleef & Arpels jewelry draped on the alluring actress Eva Marie Saint. Hitchcock's point is that wealth and luxury won't help you when you need help, but rather will iso-late you. Nevertheless, the house's wilderness isolation would have suited Neutra perfectly—though he, like Wright himself, would have sited the house more sensitively, closer to the ground. The filmmaker's choice also highlights the degree to which the modernist house, whether full-blown "futuristic" like a Neutra or with one foot still firmly in the soil of the Arts & Crafts movement like a Wright, remained the offspring of that movement, true to its exacting formal and utopian romantic impulses: all were dedicated to the patriarchal family, conceived as a unique, artistic object, usually asymmetrical and idiosyncratic, rendered by fine crafts-men in materials either fine in themselves or finely crafted, and sited if possible in splendid "natural" isolation, a monument to the taste, discern-ment, and means of its owner.

For most American homebuyers in the postwar decades, "traditional" architectural styles remained the top choice—even in California, where the ranch house held sway. The ranch house had a long, uncodified his-tory as literal ranch dwellings in the Southwest, built according to tra-dition, local materials, and practical accommodation to an arid, warm climate. The flavor was Spanish for hundreds of years, Mexican for a few decades more, American thereafter. The originals shared a loosely de-fined form: one-story, low-slung, with adobe walls and low-pitched tile roofs extending over generous eaves and covered porches and exterior walkways—*corredors,* in pre–World War II parlance. The rooms were ar-rayed in one-room thick wings flanked and connected by exterior walk-ways, each room with egress to outside spaces, an arrangement developed as practical accommodation to housing extended families, workers, and much of the animal end of the ranching business as well.

As the Southwest boomed and gained population, the form was picked up and spread as the ideal "informal" and "outdoor living," that is, suburban mode. In this period, Americans had a genial obsession with a Roy Rogers West of cowboys and Indians, horses, country music, Daniel Boone caps, and Old Mexico—romantic, bucolic imagery that the ranch house complemented effortlessly. (Roy Rogers famously lived in one with a matching horse barn.) Against this backdrop appeared the Los Angeles architect and developer Cliff May, a sixth-generation Californian who had grown up in San Diego across the street from an Irving Gill house and who had spent summer days at various 19th century adobe houses passed down by his mother's Californio family.[48] Both as an architect for others and in developing small subdivisions on his own account, May gradually launched a revolution, beginning in the late 1930s, by taking the traditional ranch house and giving it wings—literally, by running the conventional L, V, or U shapes out at odd angles to enclose more space on the generous lots of much of upscale, outer ring suburbia: he fashioned Vs, Ws, Xs, Ys, Zs, and myriad compound combinations. In his early years May more or less faithfully imitated historical precedents, down to the Spanish ironwork grilles over streetside windows. The genius of the form was the fact that nearly every room did, or could, open up to broad garden spaces lush with lawns and towering sycamore trees—often native specimens a hundred or more years old that grew in the West Los Angeles canyons he favored for his developments. At the same time, the houses could turn a blank shoulder to the street with thick walls, small windows, and big, winding driveways. May published a book, *Western Ranch Houses*, with *Sunset* magazine in 1946, which became a bestseller in the genre. He then designed the magazine's offices in Menlo Park, south of San Francisco, as a low-slung, red-tile-roofed zigzag set back from the street like a mission compound. When the book was republished in 1956, the historical bits remained, but the rustic drawings of old rancho adobes had been replaced with photos of May's own work, which began to reveal remarkable inclusions from the modern lexicon, subtly slipped in: open plans between kitchens, dining and living areas, glass walls and sliders opening to patios, and swimming pools in mod shapes. Like the modernist box, the ranch house was also built with post and beam, so it was easy to add these features while maintaining the traditional roof pitches and detailing. Soon the line began to blur.

The most interesting case was May's own house, built in 1939 and remodeled ten years later. It was a long-running sensation. The first incarnation was featured in *Sunset* in 1944 and 1945, the second in 1956 and 1958; most other top U.S. home and garden magazines picked it up, too. What he said in 1946 set the tone of the open-pollinated hybridization he was effecting: "Looking back at the old ranch houses should help you look ahead and see the real values in tomorrow's house."[49] French doors and fixed windows had been replaced with floor-to-ceiling sliders in the living room, dining room, and master bedroom. Electronic media gadgetry appeared in every room. The garden, originally rustic and "equestrian," had been revamped by Douglas Baylis into a quietly modernist statement, without the designer knickknacks of plank benches or metal scrims. A big, curving patio of pebble aggregate in a roughly five-foot grid of redwood stringers, set on the diagonal, was fitted with radiant heating that could crank up to 100 degrees—the old Neutra trick. The patio held a circular planting bed and defined the edge of a copious lawn extending to the pool. Curves were everywhere: the drive, the parking court, the elliptical swimming pool. Planting beds held large-leafed *Fatsia japonica*, the signature plants of the hip modernist landscape architects of the era. In the second edition of his book, Thomas Church's work on several May houses was photographed, as was Eckbo's.

May's updated historicism was electrifying: the ranch house became the most popular model for new, detached home construction in the West. It even came to represent America, at least in Moscow in 1959, where Nikita Khrushchev and Richard Nixon had an argument that looked a lot like a marriage spat in the kitchen of a model ranch house built by the U.S. government to show Russians how well Americans lived. The Soviet leader found ridiculous the idea that the world needed more than one brand of dishwasher, while Nixon took pride in capitalism's ready multiplication of consumer choice.[50] Americans sided with Nixon—and Cliff May.

May had pulled off a perfect triangulation, to use our anachronistic, Clinton-era word. How was it so easy? Because of function as much as fashion. The postwar suburban lifestyle's needs could be satisfied by a short list of functional requirements; any design style conceivably could do the trick, if it were amenable. Both modernism and ranch, in mid-century California, were so and had eager boosters in the media. And both were embraced by the home-buying public, in good part by digesting the salient points of the other—modernism the openness and working relationship between indoors and out of the Spanish-Mediterranean past, and ranch, that tradition's stodgy progeny, the technological and aesthetic innovations of the new designers.

Soon hybrids of the two styles were everywhere, with butted glass corner windows and spider-leg outriggers à la Neutra appearing on bad May imitations, and hipped roofs and wooden windows on glass boxes; as were odd matings of architecture and landscape: indoor-outdoor patios, long beam-supported spans enclosing atriums filled with trendy plants. Ranch was traditional, in a modern way. *Sunset* magazine featured it side by side with straight modernism for three decades as the twin models, strangely interchangeable, for the Western house, glossing over the obvious stylistic differences by claiming, ludicrously: "the ranch house is not exactly a style. Instead, let's call it an approach to living."

Was this modernism and antimodernism in bed, creating a crossbreed offspring? Or is the difference in philosophical and political outlooks implied by these words trivialized and subsumed when each extreme can be reduced to the choice between one detached, three-bedroom, two-car-garage suburban house with pool and another? At the end of the day—or the decade, or the century, depending on your point of view—what was apparent was that modernism, for all its protestations that it wasn't a style, that it transcended style, was just another style in history's bag of looks, ready to be deployed, in variously pure or adulterated forms, in different settings, to satisfy the prospective buyer. Like any of the historicist idioms that preceded it, architectural modernism found itself, when its practitioners couldn't procure larger or more utopian commissions, serving the old masters of the detached, suburban, single-family home, it's social and aesthetic aspirations subordinated just as completely as its predecessors had been to the discipline of bourgeois family isolation.

Yet, looked at another way, the modernist house in California suburbia represented the paradoxical triumph and fulfillment of the Arts & Crafts movement's original aims: to reconnect ordinary families with a more natural order, the workingman of Ruskin and Morris having been transmogrified into the commuting middle-class breadwinner of postwar America, each a master of his own self-contained idyll where close-cropped turf and possibly a swimming pool stood in for the vegetable garden and orchard of the yeoman's homestead. The evils of industrial cities had been successfully evaded, a new Eden created, within the reach of, if not the masses, then as close to that shapeshifting concept as had ever been achieved. It was the definitive style of the second half of the American century, the most innovative, surprising, intellectually engaged, and democratic—celebrating the aspirations and dignity of the middle classes, unfussy about boundaries, unafraid of embracing its opposites—in sum, as democratic a style as we've ever had, even considering its racial exclusivity. And the one for which the era will be remembered.

The story told in this chapter would not be complete without paying heed to a phenomenon that modernists and traditionalists respectively tried to ignore—tiki or Polynesian style, a lively, embarrassingly popular part of the built and cultural American environment that contradicted the aims and pretensions of the tastemakers while infiltrating their home turf. Hawaii became a state, the fiftieth, in 1959, one year after Alaskan statehood. The ratification no doubt stoked weeks of celebration and libation nationwide, but revelry in support of Hawaiian-American cultural (mis) understanding was already a long-standing tradition, with its ceremonies first laid down in sticky layers by Mark Twain in 1866 and Jack London in 1907, then refined and broadcast by a trickle-turned-torrent of American servicemen and women in the World War II era, when millions of Americans shuffled through military bases in California and Hawaii en route to the Pacific Theater, and, if they were lucky, back again. They saw things there they didn't see at home, and some of it traveled well. California, itself a kind of semi-palmy Pacific idyll for folks from colder climates and tighter social bindings, became a conduit and amplifier for the reexport of Americanized Hawaiian culture to the nether reaches of the continent. (The traffic was two-way: the Mission Revival contributed to some of Hawaii's finest—or at least most memorable—buildings, such as Bertram Goodhue's Honolulu Academy of Arts and the Royal Hawaiian Hotel, and Cliff May's triangulated ranch-modern mode was widely copied in both residential and commercial buildings during Hawaii's surging growth in the 1950s, '60s, and '70s.)

The "Polynesian" culture being trafficked was ersatz, but authentic in a certain catholic sense: a festive bouquet of imagery including visions of South Seas explorers, savage tribes worshipping wooden idols by torchlight, lovely wahines in grass skirts, and barefoot beachcombers living the easy life, sipping from coconuts while the rest of us corporate stooges sweated in tight collars back in Peoria. Tiki represented everything that the GIs and every other average postwar American craved after years of Depression and war but weren't allowed by the pedantic, puritanical modernist priests and purists who controlled the design PR machinery. It was fundamentally and loudly "about" taboo things, and it wasn't subtle: it prominently featured images of bare-breasted women—often of dark complexion—dancing in firelight, in primitive tableaux made of premodern materials such as bamboo and volcanic rock, and cocktails—lots of cocktails—mostly based on rum and with alluring monikers, such as mai tais, grogs, punches, fog cutters, Singapore slings, and scorpion bowls. Tiki first and foremost promised rewards: what one might chance into after a long sea voyage or a long war, unmediated by mother figures or librarians: rum, wahines, and song, accompanied by ukuleles and drums, and plenty of pseudo-Chinese-Malaysian food on sticks, eaten in low-slung rattan chairs. It was made simultaneously macho and intellectual by the buff Norwegian explorer-god Thor Heyerdahl's 1947 voyage in a balsa-wood raft, the *Kon-Tiki* (and 1948 book of the same name), then was made both literary and pop by James Michener's blockbuster novel *Hawaii* in 1959. Each book launched a thousand rum-boat bars. A stream of Elvis Presley movies, beginning with *Blue Hawaii* in 1961, launched a thousand more.

The tiki statue itself dovetailed perfectly with the vogue for aboriginal art among European modernists like Picasso, who cast himself as an evangelist of the "primitive." Such a posture was irresistible in the face of the overbearing self-righteousness of the modernists—even for one of the movement's biggest stars. "Ah, good taste! What a dreadful thing! Taste is the enemy of creativity," Picasso is quoted as saying. It offered a license to rebel against this other conformity: the slick, anaesthetic, cold, clinical modernist world, where no fun was allowed, no music, no women, no contact with the outside. Tiki was the outside, culturally speaking, and its natural habitat was outside, and it quickly made its way there: countless homeowners erected tiki torches and actual wooden tikis, sometimes big ones, in their yards, and planted exotic tropical-looking vegetation on the edge of the lawn. Thatched structures fitted out with wet bars appeared poolside from Palm Springs to Petaluma, melding perfectly with the hybrid architectural forms taking over coastal California, especially in the new sprawl cities of the East Bay, Orange County, the San Gabriel Valley, and South Los Angeles. On the strip boulevards, tiki mixed with the slick, *Jetsons*-esque commercial architecture of the period in hundreds of motels, restaurants, bars, liquor stores, bowling alleys, and cheap apartments featuring massive, angled cantilever roofs, glass walls, gross stone-veneered walls mimicking "lava" rock, plus a fringery of mod components such as steel beams and chrome chairs, metal fences, and plastic screens. It was aesthetic mixing of the lowest, cheapest commercial sort, but it was hugely popular, a plague of bad taste that Americans couldn't get enough of.

I can personally attest to the erstwhile popularity and ubiquity of Polynesian style. In my garden design practice, I frequently engage in a kind of archaeology, surveying, picking through, and uncovering layers of buried or forgotten stuff while looking at people's houses and gardens. Almost anything may offer clues to reconstruct the history of a property: plants that have survived from an ancient vogue, types of paving, pieces of pottery, sculpture, or art, barbeques, basins, fountains, and fences. Sometimes I find 1920s Spanish or Arts & Crafts gems, with extra luck a rim of exquisite Batchelder tile sticking up from a sea of dusty ivy; much more often I find mid-century mini-palaces of occasional debauchery, given away by clumps of enormous tropicalia like giant birds of paradise or monsteras with their joke-huge leaves and wonderful name, and especially by the festering remains of lava-rock niches, fountains, and waterfalls, covered in dirt and detritus, badly grouted and plumbed (because they were often homemade) and teeming with mosquitoes. Invariably, these haven't worked in decades, and the owners admit to no knowledge of their origins. But right there, I have no doubt, were once luaus, pool parties, swells in aloha shirts sipping stingers on the lanai, leis, lays . . . I take a picture, then call in the jackhammers. Like so many things about the postwar decades, it was bad, but good. These had been people unafraid of letting their hair down, uncowed by the guardians of good taste. I wish I had been there. Even the best designers got involved: there is a picture of a garden show installation by the firm "Armacost & Royston, West Los Angeles"—recall that Robert Royston had impeccable modernist credentials, having been a Church associate and Eckbo's sometime partner—featuring a blond girl in full Polynesian regalia surrounded by ginger, plumerias, tikis, orchids, and bamboo screens.[51] That was a stylish garden.

The party went on for many more years. I remember tiki torches burning on the lawn at Twinridge. My family sold the house in 1976 and moved to Montecito, where I lived until 1982, when my mother moved to Los

Armacost & Royston tiki garden display. (Courtesy of Oceanic Arts, Whittier, California)

Angeles County, living for the first year in a small wooden house in Malibu, tight between the Pacific Coast Highway and the beach. In winter, my mom and I would watch El Niño storms roll in; one pounding, bright day in 1984, we watched the house next to our next-door neighbor's—a little, low, pitched-roof affair, clearly from another era—wash away in the waves, broken into a slosh of kindling and boards that clattered frighteningly through our pilings before vanishing. That fall, we watched fires raging down on us from the Santa Monica Mountains, lines of forty-foot-high flames advancing over the peaks and ridges, red fire engines and crews hauling out hose lines on the PCH to make a stand. We climbed up a ladder onto our roof with the garden hose and she shared gin-and-tonics poured from a thermos into plastic cups with the neighbor and the basset hound he had hauled up the ladder, too. The firefighters saved our house, but not some other people's houses.

In 1990, we found out that Twinridge had burned to the ground in the Painted Cave fire, which started near the crest of the range and in three days burned all the way to the ocean. Most of the houses on the road weren't touched, some with their flowers continuing in bloom, but ours had vanished—the fire so hot that even the huge old oak tree was gone, leaving barely a trace.

Six

ART CONFRONTS NATURE, REDUX: TRIUMPHS AND ANXIETIES OF LANDSCAPE ARCHITECTURE (1940s–2000s)

The term *landscape architecture* . . . is odd and unhappy, seeming to signal the unease and lack of focus with which the modern profession views its activities. . . . [L]andscape architecture . . . may sometimes take its cue from architecture, being established vis-à-vis some important building. . . . But professional landscapers' use of the word *architecture* in their description seems largely the result of a feeling of acute inferiority, an inferiority that many architects have done little to relieve by their rather patronizing assumption that landscape architects are the ones who put the flowers and shrubs around *their* finished buildings. Nor has landscape architecture much more to do with "landskip" in the original sense of a painted image of some territory; indeed, the current reaction against anything "scenic" in landscape design has taken the profession even further from that original link. . . .

—*JOHN DIXON HUNT*, GREATER PERFECTIONS:
THE PRACTICE OF GARDEN THEORY, 2000

There is no better yardstick with which to measure how landscape architecture has redefined the shape of our world than the skateboard. Back in the 1970s, skateboards were used to slalom down the street or carve the walls of backyard swimming pools emptied by drought. Then came the invention of the "ollie," the deeply improbable trick of making a skateboard and its rider fly by smashing the tail of the board against the pavement and, with a deft flick of the foot, redirecting the energy to fling it upward into the air. The ollie let skaters hop over curbs and up onto stairs, railings, ledges, and benches—anything smooth and hard will do—taking advantage of changes in level to come up with ever more perilous tricks. In the process it transformed the skateboard from a suburban toy into a sharp instrument of urban exploration and opened up what had been a privileged, coastal, and largely white American activity into a multicultural and pandemically global one. It also converted skateboards into convenient diagnostic tools for observers of the built environment: where you see skaters ollying, you are likely seeing a space designed by a landscape architect. It's usually not a park of old, but a "modern" version of a park, which may or may not be simultaneously the plaza of a downtown business district, or the random, quasi-public spaces surrounding a town center, a school, a mall, or a parking garage. Its main material is concrete, its main texture is smooth, and its main color is gray. The skateboarders are interested less in its flat expanses than in its acute angles: its edges, stairs, benches, and planters, and the transitions between them, because these make up the hard canvas of their art—an art as ephemeral as music and as exacting and bone-risky as gymnastics.

This new kind of space defines not so much a place as the connective tissue between places, whether they are buildings, roads, fields, playgrounds, parking lots, or bits of infrastructure. Its function is usually circulation and demarcation: guiding people and vehicles through and around, between, from and to, to and fro. It is inhabited—if it ever is—mostly during the day, by people walking through the space on the way to something, and by clusters of workers on their lunch hour or a smoking break; at night it is usually given over to the sleeping homeless, wakeful rats, and enterprising skaters. It often has the quality of a bridge, a transition, or an in-between, with no real claim to being somewhere itself. Art is often present, usually in the form of sculpture, self-consciously but unsurely offered, its intended role not obvious. The space is normally made up of parts of a standard vocabulary of forms: trees in holes or planters arranged in lines and grids, seating, water features, steps, paving scored in repeating lines, grids, or curves, and deliberate changes in the ground plane such as mounds, tilted planes, or amphitheaters. It often boasts islands of green, presented hopefully, as if to say, "Look, here's some grass, come, relax, feel at ease, don't let all this concrete put you off." The unnaturalness of the green parts amid the hard parts points to a deep ambivalence that underlies many of these spaces: they exist uncomfortably between some residue of the traditional park or garden, meant to look like nature or at least like a seemingly undesigned rural landscape, and their typically "modern" locations around high-rises, transportation nodes, and suburban aggregations like schools and malls. Some of their design elements point to classical or traditional kinds of order—the grids of trees, square lines of paving, and expanses of verdant lawn; others point to something intended to appear more organic—the curves, mounds, and cascades of water; still others indicate an artfully modern "take" on the first two—the straight lines bent into sines, straight walls fractured into eccentric fragments, flat lawns roiled into oceanic waveforms, and computer-controlled, interactive fountains meant to inject whimsy and motion into spaces that struggle in vain to hide their commercial or bureaucratic purpose. It is the ancient ambivalence between nature and culture, amplified by a more contemporary problem: the sprawling, centerless, multinodal rural/suburban/urban agglomerations where most Americans now live, built to the measure of the automobile and the detached, single-family house, have obliterated the old relationship between private and public space and blurred the old distinction between city and country beyond recognition. The traditional place of the garden, the park, and the public square in bridging these divides no longer obtains when the vast majority live in nontraditional neighborhoods and developments, linked to one another and to any urban center only by roads. It has become far harder to define what commonalities we share, in terms of needs, identity, and community, much less to address them through the design of outdoor space, when the spaces we are left with are so utterly ambivalent and insufficient. Should a plaza in front of a bank headquarters look like Prospect Park? Especially if its location lacks a traditional park space? If not, why not? And if not, what should it look like? For better or worse, this is the sort of quandary that the designers of gardens and landscapes have had to wrestle with since the car took over the American landscape in the second half of the 20th century.

AT THE END of World War II, in most of the United States (outside of some California yards), the modernism that had by then reshaped the fine arts and architecture was nowhere to be seen in the landscape. But a shift was under way—at first only in a few ateliers and schools, where designers were rethinking and renegotiating their field's relationship to modernism and to new ideas about art and society, and to a social and physical landscape remade by the dislocations of the war. Just as in earlier eras, landscape makers interrogated their stock of models: traditional Beaux-Arts historicism, eclectic historicism such as that of the Arts & Crafts movement, "traditional" European modernism, and Eastern traditions such as China and Japan, borrowing some pieces here, rejecting others there, to fashion a new practice of making outdoor spaces. In many cases they didn't see themselves as making "gardens" but rather something different, larger, over and above the garden with its agrarian and domestic roots and associations. The concept of the garden itself became an uneasy one within the profession, which revived its old quest to try to leave the word behind and replace it with other language—*landscape*, *landscape architecture*, or *place-making*—hoping that the change of words could change the nature of the profession and its standing in the world. But to leave the "garden" behind, they first had to redefine their relationship to nature itself, to expand it in some way, to create room for their escape from the garden that, in some perverse sense, many in the field felt imprisoned it. Different designers found different stylistic means to this end, but across the board, expressing a new relationship to nature emerged as the primary preoccupation of garden/landscape makers. In so doing, they were searching for some kind of order, explicit or implicit, that might redeem the disorder of a society nearly destroyed by war and still under threat of ultimate annihilation, and heal the wounds inflicted on the earth itself. The earth itself came to play a central role—more than in any other era, landscape makers looked to the ground as a surface and material to mold and shape, and very often to literally cut into as a core part of their practice—or, as they preferred, their "art."

Three pioneer garden makers of the postwar era played crucial roles in the fruition of a new kind of landscape in the postwar decades. Two were perhaps the most important, and were certainly the most prolific American landscape architects of the 20th century, both trained initially in the Beaux-Arts canon before becoming enraptured with the emerging modernist one. One worked to reintegrate classicism and traditional architectonic order into modernism, coming to dominate and define the profession on the East Coast; the other pioneered a new, process-based, nature-patterned set of forms that epitomized the countercultural critiques and values of the West Coast. The third was a sculptor, drawn irresistibly to natural, geological forms and to gardens, beginning his career designing outside with children's playgrounds and returning to them again and again. He was by biology, circumstance, and temperament suspended between two countries and their cultures, and his career brought them together in a new synthesis between Asian and Western traditions. Among the three of them were invented most of the attitudes, ideas, and moves out of which our new common landscape was constructed, and which continue to define landscape architecture today.

WHEN DANIEL URBAN Kiley was a boy growing up in Roxbury Highlands, Boston, in the 1910s and '20s, he liked to wander through the neighborhood's matrix of connected alleys and yards: "each leading to another and another," he recalled, helping to shape his "later understanding of structural interplay and spatial relationships." He retained vivid memories: of a neighborhood lawn that was like a "single green carpet, set within the urban encasement," and of his mother scrubbing their white floor, polishing the house's brass pipes, and carefully ordering the kitchen utensils. In high school he worked as a golf caddy, which piqued his interest in golf course design and plants.[1] During the Depression years, he was lucky to land an unpaid apprenticeship with Warren Manning, Frederick

Law Olmsted's onetime assistant who had a prominent office in Boston. He was quickly promoted and spent five years in Manning's office before enrolling, in 1936, in Harvard's Graduate School of Design as a landscape architecture student (this in spite of his mentor's advice that nothing useful was to be learned there). Among his classmates were Garrett Eckbo and James Rose, who shared his dislike for the "dry" and "stiff" Beaux-Arts–inspired curriculum.

The young men were tuned to more current developments, notably the German architect Ludwig Mies van der Rohe's German Pavilion at the 1929 Universal Exposition in Barcelona (usually called the Barcelona Pavilion, the house having usurped the entire posterior significance of the event), with its bold expression of simplified, industrially derived structure in steel frames and plate glass, elegant marble and travertine details, and free flow between interior and exterior spaces. But their attempts to introduce new spatial concepts and new materials into their student landscape projects "were soundly rejected by both the landscape and architecture departments," Kiley recalled, in spite of the fact that the latter was led by former Bauhaus head Walter Gropius, an avowed modernist. The three together wrote a series of articles in *Architectural Record* loftily dividing the earth into three design problems: the urban, rural, and primeval environments.[2] Kiley soaked up other influences: for a time it was Chinese gardens—he briefly signed his name "Ki-lee"—followed by an interest in Japanese houses. In 1938 he went to Washington, D.C., to work in the government's New Deal public housing authority, where he tried in vain to inject modernist "touches" into the agency's no-frills low-income housing projects. In Washington he met the architect Louis Kahn, with whom he felt he "shared the search for magic, the latent poetry within a site or building that seeks simple, elegant expression." After leaving his government job he designed a modernist garden for a couple in Collier, Virginia, then worked as an architect designing houses in New Hampshire, where he and his wife, Anne, settled to be near the skiing. Kiley got the chance to work with Kahn in the early 1940s on several housing projects, where he contributed landscapes featuring biomorphic modernist forms. With the United States at war, Kiley returned to government service, securing a job in the Office of Strategic Services (OSS) with help from a recommendation by another architect he had met in Washington, Eero Saarinen (son of Eliel Saarinen, the celebrated Finnish architect of, most notably, the Cranbrook Academy of Art in Bloomfield Hills, Michigan). In 1945 the OSS sent Kiley to Germany with the task of rebuilding the destroyed Palace of Justice in the German town of Nuremberg and specifically designing a courtroom there for the upcoming war crimes trials.[3]

While in Europe, Kiley had a life-changing epiphany: traveling by train through the countryside, he marveled at the sense of order and natural fit that the hedges, fields, and tree-lined lanes provided; he visited Le Nôtre's Parc de Sceaux and Versailles. Years later, he would write: "THIS is what I had been searching for—a language with which to vocalize the dynamic hand of human order on the land—a way to reveal nature's power and create spaces of structural integrity. I suddenly saw that lines, *allées* and orchards/bosques of trees, *tapis verts* and clipped hedges, canals, pools and fountains could be tools to build landscapes of clarity and infinity, just like a walk in the woods." The latter comment might seem odd, since it is a rare woods that sprouts clipped hedges and formal allées, yet Kiley likened the ordered landscape to nature because both display an alternation of a number of elements: dark and light, trees and grassy areas, water and earth. What he saw in Europe, he wrote, "forever displaced arbitrary formulas from my mind," and he resolved to find ways to adapt the straight lines of neoclassical design principles to modern buildings. He saw no contradiction in "using classic elements in modern compositions, for this is not about style of decoration but about articulation of space. The thing that is modern is space. You can't touch it; it is elusive but felt. I realized that the goal was to produce the art of necessity, to avoid caprice and ambiguity."[4]

Kiley's vocabulary was coded, and loaded: *caprice, ambiguity,* and *arbitrary* meant the curvilinear and irregular forms of the modernist idiom as practiced by his peers, especially Eckbo; while *clarity, infinity,* and *necessity* connoted the forms of the neoclassical, which he would welcome back to modern landscape architecture under the guise of a new concept of "space." Dan Kiley was not alone in reembracing classical design principles; he was falling into line with his architect friends Kahn and Saarinen, who, along with Philip Johnson, were following Mies van der Rohe's "functionalist" bent of purist modernism. Functionalism was stripped of all ornament, and studiously left structural members exposed, using regularly spaced columns and steel frames to define repeating modules of wall, window, and openings. Having emigrated from Nazi Germany in 1937, Mies' classicist style soon came to dominate modernist architecture in the United States under the pseudonym the International Style. His designs for the campus of the Illinois Institute of Technology in Chicago set the tone: white-columned, classically ordered buildings, like Greek temples built of concrete, steel, and glass, arranged in rectilinear compositions that approached complete symmetry. (As a demonstration of how little modernism had penetrated landscape design at that time, the grounds for the ultramodern IIT campus were done in a naturalistic style by Alfred Caldwell, a disciple of Jens Jensen.)

Though he would later describe his experiences in Europe as decisive, it took some time for the roots of Kiley's mature style to develop into the full tree of his celebrated oeuvre. In 1946, Saarinen invited him to collaborate on a design for the proposed Jefferson National Expansion Memorial arch in St. Louis (the arch was not built until the 1960s, without Kiley's original landscape). His work in the late 1940s and early '50s revealed a slow incorporation of neoclassical elements. Saarinen recommended Kiley to work on his Osborn house, a Mies-inspired residence in Connecticut, completed in 1954. There Kiley employed an updated classical vocabulary: an allée marking the entrance drive, a maple bosque laid out on a grid, and rectilinear hedges around a gravel parking court. But Kiley's real breakthrough came when Saarinen offered another collaboration, beginning in 1953, to design the gardens for a house he and his associate Kevin Roche were building for industrial magnate Irwin Miller, in Columbus, Indiana. Saarinen called Kiley and said, "Dan, this project is for you."

It was a big parcel of level land situated along the floodplain of the Flatrock River, with little in the way of existing vegetation or conditions to consider. Kiley, then in his early forties, remembered that "this project was the first opportunity I had to fully explore ideas that had been percolating for more than a decade."[5] The house, elevated on a plinth to overlook the site, was a composition of four rectilinear volumes, or "blocks," each with a different function: master suite, children's suite, kitchen, and guest suite and garage, all arranged around a central, sunken living room. It was "quite simple and grand," judged Kiley, with his characteristically blithe yoking of opposites. First, he asked the architects to extend the plinth out twenty-five feet from the house footprint, creating a series of formal terraces off each block, then extended that block into the landscape below, using rows of trees, staggered panels of clipped arbor vitae hedge, expanses of grass, a grove of redbuds, apple orchards, and shallow pools. The drive was lined with chestnuts with clipped hedges at their bases, and an allée of honey locusts in gravel formed a long walk from a pool at one end to a sculpture at the other. The garden is a masterpiece of de Stijlesque composition: grids of trees overlap panels of grass, paving, or gravel; flat planes alternate with vertical slabs of green; solids balance against voids. Space, Kiley's modern "thing," is allowed to breathe deeply here, to full advantage. A large Henry Moore sculpture on a concrete plaza (added later, in the 1960s)[6] adds to the effect of traversing a very roomy college campus or museum grounds. Except when looking directly at the house, away from the garden, it is hard to grasp that the Miller garden is in fact a residence. What it constituted, when it was completed in 1956, was a new American villeggiatura, a modern update of the 17th century landscaped country estate.

The magazine *Architectural Forum* published the Miller house in 1958, calling it "a contemporary Palladian villa." It paired a plan of the house with one of Palladio's Villa Rotonda. The white-columned façades are certainly cousins; yet the comparison only goes so far: Saarinen's building is not centered or symmetrical, but is a pinwheel of four distinct volumes that evokes a white version of the Schindler house and Neutra's open plan room/garden permeations. What was different that Kiley brought was not the asymmetrical modern geometries, but the bag of tricks from Le Nôtre: the regular, measured structuring of space with straight lines, grids, bosques, and flat panels, extending outward from the center to give the illusion of infinite space. It fit Saarinen's architecture perfectly and beautifully, bestowing upon the whole site a clarity and grandeur that lifts the low, one-story house into a kind of mid-century modernist palace. The parallel wasn't hard to spot; indeed, the architect's huge General Motors Technical Center project, with a similar landscape by Thomas Church, was dubbed by *Architectural Forum* in 1956 "GM's Industrial Versailles."[7] The Miller house completed, in an unexpected way, two circles: it was not until this moment of 1950s American high modernism that the Palladian villa was treated to its own French royal park.

Dan Kiley went on to have perhaps the most illustrious and prolific career of postwar American landscape architects; his nine hundred realized projects by the time of his death in 2004 (another four hundred or so left on the drawing board) defined a classic modern landscape style to complement the architectural dominance of Mies and his acolytes: these included Rockefeller University (1958) and Lincoln Center (1960) in New York, Dulles Airport outside Washington, D.C. (completed 1963), the National Gallery of Art, in D.C. (1977, 1989), and the U.S. Air Force Academy in Colorado Springs, Colorado (begun mid-1950s, completed 1968). (The Air Force Academy was notable for its strong Persian influence—which seems to have been in the air then: see architect Edward Durell Stone's 1954 U.S. embassy; both were perhaps inspired by Edwin Lutyens's revival of Mughal gardens in his planned city of New Delhi, India, done from 1911 to 1931.) In addition to these institutional commissions, Kiley designed a series of corporate bank plazas in the South that helped define the form of the American corporate landscape as a grid of trees on a concrete plaza with dramatic, expensive water fountains as the main entertainment value, lending a sense of motion, grandeur, and transport to "nature"—which resided elsewhere of course, but lent its imprimatur to the bank by virtue of Kiley's artistry.

In his writings and interviews, Kiley spoke about his design process as if he were an ecologist: "landscape architecture should be a walk in the woods; it should have that sense of mystery and perpetual growth," he wrote. "I try to tap into the essence of Nature: the process is evolution;

things are moving and growing in a related, organic way." He was fond of quoting Emerson in support of his own design theory: "Nature who abhors mannerisms has set her heart on breaking up all style and tricks," was one such aphorism. "Instead, one must go right to the heart and source," Kiley continued, somewhat mystically: "the interplay of forms and volumes that, when arranged dynamically, release a continuum that connects outwards." Reliably, he found his own, geometrically ordered vision in nature, rejecting any "naturalistic" view of it as composed of curves and clumps and mixtures. Of Capability Brown he railed: "That bastard single-handedly ruined more of the beautiful classic landscapes of England than anyone," because Brown had tried to copy nature, "and, once you copy anything, it's secondhand, ersatz, fake."[8] Kiley was nothing if not convinced of the justice of his own views, and forthright. He denounced Olmsted's parks as "a bad movement" because they were "Victorian."[9] Furthermore, they were unnaturally cluttered, with too many species: "Nature would have thousands of the same tree," Kiley insisted. "Nature is continuous, not scattered." A professional ecologist would likely quibble with such a dictum, but Kiley kept to his idiosyncratic view of nature. (Perhaps he was influenced by growing up in northeastern forests, most of which are second- or third-growth, often single stands of birch or pine, or plantations of nonnatives like Norway spruce.) A better model of nature for Kiley than the disorganized pseudo-nature of the picturesque was agriculture, which remakes nature into second nature, using the same, if radically simplified, kit of parts, reordered according to function: "our intervention is the most natural act of all," he asserted, "when we shape the land to live and eat and build communities, we are nature, too." He loved cultivated landscapes—"all farmland is beautiful"—and rhapsodized over golf courses: "Look what a golf course can do. It civilizes the landscape."[10]

Pushing further, Kiley talked of finding a manifestation of the spiritual in his designs: "I am always searching for the purest connection to that which holds us all together—we can call it spirit or mystery; it can be embodied by descriptions of the universe or of religion; it takes the form of sacred geometries and infinitesimal ecologies."[11] Kiley had as philosophical an intention in the design of gardens as Thomas Jefferson in his most rarefied flights of fancy. To him, geometric order is what frees the world from chaos, what "civilizes the landscape" and gives human experience, crystallized in the Thoreauvian walk in the woods, transcendent meaning (this is why he so often quoted his New England forebears, the Transcendentalists). It is no coincidence, perhaps, that he designed the Nuremberg courtroom where the horrors of war were to be put right again, so that Europe could return to its underlying rightness and logic—"the pervading order" that Kiley searched for. In his work and view of nature one might also be seeing the care, attention, and intent that his mother showed when she polished, scrubbed, and put things in their places.

JUST FOUR YEARS younger than Kiley, Lawrence Halprin had a very similar education as a landscape architect, yet he developed in a nearly opposite direction aesthetically and philosophically, and ended up on the opposite coast of the United States, simultaneously absorbing and helping to define its regional culture. Born in New York in 1916, he grew up in Brooklyn, the grandson of Russian Jewish immigrants.[12] Between high school and college he lived on an Israeli kibbutz for three years, from 1933 to 1935. He took a bachelor's degree in horticulture at Cornell in 1939, then a master's at Wisconsin in 1941. There he met and married Anna Schuman, a fellow student and dancer. After a visit to Frank Lloyd Wright's Taliesin in Spring Green, he read Christopher Tunnard's *Gardens in the Modern Landscape* (1938) and resolved to study architecture and landscape, which he did through a scholarship to Harvard in 1942–44, studying under Gropius, Marcel Breuer, and Tunnard. While a student in Cambridge, he met the San Francisco architect William Wurster; among his classmates were Philip Johnson and I. M. Pei. In 1943 he joined the navy and shipped off to the Pacific on a destroyer. The ship was sliced in two by a Japanese kamikaze pilot at the invasion of Okinawa, and Halprin was given survivor's leave in San Francisco. After his discharge in 1945, he stayed on in the Bay Area, landing a job in Thomas Church's office. He and Anna bought a small house in the shipyard workers' town of Mill Valley, and redid the house and garden, which was published in *Sunset* and became an icon in the emerging canon of the modernist garden. (While with Church, Halprin was also closely involved with the design of the Donnell garden, completed in 1948.) The next year Halprin opened his own practice, designing biomorphic gardens in the same vein as Church and Eckbo, with the full panoply of curves, circles, grids, pergolas, and wood and concrete decks. In 1952 he built a new house in the forest of Mount Tamalpais in Marin County, across the bay from San Francisco. It comprised a series of pavilions by Wurster, around which Halprin designed a landscape conceived as a progression, or choreography—an idea he borrowed from his wife's practice—of people moving down the hillside in a sequence of garden spaces that led to a redwood deck jutting out into the trees, a treehouse-like structure that the Halprins called the Dance Deck, made expressly for Anna's modern dance workshops.

In the later 1950s, Halprin moved on from residential gardens to larger projects, where his brief became the design of whole environments: a mall in Oak Brook, Illinois, the master plan for the new University of California campus at Davis in the Central Valley, five hospitals in Appalachia, low-income housing developments in the Bay Area, a medical plaza at Stanford University, Sproul Plaza and the Student Union at the University of California at Berkeley, and outdoor spaces at Hebrew University in Jerusalem among them. He brought an innovative eye to the planning of large, multiple-use places, conceiving them as communities or organisms: "Modernism is not just a matter of cubist space but of a whole appreciation of environmental design as a holistic approach to the matter of making places for people to live in," he wrote. He sought a balance between built and open space, often clustering structures at the edges to maximize pedestrian and green space, as he did at Greenwood Common in Berkeley (1958), a complex of twelve homes around a central green, and St. Francis Square in San Francisco (1960), which consisted of three hundred units around a central garden commons.[13] Halprin even converted malls into community-centered entities, as in the celebrated 1962–65 revamp of Ghirardelli Square on the San Francisco waterfront, in which Halprin and Wurster transformed an old chocolate factory into a series of small-scale spaces over a parking garage, yielding a village-like effect.

Halprin understood that conventional planning and design—that is to say, his own profession—had serious limitations, summarized in the conclusion of a study of Manhattan his office published in 1968, called *New York, New York:* "Designed environments which are thought out, formalized, and complete are usually 'lifeless' and unapproachable." The 1960s were a time when the virtues of unplanned, organically-developed cities were gaining new appreciation from thinkers such as Jane Jacobs, whose *The Death and Life of Great American Cities,* an impassioned defense of neighborhoods like New York's Greenwich Village against the urban renewal schemes of New York City's imperial parks commissioner Robert Moses, was published in 1961. Halprin did something radical for the era: in designing communities, he worked to embrace the dimension of time, along with the uncertainties that came with it, by folding it into the planning process—in the name of improving the "creative" quality of life of the inhabitants. While planning Mililani, a new town platted on seven thousand acres of old pineapple fields on the Hawaiian island of Oahu intended for an eventual population of sixty-five thousand people, he expounded upon his philosophy: "The essential problem in establishing a new community has been to find a kind of basic order to guide its growth, within which succeeding years and people can develop wide variegation and the sense of nonregimentation and unpredictability which creative life demands."[14] He sought to plan the unplanned.

Halprin's biggest challenge came in 1961, when he was given the task of preparing a master plan for Sea Ranch, a development proposed for five thousand acres of land along the Sonoma County coast, north of San Francisco. The site was and is spectacular: windblown, fog-shrouded meadows striated by cypress hedgerows, sloping off sheer cliffs plunging into the rocky Pacific below.[15] The development company wanted something unique to help it brand and market the project, and asked Halprin, the visionary landscape architect, to locate home sites, roads, and develop a set of protocols for the first 1,800 acres of its land. To Halprin, the job became a personal mission: he had camped with his family nearby on the North Coast and had for many years spent parts of his summers in the High Sierra. California's dramatic landscapes had "become an obsession to me," he wrote in his memoirs of the Sea Ranch design process. "They have formed the bases of my aesthetic. They are my spiritual home and the source of most of my philosophical investigations."[16] He saw his task as finding a way to develop the site while simultaneously preserving it. He set out to comprehend the site in a holistic way, by camping on it, exploring it, sketching it, and analyzing its features: the wind speed and direction, the topography of hedgerows, windbreaks left over from a century of sheep ranching, with cropped meadows between, the draws and high points, and the corrugated coastline of cliffs, rock outcrops, beaches, and headlands. He made sketches with quasi-mystical labels for the different parts of the landscape: this group of rocks a "place of power," this one a "place to make offerings," this one a "place for ceremonies." He hired a "cultural geographer/ecologist" to report on the area's natural resources and how first the Pomo Indians had lived there, and later American lumbermen and ranchers. He drew an amazing map of the history of the site that he dubbed an "ecoscore": beginning in the Jurassic period, graphically plotting the progress of natural and human evolution on the site over time, on two different tracks, drawn like two different lines of music, bass clef and treble, unfolding side by side in a broadening spiral, just like a nautilus shell cut in half.

To the historical and ecological optics, Halprin added a psychological one: "the idea of group creativity," which he felt must underpin any successful plan. Influenced by Gestalt psychology and Jungian archetypes, he set up a series of workshops, called "experiments in environment," to study "the relationships of environments to community processes."[17] What he was seeking was the integration of natural and built forms into a synthesis "that expressed both." Participants, including the principal architect selected for the project, Charles Moore, and his students, were asked to collaborate in building a "driftwood village" on the beach, or to write their "personal myths" and "environmental autobiography," or were led on walks while deprived of one of their senses at a time: for ex-

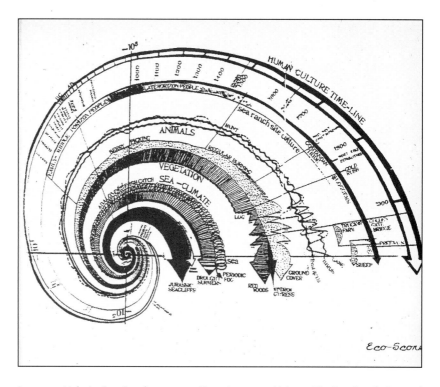

Lawrence Halprin, Sea Ranch ecoscore. (From Lawrence Halprin, *The Sea Ranch: Diary of an Idea*)

ample, hiking through the grass blindfolded in order to gain insight into how best to inhabit the land. Such intimate explorations of process became central to the way Halprin's office worked over the years, spawning a book, *RSVP Cycles*, in 1969, a classic of the genre, and a series of "Take Part" processes that was adopted by others and applied to many, unrelated issues in the Bay Area. Halprin's modus operandi was influenced by many avant-garde touchstones of the era—Anna's dance, his experiences planting trees on an Israeli kibbutz, the music of John Cage, and Jungian psychology—and was of a piece with the wide-ranging questioning of norms going on in the 1960s and '70s, nowhere more so than in the Bay Area.[18] In the field of design, he was at the forefront of innovation.

At Sea Ranch, the result was subtle and elegant, both conceptually and aesthetically: Halprin did the master plan in the form of what he termed a "locational score," prescribing that houses be clustered together, back from the bluffs and among the hedgerows, in order to keep the views open, especially from Highway 1, which runs through the upper portion of the site, and to camouflage structures to keep the sense of alteration to a minimum. Buildings would be made of unpainted wood and be in keeping with the vernacular architecture of the North Coast, from the 18th century Russian outpost at Fort Ross on the Russian River to the barns and sheds of the ranch era. The first buildings, by the San Francisco firm Moore Lyndon Turnbull Whitaker, and by Joseph Esherick, won many awards and ushered in a nationally imitated style.[19] Fifty percent of the lands were reserved as "commons," not to be built upon; the remainder, while private property, was governed by a set of restrictions on planting and fencing so that it would retain the same character as the surrounding lands. Common facilities, such as trails, stables, and recreation centers with swimming pools, would be provided, and a system of governance by the homeowners, within the restraints of a list of "covenants, codes, and restrictions," was established to guide future development. Halprin drew up a set of "basic principles" under the opposed categories "Yes" and "No": non-elitist versus elitist, rural versus suburban quality, diversity versus uniformity, design control versus no design control, modest house size versus enormous houses, simplicity versus flamboyance.

Larry Halprin had fallen in love with his creation as if it were a person: "the whole place, rather than one building or house, had a memorable and unified personality," he remembered.[20] He also talked frankly of its "utopian vision." There was no shortage of Utopias in the 1960s: hippie communes, back-to-the-land agrarian colonies, religious retreats, like the Zen ashrams proliferating along the Pacific Coast, therapeutic and self-realization retreats, like the Esalen Institute in Big Sur, on another spectacular stretch of the California coast south of Monterey, and even architectural Utopias, like Arcosanti, an ecologically focused outgrowth of Taliesin West started in 1970 in the desert north of Phoenix, Arizona, by Paolo Soleri, a former student of Frank Lloyd Wright. Sea Ranch was a version, too: self-contained, in certain ways, and self-regulated, according to a philosophy of harmony between people and nature; but it wasn't patriarchal, like Taliesin was, nor communistic, nor religious, nor a reversion to a past Golden Age, like the Arts & Crafts colonies had been—though Sea Ranch had clear Arts & Crafts inspiration in its veneration of vernacular architecture and its genuflections to rural simplicity and community values.

But for all Halprin's efforts at fostering these, the development remained a development, an enclave of private property where city dwellers could retreat to contemplate nature, if only on the weekends. In part because he didn't provide for a dense center where businesses might thrive or for interconnected roads, Sea Ranch remains a collection of second homes, dependent on cars and supplies from outside. From the beginning, Halprin and his collaborators "realized that this place would not start with a truly functional [economic] base as do most communities." Nevertheless, they felt that with adequate planning Sea Ranch would still somehow resemble an organic community: "We did not intend to become a human monoculture where everyone would be similar in age, background, and income," he would confess later.[21] Over time there was more development on the remaining acreage and Halprin's original vision faltered as land prices shot up and houses became more "enormous," more suburban, less distinctive, and crowded closer to the cliffs, blocking out more of the views. And the residents came to resemble one another more and more closely, to become closer to Halprin's unwanted "human monoculture." For all the analysis they did, the landscape architect and his team didn't consider the socioeconomic ecology of the project, and so failed to foresee how the very success of places like Sea Ranch would push the California dream of a middle-class coastal Utopia out of reach of all but a wealthy (or, like Halprin himself, who built one of the earlier houses there, lucky) few, as the state's population pushed past 30 million in 2008 toward a projected 50 million people by mid-century.

Halprin went on to help reinvent the public spaces of several city centers, as part of the surge of urban renewal sparked by federal aid to cities to replace older, supposedly "slum" areas with up-to-date downtown business districts. Often, vibrant, if low-income, mixed-use neighborhoods

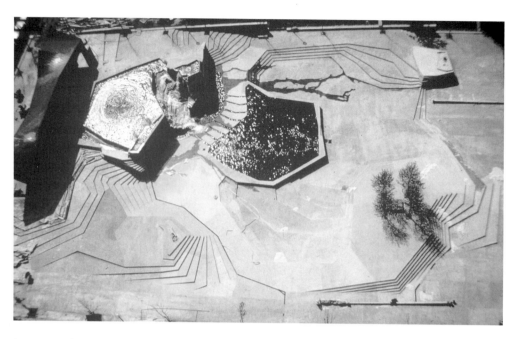

Lawrence Halprin, Lovejoy Fountain, Portland, Oregon. (Office of Lawrence Halprin)

were bulldozed to make way for sealed glass office towers and banks in the corporate International Style, surrounded by arid, lifeless plazas. Halprin committed some of this landscape architecture himself: for example, the Bank of America headquarters plaza in San Francisco in 1964, where he designed a skateboarders' heaven of an elevated, flat stone plaza joined to the street by a rank of steps dying into the grade. But his gift for making people-centered spaces was evident in a series of spectacular parks he built in the 1960s and '70s in the Pacific Northwest: the Lovejoy and Ira Keller fountain parks in downtown Portland, and Freeway Park in Seattle. In the middle of expanses of asphalt and concrete, or in the latter case, atop a huge concrete bridge over Interstate 5 in downtown Seattle, each park is a modernist distillation of the wild mountain landscapes Halprin loved: boisterous waterfalls cascade over ledges and cliffs and splash down canyons of shaped concrete; conifers and shrubs grow from concrete spires and mounts and shade pools of water that can be

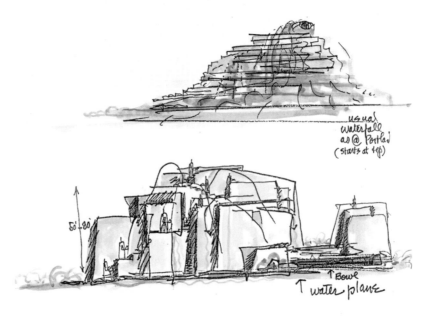

Lawrence Halprin, sketch of Ira Keller Fountain. (Halprin Landscape Conservancy)

crossed on stepping-stones or walked through, if one doesn't mind getting one's feet wet. In fact people climb all over Halprin's creations and wade in and out of the water features (surely to the horror of municipal liability attorneys). They are kinetic, sculptural spaces, but also symbolic ones: expressionistic, concrete versions of Japanese *horai* gardens, where an unusual stone is erected in a pond or sand to represent the mountain or group of islands where the immortals once lived, an earthly paradise. They are also comparable to the Chinese and Japanese way of making a small version in a garden of a mountain seen in the distance, such as Japan's Mount Fuji—in Portland it is Mount Baker, and in Seattle, Mount Rainier. And, like all of his best work, these parks have the quality of choreographing movement through them—of the flowing water and of the visitors enjoying what are in effect *events* as much as places. Halprin's art is theatrical in this sense; using new forms—quintessentially poured concrete—he revived the Renaissance garden of wonders, with its *giocchi d'acqua*, carefully sequenced passages through series of spaces, and public gathering space at the heart of the city.

Where Dan Kiley found "rightness" in extending mathematical order through space, as grids, corridors, planes, and sight lines, Halprin found it in extending experience through time, in the progression of spaces and the choreography of people, water, and communities. For him design was not the revelation or capture of a deep, permanent structure, but a continuing process—in some sense, process as an end in itself. Kiley's vision was not static: he shared with Halprin a notion of landscape as experience. And though in terms of their design vocabularies they seemed to be going in opposite directions—Kiley toward pure geometry and Halprin toward an abstracted naturalism—both talked about their work as attempts to solve the same problem: that of trying to be inspired by and to connect to nature. Where Kiley held to a kind of mysticism of deeper orders, Halprin held a belief in achieving sustainability through analysis of the site and how it is to be used; where Kiley venerated the grid, Halprin venerated what he called the "matrix of life."[22]

Each approach contributed to a distinctive American landscape architecture in the last third of the 20th century, especially urban parks and public spaces; much of the best work of the period was either theirs or was influenced by them. An enduringly successful and popular example is New York City's 1967 Paley Park, by landscape architects Zion &

Paley Park. (Courtesy of Milan Bozic)

Breen: a forty-by-one-hundred-foot "vest pocket" cut into the vertical streetscape of East Fifty-third Street in midtown Manhattan, consisting simply of a stone terrace shaded by honey locust trees, ivy-draped side walls, and a dramatic twenty-foot-high waterfall along the rear wall. Harried New Yorkers take two steps up from the sidewalk and enter a world apart: of greenery, splashing water loud enough to drown out the city sounds, and the particular freedom afforded by being able to relax in and move the park's wire tables and chairs. By combining a simple but strong distillation of nature and a slight physical remove from urban space, the park creates a remarkable psychological remove from the city. And the hot dogs aren't bad, either: the park's patron, the late William S. Paley, chief executive of the CBS radio and television network, personally chose the menu.

THE THIRD POLE of the synthesis of postwar American landscape architecture was himself a hybrid: split between two racial and cultural identities, two countries, and two artistic traditions, his career was a life's work of trying to resolve contradictions that he felt viscerally, by synthesizing the opposite poles of his experience into a new formal vocabulary for making art and gardens. Isamu Noguchi was born in Los Angeles in 1904, to Leonie Gilmour, a Bryn Mawr–educated writer whose mother was an Irish immigrant and whose American father had some Native American blood. Leonie had a brief relationship with Yonejiro Noguchi, a young Japanese poet who had come to the United States seeking to learn English. "Yone," as he was known, left her before the birth of a boy, who she named Isamu Gilmour. In 1906 Leonie decided to move with her son to Japan; there Yone, making a name for himself as an academic interpreter of America to the Japanese, would not have much to do with them. By 1910 she had moved to Chigasaki, where she supported herself and Isamu by teaching English. Yone Noguchi married a Japanese woman in 1913, making their estrangement complete. Four years later, when Isamu was thirteen, his mother sent him back to America to board at the Interlaken School in Rolling Prairie, Indiana. Isamu Noguchi wrote in his autobiography that he felt twice abandoned: first by his father, then by his mother.

Once he arrived in Indiana, his dislocation only got worse: the school was closed in the fall of 1918, when the United States entered World War I and turned it into an army training center. The boy was literally left there, alone, until the school's founder, Dr. Edward Rumely, heard of his plight and brought him to Rumely's hometown of La Porte, Indiana, where he settled the boy in the home of a local minister. Isamu attended three years of high school there. He had already fixed his sights on becoming a sculptor; Dr. Rumely secured him an apprenticeship with his friend Gutzon Borglum, who had carved Mount Rushmore, but Borglum told Isamu that he didn't possess the talent for sculpting. Encouraged by Dr. Rumely to become a physician, he enrolled in Columbia University in New York in 1923 as a premed student. Still, he wanted to be an artist. By this time his mother had moved to New York from Japan. She supported his desire, but Isamu turned away from her: "The more motherly she became, the more I resented her," he remembered.[23] He changed his surname to Noguchi—an act of rejection of his mother's identity and an appropriation of that of the father who had rejected him.

In New York, Isamu went to art school, learning academic figurative sculpture and visiting galleries. In 1926 he saw a show of sculptures by the Romanian modernist Constantin Brancusi and was "transfixed by his vision," in his words. Brancusi taught Noguchi his first lessons in minimalism: "Brancusi, like the Japanese, would take the quintessence of nature and distill it," he wrote, scrupulously keeping his work "undecorated like a Japanese house."[24] It was just one of many powerful moments of cross-cultural inspiration for him. He applied for and won a Guggenheim fellowship to study in Paris, and there, in 1927, he met Brancusi and became his apprentice for two years, though he shared no common language with the artist. Returning to New York, he supported himself by selling sculptural head portraits of friends and emerging artistic and intellectual figures he met, including the choreographer and dancer Martha Graham and the theorist Buckminster Fuller.

In 1930, he set out on a trip to Japan, in spite of the fact that he was warned in a letter from his father not to come there using his name. En route he sojourned in China for some months learning traditional calligraphy. When he at last arrived in Japan, he was met by his uncle, a Buddhist priest, and a friendly reception. He spent time studying ancient Japanese art and Zen gardens and working for five months with a traditional potter, honing the skills in clay modeling he had learned in art school and from Brancusi. Noguchi was back in New York again by 1933, where he resumed his sculpture practice and collaborated with Graham on set designs for her avant-garde dance pieces; from 1934 to 1966 he would work on twenty productions with her. In the 1930s he executed gigantic bas-reliefs in a muscular socialist style at New York's Rockefeller Center and at a Mexico City marketplace, inspired by the example of Mexican muralist Diego Rivera. He had his successes but suffered some critical snubs, including some reviews touched by an ugly racism.

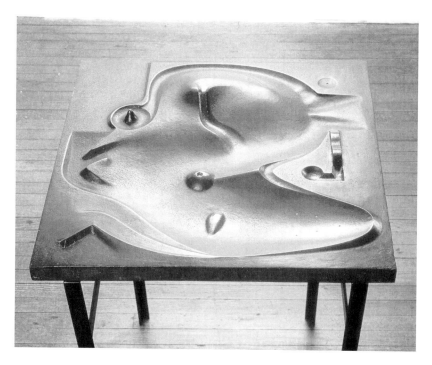

Isamu Noguchi, contoured playground. (Isamu Noguchi Foundation)

Early on, Noguchi began conceiving designs for playgrounds and earthworks, the first being 1933's *Play Mountain*, which had playful, modernist versions of swing sets and monkey bars set on an undulating and seamed ground plane. It was, he wrote later, the "kernel out of which have grown all my other ideas relating sculpture to the earth."[25] It was to prove an enduring interest. In 1940 he was commissioned by the Honolulu parks board to design playground equipment for the new Ala Moana Park, at the east end of Waikiki, but his advocate on the commission died before the work could be funded. Instead he presented the proposal to the New York City parks department, under commissioner Robert Moses, which rejected it as too dangerous because of the unorthodox whimsical and geometric shapes. The next year he revised the proposal, ostensibly to make it safer, replacing the aboveground play equipment with more variation in the ground plane—an impressive topography of long, sinuous contours, and upraised lines and berms with lips and swirls and depressions, a modern vocabulary of forms taken from surrealism and Cubism yet at the same time evoking the prehistoric earthworks, like the Great Serpent Mound, a huge Native American structure in Ohio, which captivated the artist.

With the outbreak of World War II, Noguchi watched as 112,000 Japanese-Americans on the West Coast were sent to internment camps. As a New York resident he was not required to be interned, but he felt himself affected: "With a flash I realized I was no longer a sculptor alone. I was not just American but Nisei. A Japanese-American. . . . I felt I must do something." He traveled to Washington, D.C., to try to offer his services to help ameliorate conditions in the camps. As a result of conversations there, he decided to voluntarily intern himself at the camp in Poston, Arizona, in 1942; there, for six months, he planned recreation facilities, parks, and cemeteries. Nothing he designed was built, and he became discouraged and decided to leave. It took months to get government permission, and the experience left him bitter: "I resolved henceforth to be an artist only."[26]

The war also changed his work. In 1943 he produced *This Tortured Earth,* ostensibly about the horrors of conflict. The sculpture was a square tablet of clay, shaped with oblique cuts and openings, which look on one hand geological, like berms or earth contours, or prehistoric mounds, and on the other hand supremely sensual—like nothing so much as orifices, lips, and ears, as expressive as the human body. In 1947 he made *Sculpture to be Seen from Mars:* a gigantic human face, meant to be incised into and built up out of the earth, with cones for eyes, an oval mound for a forehead, a long, raised triangle a mile long for a nose, and an oval for a mouth, its expression a combination of alarm and despair, with a hint of supplication. It may have been a response to the nightmare of nuclear war, and certainly was informed by the suicide the same year of his friend, the painter Arshile Gorky. Each of these works was designed to be contemplated from a distance, like dioramas or tableaux, or the stage sets he designed for Martha Graham. In them one can see a clear template for the future of both landscape architecture and its odd sibling in sculpture, the phenomenon that came to be called Land Art.

Noguchi remained possessed by playgrounds. In 1951 he designed one for the United Nations building in New York, but it was rejected by Robert Moses, despite support from the UN and influential neighbors. The Museum of Modern Art exhibited a project model to try to sway the commissioner, to no avail. In spite of his repeated rejections, Noguchi kept at it: none of his "playscapes" were realized until 1965, near Tokyo, and no American examples until 1976, in Atlanta.[27] The latter was commissioned to celebrate Japan's Children's Year; it was meant to last just one year, so Noguchi conceived it to express, in his words, the "inherently ephemeral nature of happiness." He found some consolation in a world trip in 1951, funded by a grant to study "leisure environments and ritual around the world." He visited prehistoric sites, dolmens, and caves in Great Britain and France, Gaudí's Barcelona, art and gardens in Italy, the Parthenon in Greece, the 18th century Samrat Yantra observatory in India, and many Kyoto gardens, from the 15th to the 17th centuries: Zen-inspired compositions of gravel, stone, grass, moss, and trees that in many ways prefigured the modernist precepts of simplicity of form and forthright expression of materials. In Japan in 1951, he received his first landscape architecture commissions: a garden for the Reader's Digest company's Japanese headquarters, which consisted of a large grassy space shaped by mounds and contours and meandering pools, and studded with stones and contorted pine trees; stark, white bridge railings for the Hiroshima Peace Park; and a memorial garden to his then deceased father at Keio University, where he had taught.

In 1952, the same year his Japanese gardens were completed, Noguchi was invited to design a courtyard garden for the Lever Brothers corporate headquarters on Park Avenue in Manhattan by the building's principal architect, Gordon Bunshaft, of the firm Skidmore, Owings & Merrill (SOM). He proposed a "marble stage": a platform with a reflecting pool, freestanding columnar sculptures, and planted beds. Though it wasn't built, it marked the first in a long series of collaborations with Bunshaft. The next was a turning point in his career as a designer of outdoor spaces:

the Connecticut General Life Insurance Company in Bloomfield Hills, Connecticut, done from 1956 to 1957, which featured a group of four interior courtyards that Noguchi filled with curvilinear, Arpesque shapes made of mounded gravel, grass, low masses of shrubs, and reflecting pools, punctuated with stepping-stones, scattered carved stones, and a tree or two—elements that added a Japanese inflection to the modernist ground planes. The compositions were simultaneously stark and sensual; part of their appeal came from the contrast between their rounded, organic forms and the rectilinear metal, glass, and marble façades of Bunshaft's International Style building.

If Church's Donnell garden defined the modernist residential landscape, Noguchi's courtyards established the paradigm for mid-century corporate and campus modernism. Noguchi achieved the benchmark of the idiom with his garden for the UNESCO headquarters complex in Paris, France, commissioned in 1956. There he designed two gardens, bridging the Secretariat building and Building 3. The first was the Patio des Délégués (Delegates' Terrace), a white stone terrace peppered with black concrete seating in the shapes of squares, inverted cones, and leaning rectangles, inspired by his mentor Brancusi, who died during the project's construction. At its center was a tall, carved, granite "source" stone, incised with Noguchi's calligraphic take on the Japanese character *heiwa* (peace), down which water flows into a pool, before running through a channel into a series of stepped pools that flow alongside the concrete entry bridge to the much larger, sunken Jardin Japonais. Noguchi called the bridge *hanamichi*: bridge of flowers or "flower path," which brought visitors into the sunken garden beneath a canopy of arching deciduous trees, a concept he borrowed from Kabuki theater.

In plan, the Delegates' Terrace garden is like a single, complex version of the Connecticut General Life courtyards: curving reflecting pools crossed with stepping-stones, interlocking with biomorphic sweeps of white gravel, raised cobblestone-paved mounds, and panels of grass planted with trees, shrubs, and protruding stones, some carved, some natural. Noguchi brought eighty tons of stone, hundreds of trees and plants, and three gardeners from Japan. The garden included traditional elements: *tobi-ishi* (stepping-stones), *horai* (the symbolic sacred mountain), *chozubachi* (water basins), and *kare sansui* (dry gardens, gravel, stones).[28] Based on the Japanese principle of the "stroll" garden, paths meander through planted banks and over stone bridges, revealing carefully framed views of water and trees, conifers alternating with deciduous broadleafs, green plants alternating with stone, open space with closed. But it was not intended to be a traditional Japanese garden. Noguchi recalled that it was a mixed thing: "I felt obligated to do a somewhat Japanese garden, a kind of homage to Japan. So it's a Japanese garden and yet it is not a Japanese garden."[29] It didn't make everyone who visited it happy: many European critics thought it was too Japanese, and many Japanese thought it too modern, with its homages to Parisian surrealism. Like all the artist's gardens, it has first and foremost a sculptural, three-dimensional quality of shaped space. But he planted UNESCO more heavily than any of his other works, and over the years the greenery has softened it and obscured the audacity of his forms, making it feel more like a traditional "garden," whether Japanese or Euro-American, than anything else he realized.

In the early 1960s, Noguchi designed several more gardens for Bunshaft's buildings, all in a similar courtyard form; the two most significant were sunken, meant to be looked on from above. For the Beinecke Rare Book and Manuscript Library at Yale University, created from 1960 to 1964, Noguchi's canvas was a space sunken below the plaza where no water was allowed (so as not to damage the books below). He designed a white marble platform incised with concentric curved lines and featuring three marble shapes: a pyramid, a ring, and a cube balanced on one point—meant to symbolize respectively the sun/energy, the past/earth, and the tenuous balance of the human condition/chance. For the Chase Manhattan Bank building in New York, begun in 1961 and completed in 1964, he designed a circular, sunken garden composed of seven stones on an undulating surface of granite cobble paving; the basin was to be dry in winter and wet in summer. It is remarkably Kyoto-like, like a curious transposition from another world in its setting in front of a steel-and-glass Manhattan skyscraper. Noguchi called it "my Ryoanji."

It is an irony that many of the ideas Noguchi developed in the 1930s, especially those for children's playgrounds, were realized only in the 1960s with Bunshaft and the big corporate budgets he commanded; instead of bringing children into contact with the earth, as Noguchi had originally intended with his playgrounds, these were contemplation gardens for corporate executives. Nevertheless, his achievement remains: in the face of such aggressive buildings—monuments to the modernist drive to elide cultural difference, place, context, and tradition, and even history itself—Noguchi delved into multiple cultures and places, from 15th century Japan to 20th century Paris and New York, to make something very personal yet with a universal appeal, something very contemporary yet rooted in history. Like Kiley and Halprin, Noguchi was responding at some level to the damage and dislocation of war and attempting to find a new vocabulary for a new world. But for Noguchi the answer would be drawn from not one tradition, but many: "I work everywhere. I feel myself equally settled wherever I am . . . since I have not got a home," he wrote.[30]

Each designer fashioned a different kind of space, characteristic of their vision and their practice. Kiley's was the surveyor's space: long, measured, meted by an essential rhythm of grid and sequence. Halprin's was the explorer's space: a journey to an unknown end, undertaken as a passage through space, in time. Noguchi's was the sculptor's space: shaped by hand into echoes of the earth and the human body, sitting in front of the viewer, distinctly centered, and almost always bounded and framed—either a courtyard, a walled area, or a completely surrounded, sunken "bowl." Noguchi's spaces are akin to Japanese *bonseki*, miniature rock gardens made on trays.[31] Over the decades, he designed a series of what he termed "landscape tables": flat stone surfaces cut into, leaving contrasting areas of worked and unworked rock. Their evocation of gardens is clear: "If my tables now suggest landscape, you must be aware that every garden is a landscape, and every garden can be considered a table, too, especially Zen gardens," Noguchi explained.[32] This notion of the table is what ties his work—seemingly so disparate, rendered in so many media—to gardens, together with his interests in myth, play, and performance: all are participatory. "There are all sorts of correlations between tables, gardens, plazas, and rituals," he wrote.

And, as with his colleagues Kiley and Halprin, the ultimate question that he struggled to come to terms with in his art was his relationship to nature. His abstractions were intended as evocations of nature, poetic echoes, synecdoches. He tried "to see nature through nature's eyes."[33] In some sense his artistic quest was like his quest for a stable identity— ultimately unachievable: "In our times we think to control nature, only to find that in the end it escapes us," he wrote. "I for one return recurrently to the earth in my search for the meaning of sculpture—to escape fragmentation with a new synthesis."[34] Still, the fragmentation of the modern, postwar condition was never fully healed or brought to unity. Noguchi understood this deep, existential irresolution in his bones, so to speak, because he embodied it. And he understood that, for the present, the problem of making gardens in the modern world could not yet be resolved. Yet he held out hope for the future:

Nature and non-nature. There will come other gardens to correspond to our changing concepts of reality: disturbing and unbeautiful gardens to awaken us to a new awareness of our solitude. Can it be that nature is no longer real for us or, in any case, out of scale?[35]

Noguchi's vision, and his question, would prove to be prescient for the profession of landscape design.

On Saturday, September 30, 1967, a gangly twenty-nine-year-old man with a gaunt, acne-pocked face and an intense stare boarded a bus at the Port Authority terminal in New York City, armed with a notebook, an Instamatic camera, and a copy of that day's *New York Times*. As the bus traveled through the Lincoln Tunnel then up and over the dark rock ridge of Weehawken and down into Secaucus, New Jersey, in the Meadowlands, he perused the newspaper, and noticed a reproduction of a painting titled *Allegorical Landscape*, by Samuel F. B. Morse. (Best known as the inventor of the telegraph, which he conceived after his wife died while he was away from home in New Haven on business in Washington, D.C., and hadn't received the news in time to return home for her burial, Morse was one of the finest portrait painters in early-nineteenth-century America.)[36] The painting depicted, in high Romantic style, a river curving through a lush landscape dotted with "Gothic" buildings, in the young man's estimation, and "an unnecessary tree" in the foreground; in the canvas, "the sky was a subtle newsprint grey, and the clouds resembled stains of sweat," he remembered. He rode on through the town of Rutherford, where he had grown up, and into the town of Passaic, where he had been born in 1938. There he got out and walked, taking notes and snapshots of things he saw: a steel-girder bridge with wooden sidewalks, a dredge derrick in the river, a parking lot, rusting pipes, a children's sandbox. There were no people in the photos.

The recording traveler was the young artist Robert Smithson, and what he was doing marked a sea change in the way Americans looked at their generic, quotidian landscape. The pictures and notes he made that September Saturday were published as a mock travelogue in the December 1967 issue of *Artforum* magazine as "The Monuments of Passaic"; the "monuments" were the mundane objects that had caught his eye: the pipes in the river became the "fountain-monument," the sandbox became "the sand-box monument" or "model desert." His descriptions were blank, deadpan, ironic, yet earnest; hilarious, occasionally ribald, as when he imagined a large dredge pipe as "a monstrous sexual organ" having an orgasm as it pumped polluted water and sand into the river. Smithson had been living in New York, working, exhibiting, and hanging around the fringes of the Manhattan art scene. He was self-taught, with a shaky drawing style, but cerebral and intense, with a gift for words. His early artwork consisted of expressionist paintings, then evolved in the early 1960s into figurative drawings of religious imagery, bodies of saints and Jesus, often rendered in red and black lines, hatched and spiraling like some form of aboriginal art. Then he became interested in the minimalist work just appearing in the galleries, such as Donald Judd's pink Plexiglas boxes, one of which Smithson thought resembled "a giant crystal from another

Robert Smithson, "The Monuments of Passaic." (Estate of Robert Smithson/Vaga, New York, NY)

planet." He was inspired by English author J. G. Ballard's 1966 novel *The Crystal World,* with its obsessive focus on the stricken, surreal landscape of an African forest slowly being crystallized by some incomprehensible process. These arresting new influences somehow stoked an interest in the landscape of Smithson's childhood in northern New Jersey. He had a feel for landscape. As a boy he had been encouraged by his parents to plan their summertime road trips, poring over maps and drafting itineraries. He had loved the dioramas at the American Museum of Natural History in New York City.

Smithson's childhood pediatrician had been William Carlos Williams, whose five-book prose poem *Paterson* he admired—it is a rending look at the town of that name, a few miles from Passaic proper, set up by treasury secretary Alexander Hamilton in 1791 under the aegis of his Society for the Establishment of Useful Manufactures, to free the nascent United States from British economic dominance by jump-starting American industry. Located at the Great Falls of the Passaic River, Paterson had seen three waves of industrialization: initially cotton, then steel, then silk. Its rise was meteoric, a driver of America's economic ascendancy in the 19th century. Then, gradually, it faltered as the industrial fortunes of the region did; then postindustrial abandonment, decay, poverty, and malaise set in.

Smithson began traveling back to New Jersey in 1966, sometimes with friends or other artists, sometimes alone. That year he wrote an essay titled "The Crystal Land," echoing Ballard, and in which he explored the idea of landscape as a cultural construct, especially of the decay and randomness of the abandoned industrial towns of his home state. He described a quarry whose sides were "cracked, broken, shattered; the walls threatened to come crashing down. Fragmentation, corrosion, decomposition, disintegration, rock creep, debris slides, mud flow, avalanche were everywhere in evidence."[37] He described the suburban landscape with the same imagery: "The highways criss-cross through the towns and become man-made geological networks of concrete. In fact, the entire landscape has a mineral presence. From the shiny chrome diners to glass windows of shopping centers, a sense of the crystalline prevails." He was searching for a new framework, a new raison d'être, for his artistic practice, and in the rudderless disarray of the "entropic" postwar, postindustrial landscape, he believed he'd found it. "A bleached and fractured world surrounds the artist," he wrote. "To organize this mess of corrosion into patterns, grids, and subdivisions is an aesthetic process that has scarcely been touched."[38]

The problem of decline consumed him. In his "Monuments of Passaic" essay, he had described a hypothetical experiment in the sandbox: half the box was filled with white sand, half with black sand; a kid running in a circle hundreds of times would mix the two together completely, but having him then run the other way could never unscramble them. In a 1968 essay, "A Sedimentation of the Mind," he wrote, "The abysmal problem of gardens somehow involves a fall from somewhere or something. The certainty of the absolute garden will never be regained."[39] For Smithson, there was no finding the Garden of Eden, because we had already fallen out of it. In New Jersey, the Garden State, which for generations embodied the promise of sylvan suburban refuge from the squalor and tumult of New York City, Eden spoiled was not a metaphor but rather a daily reality of a drab and gutted landscape. (Passaic, which he called "a Utopia minus a bottom, a place where the machines are idle, and the sun has turned to glass," is not far from Llewellyn Park, Alexander Jackson Davis's Arcadian suburban paradise.) American culture at this time was still frantically building new escapes, new Edens: golf course resorts, and irrigated suburban developments in the booming Sunbelt states but leaving behind the mess that Smithson saw all around him, as he made clear in this description of the Meadowlands: "A good location for a movie about life on Mars. It even has a network of canals that are choked by acres of tall reeds. Radio towers are scattered throughout this bleak place. Drive-ins, motels, and gas stations exist along the highway, and behind them are smoldering garbage dumps. South, toward Newark and Bayonne, the smoke stacks of heavy industry add to the general air pollution."

What to do then, as an artist? One couldn't go back to the Garden of Eden because it was a false ideology in any case: promising "a leftover Arcadia," "memory traces of tranquil gardens as 'ideal nature'—jejune Edens." But these "garden-traces" in the American mind were just a smoke screen obscuring the reality of a nearly lifeless landscape. The essay, and his work, had a sharp anti-Arcadian bent that edged into hostility: "Could one say that art degenerates as it approaches gardening?" He proposed a division, mockingly like that currently fashionable among some critics to describe minimalism, using "hot" and "cool," of art into "wet" and "dry." "The wet mind enjoys 'pools and stains' of paint," he wrote, dripping an only slightly satirical scorn: "The artist or critic with a dank brain is bound to end up appreciating anything that suggests saturation, a kind of watery effect, an overall seepage, discharges that submerge perceptions. . . ." Dry art, on the other hand, was made in the desert, "less 'nature' than a concept, a place that swallows up boundaries. When the artist goes to the desert he enriches his absence and burns off the water (paint) from his brain. The slush of the city evaporates. . . ."

One can only wonder at the psychoanalytic significance of Smithson's profound mistrust of wetness and gardens. But for American art, his formulation had wings, helping move the forefront of avant-garde practice into the landscape and fashioning a new vocabulary of forms that would irrevocably alter both art and landscape architecture. He began exhibiting Donald Judd–like faceted and stepped boxes in galleries. Beginning in 1968, he showed a series of "Nonsites" in which he collected dirt or rock from some site—usually an abandoned quarry, like those he and Judd and their wives explored together in northern New Jersey—in bins, or piled on the gallery floor. In spite of his dismissal of the possibility of regaining Eden, he was nevertheless attempting to regain some "certainty." He was trying to bring those landscapes, which were at once his former home and an irreducibly alien place to him, into the gallery and into his art, to make them realign into a comprehensible narrative of the world, to make sense again.

Smithson was not alone; he was part of a broad reassessment of the American landscape. In large part the movement was driven by a growing "environmentalist" response to the damage inflicted by centuries of unrestrained exploitation and the constant, thoughtless flight westward to the next paradise, the next frontier, after the last one was ruined. Where Jane Jacobs's *The Death and Life of Great American Cities* had been the rallying cry for preserving cities, the scientist Rachel Carson's *Silent Spring* (published the following year, in 1962), about the ravages of pesticide poisoning, sounded the same clarion for the ecosystem. There was also an aesthetic call to arms in response to the severe deterioration of the visible roadside under an assault of advertising, shoddy construction, and infrastructure. This was a notably mainstream movement, led by President Lyndon Johnson's wife, Lady Bird Johnson, who upon her husband's election in 1964 launched a nationwide beautification campaign aimed at cleaning up the mess along American roads. She persuaded the president to mention beautification and pollution in his 1965 State of the Union address outlining his vision for the "Great Society," and she herself was persuaded to expand the significance of the campaign to cities in recognition of the simmering racial tensions being felt in the country. In an interview with *US News & World Report*, she said: "Ugliness is so grim. A little beauty, something that is lovely, I think, can help create harmony which will reduce tensions."[40] In the heat of August 1965, the Los Angeles neighborhood of Watts exploded into six days of racial riots.

Lady Bird's "rebellion against ugliness," in the words of journalist James Perry, was widely shared, and received its book-length manifesto in Peter Blake's 1964 *God's Own Junkyard: The Planned Deterioration of America's Landscape*, in which the author lamented the architectural squalor of our jumbled cities and cookie-cutter suburbia, and the man-made "vandalism" of visual clutter marring the landscape—TV aerials, power lines, billboards, wires, and tanks—"a disgrace of . . . vast proportions" that he blamed on the unchecked profit motive, and lack of planning and regulation that prevailed across the country:

> *Our suburbs are interminable wastelands dotted with millions of monotonous little houses on monotonous little lots and crisscrossed by highways lined with billboards, jazzed-up diners, used-car lots, drive-in movies, beflagged gas stations, and garish motels. Even the relatively unspoiled countryside beyond these suburban fringes has begun to sprout more telephone poles than trees, more trailer camps than national parks. And the shores of oceans, lakes, and rivers are rapidly being encrusted with the junkiness of industries that pollute the water on which they depend.*

The book paired photos of good and bad landscapes, such as Jefferson's stately Range at the University of Virginia, suggesting timeless symmetry and repose, versus a photo of Canal Street in New Orleans taken in 1960, depicting a welter of cars, signs, and cables, with nary a tree in sight. "No people has inherited a more naturally beautiful land than we," he complained. "The only trouble is that we are about to turn the beautiful inheritance into the biggest slum on the face of the earth."

Blake's condemnation of the postwar American built environment was rebutted in the pages of *Artforum* by the architects Denise Scott Brown and Robert Venturi, in their 1968 article "A Significance for A&P Parking Lots, Or Learning from Las Vegas," which later became an influential book. They argued that the "roadside eclecticism" that horrified Blake in fact possessed romantic charm, interest, and a deeper order not visible to him or others held in the stiff, boring grip of orthodox modernism. Other architects and artists of Robert Smithson's generation also responded to the new, heterodox American landscape not by decrying it but by interrogating the possibility that it offered a new way of looking at the world—by thinking about the experience and qualities of the built environment, rather than its beauty or ugliness according to traditional categories. All of this was of a piece with a growing critique of commodity culture in the art world: of rejecting the selling of objects in galleries, instead taking art outside the gallery walls to engage real places, called *sites*, informed by their history and context, and the physical experience one had in them. Michael Heizer, a rising young artist from California, said, "The museum and collections are stuffed, the floors are sagging, but the real space still exists."[41] Heizer headed out to the Mojave Desert and made "drawings" with a motorcycle, its tires leaving traces on dry lake beds, and by pitching dirt and pigment from the back of a moving truck. In 1969–70 he made what is to this day considered his masterwork, *Double Negative*, two huge cuts made by bulldozer into the edges of a steep mesa face in the Nevada desert, the dirt pushed over the edge to form giant landslides down the slope, each cut lining up visually with the other across a 1,500-foot chasm. It constituted a new definition of art, and of constructed, intentional landscape—though Heizer rejected this, saying, "I don't care about landscape. I'm a sculptor. Real estate is dirt, and dirt is material."[42]

Smithson took his act outside for the first time in his 1969 *Mirror Displacements*, in which he piled salt crystals, dirt, and rocks onto square mirrors, first inside a gallery, then outdoors, memorializing the works in photos as he had done with the Passaic monuments; satisfied, he repeated the process around Ithaca, New York, then on an expedition to Mexico's Yucatan Peninsula. These efforts he photographed and exhibited in galleries, arguably negating the point of the exercise. Smithson is best known for his "masterpiece," 1970's *Spiral Jetty*, in which he bulldozed a fifteen-foot-wide track of boulders in a line 1,500 feet out from the barren shore of Utah's Great Salt Lake, before it coiled back toward shore in a tight spiral. The site is astonishing: a lifeless landscape meeting, almost imperceptibly, an expanse of still water, tinted a lurid pink by the brine shrimp that thrive in the lake. Salt crystals rim the rocks where they meet the water. It is not far from Promontory Point, where the two arms of the first transcontinental railroad met in May 1869, almost exactly one hundred years before Smithson's road came to its own end, not quite meeting itself. The sight is equally astonishing: one is struck that the artwork is impenetrably enigmatic, and that its meaning, if it possesses one, is less interesting than its impressive scale; its power due to the strange-

Robert Smithson, *Spiral Jetty*. (Soren Harward/Wikimedia Commons)

ness of the place, with its infinite vistas, and colors and textures suggesting another planet. He hated aerial photography as a reduction of artistic experience to the "gestalt" simplicity of advertising imagery, so he filmed *Spiral Jetty* by panning the camera 360 degrees. He wrote of being there: "Et in Utah Ego"—replacing Arcadia with another promised land, the Mormon's Zion of Utah, a place so dry that even its water becomes solidified into crystals of salt where it touches the air.

Another young artist, Richard Serra, who had been doing work using partly molten metal in galleries, had his own Noguchi-like epiphany in 1970 while on a world trip. He saw *Double Negative* and *Spiral Jetty* and spent six months in Japan studying Zen gardens.[43] As a result he moved his work outside, making *Shift* in King City, Ontario, from 1970 to 1972, consisting of six long, thin concrete triangles arrayed in a zigzag down a sloping, open field, like giant chopsticks strewn along the ground. He followed it in 1972–73 with *Spin Out (for Robert Smithson)* (Smithson was killed in a plane crash in 1973, while surveying the site of his last work, *Amarillo Ramp*), made of three wall-sized steel plates arrayed in a pinwheel in a wooded landscape in the Netherlands, seeming to grow from the site's topography and change it simultaneously. The question many viewers asked: "Where is the sculpture?" The answer, according to Serra, was "Where wasn't it?"[44] Serra had been looking for a way around sculpture's dissociation from its surroundings—he thought of most sculpture as "piazza art"—bad art used by bad architects to hide their failures. What he wanted to do was not put an object in a space, but alter a space using planes, lines, divisions, and demarcations, as much to define the space as to suggest its absences and voids. Serra didn't draw a plan of his works but instead drew an elevation, starting with the viewer's bodily experience of passing through space, so that he could work to affect it by blocking and steering, sometimes cutting off sight or sound, sometimes opening them up. The installations are abstract, in the sense that they don't represent anything real, but they are totally physical, too.

Smithson, when he went to visit *Shift*, had called it "picturesque," which baffled and irked Serra. The pictorial was the last quality he wanted associated with his work. But he slowly came to understand what Smithson

Richard Serra, *Spin Out (for Robert Smithson)*. (Wikimedia Commons)

meant: "I wasn't sure what he was talking about. He wasn't talking about the form of the work. But I guess he meant that one experienced the landscape as picturesque through the work." He continued: "The site is redefined, not re-presented. . . . The placement of all structural elements in the open field draws the viewer's attention to the topography of the landscape as the landscape is walked."[45] The key is that the artwork is a landscape that is walked through—a walk in the woods.

"Space is what's modern," Dan Kiley had said. But what the Land Artists (as Smithson, Heizer, and other artists working outside came to be called) were doing was a step beyond Kiley and Halprin, or what any designer of outside space had done before. It was not about evoking Arcadia, the sublime, or the eternal orders, as in the 18th century, nor about making people feel "better" by leaving the stressful city behind for an experience of nature, as in the 19th century, nor about making something beautiful or emotional. Yet it shared with these other kinds of landscapes a psychological project: it was designed to elicit feelings from the observer. But in this case it was about feeling oneself feeling—becoming aware of one's perceptions through the artwork. (Land Art shared this aim with much other so-called minimalist art of the period, and can be considered a subset of it.) Serra believed that "the biggest break in the history of sculpture in the 20th century occurred when the pedestal was removed,"[46] putting the object into the same space as the viewer, so shifting the focus from object to subject, from what is being looked at to how. The object was no longer independent, portable, or sellable (in theory) but was grounded in site, specific to place and time—whether it existed outdoors, as did *Shift*, or indoors, like one of artist James Turrell's light spaces. The work was no longer an ideal thing, being about its own form—the modernist goal. Instead it was materialist, about its own construction components and processes, but as a means to shifting the viewer's focus to herself.

WHEN PETER WALKER took his first job as a young landscape architect fresh out of school, in Larry Halprin's San Francisco office, the firm had only one nonresidential commission.[47] When he left, in 1956, Halprin had only just completed his first large commercial project, a shopping mall in Illinois. Demand for landscape architecture, especially of a modernist bent, was slow to get going in the postwar United States—and then it was mostly concentrated in the West, where distance from traditional architecture and harsh climates and a surge of new residential building opened people's minds to the need for new kinds of outdoor spaces. But the profession found itself transformed by the huge expansion of large-scale projects that picked up speed in the 1950s and hit its peak in the '60s, driven by unprecedented population growth and movement from the Northeast and Midwest to the West and South, and fueled by government spending on the military, the interstate highway system, urban development, and new suburban development. Firms grew as schools pumped out graduates like Walker to take on a growing workload, much of it for corporate projects. Many firms mimicked the corporate model, becoming large, complex integrations of planners, civil engineers, and managers as well as landscape architects. One such was Sasaki, Walker & Associates, the firm Peter Walker founded with Hideo Sasaki, a Californian who had trained and worked at Harvard. SWA, as it was called, evolved into a corporation along the lines of its corporate clients, and not coincidentally along the lines of the large architecture firms they often worked with, like SOM. In Walker's words:

> *Roads, parking, and the relationship of larger and greater numbers of buildings took the place of the simpler functional and aesthetic concerns of livable back yards. "Site planner" became the title of choice over "landscape architect." Planning, civil engineering, and managerial skills rather than visual and drawing skills gradually became the primary "products" of the larger offices. "Problem solving," "quality of services," and "process" became the buzz words heard at interviews and management meetings; and there were a lot of management meetings.*[48]

It is only natural that they should have emulated a corporate culture of specialization and efficiency in order to better serve their clients. It is equally unsurprising that the landscape architects should have emulated the architects, because of the aforementioned "slide-rule envy" so many members of the profession have ever been afflicted with—a permanent status anxiety and need to be classed alongside architecture, painting, and sculpture. The upside of landscape architecture's inferiority complex is its drive to elevate the technical, professional, and educational standards of the field in order to be accorded the same status given architects because of their perceived expertise. Its downside is its perennial denigration of horticulture, for fear of being downgraded to the level of gardeners, whom they consider little better than laborers. Frederick Law Olmsted encapsulated this syndrome for the ages when referring to his hopes for recognition from the Chicago Fair: "If people generally get to understand that our contribution to the undertaking is that of the planning of the scheme, rather than the disposition of the flower beds and other matters of gardening decoration, it will be a great lift to the profession." In a letter to his son, Rick (Frederick Jr.), he confessed the innermost desire of all landscape architects: "I want you . . . to make landscape architecture respected as an Art and a liberal profession."[49]

The results of the corporatized firms were, not surprisingly, corporate-feeling: endless bank plazas, malls, corporate campuses, and new subdivisions, competently planned and executed, often borrowing the best moves from Kiley and Halprin, not to mention Le Nôtre and Olmsted, and frequently from cutting-edge artists like Noguchi. Indeed, developers and their architects and landscape architects often borrowed the artists themselves to give their projects cachet. Noguchi was regularly commissioned to put sculptures in front of buildings like the First National Bank in Fort Worth, Texas, designed by SOM, in 1961, or his well-known *Red Cube*, placed on its point in front of New York's Marine Midland Bank building in 1968. Pablo Picasso was asked to embellish SOM's Chicago Civic Center in 1967, because, in the words of the firm's project architect, "We wanted the sculpture to be the work of the greatest artist alive."[50] Alexander Calder and Henry Moore pieces popped up across the land, functioning as celebrity-commodity fetishes, high-art fig leaves to cover the blandness of many corporate and government buildings, or even as logos for the patron companies.

Not all of the work of the big firms was soulless; some was very good—none more so than Walker's. "Why then," he asked, "do we now feel that this has been a bland or invisible period?"[51] The reason, in his estimation, was the "huge quantity of mediocre development work whose sheer size has become a symbol of the mindless market-oriented expansion of the suburban environment." There was also a lack of stylistic rigor: "Undigested and ill-fitting combinations of formalism and naturalism were produced." In a thoughtful and searching analysis, given that he was one of its leading practitioners and teachers, he admitted that the path taken by the mainstream of American landscape architecture mirrored what happened to the production of objects in general in the United States in the postwar decades: "Only household appliances, clothing, and perhaps American automobiles have had a more drastic devaluation in formal quality. Perhaps more important, the worlds of fine art and landscape design separated."[52]

ART AND LANDSCAPE would be brought back together in a most unexpected way, right in Peter Walker's front yard. One evening in the spring of 1979, Walker returned home from a business trip to find his wife, Martha Schwartz, and a group of friends drinking mint juleps on the brick sidewalk in front of their town house. The couple had first met when Schwartz interned with SWA in San Francisco in 1973; she had gone on to study landscape architecture in the graduate program at the University of Michigan. What he beheld there in their tiny front garden—a very conventional square surrounded by a low wrought-iron fence containing a gravel path edged in clipped boxwood around a central square planting bed—was her very first built landscape project. Schwartz had redesigned the front yard. She hadn't altered anything, merely added one embellishment—specifically a double row of bagels, some salt, and some pumpernickel, set down along the path. It was a practical joke and a way to defuse a certain tension that had lingered between them over who had the right to redesign the garden. Schwartz would recall later that it was little more than a "stunt," yet its significance turned out to be more momentous than anyone present could have dreamed: the "humble work," she wrote, "established me as a presence in the profession and created a mark in the sand that eventually defined the beginning of the postmodern era in landscape architecture." How could that be? One wonders. Schwartz, only half jokingly, submitted photographs of the "installation" to *Landscape Architecture* magazine, which ran it on the cover of its January 1980 issue with the title "The Bagel Garden," accompanied by an article that included spoofed working drawings, including a plan and section, and details such as "Pumpernickel Bagel: True Scale." The publication caused a brouhaha reflected in the letters to the editor section of the following issue of the magazine: many professional landscape architects felt the piece insulted their profession and trivialized their hard-won expertise and standing; a few saw the humor in it and admitted that the profession needed some rethinking.

Schwartz grew up in Philadelphia in a family of artists and architects, and had trained as an artist for ten years before going into landscape. She was influenced by minimalists like Robert Irwin, Donald Judd, and Dan Flavin, and by Pop artists Andy Warhol, Claes Oldenburg, and Robert Rauschenberg. She was wowed by the Land Artists, including Smithson and Heizer, and was especially impressed by *Spiral Jetty*, which gave her a desire "to make big art." But unlike Land Artists, she wanted to bring the work back out of wilderness and into the city.[53] Most of her classmates had a "religious fervor to save the environment," as she recalled, a gospel propagated in landscape architecture schools in the 1970s and '80s by the Scottish immigrant Ian McHarg, author of the 1969 book *Design with Nature*, which became the bible of a new environmentalist methodology that could be compared to Halprin's process-based ecological consciousness, without Halprin's poetry. But Schwartz wasn't interested in landscape design's environmental or social implications; instead she was determined that it be "at last seen again as an aesthetic enterprise and a legitimate art form," restored to some previous moment of glory, side by side with the fine arts, just as Frederick Law Olmsted had so fervently wished.

In art school she had trained as a printmaker, and a decidedly graphic orientation marked her early works, which consisted mostly of grids laid down over lawns or projected on building façades—for example, one she made with Walker in their early collaboration using tires painted white and Necco wafers on the campus of the Massachusetts Institute of Technology, in 1980, forming two offset grids on a lawn, which she described as a "clash of axes." Like Dan Kiley, Schwartz was interested in the "mystical quality of geometric forms and their relationships to each other," in her words. Her adoption of geometry rested on an odd pair of theories. The first was a clear echo of Olmsted's belief that landscapes should bring therapy: "people should derive a sense of orientation in space that produces a subliminal sense of comfort and security," she

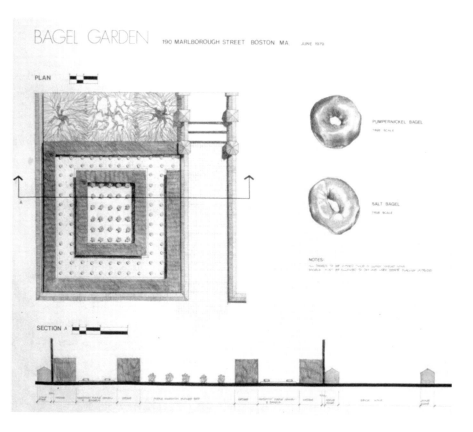

Martha Schwartz, Bagel Garden plan. (Courtesy of Martha Schwartz Partners)

explained. In her mind, the only way to instill this sense was to impose a regular, measured order on the out-of-doors: "the landscape must be depicted as architectural space so that it is recognizable and describable," using simple geometric forms, squares, and circles, because these are "familiar and memorable images." Geometry, to Schwartz, is "more humane than the disorientation caused by the incessant lumps, bumps, and squiggles of a stylized naturalism." Irregularity and roundedness were contrary to comfort and security. Her second theory is not unlike Robert Smithson's belief that the conventional "naturalism" of gardens is a narcotic that stupefies us and keeps us from dealing effectively with the hard, ugly facts of our suburban and urban reality. Geometry is more honest, she wrote, because it is just like our manufactured environment, which our romantic nostalgia for Arcadian nature obscures and distorts: "Unthinkingly, we dredge up the rolling English countryside like a universal balm," and this "has prevented us from seeing our landscape as it truly is and inhibited the evolution of an appropriate landscape approach to urbanization."[54]

It followed for Schwartz, naturally, that there should be no more making landscapes with fine materials like carved stone, but instead designers must employ "junk"—"concrete, asphalt, and plastic, the stuff with which we build our environment on a daily basis." Western society, especially its male component, is "colorphobic," she believes, and so she is fond of using very bright colors, and often overscales objects. A Schwartz design leads with a bold and deliberate artificiality that is playful and sarcastic, like the work of the Pop artists she admires, and surreal, because nothing in it is quite normal, to say nothing of natural. These qualities are the classic ones of postmodernism in art and architecture, and Schwartz indeed made what are undoubtedly the most paradigmatically postmodern "landscapes" of the 20th century—even the quotation marks are essential to understanding her work.

Again at MIT, in 1986, her design for a roof garden at the Whitehead Institute for Biomedical Research offered a paragon of the style. The Splice Garden occupies a tiny, twenty-five by thirty-five-foot space, on top of a nine-story building, open to the sky but walled in on two sides and looked into by a classroom and a faculty lounge. It was a miserable place to try to make a garden: dark, constricted, with a tiled floor that couldn't take the weight of soil or irrigation—effectively ruling out anything but potted plants—yet Schwartz's client insisted that the project be green, and quick, and cheap. Schwartz's solution was to paint the walls green, then split the square space in two on the diagonal, filling one triangular side with a cartoonish French-style parterre garden, with "hedges" made of steel frames covered in Astroturf, and the other side with a "Zen" garden of raked gravel around "rocks" that are round shrubs—fake of course, while the raked gravel is actually colored aquarium gravel. Plastic potted topiaries protrude from a wall, and plastic potted palms sit incongruously by the French hedges.

The Splice Garden, with its splice between two historically, geographically, and culturally disparate garden design traditions, speaks to the concept of gene splicing, one activity of the Whitehead Institute, presumably as a warning of its dangers. The fact that it is radically unnatural makes the garden another sort of DNA mutant: a garden with no nature in it. Schwartz views naturalism in the landscape as beside the point, not least because so-called natural landscapes are not necessarily ecological or sustainable—she holds up golf courses as examples. She sees a "great tension within the profession" because of its inherited cultural ambivalence about its role: "that humankind shouldn't violate 'nature,' and that the job of the landscape architect is to protect and save the earth from human intervention." But Schwartz insists that "the hand of man is everywhere, whether we like it or not," and so people must design their world, and not abdicate to the (false) romantic idea of an Arcadia to be imitated and paradise regained.

While Schwartz's work may have a limited appeal to fans of traditional gardens, it has captivated some people and garnered lots of press—her designs are nothing if not visually arresting. Along with a small group of like-minded designers, including Topher Delaney, of San Francisco, and Ken Smith, of New York, who formerly worked in her office, Schwartz is categorized as a Conceptualist—and like that label, has been influential but not always understood. From the Bagel Garden onward, Schwartz's work has caused scandal and faced disapproval: they are *not gardens* is a frequent complaint. But few would doubt that they are art, and this pleases Schwartz, who writes: "Today the boundary between art and landscape design has been at least partially effaced." Artists are working outside, and landscape designers are working, if not actually indoors, then well inside the conventions of art and well outside those of gardens.

Does the act of blurring boundaries, even to the point of dissolution, really change or expand the categories of art and garden, or does it simply reveal the ambitions of one side to occupy the territory of the other, a kind of imperialistic urge on the part of trespassing artists to complement the insecure status climbing of the landscape architects? Without doubt, the two share a contested dominion over their shifting intersection, a borderland where the practical and the fanciful, the earthy and the intellectual, meet and splice, and recombine. There is no way to settle the question; as Robert Smithson wrote in his cryptic footnote: "Too much thinking about 'gardens' leads to perplexity and agitation."

On the other side of the same page has been a migration of "straight" artists to the landscape, not to make "big art" per se, but simply to make gardens. In the most spectacular, expensive, visible, and puzzling case, one could watch an artist known for radical minimalism going to the opposite pole—full-dress horticulture-driven design, nearly Victorian in its obsession with plants for their forms and colors and sheer variety. In 1984, New York modernist architect Richard Meier was awarded the commission for the new Getty Center, a nearly billion-dollar art museum and research institute set high on a chaparral-covered ridge overlooking the San Diego Freeway and much of Los Angeles, and clearly visible from the city below. Meier, the most celebrated and prolific of the "White" school of stripped-down, neoclassical modernism parodied by Tom Wolfe in his book *From Bauhaus to Our House*, had designed a sprawling campus of classical-modern white buildings in geometric shapes: circles, squares, and rectangles, adjoining stone-paved piazzas and fountains of a distinctly Renaissance inspiration. For the space allotted the Central Garden, a wedge-shaped opening between the major wings of the campus (where a small canyon had been before it was destroyed by bulldozers to lay the building foundations), Meier planned a fountain at the upper plaza level, feeding into a long rill flowing down a series of stepped stone terraces, intersecting perpendicularly with an aqueduct-like peristyle (a Roman feature consisting of just columns and a roof) that would frame a dramatic sight line to the Pacific Ocean, at once interrupting and showcasing the site's panoramic view to Santa Catalina Island in the distance. Below the peristyle, the water was to empty into a bowl-shaped pool. Ever the purist, Meier described his vision: "In my mind's eye I see a classic structure, elegant and timeless, emerging, serene and ideal, from the rough hillside, a kind of Aristotelian structure within the landscape."[55]

Meier's vision for the garden was of a piece with the project as a whole, over which he exercised tight control in all its details. However, Getty Trust officials worried that the landscape conception was too purely architectural and too arid, preferring a more lush, softer, gardenlike experience to offset visitors' experience of the buildings, which were so overwhelmingly "Aristotelian." They began by bringing in landscape architects to work with Meier, yet he resented the intrusion, and Getty officials quickly realized that he "was beating up on" his intended collaborators, in the recollection of one person close to the process, "manipulating and ironing and then spitting them out, homogenizing the whole place." The trust then decided to bring in an artist, one with enough clout and independent vision to counter the architect. Their choice was an inspired one in Robert Irwin, roughly Meier's contemporary, who had grown up in Los Angeles and made his name in the 1960s with a series of careful, luminous paintings on aluminum and fiberglass meant to highlight and question the viewer's experiences of perception—in Irwin's phrase (he is good at coining phrases to describe his work) he sought an "artwork of pure phenomena." He went on to make large-room installations with changing and invisible sources of illumination, much like his fellow L.A. "Light and Space" artist James Turrell. In one series of pieces, he hung scrims in galleries to divide the spaces in interesting and provocative ways, then moved his work outdoors: in the late 1970s and early '80s he began placing long steel plates, à la Richard Serra, along lawns at commissioning college campuses and parks, such as 1981's *Portal Park Slice* in Dallas. Probably his most poetic and evocative outdoor work is *Two Running Violet V Forms*, made the next year by hanging a colored chain-link fence fifteen to thirty feet off the ground through a dense forest of eucalyptus trees on the hillside campus of the University of California at San Diego. The play of light and color through the tree canopy onto the mesh is lovely, and the contrast between the plane geometry and the shaggy vitality of the eucalyptus grove is irreducibly strange, yet familiar because of the common material. The work is breathtakingly simple yet audacious. It recalls Christo and Jeanne-Claude's *Running Fence*, a line of white cloth eighteen feet high and twenty-four and a half miles long staked across the green hills of Sonoma and Marin counties in northern California in 1976.

When Irwin began work on the Getty garden it was immediately clear that a conflict of egos was unavoidable, as the artist made no secret that he was heading in a completely different direction from Meier's conception. As the tension mounted, the trust made the decision to take control of the Central Garden away from Meier and allow Irwin autonomy. Irwin kept the watercourse and the terminal circular pool, but nothing else. He arrived with no knowledge of plants or horticulture, but, as he began to visit nurseries and look at illustrated plant books, he grew excited by the endless variety of colors, textures, leaf and flower shapes, and forms that he saw, his artist's imagination running wild with the possibilities of combination and juxtaposition. To help him with the learning curve of what would grow on this hot California site, he enlisted a cadre of nurserymen and maintenance experts and began to piece together a plant palette with which he painted a vegetal composition as madly billowing and intensely colored as anything made by Gertrude Jekyll when she approached complete blindness in her later years. Down the center of the drainage, he designed a "creek" of intricately laid stone running between boulder-studded berms and lined with a double row of plane trees. On the berms he mounded imported soil and jammed in a profusion of plants—more than five hundred species in all, with carefully sequenced seasonal progressions of colors of bloom and foliage.

During the design process he was informed by the project's disability consultants that a wheelchair-accessible ramp would be required, not just to the terraced areas or the lawns that flank the creek, but to the boulder-strewn center of the creek itself. Accordingly Irwin ran a zigzagging stone ramp back and forth through the stream feature, dictating the way most people experience the garden—descending in a series of wide swings, passing over the stream with its densely packed kaleidoscope of plants and the sound of rushing water, then out into the sunbaked lawns, as low and perfectly manicured as golf greens, that fill the spaces between the stream feature and Meier's massive stone walls, then back again, changing direction abruptly at the end of each swing like a car's windshield wiper. At the end of the creek, the water flows across a narrow terrace that sprouts six tall mushroom-shaped canopies made of rusting steel rebar and grown over with multicolored bougainvillea. At the end of the terrace the current drops over a *chadar* or tooth-surfaced inclined plane modeled on those in old Mughal gardens in Persia and India, and into a circular pool filled with azaleas planted in a bizarre design of interlocking circles that recalls an overcomplex corporate logo. The azaleas, in magenta and red, are well out of their comfort zone under the hot Los Angeles sun (they prefer light shade there). Mexican gardeners in Wellingtons wade in the clear, shallow water, keeping the azalea circles carefully pruned and dipping the leaves out of the pool. Around the pool are more garden beds, edged in the same rusted CorTen steel plates that border the zigzagging path, and planted with a riot of randomly assorted shrubs, vines, and small trees, some growing on rustic frames of the kind one would see in a cottage or kitchen garden. Down inside the bowl that is formed by the pool and the inexplicable cottage garden beds, the billion-dollar panoramic view is completely blocked by another zigzagging path edged with elbow-high steel plates, dug into a slope covered in gravel. The effect is that of Richard Serra driven mad by the disabled-access codes.

Irwin has described his garden as "a sculpture in the form of a garden aspiring to be art." The phrase has a certain ring to it, but it is hard to know just what it means. It reportedly cost more than $8 million to build—a monstrous sum that is only somewhat understandable given the intricate craftsmanship and fine materials (four kinds of rock were imported from four different states for the stream alone) that Irwin and his team achieved. But aside from the endless pumped progress of the stream from the top of the creek to the azalea bowl and back again, there is nothing that gives the design coherence or purpose—except the fact that it is a collection of plants whose only unifying characteristic is that Irwin found them visually interesting. As a designer he committed the sin of the plant collector: having to have one of everything, planted "cheek-by-jowl," as magazine garden writers like to say, arranged to be looked at up close, one at a time. It may be that the artist's genius for minimal intervention was lost in his enthusiasm for his newly discovered vegetal palette. The Central Garden works on this level—the plant forms are wonderful—but not on others. There is little shade, few places to sit (people perch on the lawn against the walls, hiding from the sun in pockets of shadow where they can find them), no view, and no perspective whatsoever on the context of the place—neither the architecture, which it is clearly a reaction against, nor Los Angeles, with its layers of unique human and natural history. Irwin didn't even use the native California sycamores for the creek, though they grow in every nearby canyon, choosing European planes instead.

When one comes to or leaves the Getty Center on the tram trains that ferry visitors from the parking garage, one passes through an odd kind of forest, conceived by Meier and executed over the objections of the office of Emmet Wemple, one of the landscape architects the trust brought in to work with Meier (and a former head of the landscape architecture program at the nearby University of Southern California). Over the rippling, steep topography of the ridges the Getty Center occupies, Meier wanted to lay a grid of trees. This required skinning the ground of the native vegetation, consisting of chaparral and coast live oak trees, virtually the only tree that can survive in the area's harsh climate and poor soils, then replacing it with a grid of straight, nursery-grown coast live oaks, underplanted with a low Australian acacia that looks and acts more or less like chaparral. At enormous expense the landscape architect replaced a beautiful, intact plant community with a kind of fantasy of itself, now regularized, ordered, and irrigated. It would seem to be an exercise in futility (even more so now, almost twenty years later, since the oaks have grown irregularly, as they will, all but obscuring the grid pattern) and in waste. But then, the unofficial motto of the Getty Trust, set up in large part as a tax write-off for an oil company, must be "Why spend less?"

There is a lesson in Meier's forest: especially in the "paper space" where most designers work out their ideas, the urge to apply geometry to our chaotic, "disorienting" real world is powerful—remaking nature in ordered form to calm our nerves or convince ourselves that we are in control. But at this extreme it goes even beyond André Le Nôtre's autocratic engineering—for that is what it is, landscape engineering. It appeals to some as art, too, but metaphysically as well as practically speaking, it is a rejection of the condition of nature and a turning it into culture. How wonderfully ironic then, that nature has taken back its terrain—since a coast live oak released from its nursery restraints will not grow straight. As Noguchi said, "In our times we think to control nature, only to find that in the end it escapes us."

What is distinctive about the urge for order as it has been expressed by so much landscape architecture is its mistrust of naturalism. Seeking to bridge our postwar, then postmodern alienation from nature, much of the profession alienated itself from the naturalistic in gardens and landscape—the only tools in its toolbox that are truly its own. For some landscape architects, this was because of their ambivalence about only being seen to be about gardens and not something larger, more significant, more serious, like art. "Nature" might be featured, but as an object, an "ecology" or "ecosystem" or other abstracted concept, once removed from the real, disorderly thing, exhibited like an exotic specimen in a cabinet of curiosities. For some artists it was a mistrust of the false promise of finding what Smithson called "a leftover Arcadia" instead of squarely facing the unpleasant reality of the hard new world we have constructed. Thus a naïve reversion to the gardenesque, such as Irwin's Getty garden, ignores that reality and ignores the painful experiences of the past century in a failed attempt to regain the "jejune Edens" of the Victorian flower garden. For some of those artists, it was necessary to build what Noguchi had prophesied: "disturbing and unbeautiful gardens to awaken us to a new awareness of our solitude." These experiments are now (mostly, one hopes) complete and have yielded a set of insights and design elements that have been productively folded into mainstream landscape design. What seems less austere and more promising is the unplanned, disordered path of reflective, abstracted naturalism followed by Halprin and at times Noguchi, searching for a partial reintegration of nature and culture even in the face of the certainty that a complete reconciliation may not be possible. What this exploration will yield is the other half of the task Noguchi set the garden maker: always working to conceive "other gardens to correspond to our changing concepts of reality."

Seven

ALL OUR MISSING PARTS: MONEY AND VIRTUE IN THE GO-GO YEARS

Landscaping makes an imaginary world come true, or, rather, appear to be true.

—MICHEL CONAN, INTRODUCTION TO
Environmentalism in Landscape Architecture

That is our story here . . . of a little girl who never got over what life had never given her and wound up inventing for herself a past she had never known—a hologram of life so powerful that it not only convinced her personally but mesmerized the world. In this way, the quiet little girl from the house on Elm Place became, in time, the richest self-made businesswoman in America, by selling the world all her missing parts.

—CHRISTOPHER BYRON, *Martha Inc.:*
The Incredible Story of Martha Stewart Living Omnimedia

There she is in a scene from a video: Martha, with her trademark deep voice and charming smile, her blond hair looking lightly combed but not coiffed, clutching against her canvas jacket Vivaldi, a fat furball cat that wears a taciturn expression—"One of my favorite Himalayas," she says admiringly. Martha is telling us how to plant lily bulbs, preparing us for the task; then she demonstrates the form: pushing each bulb deep into her lusciously prepared soil with her foot on a bulb planter. Next she shows us how to plant primroses: kneeling, in her informal but WASPy jeans and sweater, digging with her hands in the dark dirt. She explains how to do "early spring feeding," throwing fertilizer; then she builds a trellis for sweet peas. Birds are chirping noticeably loudly in the background. She shows us how to prune fruit trees in her orchard, confidently nipping off branches with her loppers. She talks admiringly of the tools she uses. She is genial, familiar, sometimes confidential, always speaking directly to us. Of the herb garden she built she confides: "I always wanted a classic herb garden," then explains how, at her Connecticut home in 1993, she had men dig out part of her driveway with a backhoe and bring in mounds of compost to make lovely, dark, loamy soil in which she planted fifteen varieties of basil. She is always sunny, with controlled enthusiasm: dividing hellebores on her TV show, she exclaims, "this is a *very* handsome clump!" And she often gives us the satisfaction, the payoff, of her labors, and our attention—she shows us how to cook up the fruits of the garden: a rhubarb crisp, a fontina and asparagus bruschetta. Delicious.

This is the Martha Stewart who is irresistible to millions. The Martha Stewart who rose from being just another blond Westport, Connecticut, housewife in the 1970s with a part-time catering business to straddling the pinnacle of American media, building an empire of lucrative books, magazines, videos, television shows, and a line of branded products sold nationwide. It was all based on her image, her personality, her name, *Martha;* when her company made an initial stock offering in October 1999, that name was valued by Wall Street at more than a billion dollars.[1] In the process she altered the taste, expectations, and buying patterns of millions of Americans. She fueled her cult by becoming the high priestess of class anxiety, spotlighting it where few were even aware it existed in them, provoking it where it didn't, then assuaging it by showing her audience the example of her own confidence and success so that they might emulate her. For someone who makes her living off getting others to buy into her taste prescriptions, it is a brilliant strategy—like the firefighter who secretly starts a fire, then leaps into action to put it out and gets covered in glory for saving the day.

After building a successful catering company, initially in Westport but soon reaching into the world of New York media and business that many Westporters, her husband, Andy, included, commuted to daily, Martha made her own publishing play—beginning with the 1982 book *Entertaining*. Padded with recipes and photos of Martha, and propelled by her increasingly visible image, it was an improbable bestseller—the largest-selling cookbook since Julia Child's *Mastering the Art of French Cooking* came out in 1961. It was followed like a steady series of dead-eye gunshots by *Quick Cook* in 1983, *Hors d'Oeuvres* in 1984, *Pies & Tarts* in 1985, *Weddings* in 1987, *The Wedding Planner* and *Quick Cook Menus* in 1988, and *Martha Stewart's Christmas* in 1989, all of which she flacked with a relentless publicity schedule. Her talent for self-promotion was matched by her appeal: her talks and appearances attracted huge crowds of (mostly) women who wanted to see Martha. Her appeal was only burnished by her ever-increasing success, as she repeatedly exceeded the expectations of the (mostly) male business establishment. After her string of blockbuster books, she talked skeptical executives at Time Warner into paying for the launch of a glossy magazine, *Martha Stewart Living*, constructed around the unusual premise of a magazine all about Martha, all the time: she would be the editor, commentator, and subject all at once, framing each issue and each individual topic with reminiscences of her happy childhood and marriage, illustrated with pictures of her in action. Her face would even go on the cover. When the first issue hit the newsstands, in November 1990, the Time executives who had bankrolled half a million 130-page color copies held their breath. It was a huge hit, surprising them and nearly everyone else—but not surprising Martha.

Martha clearly had the touch: she understood that what a large slice of Americans (again, mostly women) wanted was advice and guidance in their home spheres: what to do, when to do it, and how to do it. Martha's knowledge was encyclopedic—she knew how to do everything, from gardening to cooking, entertaining, and keeping house, and she delivered her lessons with a total, breezy self-assurance that instilled confidence in the most timid and inexperienced in the domestic realm. Her dicta were absolute, and absolutely cheerful: "A house is not a home until it is full of color," she instructed.[2] She taught how to force hyacinths, polish silver, buy garden antiques, grow heirloom tomatoes, make seasonal drinks, pickle vegetables, and keep chickens—in case her 20th century middle-class but upwardly mobile suburban audience had forgotten the fine points of being a 19th century middle-class but upwardly mobile suburban wife. She invented, or at least popularized, a rubric, *homekeeping*, for all the disappearing but critical folk sciences of washing linens, removing stains, and the simultaneously efficient and aesthetically pleasing packing of suitcases. Her instructions were studiously, some would say relentlessly, practical. The pictures always showed Martha doing the job herself: guiding the rototiller, squeezing the pruner, climbing the ladder, kneeling in the dirt, shoveling. Martha with her hands in the dirt was her ubiquitous, signature image, featured and repeated over and over.

But Martha's world was inescapably also *not* practical; instead it was an elaborate fantasy world that no normal woman or man without infinite time and resources on their hands could inhabit. The stage set for most of her photo shoots, her own house and garden in Westport, which she called Turkey Hill, was the picture of a homeowner and gardener's afterlife: a prim white clapboard colonial house surrounded by a swimming pool, an orchard, a kitchen garden, and a seemingly endless perennial garden bursting with irises, poppies, peonies, roses, and clematis. She had three hundred varieties of roses in her garden; she demonstrated how to gild pumpkins with two baths of metallic paint for Halloween décor and how to make tiny, impossibly delicate chocolate flowers for Christmas; she went fly-fishing in Alaska by floatplane; she made the perfect burger. Fresh-cut bouquets of flowers were everywhere, captured in luscious close-up vignettes—a shameless flower porn that Martha perfected. Gamboling in an endless green garden with its owner, another, nearly identical blond woman, the two of them in white dresses, she threw a summer tea party and cut the crusts off the sandwiches. To many, Martha Stewart became something of a mysterious joke: Yes, Martha showed us how to do all these things, but who actually could, or would? To others she was seductive but maddening. Watching Martha do her thing on an appearance on the morning TV talk show *Live with Regis and Kathy Lee*, co-host Kathy Lee Gifford deadpanned to Regis Philbin, in simultaneous admiration and exasperation at Martha's Stepford Wife–like performance: "She is Martha Stewart. And you're not. And I'm not! And it makes me crazy." People had strong opinions about Martha; many either loved or loathed her. But her success continued unabated, and her influence spread: knockoffs of her magazine sprouted like mushrooms after rain—*Garden Design* and a revived *House & Garden*, just to name two high-end competitors inspired by her. A parody volume titled *Is Martha Stuart Living?* appeared on newsstands in 1995, with feature stories: "How to Dominate a Tag Sale, Making Water from Scratch, Collecting Glue Guns, Stenciling the Driveway."

The secret of her appeal was that, though few of her fans probably did much of what Martha showed them, they wanted to see how to do it, to have access to the knowledge, just in case. Martha understood this. In her editor's introduction to the February/March 1992 issue of the magazine, she wrote: "I have finally found the right word to sum up what we are trying to accomplish here at the magazine. It's *demystification.* . . . There are so many things in this complex world of ours that are intimidating simply because we don't understand them." By explaining not only *how* to do things, but *which* things to do, Martha gave her audience a form of empowerment well worth the cover price, even if it was made of a good dose of imaginary wish fulfillment and fantasy.

This is what Martha Stewart understood: *desire*. The night before her first, self-titled TV program debuted in 1993, the show's producer, a hardened TV veteran named Richard Sheingold, was gripped with doubt: surely it would be a flop, since there was Martha, standing in her garden, earnestly advising her audience not to cut their roses in the heat of noon but in the evening, when the first dew appeared on the leaves, so that they would stay fresh-looking longer. He pointed out to her that the target audience markets were urban: "They're working-class people. These people don't even *have* gardens." Martha answered him coolly: "Yes, but they want them."[3] The show, initially a weekly half-hour segment, quickly gained a national following and grew to one hour, then became daily, then added half-hour segments on weekends; soon Martha was also guesting on CBS's *The Early Show* and starring in holiday TV specials. In some sense Martha invented modern reality TV. Not that she invented the genre of the domestic how-to show—Julia Child had perfected that two decades earlier—but *Martha* expanded from the kitchen counter to swallow the entire domestic universe, inside and outside, every nook and cranny expertly tamed by her ubiquitous personality. In 1995, *New York* magazine put her on the cover, pronouncing her "the definitive American woman of our time." Martha had become a cult of vicarious perfection for "the" American woman of the time. She explained why to a reporter in 1998: "I am first and foremost a housewife with a home, with a garden, with everything that everybody wants."[4]

What Martha Stewart was selling was a dream of a genteel, beautiful country house life, with all the supposed WASP trappings of the deep-rooted northeastern establishment. It was none other than the old dream of rural repose, retailed by poets and media personalities since at least Virgil, and updated for each century by some energetic, magnetic entrepreneur, whether Alexander Pope, Capability Brown, Andrew Jackson Downing, or Martha Stewart, née Martha Kostyra, born into a working-class family of eight in August 1941, in Jersey City, New Jersey, soon moving to 86 Elm Place in Nutley, New Jersey, a no-frills town near Newark. Her father, Eddie, was by all accounts an angry, alcoholic, and occasionally abusive man who held a succession of blue-collar jobs and seethed at the fact that he had not risen in life as high as he felt he should have. Martha graduated from Nutley High School in 1959, a year when the girls in the yearbook wore sweaters and pearls and shoulder-length hair and listed as their interests gardening, cooking, and homemaking. She began her rise then, getting a job as a clothes model at the Bonwit Teller department store in Manhattan, possibly on the strength of a photo portfolio her father took and printed of her. She got a place at Barnard College, uptown at 116th Street, the women's school across Broadway from its then still all-male counterpart, Columbia University. For a time she held a job on Fifth Avenue on the wealthy Upper East Side, getting a stipend, room, and board in exchange for housework and cooking. It was to prove good training for a future business tycoon. In 1961, *Glamour* magazine listed Martha Kostyra as one of the "Best Dressed College Girls" of the year; she had submitted her own photos, wearing clothes she had made herself. As a Barnard freshman she'd met Andy Stewart, who seemed the perfect catch, from a family that by all appearances was WASP and old money. They were married in July 1961 and Martha put her career on hold to move to New Haven, Connecticut, while he went to Yale Law School. In short order there would be frustration: it turned out that Andy was not WASP after all, not rich, but instead from a Jewish family of failing fortunes. Martha would still have to make her own way in the world, and she kicked hard on the door: from 1968 to 1973 she worked on Wall Street for an upstart brokerage firm, one of few women on the Street selling stocks. She later recalled that she was a good seller, not incidentally because she wasn't afraid to wear short skirts and leggings, deploying her long legs to good advantage.[5]

In the spring of 1971, she and Andy found an abandoned six-room farmhouse, at 48 Turkey Hill Road South, in Westport. Built in 1805,[6] it was something of a wreck, but they could afford it at $33,750. (Christopher Byron, the author of an unauthorized biography, reported that he and his wife had also looked at the property and passed because of its state of disrepair.) The marriage was stressed, and soon, in 1973, Martha's job vanished as the brokerage firm sank in the wake of stock market turmoil. She threw herself into renovations and started selling pies at a local gourmet food shop; when demand rose, she paid other women to make her "homemade" pies, which she then sold for up to twenty dollars a pop. Soon she started a catering company with a partner—whom she later came to alienate, in part by taking jobs on the side, and bought out of the company, according to Byron. Martha called it "The Uncatered Affair"—and marketed her prowess at delivering all the food, serving gear, and décor, then staging it and vanishing into the background so that a hostess might appear to have done it all herself. It set itself up to be exactly what it wasn't, providing a lovely illusion to mask the stresses that many women in places like Westport, Connecticut, felt in the 1970s. Especially in upscale suburbs, the 1970s seemed an exaggerated pendulum swing back from the experimentation and questioning of traditional social roles of the 1960s—there was a renewed emphasis on home, family life, and the role of women as homemakers, though increasing numbers of them also needed or chose to work.

Here were the beginnings of the double bind of modern American womanhood: caught between the pincers of the women's movement on one hand, with its rising demands of women's career and earning parity with men, and on the other hand an antifeminist backlash that reinstated traditional social expectations that married women must fulfill the highest standards of their traditional gender role in tending the home and children. This was the era of triumphant women's lib: think of tennis player Bobby Riggs challenging and losing to Billie Jean King; and of the pushback against it: think of the national campaign to pass the Equal Rights Amendment, which would have outlawed gender discrimination, defeated by conservative forces led by Phyllis Schlafly. Add to that rising living standards among the social class Martha moved in and an attendant rising consumerism—the mid–1970s was the beginning of a pre-Yuppie suburban status escalation among the upwardly mobile middle and upper middle classes, as fondue replaced Hamburger Helper at the table and BMWs replaced Buicks in the driveway. By the 1980s the trend was national and moving down the tax bracket ladder: an appetite for mid-luxury trappings and a vision of a vaguely European, upper-class existence was encouraged by national ad campaigns: think of the TV commercial where one British gentleman in a Rolls-Royce stops another and asks, "Pardon me, would you have any Grey Poupon?"

The 1980s, for a certain social strata, namely white urban and suburban boomers, was the beginning of a stretch of good years. Money was being made in professional careers, houses in the tonier suburbs bought. They needed to be gardened, decorated, and entertained in. Few Americans in these circumstances could draw on family traditions or education to instruct them on the new standards being shown them in the media. Thus there was both appetite, and anxiety—what to do to show the world that you knew what to do with money, to show that, in essence, you belonged? Martha Stewart, herself a pure product of this wave of upward mobility and possibility of personal transformation, understood both the superb ironies of the situation and how to profit from it by working both angles: like her catering company name, she mastered a kind of double-speak that at the same time addressed the two forces pulling at so many American women—the feminist critique of homemaking and the practical and psychological necessities of it. "I consider myself one of the original feminists. I'm trying to help give women back a sense of pleasure and accomplishment in their homes,"[7] she said. And she provided an entire thesis that seemed to lace the two separating poles back together:

> *What I try to do is bring back a way of life that we've forgotten. It began to change in the 1970s with the "Me Generation." But now we're looking for a balance with our career, homes, gardens, family and pets. I try to show a comfortable and gentle lifestyle from the moment you wake up until you go to bed in a very nice way that's not expensive and from a woman's way with the subject of life.*[8]

Martha's program was a replay of Downing's: her message was a 20th century reprise, with electric glue guns and diesel backhoes, of the 19th century's "playing farmer" in the genteel suburbs while the husband commutes on the train to his Manhattan office job. Like Downing (and Loudon, and Repton, and so on), she adroitly used the media to build a franchise based on personality, expertise, and authority as a taste maven to help the confused, unconfident upwardly mobile upper middle classes figure out how to comport themselves for others' benefit. Like Downing, born in Newburgh, New York, just as the Hudson Valley and the major urban areas of the country saw a wave of suburbanization, Martha also saw success come about in part through being in the right place at the right time. Westport was then (and remains today) home to many people in New York publishing—people who knew and perhaps hired her as a caterer. Her husband, Andy, had ended up running, more or less by accident, the Random House publishing company imprint Harry N. Abrams, where he found himself with a surprise blockbuster on his hands with the American edition of a quirky Dutch children's book called *The Secret Book of Gnomes* in 1977. It was Andy, suddenly a publishing genius, who passed Martha's proposal for *Entertaining* to another Random House imprint, Crown Books—and the rest is history. And Martha's flowery, nostalgic aesthetic was perfect for the era: it was an (appropriately stiffer and glossier) American variant on the British shabby chic phenomenon of replicating old, faded, cluttered country house elegance in more modest dwellings, and anticipated the gauzy romanticism of Republican presidential candidate Ronald Reagan's "Morning in America" TV ads of 1984, with their impressionistic, slow-motion scenes of Regular Joes going to work, brides in white wedding dresses, misty country roads, and bucolic fields. Martha's world, where women kept a perfect, beautiful home, fit in beautifully with this mood of social and aesthetic retrenchment.

At the same time, her persona perfectly hit the notes of a new assertiveness in American business culture, in which women were beginning to participate in increasingly visible ways. Martha didn't wear the boxy, padded-shoulder Armani suits that many professional women put on in the 1980s and '90s (she preferred a no-nonsense WASP country weekend look of jeans and sweaters), but she embodied the all-business ethic they were meant to signal. In spite of her best efforts at making her activities seem effortless, Martha was obviously, strenuously, implacably about work. There was something awesome in the spectacle of her mastery and prodigious productivity—she was the überhousewife, though clearly more house master than mistress, subservient to no one (it is worth noting that in her perfect home, men were conspicuously absent, except as occasional helpers, running backhoes, for example). She not only ran her home like a well-oiled business machine, but ran a deadly serious business empire from her home. She had found a way to bridge the widening gulf between work and home, and in that was an impressive display of female empowerment. But for some people it came at too high a price of aggressiveness and overkill: she told her readers how to plan cocktails for twenty-five guests, and for fifty, and for two hundred, and how to whip up a midnight omelette "supper" for thirty—or sixty. How could one not feel intimidated, even a little bullied, by such prescriptions?

Newsweek magazine called Martha's shtick "the art of showing off," giving voice to many onlookers' objections to Martha's message and her success. It's not surprising that when the press increasingly reported on accounts of Martha's nastiness to neighbors in Westport and abusive behavior toward employees and business partners, the stories got wide play. She was reported to have cursed at people for driving too slowly and neighborhood kids for accidentally sending a ball into her yard. Behind the smile for the cameras she was said to have a hard edge that often turned to rage. At one of the nine houses she eventually owned,[9] a modern house on the Hamptons' exclusive Georgica Pond (designed by Gordon Bunshaft, Isamu Noguchi's old collaborator), she became embroiled in a fight with her neighbor over the placement and height of hedges and blocked views, a spat that escalated in a tit-for-tat of midnight plantings and tearings out, of legal attacks and counterattacks, including a contretemps with a landscaper employed by the neighbor in which he accused Martha of cursing at him and running into him with her car (their dispute was settled out of court). Some former employees said that she often treated Andy Stewart with scorn. Behind the carefully crafted image of domestic bliss, Martha was acting like Eddie Kostyra had, controlling and lashing out at those around her.

None of this diminished her drive, or her success. She inked a deal with Kmart to sell a Martha Stewart line of home furnishings, and talked executives at Time Inc. into selling her the magazine business for what was calculated to be a cash commitment of only $2 million. That investment paid off in spectacularly improbable and typically Martha Stewart fashion when the public stock offering of her aptly named company, Martha Stewart Living Omnimedia, returned a market valuation of $1 billion in 1999.[10] If anything, Martha's ruthlessness and business acumen gained her admirers, and she played her reputation to her own advantage. She told Oprah Winfrey in one appearance on Oprah's show: "I can almost bend steel with my mind. I can bend anything if I try hard enough.

I can make myself do almost anything." And Oprah seemed to agree, telling an interviewer that "Martha and I are not in competition with each other because Martha is the queen of external creations, which I am not. I am really more interested in getting them to look inside themselves and to try to excavate, pull back the layers of their lives, and then fix up their house."[11]

Martha wasn't interested in excavating the self, just in fixing up the house and showing it off with a big, lavish party designed to make her rivals squirm at their inadequacy. After being convicted of lying to investigators about money made on a stock sale, and serving five months in a federal prison, Martha staged a comeback in grand style: she went back on the air with *The Martha Stewart Show* and *The Apprentice*: *Martha Stewart*, a version of the popular TV series about working for difficult bosses that also featured Donald Trump; and she launched a new line of housewares with Macy's department stores. The stock price of her company rose, and by 2006 it was profitable again, aided by a second magazine, *Martha Stewart Weddings*, and a new spate of books—three at last count. As icing on the cake—and the most delicious kind of irony, where real life perfectly mirrors a cartoon critique of it—she created a line of Martha Stewart signature suburban houses sold by national suburb builder KB Home, available in four color-coordinated configurations: "Katonah," based on her houses in Westport and Katonah, New York, "Lily Pond," based on her Shingle-style house in the Hamptons, "Skylands," based on her house of that name on the Maine coast, and "Dunemere," supposedly inspired by the Bahamas. The designs are offered in seven themed developments in five Sunbelt states, turnkey-ready so that the buyer can, if not actually be Martha, at least live a perfectly replicated Stepford Wife version of her life. It is life as reality TV: starring in one's own *Martha Stewart Show*.

NONE OF MARTHA'S notoriety or business machinations can diminish the profound effect she has had on taste in America. She was by no means alone in selling home and garden style, nor did she invent or even contribute anything new to either, but she was the most prodigious popularizer of a pastiche aesthetic that has, with her help, become so ubiquitous in the United States as to be invisible: a kind of modernized, plushed-up version of the late Victorian Colonial Revival Style. Like Andrew Jackson Downing's, Martha's look is a domesticated form of Romantic naturalism, comforting and lavish at the same time, which aims to evoke an unstudied gentility and links to an imagined WASP cultural past. Next to its avatar, her Turkey Hill garden, the style is best exemplified in the garden she had restored at Skylands, near Seal Harbor, Maine, a woodland fantasy designed by Jens Jensen in 1925 for Edsel Ford. From Jensen's plans, Martha replanted the woods, paths, and native rockwork with ferns and perennials and constructed a stone council circle (which is much more cleanly built than any of Jensen's) with a fire pit in the center. Besides the plants, the sheer size of the property is the star of the show.

The garden at Skylands is a link to the Gilded Age, and it is appropriate that Martha Stewart—a Polish girl from working-class New Jersey who acquired a Scottish surname by marrying a Jew and became a self-made billionaire (for a while anyway, on paper) by selling a lifestyle she had never enjoyed herself until she seized it with sheer chutzpah—should have resurrected it. During her ascendancy gardens again became potent status symbols and markers of the arrival of new money. If the first Gilded Age's hotbed of houses and gardens for newly minted millionaires was Newport, that of the second Gilded Age of the 1980s and '90s and early 2000s was the Hamptons, on Long Island's East End. Had he visited in this period, Henry James would have immediately recognized its hothouse mixture of architecture, gardens, money, and class anxiety, as the Hamptons were and are all about new money trying to simulate the patina of old money by making a fantasy version of WASP culture. Big, muscular houses copied from the Shingle style of McKim, Mead, and White are the thing, surrounded by big hedges, big flower borders, big lawns, and big, expensive specimen trees—an obsession about which Martha joked: "It's pretty funny hearing so many wealthy guys bragging about the size of their weeping copper beeches and taxus yews. My theory is it's about midlife crisis. I've noted that when they glimpse a rare tree and a pretty girl at the same time, they often look a lot more excited about the tree."[12]

Especially in gardens in the northern tier of the United States, the past few decades have been marked by a focus on plants, less than on design, yielding a look that owes much to the Arts & Crafts garden, especially its William Robinson and Gertrude Jekyll–influenced plantsmanship. One of the most impressive achievements of the era was Frank Cabot's Les Quatre Vents, on the north shore of the Saint Lawrence River in Quebec, which became widely influential in the garden world, a kind of Mecca for garden fanciers lucky enough to make the pilgrimage. Cabot's grandparents and parents began with a summerhouse in 1928, adding to it and transforming it over the years, including setting out an axial formal garden and a white garden in the 1930s, under the influence of Sissinghurst Castle Garden in England. Since 1975, Cabot and his wife, Anne, have gardened especially industriously, expanding out from the central formal pieces to create a sprawling Arts & Crafts–style masterpiece with curious echoes of the English picturesque. Surrounding the steep-roofed, French Colonial Revival house are allées, formal lawns, knot gardens, hedges, a rockery, terraces complete with circular steps copied from Lutyens and Jekyll, perennial borders, and a rose garden; beyond them are flowering meadows, pastures, and woodlands, here and there punctuated with follies that could have been built in the 18th century—a red lacquered Japanese-style bridge, a vaguely neoclassical music pavilion, a Chinese-style moon bridge over a meandering watercourse, Nepalese rope bridges across a small ravine,[13] two exquisite Japanese wood and paper pavilions in their own Japanese garden complete with a pond, and a "pigeonnier" tower straddling a canal, which tower resembles a cross between a corner fallen off a French baroque château, a medieval water mill, a dovecote, and the Taj Mahal. Like a good garden anthologist, Frank made no apologies for copying things he and Anne liked: "plagiarism is the life's blood," he explained.[14] And they copied with uncommon imagination and skill. The whole is utterly spectacular and would have made even a Vanderbilt or duPont jealous. What is most significant about the garden is not its scale but its plantsmanship: Les Quatre Vents is a sustained horticultural symphony, performed at the highest level. It has been widely admired for the Cabots' collection of Asian rarities, including the blue Himalayan poppy, *Meconopsis betonicifolia*, a temperamental fetish object of gardeners in temperate zones worldwide that happens to like southern Quebec and propagates readily there. The same floral tour de force was on view at the Cabots' smaller, twelve-acre garden in Cold Spring, New York, called Stonecrop, which became public in 1992. In the Gilded Age tradition, these residential gardens were in effect private botanical gardens, showcasing their owners' skill, resources, and ambition, and comparing favorably with much bigger institutions like Longwood Gardens in Delaware or Wave Hill in the Bronx. Their influence on gardening style, especially in the East, has been enormous, reinforcing a general trend toward plant-driven design.

An even more visible and popularly influential garden was Lynden Miller's resurrection of the 19th century Conservatory Garden in New York's Central Park. In the 1980s, a friend of Miller's involved with city planning suggested that the painter and weekend gardener spearhead the renovation of the dilapidated six-acre garden that stretches along the eastern edge of the park, with its entrance at Fifth Avenue and 105th Street. Originally the site of a huge greenhouse for Central Park plants, the garden had later been laid out as a triptych of formal schemes, nominally Italian, French, and English, featuring fountains with Arts & Crafts bronze figures, a curving wisteria arbor, a hedged lawn, and a double allée of twisted, spreading crab apple trees. By the late 1970s and early '80s, with New York City suffering from high crime, white flight to the suburbs, and fiscal ruin, its international image of decline and chaos fixed by the Blackout of 1977 with its looting and arson, the garden had gone to rack and ruin and saw more hustlers and addicts than Sunday strollers. Miller, who in addition to being a redoubtable fundraiser and navigator of the city bureaucracy was a gifted plantswoman and designer, transformed the sad place into a showplace worthy of Winterthur: restoring the knots, hedges, fountains, and bluestone paths and planting the beds to overflowing with rudbeckias, grasses, tulips, hydrangeas, and her signature plant, the purple smokebush, Cotinus. When she was through, the garden deserved the name again, offering a serene oasis apart from the rush and noise of Manhattan's streets. It also needed to be fed: gardening like this is an expensive proposition, requiring constant inputs of soil, plants, and labor—and therefore, fund-raising. Like the giant pair of ornate iron gates that guard the entrance from Fifth Avenue (originally from the Vanderbilt Mansion at Fifth Avenue and Fifty-eighth Street, which was demolished in 1927, and the gates moved here in 1939), the Conservatory Garden is redolent of the Gilded Age. In fact, its renovation signaled the advent of a new one and was a tangible manifestation of the restoration of New York City as a place the upper middle class and the truly rich could again be proud to call home. After its nadir and with the financial markets improving, the city's elite began to take control of its public space again, applying the "broken windows" theory, published in the *Atlantic* in March 1982 by criminologists James Q. Wilson and George Kelling, to cleaning up the subways, fighting graffiti, arresting "squeegee men," and, after Rudolph Giuliani was elected mayor in 1993, applying a "zero tolerance" policy to petty crime. Following Lynden Miller's success in the Conservatory Garden, she and the privately funded Central Park Conservancy applied the treatment to the rest of the park. The transformation over the years was remarkable: in a given corner of the park—perhaps a scruffy, balding patch of lawn or a bed with a few anemic shrubs—little fences would appear, meant to keep people out, then Gardening would commence in earnest, with tulips and taxus planted and turf reseeded. Corner by corner, the park was turned into a garden. More police came with the perennials, and more people of the prosperous, orderly type began using the park, until today Central Park is filled with (mostly) law-abiding people, day and night, and is no longer the byword for muggings and rapes that it was for a generation. Little fences are still up, keeping the happy hordes in their places and out of the flower beds. Become something of a heroine, Miller was asked to work her magic on Bryant Park, Madison Square Park, part of the New York Botanical Garden, and Columbia and Princeton universities, among other projects.

This sort of horticultural splash and intensity as the prime directive of garden design was propagating by the early 1990s throughout the media that concerned itself with gardens, and not just in *Martha Stewart Living*. Ken Druse, a garden photographer and writer based in Brooklyn,

Conservatory Garden, Central Park. (Sookie Tex)

spotlighted new plants in the *New York Times* and published a series of well-received books that amounted to a kind of flower porn for plant collectors: *The Natural Garden* (1989), *The Natural Shade Garden* (1992), *The Natural Habitat Garden* (1994), and *The Collector's Garden* (1997). Druse's books could have been designed by William Robinson, illustrated with luscious color photos: there were wildflowers, woods, brilliantly variegated leaves, and no end of hostas, ferns, columbines, trilliums, delphiniums, and clematis. The images offer a sense of infinite expanse, with views into unbroken woods and meadows, meandering paths, and a conspicuous absence of neighbors and buildings, save the occasional genteel, invariably cottagey-looking house. Yet the style appeared all over New York and other eastern cities: in pocket parks, in narrow beds in front of Park Avenue buildings, and in tiny Brooklyn backyards, like Druse's own, each one becoming an evocation of a natural woodland harmony that must exist somewhere out there, in "nature."

The repetition of the word *natural* in Druse's titles was a sign of an increasingly focused awareness in the zeitgeist of environmental issues and the garden's capacity—or, some thought, responsibility—to engage them. All over the map, even in the Hamptons, along the dunefront megamillion-dollar houses of Gin Lane and Further Lane, between the habitual opulence and the clipped hedges, a growing naturalism was on display, drawing on the look of the dunes and marshes, with their grasses, pines, and scrub oaks. This emerging aesthetic received a big push from the landscape architecture firm Oehme, van Sweden, based in Washington, D.C., which made a splash with what it called "the New American Garden": sweeping curves, lawns edged with bermed beds with massed plantings of big, brightly colored textural plants like rudbeckias, coneflowers, joe-pye weed, and tall ornamental grasses. The style had a naturalistic feel yet was manicured at the same time: nothing was clipped, nothing was straight, but the plantings were reassuringly controlled, like a meadow scene as composed by a color-field painter.

An irony of the New American Garden was that it, like Jens Jensen's before it, had been imported from northern Europe, along with the grasses that were the signature progressive plants of the era. In Europe, they had become key to a resurgent naturalistic style reminiscent of the native plant movement in gardening of the early 20th century that had influenced the young Dane. This time the European immigrant who carried the movement to America was the nurseryman and designer Kurt Bluemel, and the epicenter was not Chicago, but Maryland. Born in 1933 in German Sudetenland (now part of the Czech Republic), young Kurt and his family were forced to flee to Germany after the war. As a young man he worked in the nursery trade, and came to the United States from Switzerland in 1960, to Monkton, Maryland, where he took a job at a nursery and moonlighted as a grave digger (which paid better). There he met the landscape architect Wolfgang Oehme, who had arrived from Germany three years earlier and shared his passion for plants. The two started their own nursery in 1964. Oehme sold his share to Bluemel two years later to go into a design partnership with James van Sweden, and the men began designing gardens using new perennials and grasses being imported by Bluemel from Germany and Switzerland. His most popular commercial introductions included various dramatic forms of *Miscanthus sinensis*, a tall Japanese silver grass with tufted flowers that wave like pompoms, the gray-green switchgrass *Panicum virgatum* "Heavy Metal," and the little bluestem grass *Schizachyrium scoparium* "The Blues." Oehme and Van Sweden combined loose plantings with fine materials like cut bluestone and cobbles, used for swimming pool copings, decks, paths, and walls, studded with crops of embedded boulders. The look was perfect for East Coast summerhouse climes: reminiscent of the dunes, sounds, estuaries, woods, and meadows of semirural second-home-urbia. In the Hamptons, successful society designers like Deborah Nevins and Edwina von Gal worked it into their repertoires of lawns and hedges, and the look became a backdrop for countless Ralph Lauren and Calvin Klein clothing ads.

The naturalism creeping into the gardens of the summer colonies of the leisure class was part of a spectrum of ideas that reached all the way from progressive politics to conservation biology. It meshed with and fed on a growing critique of the American obsession with lawns, which was memorably expressed by author Michael Pollan in his book *Second Nature* as a doctrine of not imposing our will on nature, but interacting with the forces of nature to make gardens. Designer, nurseryman, and author John Greenlee in California searched for alternatives to traditional turf grass, instead making meadows using low sedges, buffalo grass, and other species needing less water and fertilizer and less or no mowing than a lawn. What Greenlee began practicing in people's yards echoed on a small scale broader themes in landscape management and environmental theory. In figuring out how to remediate abused or polluted landscapes and redevelop abandoned industrial areas, known as "brownfields," government planners worked with scientists and landscape architects to do

ecological restoration. Conservation biologists began to point out the
need to set aside large areas of remaining wild lands in North America
and link them with restored corridors of "rewilded" lands in order to preserve the DNA of threatened plant and animal populations. They began
drawing maps showing huge swaths of territory, hitherto occupied by
towns, roads, and agriculture, put literally back to nature by large-scale
landscape engineering—a kind of reverse settlement of the continent.
This line of thinking had its most singularly elegant and controversial idea in the Buffalo Commons, a proposal put forth in 1987 by the
academic couple Frank and Deborah Popper, arguing that conventional
farming and ranching are unsustainable on the dry parts of the Great
Plains, testified to by the depopulation of the region since the 1920s, and
advocating the restoration of native prairie and bison herds on roughly

John Greenlee's first grass garden, Pomona, California. (By Saxon Holt)

140,000 square miles of land in ten states. It would be "natural gardening" on a continental scale.

In 1978, on the corner of La Guardia Place and West Houston Street in New York's Greenwich Village, at the intersection of landscape and art, a postage-stamp-sized precursor of the Buffalo Commons appeared. It was a dirt rectangle twenty-five feet by forty feet, circumscribed by concrete sidewalks, between an apartment complex and a market; the only indication that it was anything other than a weedy strip was a plaque explaining the intention of its creator, Alan Sonfist. Sonfist had grown up in the South Bronx near a section of the Bronx River that was still covered in forest, in which he played as a child. Then the authorities "decided it was dangerous and poured concrete over it," according to him. He never got over it. He wanted it back. When he later studied to become an artist, it occurred to him that one might be able to peel away some of that concrete that buried New York and replant the childhood paradise—and call it art. In 1965, when he was twenty-one years old, Sonfist first proposed the idea behind *Time Landscape*, altering fifty sites in the city to re-create pre-European landscape conditions. Later, around 1968 or '69, he met the artists Robert Smithson and Gordon Matta-Clark, both of whom had sketched out ideas for islands, covered in trees, floating off Manhattan—Matta-Clark's was a series of barges anchored in the harbor, stationary, while Smithson's was an island to be towed around Manhattan Island continually, like a piece of Central Park spun off into a satellite in orbit. Encouraged by members of the art world but stymied by city government, Sonfist did not find his vision achieved until 1978, and then only on the one Village site. He researched historical records for clues to the area's pre-settlement state. An English document described a trout stream just off Broadway, and he learned that Canal Street was so named because the street was once a waterway. He determined that the location at La Guardia and Houston once would have supported a forest of beech trees on rocky ground and sandy hills covered in wildflowers and junipers, so that is what he planted. The trees were at first no more than three feet tall; some of the plantings were just a few inches high. By the late 1980s *Time Landscape* had grown into a dense thicket, fenced off from the homeless and peppered with blown trash. But its influence, and its status as a harbinger of a flood, were real.

Ecology and natural processes soon came to be dominant preoccupations of landscape architects, especially academics such as Harvard Graduate School of Design professor Michael Van Valkenburgh, whose work has become canonical, including the *Ice Wall* series at Radcliffe College (1988–90), made of metal screens sprayed with water in the winter months to form translucent sheets of ice along walkways, and Mill Race Park, in Columbus, Indiana (1989–93), a sequence of pools, sluices, and raised areas designed to dramatize the seasonal rise of the nearby White River that floods most of the park. Following earnestly in Isamu Noguchi's contoured traces, the new, ecological landscape architecture was all about landform, about cutting and gouging to simulate nature. A fine example is George Hargreaves's Guadalupe River Park, in San Jose, California, conceived in 1988 as a solution to another river flooding problem in a developed area. Alongside a stretch of channelized river, Hargreaves sculpted a series of crescent-shaped berms of "sediment," with cuts in between them, mimicking a fluvial landscape of braided overflow paths on either side of the main channel. This one was manufactured with bulldozers. Appropriately, the forms are stylized, not meant to look precisely natural—rendering them a descendant of Halprin's Portland fountains. But Hargreaves's version of geomorphology is functional, replacing what would have been seventeen-foot-high concrete walls with a floodable park that allows water to safely spill over the banks during storms.

The San Jose park and hundreds of projects like it built since are visionary moves toward reclaiming natural processes in the built environment, allowing city and nature to better coexist. Most important, it was designed to allow for change over time, fulfilling Robert Smithson's dictum that parks and landscapes ought not seek to be perfect, final, and unchanging: "Parks are idealizations of nature, but nature in fact is not a condition of the ideal. . . . Nature is never finished. . . . Parks and gardens are pictorial in the origin—landscapes created with natural materials rather than paint. The scenic ideals that surround even our national parks are carriers of a nostalgia for heavenly bliss and eternal calmness."[15] Post-Noguchi, landscape architecture works at mimicking nature, just as Capability Brown and Olmsted did—for aesthetic pleasure, but also for moral pleasure: righting the wrongs of industrial, engineered civilization that had committed crimes against nature. It promised living better through better-designed space.

Even at the other pole of the profession, among the conceptualists, stylized versions of ecology began to appear everywhere, such as Toronto's Village of Yorkville Park, created from 1991 to 1996 by Martha Schwartz, Ken Smith, and David Meyer. On a one-acre site adjacent to a row of town houses, they designed a linear series of "boxes," each one displaying the characteristic plants of seventeen different ecosystems that occur in the province of Ontario. On one end is an enormous, rounded rock outcrop on which people climb and sit, evoking the rocky landscape of Central Park. The Yorkville park has been described as an "ecological curio case," a collection, as in a botanical garden, but one of "systems," not specimens, referents to a supposed ecological balance that exists somewhere else. The idea is almost Victorian—a new, environmentalist anthology garden. Bringing native plants into the city here serves a moral purpose—naturalizing the city, putting us back in touch with nature, as Olmsted did—though what is being remediated in Toronto is not (only) the frazzled nerves of the city dweller, but his and her consciousness and conscience. The garden is lovely, relaxing, and didactic. In her design for the Minneapolis Federal Courthouse Plaza, built in 1998, Schwartz followed a similar procedure, using grass-covered berms, arrayed in a wave pattern, like Hargreaves's, some with jack pines growing out of them, and silver-painted logs to conjure a stylized version of Minnesota's historical landscape and lumbering economy.

SOME OF THE best syntheses of contemporary landscape design's kit of parts—the ecological mimicry, naturalistic style, fields of grasses, and elaborate, self-conscious ground-shaping—are to be found in the work of Kathryn Gustafson and her partners. The first thing that strikes one about Gustafson's gardens is the liveliness of the ground: it swoops, folds, and falls in mounds, banks, crevices, and sinuous curves. The landform is sometimes bare, with just a covering of close-mowed turf; sometimes it's combined with sophisticated plans of intersecting panels of water, grass, and stone with trees and paths laid out in carefully modulated sine curves. At its most complex, in the Lurie Garden in Chicago's Millennium Park, opened in 2004, designed with Dutch plantsman Piet Oudolf, known for ornamental grass landscapes, it is a virtuoso weaving of curving paths, lines of water, arcing stone walls, wildflower meadows, and bosques of trees set on an undulating ground plane that mimics a prairie landscape, though it is constructed over a giant parking garage.

The path Gustafson followed to her mature style is surprising. She grew up in Yakima, in eastern Washington state's high desert plateau, where folded, tawny, grass-covered hills form a backdrop for a river curving through town—a tableau echoed in some form in many of her gardens. She first studied fashion design in New York City before moving to France at the age of twenty. Soon she found herself captivated by landscape making and enrolled in the Ecole Nationale Supérieure du Paysage at Versailles, site of André Le Nôtre's monumental royal gardens surrounding the palace of King Louis XIV. Le Nôtre's masterpiece had a big influence on the young American; it's still her favorite garden, and she revisits it every year. What inspires her in it is not what it's typically celebrated for—the gigantic, radial geometry, the stark rationality. Her take on it is novel: "I think that one of the most modern gardens in the world is Versailles, it's fantastically contemporary," she said, with "very subtle land movement, terracing, and scale changes that create totally different spaces. Mine may not be as rectilinear, but I think there are a lot of lessons from historical landscapes."

Deciphering these lessons is central to her practice. By example, she asked: "Why do you like to walk down a canal in Europe? What are the three major elements of them?" She answers. One: "It's linear, you know where you're going; it has an edge that you can walk on." Two: "It has trees that provide you shade and dappled light." And three: "It has two different kinds of smell, vegetation and water." The Lurie Garden is an

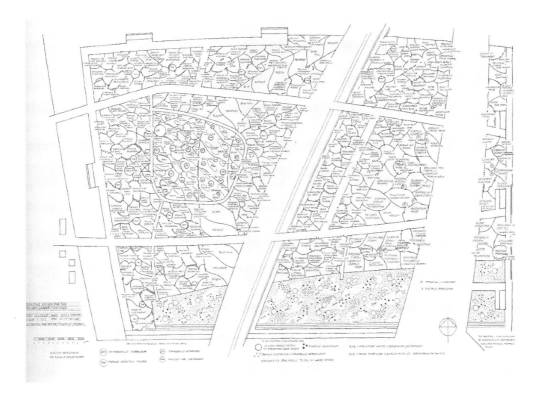

Lurie Garden planting plan. (Courtesy of Gustafson Partners)

example of all three: the edge being the water "seam" that represents the ghost of the old Chicago lakefront that was once right below it before the rail yard was built with landfill. The result is the ability to make visiting her gardens feel like taking a private journey in a public space.

After receiving her diploma in 1979, she opened an office in Paris. Her first commissions were for government transportation projects: tunnel entrances, reservoir tailings, and expressway interstices—seemingly random, lifeless spots that she reworked into dramatic, flowing compositions of contoured, terraced, but still organic-seeming shaped grassy ground. These led to arresting work at corporate headquarters for L'Oréal, Shell, and Esso in France, with sweeping, undulating grassy surfaces edged

Kathryn Gustafson, Shell Oil headquarters, France. (Courtesy of Gustafson Guthrie Nichol Ltd)

and studded with concrete ribbons or slabs protruding from the ground, à la Richard Serra. They achieved an uncanny modulation between an organic feel, like hills or folds of flesh, and the intentionally contrived abstractions of artistic postminimalism. From there her career skyrocketed, with invitations to do public work all over: including the North End Parks in Boston, the Square of the Rights of Man in Evry, France, the Diana, Princess of Wales Memorial Fountain in London's Hyde Park, the Seattle Civic Center, the garden for the Ross Planetarium at New York's American Museum of Natural History, a garden at the Art Institute of Chicago, and the Lurie Garden. Today she splits her time between homes in Seattle and Paris and partner firms in Seattle and London. She is an American who holds French nationality and considers France "home"—a uniquely hybrid outlook that shapes her work. "The best way I can explain it is my moral education is American and my intellectual education is French," she told me.

The primacy of shaped ground in her work stems from the design process itself, which begins with models she hand-sculpts in clay (later they are translated into computer software to guide construction). The spirit of Noguchi is close in these models, as is that of Polish sculptor Igor Mitoraj, who first urged Gustafson to take her modeling seriously and gave her the actual sculpting tools to do it. The unadorned clay panels are in many ways the purest form of her vision: precise, perfectly smooth, monochrome reliefs that look as though they could be still photographs of rippled water, or human flesh. It's more than an analogy: Gustafson is keenly aware of the relationship between landform and the body. "I think it's because it is organic and we're organic, we're basically made of the same stuff. I think that part of my fascination with it is that it's so connected to who we are," she said. "Everybody touches the land, you walk on it, so it's your immediate first connection. If somehow you can translate your concept through that connection, then the creating the space only gets heightened by the other objects," such as trees, plants, and built features. And experience is at the heart of Gustafson's design philosophy: she is interested in creating spaces that draw people to them and through them, in the process creating "ambiences," in her words, "that make you feel a certain way or function a certain way."

Working first in clay, not paper, the normal medium of landscape design, gives the gardens a thickness—call it fullness—that "thinking in *section*," as she puts it, can give, where thinking only in *plan* can't. The result is like Land Art, yet her version is more feminine, less interventionist, less about sticking things (like Cadillacs or rusting steel plates) into the ground or scraping it with bulldozers than in realizing the ground's potential to evoke emotion in us as we walk across it. It feels like nature, though it might be built over a parking garage or a rail yard, as at Millennium Park. Seeing the maquettes shows the sophisticated interplay of "natural" organic form, curves, bumps, meanders, and gridding, though the grids are generally torqued and curved so that they're not legible as

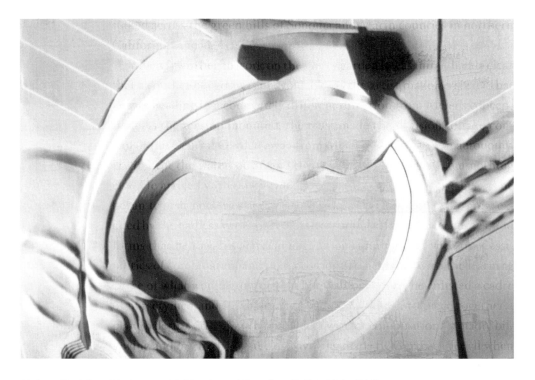

Kathryn Gustafson, Morbras model. (Courtesy of Gustafson Guthrie Nichol Ltd)

such. Without benefit of the overhead plan view, moving through one of her gardens feels just like a walk in the park.

AND HERE IS the nexus point of contemporary American landscape design: the shaped landform, and, ironically, close-cropped grass. In spite of all the powerful environmental critiques of lawns promulgated from academia to the popular media, the American garden can't escape from turf. Much of Kathryn Gustafson's work is a more ethereal, feminine translation of Noguchi's three-dimensional stone surfaces into lawn. At another aesthetic extreme, what might be called the postminimalist garden, supremely self-consciousness and referential, are the gardens made by the American postmodernist architectural theorist and landscape designer Charles Jencks, among them the turf-covered spiral mound called

Landform Ueda at the Scottish Gallery of Modern Art in Edinburgh (1999–2002), and the Garden of Cosmic Speculation, also in Scotland, which he designed over several decades with his wife, Maggie Keswick (the author of an authoritative history of Chinese gardens), a truly eccentric and wonderful composition of spiral mounds and curving terraces, all in close-cut turf, intersecting with planes of water and swooping steel bands. Jencks's work may be inspired by physics and mathematical chaos theory, but it is enabled by bulldozers and lawnmowers. As the anti-lawn movement complained, the perfect greensward remains stubbornly and deeply lodged in the American (and British) psyche.

While these examples of gardens are rarefied indeed, all touch and resemble the most mundane and ubiquitous product of American land-

Charles Jencks, the Garden of Cosmic Speculation, Scotland. (Wikimedia Commons/GNU Free Documentation License)

scape architecture: the golf course. Rarely mentioned in the same breath as proper landscape architecture or gardens, golf courses nevertheless share the same physical and cultural space as those supposedly more legitimate and "artistic" activities. Like the bits and strips of designed and maintained greenery along roads, in medians, and in the borders between buildings, malls, freeways, parks, and schools, all share in the psychological and physical form of the American landscape; they are often no less intentional, and no less meaningful; often they are more functional and more visually satisfying than their more exalted cousins.

English-speaking (and Scots-speaking) people have been designing golf courses for five hundred years, working out contour, texture, flow, sequence, planting, and maintenance in ever more sophisticated ways. Eighteenth century greenskeepers in Britain were functionally no different than Capability Brown, except in the social ecology of their professions. This status difference changed in the late 1960s, and due in good measure to the influence, personality, and visibility of one man: Jack Nicklaus, a prodigy golfer from Columbus, Ohio. In 1965, having already won the U.S. Open, the Masters, and the PGA Championship by the age of twenty-five, Nicklaus joined former amateur competitor Pete Dye to help design a course for the Golf Club in New Albany, Ohio. Eventually the two formed a partnership. Jack liked the work, and by the early 1970s was on his own, winning praise for course designs that "thought" the way good golfers did. Dye said of him that he was "a second-shot thinker," convinced that the approach to the green, not the tee shot, ought to guide a golfer's strategy and a course designer's.[16] Nicklaus used his experience as a competitor, having played on hundreds of courses all over the world, to think through the movement and flow of each hole, where trouble should lie and where safety, fitting the choreography of strokes into the topography. He became known for very prominent bunkers, and holes that "faded" from left to right (a shot he himself excelled at), and for remarkably beautiful courses that fit in with their surroundings. Known as the greatest professional golfer of all time, Nicklaus won seventy-three PGA tour events and eighteen major championships over a twenty-five-year career. It is less well known that he and his company have designed more than three hundred courses—roughly 1 percent of all the golf courses on earth.

When he approached a new design, he would "consider it from four angles," asking himself these questions:

1. *Who is going to play the course?* Would they be predominantly pros or amateurs, women or men, old or young?

2. *How sensitive is the environment?* Nicklaus often has been called on to put courses on old dumps or mine tailings, and has developed real skills in ecological restoration.

3. *How can I balance the demands on a player's intelligence with demands on his strength?* The designer's challenge is putting enough variety in the course so that a smarter player has a fair chance against a longer hitter. In his book, *Nicklaus by Design: Golf Course Strategy and Architecture,* he explained: "One of the really overlooked battlegrounds in the war between power and placement is the driveable par-4," naming the tenth hole at Riviera Country Club in Los Angeles as an example.[17]

4. *How will it look?* Here is Nicklaus's philosophy: "It sounds basic, but a golf course has to be pretty."

At the aesthetic level, Nicklaus has an unusually subtle understanding of fit and blending in—far greater than most landscape architects. Along with his prodigious output, this ought to make him one of the most important, and the most unheralded, landscape designers in history, one whose methods ought to be studied. "A well-designed course can't be separated from its surroundings—it's part of them," he wrote. "In designing a golf course, it's critically important to infuse the course with the surroundings and view. You have to look at the mountains, the vegetation, the lakes, the indigenous grasses—see what you've got and try to bring that through in the finished layout. That tying of what you might call the themes or rhythms of the land into the design is what separates an ordinary golf course from a beautiful one.

"If I'm working in a mountain setting, I'll try to mirror the forms of the surrounding mountains in the mounding on the course. I'm not trying to replicate the mountains, and most players don't even notice it on a conscious level, but it's a technique that allows the course to fit in, to match. It's not unlike matching a shirt and tie." He will echo a distant line of treetops, or a texture, like that of palmettos in an adjacent savannah, or a shade of green, on the course. "Even in an area that has few cues, such as the desert, I try to bring the rhythm and flow of the land itself into the design."[18] A lovely example of this technique is visible at his PGA West course, at La Quinta, near Palm Springs, California, where the scalloped line of small grassy drop-offs on the side of the fairway repeats in miniature the contours of a line of hills in the desert beyond, catching sunlight and casting shadows in precisely the same way, so that the completely artificial foreground landscape seems of a piece with the natural backdrop. The balance between the naturalistic and manicured, the miniaturization, and the way the distance is pulled in with *shakkei* recall Japanese gardens, yet the modern golf course is a consummately American form.

All golf courses are beautiful in some way, because they are at the confluence of nature and the human mind; they are an edge, a pleasing contiguity between grass and trees, between the terrain we walk through that we make and the terrain beyond that we don't. As Kathryn Gustafson noted about walking along a canal, the edge also provides a path to follow on our journey. The golf course, with its numbered chain of holes, makes a game of it. Golf course making and "serious" garden making are joined on the field of play: after his 1933 proposal *Monument to the Plow*, Noguchi's first expressions of earth sculpting were his playgrounds, intended to make children feel closer to the earth. The first artist's earthwork is generally recognized to be Herbert Bayer's *Grass Mound*, made in 1955 at the Aspen Art Institute by the Bauhaus-era German architect who came to the United States in 1938, followed by his Anderson Park, also in Aspen, both of which look like a golf course and a Noguchi playground genetically spliced. A golf course and an earthwork are adult playscapes.

I can recall watching, in about 1992, bulldozers shape a field of hideously jagged black lava on the Big Island of Hawaii into what would become the softly contoured banks, bunkers, and fairways of the Hualalai course—one of Jack Nicklaus's more dramatic creations: a Joan Miróesque tapestry of smooth green and white amoebas (fairways, greens, and sand traps) splattered across a black lava field as sharp as broken glass, laid alongside the deep blue waters off North Kona. The sight of the clanking machines performing this miracle was awesome and beautiful, and gratified some childish urge to shape the ground with one's hands, like making sand castles on the beach. Earthmoving is the essence of the garden art form, because it precedes planting and prepares for it, taking land and making it more like "nature": that is, like the mental image of nature specific to the imaginer and his cultural framework. This is what Olmsted did in Central Park, according to Robert Smithson: he "brought a Jeffersonian rural reality into the metropolis."[19] This too is what Nicklaus, Schwartz, and Gustafson are doing, each in their own way.

Golf, of course, has its social meaning, too, which can't be separated from its physical forms. It has a well-deserved reputation for elitism, and historically, racism, due to its association with restricted-membership country clubs. From their earliest importation into this country, golf courses have been profitably attached to exclusive residential subdivisions, with the course serving as status marker—the owner's share of a huge, quasi-communal Arcadian landscape—and a recreational and social amenity. A golf-course-centered enclave provides a paradoxical sort of town and society in a purely anti-urban and antisocial form. We Americans seem to carry with us an ancient British attachment to verdant green lawns wherever we go. It's easy enough to re-create an approximation of England in rainy Pennsylvania or Ohio, but greenskeeping becomes more difficult as one moves west and the climate becomes more extreme, and drier. But we have never let that stop us: since the middle 19th century, the quintessential American form of settlement is the irrigation colony in the desert, repeated countless times by people fleeing the constricted realities of eastern cities. From the Mormon Zion that Brigham Young planted in the Utah desert in 1847, to the Union Colony at Greeley, Colorado, founded in 1869 as a Utopia for those of "high moral standards," to the orange groves of a hundred thousand hobby farmers escaped to sunny Southern California, Americans have excelled at moving water from one place to another to overcome local conditions and re-create the ancestral greensward.

The irrigation colony's contemporary form par excellence is the gated community built around a golf course (or two, or three) in the desert. Think of southern Arizona, whether Tucson, Scottsdale, or Phoenix, where Nicklaus developed one of his most visually arresting courses, the Cochise Course at Desert Mountain (named for the legendary Apache raider who bedeviled the U.S. Army for a decade), in the delightfully named wealthy suburb of Carefree. Or think of Southern California, especially Palm Springs, and its newer neighbor, Palm Desert, where square-mile-sized blocks of pristine desert have been transformed into what must be, from a certain perspective, the achievement of paradise on earth. In a typical upscale golf community, concrete walls a mile long, festooned with brightly flowering bougainvillea, wall off massive, empty, palm-lined boulevards and wall in a maze of serpentine streets lined with vaguely Spanish-style stucco houses, apparently only every tenth one occupied at any given time by owners and renters from far away. The curving rows of houses follow the DNA helixes of the fairways, onto which their living rooms and patios open, shaded by palms and misted by the overspray of the sprinklers that keep everything a lush, otherworldly Irish green. Down the middle of the fairways run streams, every so often burbling over rocky falls, the water circulating the length of two eighteen-hole courses before being pumped back up to the beginning to make the circuit again. The hiss of irrigation is mixed with the hum of electric golf carts and blotted out by the gas trimmers of Mexican gardeners tending the odd-shaped "meatballs" they have made of the variety of evergreen shrubs planted everywhere, free-form topiary. The gardeners, mostly poorly paid illegal immigrants, move in a businesslike hurry, like worker ants checking the aphids, their slightly desperate pace and purpose at odds with the stiff tranquility of the surroundings. When they move on, there can be stillness, and space to take in the views of distant mountains. The quiet might be interrupted by a sandstorm, turning the air yellow with grinding dust and blowing fallen palm fronds sideways, bouncing along the greens as if in a gale on a Pacific island. A sandstorm is a jarring reminder of how tenuous this privileged, perfected world is: the source of all this water, pumped out of the Colorado River east of here in the desert, is the Rocky Mountains, seven hundred miles away, and the river threatens to run dry from overuse and a drying climate. While it is real for now, Palm Desert is a fantasy world—bending the physical world to our will. It has existed for only a few decades, and it may not be sustainable.

Then again, we Americans are very good at this transportation: bringing a domesticated Jeffersonian rural fantasy to Central Park or to the Mojave Desert, bringing along everything settlers might need or want for implanting a new life in new worlds—hostile, unknown, arid, or tropical, it matters not, since we will re-create the world we want in any case. The *Mayflower* was such a transport vehicle, and the covered wagon; so is the armed fort of the English colonists or the U.S. Army cavalry that brought in Cochise and Geronimo. The irrigation settlement, the Panama Canal Zone, even Baghdad's Green Zone (while not a garden, it is a walled exclosure built on the site of the old Garden of Eden, just like it, to keep its inhabitants safe from the dangerous world outside) are all examples of American islands, private estates, gated havens. To this list should be added the Apollo missions, with their command modules, lunar landers, and return capsules—and golf clubs. Who can forget that the astronaut Alan Shepard, the first American in space and fifth man to walk on the moon as commander of the Apollo 14 mission, brought a six-iron with him and took two shots, one-handed because of his stiff spacesuit. The first fizzled, so he took a mulligan, dropped a second ball, and drove it a few hundred yards, setting the course record.

It is fitting that a spot in the Arizona desert outside ever-expanding Phoenix was chosen as the site for Biosphere 2, the $200 million glass vivarium built from 1987 to 1991, at 2.5 football fields long the largest closed system ever constructed. It was meant to be a veritable Garden of Eden, a self-contained habitat where a group of scientists could learn how to manage miniature scripts of Earth's support systems. It had a living area, a farm, plus versions of nature, something of an anthology of ecosystems, not unlike Martha Schwartz and company's Yorkville garden or the Huntington Gardens in Pasadena, with its Australian section, desert section, and New World tropics section. Biosphere 2 contained a rain forest, a coral reef, a mangrove forest, a savannah, and a fog desert. It was a sealed experiment, designed to teach how to colonize space, presumably the moon first. (It did not contain a golf course, but there were scores of them nearby.) Two immersions were carried out with a scientific team and a doctor: from 1991 to 1993, and a part of 1994. Scientific and financial troubles put an end to the project, but it was paradigmatic, in some sense the perfect American garden because perfectly autonomous, in theory. Appropriately, the surrounding 1,650-acre site was sold in 2007 by Biosphere 2's receivers to pay its debt—to a developer planning to build a residential golf community and a resort hotel.

IN THE PROSPEROUS residential neighborhoods of coastal California in the 1970s, gardens tended to follow the later style of Thomas Church, who passed on in 1978 but whose ghost continued to design the region's gardens well into the 1980s: open layouts of lawn with curved edges, expanses of brick or flagstone paving studded with raised planters for medium-size evergreen trees like the Melaleuca paperbarks, ficus, Brazilian peppers, and Queen palms, all bordered by beds filled with vaguely exotic shrubs like nandina, rhaphiolepis, ferns, and strap-leaved African corms like agapanthus and clivia, all of which could take the shade that had overtaken California's suburban yards since their raw beginnings. The feel was a cross between a cleaned-up woods and the modernist diagram of curves, clumps, and masses, with a nod to the Spanish tradition thrown in by using brick hardscape.

By the late 1980s and early '90s, a resurgence of more angular, sleek modern architecture in the Neutra vein nudged some garden designers toward a graphic, color-contrasting palette, inspired by the garden at Neutra's Tremaine House and by Lotusland: heavy on succulents and strikingly colored plants, including many being introduced from New Zealand, with its phormiums, of which a rainbow of new cultivars appeared with names like Maori Princess and Dark Delight in intense hues and striped variegations, and a raft of variegated pittosporums, and from Australia, with its wonderfully bizarre Kangaroo Paws and Protea family oddities like banksias and grevilleas. Jay Griffiths in Venice, Pamela

Burton in Los Angeles, and Isabel Greene (a granddaughter of Henry Greene of Greene & Greene, the Arts & Crafts architects in Pasadena) in Santa Barbara were prominent designers in this idiom, which mixed the by-then old modernist arsenal of concrete, metal, wood slats, and glass with a postmodern plant collector's palette worthy of Dr. Seuss into a very unique and recognizable regional style to complement its ubiquitous modern architecture.

But because Californians had never stopped building in the Spanish Colonial and other revival flavors, the market for formal gardens never disappeared. In the same period, a renewed interest in the California classicism of the 1910s and '20s was visible, relearning its melding of voluptuous horticulture and rigorous formal design, and rediscovering the genius of Lockwood de Forest, Bertram Goodhue, Paul Thiene, Edward Huntsman-Trout, Florence Yoch, and others. The standout on this historicist side of the equation was a conventionally untrained former interior designer, Nancy Goslee Power. Growing up on the eastern shore of Delaware in a small-town world that still preserved the culture of that northern outpost of the South, she made gardens from a young age, alongside a grandmother who grew mounds of delicious organic produce that fed the family and a mother who didn't care to grow food but instead brought a perfectionist's intensity to coddling her collection of rare and exotic plants. In college Power spent two transformative years in Florence, Italy, studying art and history and eagerly imbibing the formal framework of the region's traditions and appreciating its relaxed, generous, gracious style of living. The experience transformed her into what she calls a "born-again Italian," and it showed thereafter and still shows in the strong bones, loose, overflowing plantings, and emphasis on food and outdoor living that marks her work.

After her Italian sojourn, she had a thriving career as a decorator in New York City, before moving to Santa Monica with her small son and husband, who was in the movie business and wanted to be in Los Angeles. Before long she was making gardens again, now energized by the freedom afforded by the warm climate, endless plant palette, and Mediterranean style of much of the Los Angeles area's architecture. One of her first, the garden around her small Spanish-style Santa Monica house, linked tiled patios, fountains, an outdoor fireplace, a sturdy, masonry-columned pergola, and a geometric kitchen garden into a series of walled garden rooms, planted with an Arts & Crafts–like profusion of plants common and rare. Like that tradition, Power's work is built on interlocking rooms, deliberate transitions and sight lines, and carefully revealed surprises, all scaled to actual human dimensions, never too close for comfort nor too large for contact, whether the site is expansive or cramped.

As she explained it, "My goal is to make gardens and parks that are tranquil outdoor places apart from the chaotic, noisy, machine-driven environments where most of us work and live. Most of all I make beautiful places to be in love. I am a diehard romantic, but a practical one." This could have been written by Gertrude Jekyll or Beatrix Farrand. Indeed, Power is their clear descendant, her work a synthesis of formal and naturalistic, intended to elicit sensory and emotional experience. Power's is a new fin-de-siècle version of the Arts & Crafts apogee, historically conscious, especially when paired with revival architectures from that period. She has an unusual grasp of history, culled in part from a huge library that she consults with simultaneous respect and opportunism, not unlike Frank Cabot's—copying a set of stairs from Dumbarton Oaks, a bed layout from de Forest, or a color scheme from Jekyll, always gratefully acknowledging her debt.

At the same time, Power's style is very much engaged in the present, meshing in surprising ways with some of the most challenging modern architecture Southern California has produced. In the early 1990s she got an opportunity to work with her neighbor Frank Gehry, whom she knew because their kids played together. (I got the opportunity to work with her then, as a young associate in her office, learning the ropes of garden making on the job and from her extraordinary mentoring, as she had before from masters like the legendary Santa Monica plantsman Phil Chandler.) Gehry asked Nancy to help him with his own house, a characterless box that he had exploded, using off-the-shelf plywood, two-by-four studs, asphalt, and glass to reconfigure it with odd angles and volumes jutting out, creating more usable space and light for himself and his family. In the process he had horrified more conservative neighbors, who worried that the renegade architect's alien efflorescence on their mundane block would ruin their property values, and had enthralled a growing tide of architecture tourists, including at least one busload of Japanese, who would pile out of their vehicles, walk right up to his windows—he hadn't done any landscaping—and aim their cameras into his kitchen, sometimes getting him in the shot as a bonus. Power's approach was first to look at what grew in the neighborhood, both in order to sew the unique house into the fabric of the area and to see what worked, in a Darwinian sense: what thrived in the soil, temperature, and light, one side of the house being deeply shaded by the deodar cedars that grow along the street. She discovered that many of the classic, "workhorse" Los Angeles plants—*Aloe arborescens*, soft Mexican agaves, and birds-of-paradise—did the trick and were texturally bold enough to respond to Gehry's gestures if used in intentional, big ways. Planted on top and below the patio wall, they spill over in asymmetrical masses that echo the house's fragmented volumes. Over time, and not quickly enough for Frank, the garden grew in, though the tourist traffic only increased—along with the property values, bolstered by the growing international fame of the 1990s' first "starchitect."

A few miles away, Gehry designed an involved, eccentric house for Rock and Marna Schnabel, constructed of stark white stucco, glass, exposed wood framing, and seamed, paneled metal roofs. Nancy knew that Gehry, like many modern architects, preferred minimal or no landscaping to obscure his buildings. Yet Marna told her that she wanted an "English" garden, full of flowers and colors. How to reconcile these mutually exclusive demands? Power's inspiration came from a picture of a border included in a 1931 book, *California Gardens*, by Winifred Starr Dobyns, which she re-created along the house's entrance walk complete with its old-fashioned cannas, but zinged into the late 20th century with spiky purple cordylines and dark New Zealand flax, black Aeonium succulents, and purple-flowered sea lavender. Elsewhere she furthered the effect by using blue agaves and silver Butia palms, whose sculptural forms answered Gehry's. Vines and flowers climbed against the stucco and metal. Power's solution had been to dip into the old California version of the Arts & Crafts style. What made it a perfect match was the fact that Frank Gehry's architecture owes at least as much to the Arts & Crafts as it does to the Bauhaus—the Schnabel house is a modern Saracenic fantasy, with separate, asymmetrical pieces linked by catwalks, a tower, terraces, a bedroom set down in the middle of a lake, and a copper-domed pavilion that would have looked at home in British India. The house and garden worked beautifully together, each piece of Gehry's quirky complex staged and only gradually revealed by the planting.

The very success of the pairing explains why modernism failed as a social reform project, and why the Arts & Crafts movement did before it—each for the same reason: both started with the intention of returning quality and distinctive design to the middle and working classes through mass production, but both quickly succumbed to market realities and became cottage industries purveying luxury craftsmanship, creating one-off status objects, not far removed from the making of fine jewelry. After the Schnabel house, Gehry went on to design a series of instantly famous works that are less like buildings than like huge jewels: the Guggenheim Museum in Bilbao, Spain, and the Walt Disney Concert Hall in Los Angeles among them, resplendent in their urban settings, the big diamonds in tiaras. Most of them fail to acknowledge or incorporate anything of their specific contexts (only when touching others in a circumscribed urban situation, like his *Fred & Ginger* in Prague, are Gehry buildings not totally autonomous). Fittingly, he now designs a line of exquisite metal jewelry for Tiffany & Company that would have impressed William Morris—or Eva Marie Saint.

When Gehry was asked to renovate the galleries at Pasadena's Norton Simon Museum of Art in 1995, Power's office was brought in as well. Again the results could not have been predicted, and were spectacular. What was there was unique, and uniquely challenging: a bizarrely shaped low building, completed in 1969 by the architects Thornton Ladd and John Kelsey, with a plan that can only be compared to a Klingon battlecruiser from *Star Trek*, and a nearly windowless exterior clad in rectangular dark brown tiles. The garden consisted of lawns with a few paired koelreuteria

Nancy Goslee Power, Schnabel House. (Courtesy of the author)

and ficus trees sitting in broad beds of ivy, a straight concrete entrance walk, and a long, straight, rectangular concrete pool in the back, something Dan Kiley might once have done had he been deeply uninspired or down with the flu. Gehry wisely left the unusual building largely alone, but punched out skylights and otherwise improved the lighting, replaced the walls and floors with brighter materials, and expanded some exhibition spaces. The effect was to light and lighten the corners, replacing the galleries' earlier sense of gloom with a mood more suited to viewing the impressive art on display.

Outside, Nancy pondered her share of the problem. She knew the pool had to go but needed to be replaced with another water feature. The late collector and philanthropist Norton Simon's wife was the actress Jennifer Jones, a star of the 1940s and '50s big screen who won an Academy Award for her role in *The Song of Bernadette* in 1943, and went on to play opposite most of Hollywood's leading men: Humphrey Bogart, Montgomery Clift, Charlton Heston, William Holden, Gregory Peck, and Rock Hudson to name some. Jennifer told Nancy that she wanted the garden to look like Monet's in Giverny. So Power gave her a California version of just that, with a winding lake draped with water lilies and bristling with cannas and rushes, overhung with Montezuma cypresses instead of weeping willows, and shaded by tulip trees and eucalyptus. In spite of its exotic species, the plantings re-create the exuberance of Monet's garden, with a riot of color inspired by J. M. W. Turner's watercolors and organized according to Gertrude Jekyll's principle of grouping the hots in the center and moving toward the cooler colors at the periphery. Power and her team repositioned the museum's sculpture collection along a meandering path, putting the pieces on chunks of rock they found in an old quarry in the Sierra foothills and tucking them behind trees and in hidden pockets, to transform the walk around the garden into a series of intimate surprises—appropriate, as Jones and Power had talked about how to make special places in the garden for trysting. Gehry had also designed a teahouse to go in the garden, colored peach like the negligee Jones wore in the 1946 film *Duel in the Sun*, but it never got built—which was just as well, as it left more room for plants. The new garden performed what might seem an impossible task—turning an irreducibly modern building and landscape into a magical world out of an Impressionist painting. Power's bold moves succeeded in part because Ladd and Kelsey's building, like Gehry's, was already a kind of Arts & Crafts object, hiding in plain sight but invisible because it wore a reflexive modernist label.

Always curious, Power has traveled all over the world looking for inspiration, to the cores of many of the world's great garden traditions: in the Mediterranean, to Spain, Italy, and the mother-garden culture, Iran; in Asia, to Bali, Java, Sri Lanka, and India; and the new worlds, to Brazil, Australia, and New Zealand. At her second house, also in Santa Monica, she made an intricate, welcoming garden inspired by a visit to the home of the Brazilian landscape designer and artist Roberto Burle Marx and brightened with the colors of Brazilian colonial towns. In her mature style, all of these influences may be thrown in, depending on the site, the building, and the client—the all-important client.

When I asked Nancy Power, "What do people want in their garden?" she responded immediately: men want big views and lots and lots of grass. And, if they can afford it, they want visibly fine craftsmanship and fine objects. The most traditional, and masculine, garden she has made in recent years is a Santa Barbara estate for the late New York financier Bruce Wasserstein. Wasserstein had purchased a Hope Ranch property with fabulous views to the Pacific, on fifteen acres of old, poorly maintained avocado and cherimoya orchards, and asked Power to design the gardens for him. She recommended architect Buzz Yudell, a principal in the Santa Monica firm Moore Ruble Yudell, cofounded by Charles Moore, to design a modern take on the client's favorite style, the 1920s Spanish-style houses of Palm Beach, Florida, by Addison Mizner, who had built ornate, arch-windowed mansions for the investment titans of his day. She laid out a Mediterranean fantasy that would have dropped Bertram Goodhue's jaw: the orchards were replanted and shot through with long allées of palms and olives, hiding intimate courts centered on fountains made of custom-fired tiles with agave motifs, a swimming pool with a view of the Channel Islands, and a hand-carved sandstone water staircase. There are stunning ocean views, yes, but also secret, shaded garden rooms, long walks flanked with aloes and agaves, intersecting at eccentric angles and terminating at an exquisite fountain or 18th century oil jar. It was a private Alhambra for a modern sultan, channeling the spirit of Madame Walska at Lotusland, though more masculine and magnificent. The owner rarely found time to come to his western domain, so Power's staff would send figs and avocados from the garden to him in New York. For what those figs, finer and far fresher than any he could buy at Dean & DeLuca on Manhattan's Upper East Side, actually cost him, he could buy Dean & DeLuca. Which just goes to show that there are other things at work in the way we make gardens than rational calculation—other passions, and other satisfactions.

By contrast, Power said that women often seek privacy and protection in a garden. They are less interested in seeing out of the garden, or in people seeing into theirs. Sometimes this reflects a desire to withdraw from the world, and some women, she said, suffer from the isolation they build into their worlds. In general they appreciate smaller spaces more than men do for their intimacy, understanding their sufficiency for most of the garden's pleasures. Those with an active romantic bent see gardens like Jennifer Jones did: as places with the possibility of magic, the privacy serving the potential—for love, perhaps, or to evoke emotions and memories, to return us to that state of remembered or imagined bliss.

What I have found in my practice is that people want extensions of their own qualities in their gardens—especially their good qualities, or the qualities they would like to have, or wish they had, or delude themselves into thinking they had. A garden is often a good indicator of other things true of its maker, owner, inhabitant, or gardener. Practical people want practical things: a table and grill if they cook, a lawn for their kids to play on if they have them. Modest people resist ostentation. People who think themselves grand want their surroundings to mirror them. Slightly depressive people like lots of color. So do people who are very cheerful. Liking color is not diagnostic by itself of any personality state, but it is useful to know, if you are designing a garden for someone, which colors they like, since most people profess to not like or "hate" at least one color. No one ever cites a reason for this animosity. People who are bohemian like a few rough edges, some minor dishevelment, so that things won't appear to be too perfect. People who want to save the world want their surroundings to show that commitment, and that vision: with drought-tolerant or low-maintenance plants, even if they can't resist watering them liberally and their gardeners blast everything with gas-powered blowers anyway, at minimum they want to have the promise of such virtues. Gardens are expressions of self, and self-image, signals meant to be seen and understood. Most people are limited by the architecture of their house and their budget to one garden trope, unable to collect a pile of different gardens in one place, like a Huntington or a duPont.

Not so everyone. One entertainment industry personality, having become very successful, began to add properties around the house they owned in the hills, purchasing each additional one as it happened to come on the market, with no greater plan than acquisition. Each new house and its landscape was different, none very distinguished, so the task became linking all of them together and back to the original, central house, by means of gardens. Yet, absent a cohesive vision, idiom, or plan, a series of ideas for things that would "be cool to have," grasped seemingly at random, like impulse buys on the way to the checkout, grew into another collection of garden styles: here was an Adirondack camp, with a wooden deck and pergola that were rusticated but somehow slick; there was a Spanish courtyard with a tiled fountain; in the center was a vast lawn around a bluestone-decked swimming pool that had an eastern country club quality to it; there, in a ravine, grew a tropical forest of palms and large-leaved plants, dense and dark, with sprinklers running all the time to keep it moist; and over there in another, more distant piece of ground was a theoretically drought-tolerant grass meadow. The whole aimed to be sunny, easygoing, and relaxing, but the effect was forced by the sheer expense and rush of it and the ways the pieces didn't fit together properly, weren't integrated. This lack of integration mirrored the owner's personality: they tried mightily to be funny, cheery, and friendly, when not very far beneath that tanned, smiling exterior was a person controlling, anxious, distrustful to the point of being mildly paranoid, and not very happy, seemingly always overcaffeinated, and too busy, living life at too high a speed to actually relax and enjoy the amenities their success had purchased. Perhaps they were outrunning their demons and could not risk slowing down. In any event, it's a common syndrome, or predicament, and struck me as both a diagnosis and a metaphor for our society in the last couple of decades.

What most people, myself included, want in the garden is what we remember from childhood; but now childhood goes on much longer than it used to, it seems. The cultural response of the late 19th and early 20th centuries to fears about industrialization and urbanization was withdrawal to fantasies of a premodern, agrarian childhood, where there were no adults around and we had furry animals for friends and a little house sized just for us. Now, at the beginning of the 21st century, when it seems we have lost control of our shrinking world to globalized technologies and capital flows, our cultural response is to flee backward, but this time re-creating tableaux of an extended childhood, of teenagers and young adults: the ideal summertime of teenagers in the well-to-do suburbs, at the country club, the beach holiday, the lakeside resort, the sports camp. Maybe the place where we first fell in love, which might have been a garden—think of the refrain from the quintessential baby boomer Van Morrison's song: "We felt the presence of the youth of eternal summers, in the garden. . . . In the garden, wet with rain." The *New York Times* reported how a wealthy designer for Nike shoes built a getaway in Idaho modeled on a summer camp, complete with a mess hall for communal eating. I have noticed among my generation a noticeable number of families taking on the identities of their parents' or even grandparents' generation, "retiring" while still in their prime working life to the gated community, joining the country club, and wanting a bigger lawn at home.

For slightly more mature effects, some people seem to want to re-create a scene from an overseas vacation, before they had kids, perhaps where they fell in love the second time—if not with someone, then with some place. The major tropes, as they were in the first Gilded Age, are Italy and Japan. Since the beginning of American time, Italy has proved an irresistible image for many, and its magic hasn't waned. All over upper-middle-class exurbia, patches of grapevines strung on wires have sprouted on backyard hillsides, sometimes ludicrously small, which doesn't diminish the size of the ardor they display. New second-home developments are appearing all over the country centered around vineyards, replacing the golf course version of Arcadia with a Mediterranean viticultural one; instead of lining the fairways with Spanish or English colonial style houses, the contoured lines of vines are overlooked by Italian-themed mansionettes.

The influence of Japan continues as strong as ever, especially in a vein of modernist architecture that melds a Neutra-derived embedding and stacking of glass-walled boxes with rich, dark wood elements descended from the Craftsman bungalow. One can see the epitome of this style in the pages of *Dwell* magazine and along the streets of Venice, California, where the original tiny clapboard bungalows of this Italian-themed beach resort have been systematically replaced with hulking, two-story postmodern renditions full of polished concrete, smoked glass, and acres of "ironwood" horizontal slatting and flooring—referring to one of several types of tropical hardwoods that have come into the American market in the past decade and have become ubiquitous in high-toned design, inside and out. (Most are supposedly sustainably harvested, but how can one know for certain that rain forests aren't being cleared somewhere in Borneo to build one's new garden yoga platform?) More often than one might hope, there will be a Buddha's head or torso placed in the garden. These remind us not so much of Japan as Bali, the Shangri-la of late 20th and early 21st century seekers of perfect surf and upscale spiritual discovery. (Many owners of these houses in Venice are in fact surfers, grown wealthy creating advertisements for new-economy clients like Apple Computer.) Almost as often, there will be a gas-flame fire element, green-yellow tongues of flame licking up immaculately and sootlessly from a bed of colored glass pebbles, for example. The aesthetic is a chicer update on the old South Seas tiki vibe. It owes as much to actual Balinese vacations, where one can soak up that island's sexy Hindu-Buddhist iconography, intricate wooden architecture, and colorful, flower-decked offerings to the deities that adorn seemingly every sidewalk and fencepost, as it does to the luxe version spread to all corners of the world by "boutique" hotel chains like the Aman resorts and their imitators, with the more rustic Balinese elements laid onto a polished, minimalist architecture and attitude that seem to come from Japanese "Zen" but have nothing whatsoever to do with it in practice. Whether in hotels, where Buddha's head and a dancing fire pit preside over bars serving twenty-dollar designer cocktails, or in the million-dollar bungalows of the surfer/creative elite, this new, accessorized Japanism appears to be less a conscious aesthetic choice than an assertion of mental and lifestyle hygiene: the simple, smooth surfaces seem to promise some kind of purity, honesty, or clarity; though their opulence points in the other direction. It is never an easy task to reconcile money and virtue.

Once again it is Martha Stewart who painted the perfect picture of what many of us want from a garden, in her case combining clichés from West and East and throwing in an improbable do-it-yourself project to show she's still the boss. Asked, in a potted interview published in *Vanity Fair* in November 2009, "What is your idea of perfect happiness?" she answered (one hopes with her tongue firmly in her cheek): "A verdant landscape filled with beautiful animals of all kinds, harp music, cumulus clouds in a bright-blue sky, and happy people conversing pleasantly, sipping cold sake from homemade bamboo cups."

THE SAME YEAR that Martha and Andy Stewart bought the run-down house at Turkey Hill Road, another revolution in American style and ideas marked its beginning: in 1971, in Berkeley, California, across the bay from San Francisco, Alice Waters, a woman in her late twenties, along with investors, opened the restaurant Chez Panisse, serving French food using unremarkable techniques but a completely unorthodox supply chain—for the postwar United States. Inspired by visits to France, Waters insisted on finding local producers of high-quality, organic food. She scoured farmers' markets, and in some cases, had to talk farmers into growing what she sought. The result, dubbed "California cuisine," was sensational: the food was bright and surprising; the menus were famously fluid, changing with the seasons and the producers' rhythms, setbacks, and windfalls. Such a reversion to premodern, pre-agribusiness foodways was then unheard-of in the United States and defined a new gospel of production and consumption. It implied a strong critique of American society: we had become dependent, unhealthy, unaware of where our food came from and unconnected to the land and our own communities. Eating at Chez Panisse or one of its growing legions of imitators allowed us to regain part of our identity as Americans: agrarian, self-sufficient, modest, hardworking, productive—if only by supporting the idealistic, subaltern agriculture Chez Panisse rested on. Waters's influence over the years grew to be incalculable, helping spark and guide a revolution among educated people, especially of a liberal bent, but by no means limited to them—Montana survivalists are just as likely as Berkeley professors to want to grow their own food.

Of course, vestiges of a prewar, precorporate food system have persisted here and there, in small farms and collectives, and in family-run stores and restaurants. But their days surely looked to be numbered in 1971, from the point of view of any conventional assessment of America's trajectory. Agrarian ideals have defined a portion of America's ideals since the dawn of European settlement on this continent, but their real-world fortunes have ebbed and flowed. Jefferson's own career demonstrated this: an eloquent proselytizer for the faith and practitioner of integrated, organic gardening and gourmandizing of the highest caliber, he nevertheless suffered ultimate defeat in the face of an international system of debt finance and export (wheat) monoculture. At the high point of World War II, first lady Eleanor Roosevelt's White House Victory Garden was just one of tens of millions, which together grew 40 percent of the nation's produce. But once the war was won, the tide reversed radically and irresistibly, until, by 2009, 96 percent of our food was grown, shipped, marketed, sold, and distributed by Big Food, an agribusiness cartel fattened on the milk of interlocking government subsidies and supports—the tip of the iceberg being the annual behemoth farm bill, 2008's weighing in at $286 billion—all of which encourages overproduction of soybeans and corn, much for animal feed, much for the high-fructose corn syrup that saturates our kids' diets, and much of the rest now for corn-based ethanol, whose distortions of food markets ripples throughout the world, leading to food riots and starvation. Pollution from pesticides, fungicides, herbicides, and hormones poisons our wells and our cells; nitrogen fertilizers kill our oceans, turning vast areas into dead zones. Today there are just 2.2 million farm owners, down from 6.3 million in 1940, and too many of our farmers are as dependent on workers living in abysmal conditions on starvation wages—now likely to be illegal immigrants—as was Jefferson on his slaves.

In opposition to this tide, a full-throated movement of organic agriculture has long labored on the sidelines, led by Jerome Rodale's institute and publishing company, founded in Pennsylvania in the 1940s. The George W. Bush years gave the movement new cause for alarm and new conviction to fight for reform: the environmental consequences of big

American agribusiness had become too large and damaging to ignore: massive air, water, and soil pollution, the uncontrolled spread of genetically modified, patent-protected seeds, monopolistic supply chains that drove small farms and distributors out of business, dependence on low-wage labor, and the ignominious end result of a population racked by childhood obesity, diabetes, and heart disease. Books such as Michael Pollan's *The Omnivore's Dilemma* and movies such as *Supersize Me* brought the critique to a wider audience. Gardeners and even garden designers began to get back to basics, returning agriculture to the center of domestic landscapes for the first time in nearly a century. Even the art world joined in: Fritz Haeg's *Edible Landscapes* project encouraged homeowners to tear out their lawns and plant kitchen gardens, then report on the results as if they were a form of agitprop, with several of them published as a volume with the same name and the provocative subtitle *Attack on the Front Lawn*. (Like Alan Sonfist, Haeg had hit on the novel idea of planting something that once was guilelessly common but had disappeared, then calling it art.)

The subprime mortgage crisis of 2007 and the economic crash it kicked off in 2008 lent real urgency to calls for change. Change reached the White House grounds in April 2009, just months after Barack Obama took up residence there, as first lady Michelle Obama presided over the groundbreaking for a new Victory Garden. Planted for a reported two hundred dollars in seeds and supplies, growing fifty-five varieties and boasting two hives for honey, it measured in at 1,100 square feet—no rival to Jefferson's, which covered eighty thousand square feet at its zenith. But the third president had to feed what was in effect a village, while the forty-fourth uses it to add a few meaningful beans and greens to otherwise market-bought White House luncheons. Michelle was reviving a long tradition. John Adams had planted a vegetable garden at the White House, since presidents then had to feed their own households. Woodrow Wilson had sheep grazing on the South Lawn during World War I to save on gas and rubber for mowing the grass, while first lady Edith had a kitchen garden first dubbed a Liberty Garden, then, when the Allies started winning, renamed a Victory Garden. Eleanor Roosevelt planted another in her time as economic depression and war came again. And the Obamas' small patch wasn't small potatoes: Michelle Obama was sending a powerful message when she told Oprah that "we want to use it as a point of education," to link diet and health, diabetes and childhood obesity, and especially to reach out to kids—from her daughters and the fifth graders at Bancroft Elementary in Washington, D.C., who helped her pick seventy-three pounds of lettuce and twelve pounds of peas, to the millions who saw her on *Sesame Street* extolling the virtues of fresh vegetables.

The first lady was very adeptly picking up the baton from her predecessors, and her example may influence enough people to raise organic food's market share from its basement, in 2010, of 4 percent nationally. But just as the wartime Victory Gardens gave way in the years of prosperity that

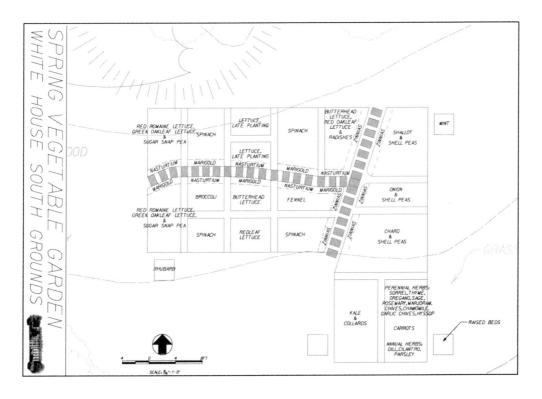

Obama White House kitchen garden layout. (The White House Blog)

followed to Big Food abundance—decades of Twinkies and Pepsi—so too can the current mood of national virtue and self-reliance fade. Yet this pendulum swing back to the pole of agrarian self-sufficiency feels no less deep and heartfelt than earlier ones: one can see it cropping up everywhere, from community gardens on reclaimed vacant lots, to school gardens, such as the Edible Schoolyard, started by Alice Waters in 1995 at Martin Luther King, Jr., middle school in Berkeley, California, a one-acre growing ground linked to the school's classroom curriculum and lunch program, allowing urban children who have perhaps never seen a farm to participate in food production from seeds to table. Waters's example has inspired hundreds of others around the country, as well as efforts to reform school lunch programs at the local, state, and federal levels. And interest in having kitchen gardens has reached all strata of American gardening culture, even in the estate gardens of the wealthy, who increasingly commission designers to integrate kitchen gardens into their grounds. Nancy Goslee Power has made it a specialty to design extensive, elegant kitchen gardens and orchards with formal plans that are at once beautiful and truly productive, in the tradition of Jefferson's at Monticello.

The movement is most visible in middle-class districts, and most tellingly in the inner-ring suburbs of our cities being revived in the past few decades by an extraordinary in-migration of young people. It is a new, *pastoral urbanism*: committed to greater self-reliance and minimum impact on the environment, often using organic methods, replacing traditional lawns with vegetable beds and fruit trees, berries, and vines, raising chickens and tending beehives, composting, and capturing rainwater in barrels—all within cities, often in their formerly abandoned cores. Such gardens are still sites of leisure and pleasure, but the pleasure their owners derive comes increasingly from productive, not just aesthetic, values—in pointed contrast to the conspicuous consumption of mainstream garden culture in the past several decades. (Of course, in the hands of some practitioners the drive toward virtue goes overboard, is too manifest, too much, verging on conspicuous production—a tactic of social positioning not so far removed from Martha Stewart's do-it-yourself power-hostess-with-the-mostest program, even while it is clothed in more self-consciously progressive politics of environmental stewardship and jettisons the pantomime of traditional domesticity and gender roles.)

From a cynical point of view, and in view of the cyclical nature of American history, it would be wise to have doubts about the depth or longevity of such a phenomenon. After all, the Liberty and Victory gardens of World War I quickly gave way to unbridled opulence in the Roaring Twenties, and the Great Depression's community gardens and the Victory Gardens of World War II gave way, when prosperity returned, to the biggest surge of middle-class suburbanization in history, with gardens mostly given over to the display of leisure *as* a style. The devotion to leisure worked against growing food in gardens, since it required more effort than driving to the supermarket and therefore seemed to be downwardly mobile. And the back-to-the-land movement of the late 1960s and '70s, which its adherents trumpeted as a millennial calling, promising to change the world for good, gave way to almost four decades of bling and debt-leveraged personal indulgence, turning away from notions of community, sustainability, balance, or responsibility. This retrenchment, beginning in the late 1970s, found its outdoor expression in more and more ostentatious gardens, reflecting—even if, like Martha's, they were draped in cryptoconservative colonial lace and old roses—the acquisitive, consumerist, solipsistic direction of late 20th century American society.

The late resurgence of edible gardens has been matched by an unprecedented naturalism in gardens and landscape. After three decades of proselytizing, John Greenlee, the grass and natural lawn guru, has seen his gospel accepted into more and more Americans' hearts and meadows sown in place of their turf, including Hollywood bigwigs like Steven Spielberg, Ellen Degeneres, and Kathryn Bigelow—slowly (but hopefully, surely) reversing the march of the monocultural lawn launched by Loudon and Downing a century and a half before. In the heart of New York City, the naturalistic aesthetic has seen its most remarkable manifestation yet in the High Line Park, made by upgrading, at considerable cost, an abandoned elevated freight railroad that once ran through parts of Manhattan's West Side into a chic aerial promenade. Long disused, rusting, and covered by trash, graffiti, and weeds, the tracks had run through a formerly industrial part of the city that had languished for decades as a refuge of meatpacking companies and warehouses by day and transvestite prostitutes and their acolytes by night. By the turn of the 21st century, the relentless gentrification of Manhattan had turned the former lead of decaying Chelsea and the West Village into real estate gold, and the improbable dream of a few aficionados and visionaries who had clambered on top of the decrepit elevated line soon after became an even more improbable reality: a narrow walkway raised above the surrounding streets, extending for a mile or so along the West Side through poetically wild-looking meadowscapes by the Dutch plantsman Piet Oudolf (who had previously collaborated with Kathryn Gustafson on the Lurie Garden at Chicago's Millennium Park), with stunning views of the Hudson River, the New Jersey skyline, and nearby buildings. Recent development has transformed the face of the area with glass mini-towers in the latest, signature architectural styles, including a triplex of utmost-luxury transparent condominium buildings along the riverfront by Richard Meier, a de Stijl façade of sequinlike windows by Jean Nouvel across the street from an incongruously curvy stack of frosted glass office boxes by Frank Gehry, and the two glass slabs of the Standard Hotel, one of which bridges out over the High Line itself—reportedly providing alert walkers with glimpses of the intimate doings of some uninhibited hotel guests. At least as much as the contemplation of plantings carefully designed to resemble the scrappy flora that the wind once blew in unaided, voyeurism of the lifestyles of the rich and hip is essential to the experience of the High Line. *The New Yorker* magazine architectural critic Paul Goldberger, in a March 2010 radio interview, admitted, somewhat defensively: "It's a place that recognizes that the city is in part about looking at itself, and there's nothing wrong with that. That a little bit of urban narcissism is not the worst thing in the world, as long as you can share it. It's sort of democratic narcissism, I guess you could say."[20]

It is fitting that this new celebration of wild nature in the heart of the postindustrial city has been staged on a defunct railroad line, since the railroad is what allowed American cities to grow from compact, walkable centers up until the early 19th century into crowded metropolises with smoking factories and slums at their cores, and then in turn allowed the well-to-do to flee to new garden suburbs, followed by the middling orders of people, and then by industry, all evacuating the central cities in favor of peripheral sites closer to purifying nature, abandoning the grubby cores to immigrants, people of color, and economic devastation. Now, of course, several decades of public and private effort have paid off in reversing the outward tide, leading to the recolonization of the central cities by the middle and upper classes. The High Line is a jewel in that migration's crown, no less than it is a consummate homage to the idea of nature—a nature celebrated by the park for its picturesque ability to recolonize the same decaying industrial real estate as its upwardly mobile creators, patrons, and visitors. In the "weedish" plantings (in Goldberger's parlance), studiously curated amid the rusting rails left in place in parts of the park, 21st century New Yorkers, many of them also transplants, may see themselves in an optimistically romantic and yet still satisfyingly, if superficially, gritty setting. No less than Central and Prospect parks before it, not so many miles away, the High Line is a triumph of America's urban culture—and "democratic narcissism." The question is, is this new park just another bauble of gentrification, another amenity for the wealthy, as the reclaimed Conservatory Garden was before it?

Yet the new pastoral urbanism is also grounds for hope: that now, more than four hundred years into the experiment, we Americans have come close to reconciling the contradictions of our existence—living in cities in the midst of a tantalizing wildness, a garden of possibility that cannot be attained by continuously fleeing from civilization. What is different perhaps in this round of proto-agrarian earnestness is that it coincides with a real, sustained return to cities—the first in American experience—a recolonization, a reinvestment, one not limited to New York or Los Angeles, but taking place everywhere, multigenerational, multicultural, a deep current, building over several decades. This migration, this mind-set, is pro-urban *and* pro-nature—in sum, pro-garden. Our people, in Emerson's phrase, are no longer "lighting out for the territory," as Mark Twain's Huck Finn did, but sticking, settling, and maybe, just maybe, coming to grips with the urban and capitalist nature of our actual cultural landscape and resolving to make it functional on its own terms, no longer fleeing for greener pastures, no longer turning real pastures into fake ones.

Thomas Jefferson would have understood—both the challenge, and the determination to stick it out and try to sow something beautiful in the midst of economic and philosophical difficulties, to stay true to our idealistic American values, even if they become compromised in the doing. He might have quoted the Frenchman Voltaire, whom he much admired, from the novel *Candide:* "when man was put into the garden of Eden, it was with an intent to dress it; and this proves that man was not born to be idle," said Pangloss. Candide agreed, thus: "Il faut cultiver notre jardin"—We must cultivate our garden.

ACKNOWLEDGMENTS

Let us be grateful to people who make us happy; they are the charming gardeners who make our souls blossom.

—MARCEL PROUST

Thanks to the people who inspired me, sustained me, and bore with me during the writing of this book, and those who helped by reading, editing, and sharing their wisdom and their gardens—often the same people. Beginning with my editor at HarperCollins, Jennifer Barth, here is just the top of a long list: Nora Bateson, Lakin Crane, Charles Donelan, Ann Ehringer, Brent Forrester, Otis Graham, David Kuhn, Bruno Louchouarn, Corey Madden, Jeff Martin, Rowan Pelling, Nancy Power, Jason Sack, Mitie Tucker.

NOTES

INTRODUCTION: THE POLITICS AND PASSIONS OF GARDENS
1.   John Claudius Loudon, *Encyclopedia of Architecture*, 1839.

CHAPTER I: FOUNDING GARDENS (1600–1826)
1.   Ralph Griswold and Frederick Nicholls, *Thomas Jefferson, Landscape Architect* (Charlottesville: University Press of Virginia, 1978), 126.

2.   Thomas Jefferson, *The Garden and Farm Books of Thomas Jefferson,* ed. Robert C. Baron (Golden, CO: Fulcrum, 1987), 45.

3.   Peter Loewer, *Jefferson's Garden* (Mechanicsburg, PA: Stackpole, 2004), 14.

4.   Jefferson, *Garden and Farm Books,* 46.

5.   Peter Martin, *The Pleasure Gardens of Virginia from Jamestown to Jefferson* (Princeton, NJ: Princeton University Press, 1991), 134.

6.   Griswold and Nicholls, *Thomas Jefferson, Landscape Architect,* 69.

7.   Joyce Appleby, *Thomas Jefferson* (New York: Times Books, 2003), 149.

8.   Loewer, *Jefferson's Garden,* 16.

9.   Jefferson, *Garden and Farm Books,* 4.

10.   Martin, *The Pleasure Gardens of Virginia,* 109.

11.   Denise Otis, *Grounds for Pleasure: Four Centuries of the American Garden* (New York: Harry N. Abrams, 2002), 14.

12.   Otis, *Grounds for Pleasure,* 15.

13.   Martin, *The Pleasure Gardens of Virginia,* 7–10.

14.   Martin, *The Pleasure Gardens of Virginia,* 20.

15.   Martin, *The Pleasure Gardens of Virginia,* 4.

16.   Ann Leighton, *American Gardens in the Eighteenth Century: "For Use or for Delight"* (Amherst: University of Massachusetts Press, 1986), 42–43.

17.   Martin, *The Pleasure Gardens of Virginia,* 4.

18. Martin, *The Pleasure Gardens of Virginia,* 148, 153.

19. David Hackett Fischer, *Albion's Seed: Four British Folkways in America* (New York: Oxford University Press, 1989), 633–39.

20. Fischer, *Albion's Seed,* 25.

21. Richard Bushman, *The Refinement of America: Persons, Houses, Cities* (New York: Knopf, 1992), vi.

22. Bushman, *The Refinement of America,* 15.

23. Martin, *The Pleasure Gardens of Virginia,* 30.

24. Martin, *The Pleasure Gardens of Virginia,* 37; John Reps, *The Making of Urban America: A History of City Planning in the United States* (Princeton, NJ: Princeton University Press, 1965), 103–14.

25. Martin, *The Pleasure Gardens of Virginia,* 3.

26. Martin, *The Pleasure Gardens of Virginia,* 53.

27. Martin, *The Pleasure Gardens of Virginia,* 53.

28. Martin, *The Pleasure Gardens of Virginia,* 54.

29. John Dixon Hunt, *Garden and Grove: The Italian Renaissance Garden in the English Imagination, 1600–1750* (Princeton, NJ: Princeton University Press, 1986), 12, 81.

30. Hunt, *Garden and Grove,* 104–5.

31. Norman T. Newton, *Design on the Land: The Development of Landscape Architecture* (Cambridge, MA: Belknap Press of Harvard University Press, 1971), 183–84.

32. Hunt, *Garden and Grove,* 113.

33. Jenny Uglow, *A Little History of British Gardening* (New York: North Point Press, 2004), 56–57, 82.

34. Uglow, *A Little History of British Gardening,* 104, 143; Hunt, *Garden and Grove,* 143.

35. Hunt, *Garden and Grove,* 177.

36. Hunt, *Garden and Grove,* 153.

37. Griswold and Nicholls, *Thomas Jefferson, Landscape Architect,* 9.

38. Fiske Kimball, *Thomas Jefferson, Architect: Original Designs in the Coolidge Collection of the Massachusetts Historical Society* (New York: Da Capo, 1968), 24.

39. Margherita Azzi Vicentani, "Palladio in America, 1760–1820," in Irma B. Jaffe, ed., *The Italian Presence in American Art, 1860–1920* (New York: Fordham University Press, 1992), 232–39.

40. William Beiswanger, "The Temple in the Garden: Thomas Jefferson's Vision of the Monticello Landscape," *Eighteenth Century Life* 8 (January 1983), 170–88.

41. Jefferson specified that these lines, instructing the grotto's resident nymph to keep quiet, be inscribed inside:

> Nymph of the grot, these sacred
>   springs I keep,
> And to the murmur of these waters
>   sleep;
> Ah! spare my slumbers! gently tread
>   the cave!
> And drink in silence, or in silence lave!

Griswold and Nicholls, *Thomas Jefferson, Landscape Architect,* 95.

42. Beiswanger, "The Temple in the Garden," 172.

43. John Dixon Hunt, *The Genius of the Place: The English Landscape Garden, 1620–1820* (London: Elek, 1965), 289.

44. Hunt, *The Genius of the Place,* 289–97.

45. John Dixon Hunt, *The Picturesque Garden in Europe* (New York: Thames & Hudson, 2002), 25.

46. John Dixon Hunt, *Gardens and*

the *Picturesque: Studies in the History of Landscape Architecture* (Cambridge, MA: MIT Press, 1993), 122.

47. Hunt, *The Picturesque Garden in Europe*, 14–16, 95.

48. Griswold and Nicholls, *Thomas Jefferson, Landscape Architect*, 80.

49. Hunt, *The Genius of the Place*, 337.

50. Kimball, *Thomas Jefferson, Architect*, 34.

51. Hunt, *Garden and Grove*, 197.

52. Hunt, "Pope's Twickenham Revisited," *Eighteenth Century Life* 8 (January 1983): 26–35.

53. Hunt, *The Genius of the Place*, 293–94.

54. Hunt, *Gardens and the Picturesque*, 46.

55. Leighton, *American Gardens in the Eighteenth Century*, 144.

56. Arthur Weitzman, "An Eighteenth Century View of Pope's Villa," *Eighteenth Century Life* 8 (January 1983), 36–38.

57. Beiswanger, "The Temple in the Garden," 174.

58. Roger G. Kennedy, *Architecture, Men, Women, and Money in America, 1600–1860* (New York: Random House, 1985), 11.

59. James D. Kornwolf, "The Picturesque in the American Garden and Landscape before 1800," *Eighteenth Century Life* 8 (January 1983): 96–99.

60. Griswold and Nicholls, *Thomas Jefferson, Landscape Architect*, 96.

61. Griswold and Nicholls, *Thomas Jefferson, Landscape Architect*, 139–40.

62. Frank O'Neill, "The Great Iconoclast," *Garden & Gun*, Spring 2007, 77.

63. Peter Martin, "'Long and Assiduous Endeavors': Gardening in Early Eighteenth-Century Virginia," *Eighteenth Century Life* 8 (January 1983): 114.

64. Beiswanger, "The Temple in the Garden," 179.

65. Griswold and Nicholls, *Thomas Jefferson, Landscape Architect*, 138.

66. Joseph Ellis, *American Sphinx: The Character of Thomas Jefferson* (New York: Knopf, 1997), 129, 134.

67. May Brawley Hill, *On Foreign Soil: American Gardeners Abroad* (New York: Harry N. Abrams, 2005), 24–25.

68. Ellis, *American Sphinx*, 82.

69. An engraving of her hangs in the family sitting room at Monticello, while a painting of Jefferson by John Trumbull that she owned now hangs in the White House. Her brother, George Hadfield, worked on the U.S. Capitol building and was the architect of Arlington House, in Virginia, built for George Washington Park Custis, stepgrandson of the first president; the house was later owned by General Robert E. Lee, who married Custis's daughter.

70. Ellis, *American Sphinx*, 110–12; Griswold and Nicholls, *Thomas Jefferson, Landscape Architect*, 78.

71. Ellis, *American Sphinx*, 114.

72. Kimball, *Thomas Jefferson, Architect*, 38.

73. Loewer, *Jefferson's Garden*, 18.

74. Griswold and Nicholls, *Thomas Jefferson, Landscape Architect*, 77.

75. Griswold and Nicholls, *Thomas Jefferson, Landscape Architect*, 81.

76. Kornwolf, "The Picturesque in the American Garden and Landscape before 1800," 100.

77. Martin, *Pleasure Gardens of Virginia*, 147.

78. Loewer, *Jefferson's Garden*, 21.

79. Griswold and Nicholls, *Thomas Jefferson, Landscape Architect*, 139.

80. Ellis, *American Sphinx*, 135.

81. Ellis, *American Sphinx*, 32.

82. Appleby, *Thomas Jefferson*, 15, 16.

83. Ellis, *American Sphinx*, 131.

84. Letter of August 1, 1816.

85. Appleby, *Thomas Jefferson*, 34.

86. Ellis, *American Sphinx*, 146–47.

87. Ellis, *American Sphinx*, 139–40.

88. Ellis, *American Sphinx*, 159.

89. Appleby, *Thomas Jefferson*, 135.

90. Ellis, *American Sphinx*, 163.

91. Ellis, *American Sphinx*, 164–65.

92. Griswold and Nicholls, *Thomas Jefferson, Landscape Architect*, 94.

93. Kennedy, *Architecture, Men, Women, and Money in America, 1600–1860*, 18–40.

94. Charles Quest-Ritson, *The English Garden: A Social History* (Boston: David R. Godine, 2003), 6.

95. Bushman, *The Refinement of America*, 198.

96. Ellis, *American Sphinx*, 100.

97. Ellis, *American Sphinx*, 181.

98. Appleby, *Thomas Jefferson*, 44–45.

99. Ellis, *American Sphinx*, 233.

100. Griswold and Nicholls, *Thomas Jefferson, Landscape Architect*, 107.

101. Beiswanger, "The Temple in the Garden," 181.

102. Kimball, *Thomas Jefferson, Architect*, 70.

103. Beiswanger, "The Temple in the Garden," 183.

104. Griswold and Nicholls, *Thomas Jefferson, Landscape Architect*, 86.

105. Griswold and Nicholls, *Thomas Jefferson, Landscape Architect*, 161.

106. Griswold and Nicholls, *Thomas Jefferson, Landscape Architect*, 134.

107. O'Neill, "The Great Iconoclast," 79, citing Peter Hatch, *The Gardens of Thomas Jefferson's Monticello* (Charlottesville, VA: Thomas Jefferson Memorial Foundation, 1992).

108. Joan L. Horn and Corporation for Jefferson's Poplar Forest, *Thomas Jefferson's Poplar Forest: A Private Place* (Forest, VA: Corporation for Jefferson's Poplar Forest, 2002), 85.

109. Beiswanger, "The Temple in the Garden," 185.

110. O'Neill, "The Great Iconoclast," 75.

111. Ellis, *American Sphinx*, 238–39.

112. Griswold and Nicholls, *Thomas Jefferson, Landscape Architect*, 27.

CHAPTER 2: A WALK IN THE PARK: SUBURBIA AND THE SUBLIME (1820–1890)

1. Witold Rybczynski, *A Clearing in the Distance: Frederick Law Olmsted and America in the Nineteenth Century* (New York: Scribner, 1999), 43.

2. Rybczynski, *A Clearing in the Distance*, 60.

3. David Schuyler, *Apostle of Taste: Andrew Jackson Downing, 1915–1852* (Baltimore: Johns Hopkins University Press, 1996), 220.

4. Schuyler, *Apostle of Taste*, 72.

5. Schuyler, *Apostle of Taste*, 222.

6. Schuyler, *Apostle of Taste*, 107.

7. Schuyler, *Apostle of Taste*, 14–15.

8. Judith K. Major, *To Live in the New World: A. J. Downing and American Landscape Gardening* (Cambridge, MA: MIT Press, 1997), 3.

9. Published in *New-York Farmer and Horticultural Repository* 5 (September 1882): 329–30; Schuyler, *Apostle of Taste*, 34, 264n20.

10. Roderick Nash, *Wilderness and the American Mind* (New Haven, CT: Yale University Press, 1967), 72.

11. Nash, *Wilderness and the American Mind*, 77.

12. Nash, *Wilderness and the American Mind*, 97.

13. Nash, *Wilderness and the American Mind,* 85.

14. John Stilgoe, *Borderland: Origins of the American Suburb, 1820–1930* (New Haven, CT: Yale University Press, 1988), 7.

15. Schuyler, *Apostle of Taste,* 54; Alexis de Tocqueville, *Democracy in America,* ed. Phillips Bradley (New York: Knopf, 1945), 2: 144–45.

16. Stilgoe, *Borderland,* 93; Schuyler, *Apostle of Taste,* 10, 54.

17. Major, *To Live in the New World,* 3.

18. Oliver Larkin, *Art and Life in America* (New York: Holt, Rinehart & Winston, 1960), 156–62.

19. Kornwolf, "The Picturesque in the American Garden and Landscape before 1800," 101.

20. Uglow, *A Little History of British Gardening,* 129, 159.

21. Larkin, *Art and Life in America,* 170.

22. Hunt, *Gardens and the Picturesque,* 163.

23. Hunt, *Gardens and the Picturesque,* 157.

24. Uglow, *A Little History of British Gardening,* 172.

25. Uglow, *A Little History of British Gardening,* 171, 182–88, 220.

26. Uglow, *A Little History of British Gardening,* 161.

27. Ann Leighton, *American Gardens of the Nineteenth Century: "For Comfort and Affluence"* (Amherst: University of Massachusetts Press, 1987), 159.

28. Andrew Jackson Downing, *Landscape Gardening and Rural Architecture* (New York: Dover, 1991), 46.

29. Downing, *Landscape Gardening and Rural Architecture,* 47.

30. Downing, *Landscape Gardening and Rural Architecture,* 53.

31. Schuyler, *Apostle of Taste,* 38, 74.

32. Leighton, *American Gardens of the Nineteenth Century,* 166.

33. George B. Tatum, introduction to Downing, *Landscape Gardening and Rural Architecture,* xii.

34. Schuyler, *Apostle of Taste,* 45.

35. Tatum introduction to Downing, *Landscape Gardening and Rural Architecture,* xiii.

36. Wayne Andrews, *Architecture, Ambition, and Americans: A Social History of American Architecture* (New York: Free Press, 1978), 102–114.

37. Schuyler, *Apostle of Taste,* 53.

38. Major, *To Live in the New World,* 9.

39. Major, *To Live in the New World,* 10.

40. Bushman, *The Refinement of America,* 240.

41. Schuyler, *Apostle of Taste,* 63.

42. Schuyler, *Apostle of Taste,* 75–76.

43. Schuyler, *Apostle of Taste,* 64.

44. Schuyler, *Apostle of Taste,* 74–75.

45. Schuyler, *Apostle of Taste,* 72.

46. Schuyler, *Apostle of Taste,* 72.

47. Schuyler, *Apostle of Taste,* 71–72.

48. Stilgoe, *Borderland,* 38.

49. Stilgoe, *Borderland,* 53.

50. Schuyler, *Apostle of Taste,* 113.

51. Schuyler, *Apostle of Taste,* 113–17.

52. Schuyler, *Apostle of Taste,* 92.

53. Schuyler, *Apostle of Taste,* 117; Leighton, *American Gardens of the Nineteenth Century,* 148.

54. T. J. Jackson Lears, *No Place of Grace: Antimodernism and the Transformation of American Culture, 1880–1920* (New York: Pantheon, 1981), 71.

55. Tatum introduction to Downing, *Landscape Gardening and Rural Architecture,* ix.

56. Schuyler, *Apostle of Taste,* 112.

57. Stilgoe, *Borderland,* 70.

58. Stilgoe, *Borderland,* 67, 76.

59. Stilgoe, *Borderland,* 99, 110.

60. Noël Kingsbury and Tim Richardson. *Vista: The Culture and Politics of Gardens* (London: Frances Lincoln, 2005), 88–89.

61. Schuyler, *Apostle of Taste,* 100.

62. Schuyler, *Apostle of Taste,* 104.

63. Stilgoe, *Borderland,* 33–34.

64. Ann Douglas, *The Feminization of American Culture* (New York: Knopf, 1977), 5, 6, 12.

65. Otis, *Grounds for Pleasure,* 138.

66. Nash, *Wilderness and the American Mind,* 91.

67. It is hard to distinguish between the two, since they bleed into one another. John Stilgoe called the latter "the borderland," but the title of his great book *Borderland: Origins of the American Suburb* admits the difficulty. For my purposes, the suburb and the more-distant second home zone partake of the same motivations, effects, and structure—the one being only more dense than the other, so I will lump them together under "suburb."

68. Thomas Bender, *Toward an Urban Vision* (New York: Columbia University Press, 1975), 49.

69. Leo Marx, *The Machine in the Garden: Technology and the Pastoral Ideal in America* (New York: Oxford University Press, 1964), 17.

70. Stilgoe, *Borderland,* 24.

71. Stilgoe, *Borderland,* 31.

72. Leighton, *American Gardens of the Nineteenth Century,* 153.

73. Newton, *Design on the Land,* 220–24; Uglow, *A Little History of British Gardening,* 183.

74. Nathaniel Hawthorne, "Our Old Home: A Series of English Sketches," in *The Works of Nathaniel Hawthorne* (New York: Thomas Crowell, 1906), 201.

75. Eric Homberger, *The Historical Atlas of New York City: A Visual Celebration of Nearly 400 Years of New York City's History* (New York: Henry Holt, 1994), 71.

76. Schuyler, *Apostle of Taste,* 158.

77. Schuyler, *Apostle of Taste,* 160.

78. Rybczynski, *A Clearing in the Distance,* 45.

79. Hawthorne, "Our Old Home," 204.

80. John McPhee, *Annals of the Former World* (New York: Farrar, Straus & Giroux, 1998), 161.

81. Leighton, *American Gardens of the Nineteenth Century,* 135.

82. Bushman, *The Refinement of America,* 165.

83. Douglas, *The Feminization of American Culture,* 210.

84. Leighton, *American Gardens of the Nineteenth Century,* 140.

85. Bender, *Toward an Urban Vision,* 161.

86. Schuyler, *Apostle of Taste,* 202.

87. Schuyler, *Apostle of Taste,* 20.

88. Homberger, *The Historical Atlas of New York City,* 70.

89. Rybczynski, *A Clearing in the Distance,* 85.

90. Bender, *Toward an Urban Vision,* 164–66.

91. Rybczynski, *A Clearing in the Distance,* 93.

92. Rybczynski, *A Clearing in the Distance,* 98.

93. Rybczynski, *A Clearing in the Distance,* 156.

94. Bender, *Toward an Urban Vision,* 179.

95. Bender, *Toward an Urban Vision,* 171.

96. Rybczynski, *A Clearing in the Distance,* 261.

97. Rybczynski, *A Clearing in the Distance,* 271.

98. Rybczynski, *A Clearing in the Distance,* 283.

99. Nash, *Wilderness and the American Mind,* 108.

100. Christian Zapatka, *The American Landscape* (New York: Princeton Architectural Press, 1995), 79.

101. Kenneth Jackson, *Crabgrass Frontier: The Suburbanization of the United States* (New York: Oxford University Press, 1985), 76–77.

102. Susan Fenimore Cooper, *Rural Hours* (Syracuse, NY: Syracuse University Press, 1995), 68.

103. Jackson, *Crabgrass Frontier,* 81.

104. Rybczynski, *A Clearing in the Distance,* 348.

105. Wade Graham, "The Grassman," *The New Yorker,* August 19, 1996.

106. Virginia Scott Jenkins, *The Lawn: A History of an American Obsession* (Washington, DC: Smithsonian Institution Press, 1994), 24.

107. Jenkins, *The Lawn,* 107.

108. Jenkins, *The Lawn,* 61.

109. Lewis Mumford, *The Brown Decades: A Study of the Arts in America, 1865–1895* (New York: Dover, 1955), 88.

CHAPTER 3: THE GOLDEN AGE: MODERNITY AND ITS DISCONTENTS (1880–1915)

1. Barbara Babcock Millhouse, *American Wilderness: The Story of the Hudson River School of Painting* (Hensonville, NY: Black Dome, 2007), 159.

2. Larkin, *Art and Life in America,* 242.

3. Larkin, *Art and Life in America,* 175.

4. Larkin, *Art and Life in America,* 235, 239–40.

5. Larkin, *Art and Life in America,* 247.

6. Lewis Mumford, *Sticks and Stones: A Study of American Architecture and Civilization* (New York: Dover, 1955), 105.

7. Leighton, *American Gardens of the Nineteenth Century,* 245.

8. Keith N. Morgan, *Charles A. Platt: The Artist as Architect* (Cambridge, MA: MIT Press, 1985), 36–37.

9. Morgan, *Charles A. Platt,* 23.

10. Hill, *On Foreign Soil,* 59.

11. Morgan, *Charles A. Platt,* 13–14.

12. Robin Karson, *The Muses of Gwinn: Art and Nature in a Garden Designed by Warren H. Manning, Charles A. Platt & Ellen Biddle Shipman* (Sagaponack, NY: Sagapress, 1995), 15.

13. Morgan, *Charles A. Platt,* 101.

14. Morgan, *Charles A. Platt,* 21.

15. Larkin, *Art and Life in America,* 179.

16. Hill, *On Foreign Soil,* 36.

17. Hill, *On Foreign Soil,* 35.

18. Henry Adams, *The Education of Henry Adams* (New York: Modern Library, 1931), 89.

19. Larkin, *Art and Life in America,* 293.

20. Morgan, *Charles A. Platt,* 22.

21. Karson, *The Muses of Gwinn,* 16–17.

22. Leland M. Roth, *McKim, Mead & White, Architects* (New York: Harper & Row, 1983), 33.

23. Larkin, *Art and Life in America,* 296–99.

24. Morgan, *Charles A. Platt,* 78.

25. Charles A. Platt, *Italian Gardens* (Portland, OR: Sagapress/Timber Press, 1993), 15–16.

26. Morgan, *Charles A. Platt,* 116.

27. Otis, *Grounds for Pleasure,* 39.

28. Morgan, *Charles A. Platt,* 52.

29. Larkin, *Art and Life in America,* 311.

30. Rybczynski, *A Clearing in the Distance,* 385.

31. Rybczynski, *A Clearing in the Distance*, 313.

32. Roth, *McKim, Mead & White*, 177.

33. Larkin, *Art and Life in America*, 311.

34. Rybczynski, *A Clearing in the Distance*, 398.

35. Kenneth H. Cardwell, *Bernard Maybeck: Artisan, Architect, Artist* (Santa Barbara, CA: Peregrine Smith, 1977), 31.

36. Larkin, *Art and Life in America*, 315.

37. Adams, *The Education of Henry Adams*, 315.

38. Rybczynski, *A Clearing in the Distance*, 387.

39. Larkin, *Art and Life in America*, 339–40.

40. Adams, *The Education of Henry Adams*, 339–40.

41. Stilgoe, *Borderland*, 114.

42. Larkin, *Art and Life in America*, 285.

43. Overall argument from Lears, *No Place of Grace*.

44. Mumford, *Sticks and Stones*, 127–28.

45. May Brawley Hill, *Grandmother's Garden: The Old-Fashioned American Garden, 1865–1915* (New York: Abrams, 1995), 66–67.

46. Hill, *Grandmother's Garden*, 66.

47. Stilgoe, *Borderland*, 28.

48. Hill, *Grandmother's Garden*, 35.

49. Hill, *Grandmother's Garden*, 22.

50. Hill, *Grandmother's Garden*, 61.

51. Leighton, *American Gardens of the Nineteenth Century*, 81.

52. Celia Thaxter, *An Island Garden* (Boston: Houghton Mifflin, 1988), 4.

53. Hill, *Grandmother's Garden*, 65.

54. Martin, *The Pleasure Gardens of Virginia*, 140.

55. Hill, *Grandmother's Garden*, 143.

56. Hill, *Grandmother's Garden*, 66.

57. Hill, *Grandmother's Garden*, 147.

58. Charles E. Aguar and Berdeana Aguar, *Wrightscapes: Frank Lloyd Wright's Landscape Designs* (New York: McGraw-Hill, 2002), 11.

59. Larkin, *Art and Life in America*, 311.

60. Vivian Russell, *Edith Wharton's Italian Gardens* (London: Frances Lincoln, 1997), 9.

61. Russell, *Edith Wharton's Italian Gardens*, 9–10.

62. Russell, *Edith Wharton's Italian Gardens*, 11.

63. Russell, *Edith Wharton's Italian Gardens*, 12.

64. John Dixon Hunt, introduction to Edith Wharton, *Italian Villas and Their Gardens* (New York: Century, 1903).

65. Hill, *Grandmother's Garden*, 31.

66. John M. Bryan, *Biltmore Estate: The Most Distinguished Private Place* (New York: Rizzoli, 1994), 11.

67. Henry James, *Italian Hours* (New York: Horizon, 1968), 306–7.

68. Mac Griswold and Eleanor Weller, *The Golden Age of American Gardens: Proud Owners, Private Estates, 1890–1940* (New York: H. N. Abrams, 1991), 13.

69. Hill, *On Foreign Soil*, 101–2.

70. Griswold and Weller, *The Golden Age of American Gardens*, 13.

71. R. W. B. Lewis, *Edith Wharton: A Biography* (New York: Harper & Row, 1975), 121.

72. Lewis, *Edith Wharton*, 312.

73. Griswold and Weller, *The Golden Age of American Gardens*, 40; Otis, *Grounds for Pleasure*, 176; Morgan, *Charles A. Platt*, 48–49.

74. Morgan, *Charles A. Platt*, 69.

75. Larkin, *Art and Life in America*, 338.

76. Lewis, *Edith Wharton*, 136.

77. James, *Italian Hours,* 224.

78. Andrews, *Architecture, Ambition, and Americans,* 145.

79. Larkin, *Art and Life in America,* 283.

80. Griswold and Weller, *The Golden Age of American Gardens,* 28.

81. Mrs. Mariana Griswold Schuyler Van Rensselaer, *Art Out-of-Doors: Hints on Good Taste in Gardening* (New York: Charles Scribner's Sons, 1893), 175–76.

82. Edith Wharton, *The House of Mirth* (New York: New York University Press, 1977), 3.

83. Quest-Ritson, *The English Garden,* 220.

84. Hill, *On Foreign Soil,* 79, 90.

85. Bryan, *Biltmore Estate,* 16.

86. Bryan, *Biltmore Estate,* 41–42.

87. Bryan, *Biltmore Estate,* 94.

88. Rybczynski, *A Clearing in the Distance,* 404.

89. Rybczynski, *A Clearing in the Distance,* 410.

90. Griswold and Weller, *The Golden Age of American Gardens,* 298.

91. Newton, *Design on the Land,* 413, 415.

92. Mumford, *Sticks and Stones,* 130.

93. Henry James, *The American Scene* (Bloomington: Indiana University Press, 1968), 322.

94. Griswold and Weller, *The Golden Age of American Gardens,* 89; Otis, *Grounds for Pleasure,* 39–40.

95. Clay Lancaster, *The Japanese Influence in America* (New York: W. H. Rawls, 1963), 4.

96. Otis, *Grounds for Pleasure,* 44.

97. Lancaster, *The Japanese Influence in America,* 256.

98. Hill, *On Foreign Soil,* 60.

99. Lancaster, *The Japanese Influence in America,* 33–34.

100. Lancaster, *The Japanese Influence in America,* 256.

101. Lancaster, *The Japanese Influence in America,* 206.

102. Lancaster, *The Japanese Influence in America,* 36, 47, 137.

103. Lancaster, *The Japanese Influence in America,* 207.

104. Lancaster, *The Japanese Influence in America,* 97.

105. Kendall Brown, *Japanese-Style Gardens of the Pacific West Coast* (New York: Rizzoli, 1999), 19.

106. Gray Brechin, *Imperial San Francisco: Urban Power, Earthly Ruin* (Berkeley: University of California Press, 1999), 134.

107. Lancaster, *The Japanese Influence in America,* 97.

108. Kevin Starr, *Material Dreams: Southern California Through the 1920s* (New York: Oxford University Press, 1990), 294.

109. Starr, *Material Dreams,* 252.

110. Brechin, *Imperial San Francisco,* 122.

111. Brechin, *Imperial San Francisco,* 123.

112. Starr, *Material Dreams,* 239.

113. Starr, *Material Dreams,* 290–91; Newton, *Design on the Land,* 418.

114. Brechin, *Imperial San Francisco,* 153.

115. Brechin, *Imperial San Francisco,* 145.

116. Newton, *Design on the Land,* 417.

117. Newton, *Design on the Land,* 416–17.

118. Griswold and Weller, *The Golden Age of American Gardens,* 314–16.

119. Brechin, *Imperial San Francisco,* 143.

120. Brechin, *Imperial San Francisco,* 157.

121. Brechin, *Imperial San Francisco,* 160.

122. Lancaster, *The Japanese Influence in America,* 206.

123. Brechin, *Imperial San Francisco,* 167.

124. Brechin, *Imperial San Francisco,* 274.

125. Brechin, *Imperial San Francisco,* 150.

CHAPTER 4: FORWARD TO THE PAST:
THE LONG ROMANCE OF THE ARTS &
CRAFTS GARDEN (1850–1945)

1. Mumford, *Sticks and Stones*, iii, 35.

2. Mumford, *Sticks and Stones*, 22.

3. Wendy Kaplan, *The Arts and Crafts Movement in Europe & America: Design for the Modern World* (New York: Thames & Hudson, 2004), 247, 273.

4. Kaplan, *The Arts and Crafts Movement in Europe & America*, 42.

5. Kaplan, *The Arts and Crafts Movement in Europe & America*, 247.

6. Lears, *No Place of Grace*, 74. "Craft ideologues tended to infer the social problem from its aesthetic effects."

7. Derek Fell, *The Gardens of Frank Lloyd Wright* (London: Frances Lincoln, 2009), 29.

8. Mumford, *Sticks and Stones*, 118.

9. Judith B. Tankard, *Gardens of the Arts and Crafts Movement: Reality and Imagination* (New York: Harry N. Abrams, 2004), 33.

10. Tankard, *Gardens of the Arts and Crafts Movement*, 38.

11. William Robinson, *The Wild Garden* (Portland, OR: Sagapress/Timber Press, 1994), 9.

12. Reginald Blomfield, *The Formal Garden in England* (London, Macmillan, 1901), 7.

13. Blomfield, *The Formal Garden in England*, 9.

14. Blomfield, *The Formal Garden in England*, 12.

15. Blomfield, *The Formal Garden in England*, 10.

16. Blomfield, *The Formal Garden in England*, 10.

17. Blomfield, *The Formal Garden in England*, 233.

18. Rick Darke, *In Harmony with Nature: Lessons from the Arts & Crafts Garden* (New York: Friedman/Fairfax, 2000), 13.

19. Judith Tankard, introduction to Robinson, *The Wild Garden*, xi.

20. Quoted by Jane Brown, introduction to Gertrude Jekyll and Sir Lawrence Weaver, *Gardens for Small Country Houses* (New York: Charles Scribner's, 1927), 11.

21. Aguar and Aguar, *Wrightscapes*, 13.

22. Kingsbury and Richardson, *Vista*, 15.

23. Darke, *In Harmony with Nature*, 80–81.

24. Diana Balmori, Diane Kostial McGuire, and Eleanor M. McPeck, *Beatrix Farrand's American Landscapes: Her Gardens and Campuses* (Sagaponack, NY: Sagapress, 1985), 14.

25. Judith B. Tankard, *The Gardens of Ellen Biddle Shipman* (Sagaponack, NY: Sagapress, 1996), xv.

26. Balmori, McGuire, and McPeck, *Beatrix Farrand's American Landscapes*, 24.

27. Balmori, McGuire, and McPeck, *Beatrix Farrand's American Landscapes*, 22.

28. Balmori, McGuire, and McPeck, *Beatrix Farrand's American Landscapes*, 24.

29. Van Rensselaer, *Art Out-of-Doors*, 160, 167.

30. Hill, *On Foreign Soil*, 106–7; Griswold and Weller, *The Golden Age of American Gardens*, 40.

31. Tankard, *The Gardens of Ellen Biddle Shipman*, 22.

32. Tankard, *The Gardens of Ellen Biddle Shipman*, 152.

33. Wharton, *Italian Villas*, 42.

34. Karson, *The Muses of Gwinn*, 11.

35. Nancy Fleming, *Money, Manure & Maintenance: Ingredients for Successful Gardens of Marian Kruger Coffin, 1876–1957* (Weston, MA: Country Place, 1995), 9.

36. Fleming, *Money, Manure & Maintenance*, 61.

37. Fleming, *Money, Manure & Maintenance*, 5.

38. Tankard, *The Gardens of Ellen Biddle Shipman*, 3–4.

39. Tankard, *The Gardens of Ellen Biddle Shipman*, 7.

40. John Wedda, *Gardens of the American South: Grace, Beauty, History and Romance in Text and Pictures* (New York: Galahad, 1971), 48.

41. Wedda, *Gardens of the American South,* 22; Griswold and Nicholls, *Thomas Jefferson, Landscape Architect,* viii; Otis, *Grounds for Pleasure,* 46.

42. Frank Lloyd Wright, *Testament* (New York: Horizon, 1957), 19.

43. Marco Dezzi Bardeschi, *Frank Lloyd Wright* (New York: Hamlyn, 1972), 12.

44. Wright, *Testament,* 17.

45. Wright, *Testament,* 33.

46. Wright, *Testament,* 16.

47. Wright, *Testament,* 22.

48. Wright, *Testament,* 21.

49. Wright, *Testament,* 219.

50. Tankard, *Gardens of the Arts and Crafts Movement,* 169.

51. Bardeschi, *Frank Lloyd Wright,* 35.

52. Bardeschi, *Frank Lloyd Wright,* 35.

53. Lancaster, *The Japanese Influence in America,* 85–88.

54. Fell, *The Gardens of Frank Lloyd Wright,* 33.

55. Aguar and Aguar, *Wrightscapes,* 98–99.

56. Fell, *The Gardens of Frank Lloyd Wright,* 33.

57. Aguar and Aguar, *Wrightscapes,* 100.

58. Fell, *The Gardens of Frank Lloyd Wright,* 133–14.

59. Wilhelm Miller, *The Prairie Spirit in Landscape Gardening* (Amherst: University of Massachusetts Press, 2002), xiii.

60. Miller, *The Prairie Spirit in Landscape Gardening,* xvii.

61. Fell, *The Gardens of Frank Lloyd Wright,* 111.

62. Wright, *Testament,* 227.

63. Fell, *The Gardens of Frank Lloyd Wright,* 33.

64. Fell, *The Gardens of Frank Lloyd Wright,* 38.

65. Fell, *The Gardens of Frank Lloyd Wright,* 14, 18, 46–7.

66. Edgar Kaufmann, Jr., *Fallingwater: A Frank Lloyd Wright Country House* (New York: Abbeville, 1986), 38.

67. Aguar and Aguar, *Wrightscapes,* 178.

68. Kaufmann, *Fallingwater,* 36–49.

69. Kaufmann, *Fallingwater,* 31.

70. Kaufmann, *Fallingwater,* 22.

71. Kaufman, *Fallingwater,* 49.

72. Bardeschi, *Frank Lloyd Wright,* 12.

73. Wright, *The Disappearing City,* 1932, quoted in Catherine Howett, "Modernism and American Landscape Architecture," in Marc Treib, ed., *Modern Landscape Architecture: A Critical Review* (Cambridge, MA: MIT Press, 1993), 26.

74. Lucia Howard and David Weingarten, *Ranch Houses: Living the California Dream* (New York: Rizzoli, 2009) 8–11.

75. Romy Wyllie, *Bertram Goodhue: His Life and Residential Architecture* (New York: Norton, 2007), 40.

76. Wyllie, *Bertram Goodhue,* 47.

77. Seth Lerer, *Children's Literature: A Reader's History, from Aesop to Harry Potter* (Chicago: University of Chicago Press, 2008), 254.

78. Lerer, *Children's Literature,* 257.

79. Virginia Hayes, "The Other Men," *Santa Barbara Independent,* March 5, 2009.

CHAPTER 5: CALIFORNIA AND THE
MODERN GARDEN (1920–1960s)

1. Thomas Dolliver Church, *Gardens Are for People: How to Plan for Outdoor Living* (New York: Reinhold, 1955), 7.

2. Church, *Gardens Are for People,* xi.

3. Church, *Gardens Are for People,* xii.

4. Church, *Gardens Are for People,* xii.

5. Marc Treib, *The Donnell and Eckbo Gardens: Modern California Masterworks* (San Francisco: William Stout, 2005), 22.

6. Jackson, *Crabgrass Frontier,* 190.

7. Jackson, *Crabgrass Frontier,* 162–63, 175.

8. Jackson, *Crabgrass Frontier,* 248.

9. Jackson, *Crabgrass Frontier,* 164.

10. Jackson, *Crabgrass Frontier,* 172.

11. Jere Stuart French, *The California Garden: And the Landscape Architects Who Shaped It* (Washington, DC: Landscape Architecture Foundation, 1993), 153.

12. French, *The California Garden,* 146.

13. Jane Brown, *The Modern Garden* (New York: Princeton Architectural Press, 2000), 29.

14. Treib, *The Donnell and Eckbo Gardens,* 24–25.

15. David Gebhard, *Schindler* (New York: Viking, 1971), 9.

16. Pamela Burton, *Private Landscapes: Modernist Gardens in Southern California* (New York: Princeton Architectural Press, 2002), 8.

17. Gebhard, *Schindler,* 32.

18. William J. R. Curtis, *Le Corbusier: Ideas and Forms* (London: Phaidon, 1986), 102.

19. Reyner Banham, *Los Angeles: The Architecture of Four Ecologies* (New York: Harper & Row, 1971), 164.

20. Esther McCoy, *Richard Neutra* (New York: Braziller, 1960), 9.

21. Barbara Mac Lamprecht, *Richard Neutra: Complete Works* (New York: Taschen, 2000), 12.

22. Gebhard, *Schindler,* 62.

23. Richard Neutra, *Mysteries and Realities of the Site* (Scarsdale, NY: Morgan & Morgan, 1951), 60; Lamprecht, *Richard Neutra,* 18.

24. Neutra, *Mysteries and Realities of the Site,* 40.

25. Neutra, *Mysteries and Realities of the Site,* 51.

26. Neutra, *Mysteries and Realities of the Site,* 55.

27. Neutra, *Mysteries and Realities of the Site,* 24.

28. Neutra, *Mysteries and Realities of the Site,* 62.

29. Arthur Drexler, head of design, Museum of Modern Art, in *The Architecture of Richard Neutra,* quoted in Lamprecht, *Richard Neutra,* 11.

30. Sylvia Lavin, *Form Follows Libido: Architecture and Richard Neutra in a Psychoanalytic Culture* (Cambridge, MA: MIT Press, 2004), 30–32.

31. Lavin, *Form Follows Libido,* 79.

32. Neutra, *Nature Near,* quoted in Lamprecht, *Richard Neutra,* 10.

33. Treib, *The Donnell and Eckbo Gardens,* 29.

34. French, *The California Garden,* 160.

35. Marc Treib and Dorothée Imbert, *Garrett Eckbo: Modern Landscapes for Living* (Berkeley: University of California Press, 1997), 73.

36. Treib and Imbert, *Garrett Eckbo,* 33.

37. Garrett Eckbo, *Landscapes for Living* (New York: Architectural Record with Duell, Sloan & Pearce, 1950), 1.

38. Brown, *Japanese-Style Gardens of the Pacific West Coast,* 87.

39. Jackson, *Crabgrass Frontier*, 179, 250.

40. French, *The California Garden*, 168.

41. The main beneficiary of $119 billion in FHA loans and mortgage insurance in the agency's first four decades was suburbia; half of all housing in the suburbs had FHA or VA financing, whereas the inner cities saw very little. These agencies lowered down-payment requirements from 30 to 50 percent or more to 10 percent or less, and extended the repayment period to twenty-five to thirty years. The tax subsidy to homeowners, concentrated in the suburbs, through the property tax and mortgage interest deductions, amounted to four to five times the actual outlay of all the housing programs combined—$53 billion in 1984 alone. It has been calculated that average housing subsidies in affluent suburbs are several times higher than the subsidies extended to welfare recipients in the cities. Kenneth Jackson, *Crabgrass Frontier: The Suburbanization of the United States* (New York: Oxford University Press, 1985), 203–18.

42. Jackson, *Crabgrass Frontier*, 205, 241.

43. The structure of loan programs encouraged single-family homes—that is, mostly suburban—but discouraged the multifamily projects typical in denser city cores by making it easier to build new than to fix old structures. "Redlining" by lenders, the classification of neighborhoods by racial/ethnic composition and the likelihood of change, discriminated against multiple use, higher densities, and older structures. Such racist policies stoked white flight, accelerating the hollowing out of huge areas of cities like Detroit and accelerating ghettoization in communities large and small across the country. Jackson, *Crabgrass Frontier*, 195–203.

44. Jackson, *Crabgrass Frontier*, 241.

45. Diane Harris, "Race, Class, and Privacy in the Ordinary Postwar House, 1945–1960," in Richard H. Schein, ed., *Landscape and Race in the United States* (New York: Routledge, 2006), 136.

46. Harris, "Race, Class, and Privacy," 136.

47. Harris, "Race, Class, and Privacy," 138–39.

48. Howard and Weingarten, *Ranch Houses*, 12.

49. Howard and Weingarten, *Ranch Houses*, 12.

50. "The Politics of Plenty," *Economist*, May 26, 2007, 33.

51. Sven A. Kirsten, *The Book of Tiki: The Cult of Polynesian Pop in Fifties America* (Koln: Taschen, 2000), 230.

CHAPTER 6: ART CONFRONTS NATURE, REDUX: TRIUMPHS AND ANXIETIES OF LANDSCAPE ARCHITECTURE (1940s–2000s)

1. Jane Amidon and Dan Kiley, *Dan Kiley: The Complete Works of America's Master Landscape Architect* (New York: Bulfinch, 1999), 10.

2. Treib and Imbert. *Garrett Eckbo*, 25.

3. Gregg Bleam, "Modern and Classical Themes in the Work of Dan Kiley," in Treib, ed., *Modern Landscape Architecture*, 223.

4. Bleam, "Modern and Classical Themes in the Work of Dan Kiley," 223.

5. Amidon and Kiley, *Dan Kiley*, 20.

6. Bleam, "Modern and Classical Themes in the Work of Dan Kiley," 221, 231, 235.

7. Bleam, "Modern and Classical Themes in the Work of Dan Kiley," 227–30.

8. Calvin Tomkins, "The Garden Artist," *The New Yorker*, October 16, 1995, 136.

9. Tomkins, "The Garden Artist," 143.

10. Tomkins, "The Garden Artist," 136, 144.

11. Amidon and Kiley, *Dan Kiley*, 8.

12. Melanie Simo and Peter Walker, *Invisible Gardens: The Search for Modernism in the American Landscape* (Cambridge, MA: MIT Press, 1994), 148.

13. Richard Sexton, *Parallel Utopias: Sea Ranch and Seaside: The Quest for Community* (San Francisco: Chronicle Books, 1995), 32.

14. Lawrence Halprin, *Changing Places: San Francisco Museum of Modern Art, 3 July–24 August 1986* (San Francisco: The Museum, 1986), 125.

15. Lawrence Halprin, *The Sea Ranch: Diary of an Idea* (Berkeley: Spacemaker, 2002), 3.

16. Halprin, *The Sea Ranch*, 1.

17. Halprin, *The Sea Ranch*, 11.

18. Simo and Walker, *Invisible Gardens,* 154–55.

19. Sexton, *Parellel Utopias,* 33.

20. Halprin, *The Sea Ranch*, 29.

21. Halprin, *The Sea Ranch*, 33.

22. Simo and Walker, *Invisible Gardens,* 167.

23. Ana Maria Torres, *Isamu Noguchi: A Study in Space* (New York: Monacelli, 2000), 14.

24. Isamu Noguchi, *Isamu Noguchi: Space of Akari and Stone* (San Francisco: Chronicle Books, 1986), 9.

25. Bruce Altshuler, *Isamu Noguchi* (New York: Abbeville, 1994), 26.

26. Torres, *Isamu Noguchi,* 53.

27. Torres, *Isamu Noguchi,* 30.

28. Altshuler, *Isamu Noguchi,* 62.

29. Marc Treib, *Noguchi in Paris: The UNESCO Garden* (San Francisco: William Stout, 2003), 107, 128.

30. Torres, *Isamu Noguchi,* 10.

31. Treib, *Noguchi in Paris,* 116.

32. Treib, *Noguchi in Paris,* 117.

33. Altshuler, *Isamu Noguchi,* 14.

34. Noguchi, *Isamu Noguchi,* 9.

35. Treib, *Noguchi in Paris,* 128, from Isamu Noguchi, "New Stone Gardens," *Art in America,* June 1964, 89.

36. Jack Flam, ed., *Robert Smithson: The Collected Writings* (Berkeley: University of California Press, 1996), 68–69.

37. Eugenie Tsai, ed., *Robert Smithson* (Berkeley: University of California Press, 2004), 20.

38. John Beardsley, "Earthworks: The Landscape after Modernism," 111, in Stuart Wrede, *Denatured Visions: Landscape and Culture in the Twentieth Century* (New York: Museum of Modern Art, 1991).

39. "Note 1. The sinister in a primitive sense seems to have its origin in what could be called 'quality gardens' (Paradise). Dreadful things seem to have happened in these half-forgotten Edens. Why does the Garden of Delights suggest something perverse? Torture gardens. Deer Park. The Grottoes of Tiberius. Gardens of Virtue are somehow always 'lost.' A degraded paradise is perhaps worse than a degraded hell. America abounds in banal heavens, in vapid 'happy-hunting grounds,' and in 'natural' hells like Death Valley National Monument or The Devil's Playground. The public 'sculpture garden' for the most part is an outdoor 'room,' that in time becomes a limbo of modern isms. Too much thinking about 'gardens' leads to perplexity and agitation. Gardens like the levels of criticism bring one to the brink of chaos. This footnote is turning into a dizzying maze, full of tenuous paths and innumerable riddles. The abysmal problem of gardens somehow involves a fall from somewhere or something. The

certainty of the absolute garden will never be regained." Robert Smithson, "A Sedimentation of the Mind: Earth Projects" (1968).

40. Lewis L. Gould, *Lady Bird Johnson: Our Environmental First Lady* (Lawrence: University of Kansas Press, 1999), 51–52.

41. Beardsley, "Earthworks," 111.

42. Beardsley, "Earthworks," 111.

43. Hal Foster and Gordon Hughes, eds., *Richard Serra* (Cambridge, MA: MIT Press, 2000), 60.

44. Foster and Hughes, *Richard Serra,* 64.

45. Foster and Hughes, *Richard Serra,* 60.

46. Foster and Hughes, *Richard Serra,* 179.

47. Peter Walker, "The Practice of Landscape Architecture in the Postwar United States," in Treib, ed., *Modern Landscape Architecture,* 251.

48. Walker, "The Practice of Landscape Architecture in the Postwar United States," 255.

49. Rybczynski, *A Clearing in the Distance,* 395, 397, 401.

50. Harriet F. Senie, *Contemporary Public Sculpture: Tradition, Transformation, and Controversy* (New York: Oxford University Press, 1992), 95.

51. Simo and Walker, *Invisible Gardens,* 255.

52. Walker, "The Practice of Landscape Architecture in the Postwar United States," 256.

53. Martha Schwartz, "Landscape and Common Culture Since Modernism," in Treib, ed., *Modern Landscape Architecture,* 263.

54. Schwartz, "Landscape and Common Culture Since Modernism," 264.

55. Lawrence Wechsler, *Robert Irwin Getty Garden* (Los Angeles: J. Paul Getty Museum, 2002), 3.

CHAPTER 7: ALL OUR MISSING PARTS: MONEY AND VIRTUE IN THE GO-GO YEARS

1. Christopher Byron, *Martha Inc.: The Incredible Story of Martha Stewart Living Omnimedia* (New York: Wiley, 2002), 269.

2. *Martha Stewart Living,* April/March 1992.

3. Byron, *Martha Inc.,* 212.

4. Associated Press, August 1, 1998, quoted in Bill Adler, ed., *The World According to Martha* (New York: McGraw-Hill, 2006), 15.

5. Adler, ed., *The World According to Martha,* 4.

6. *Martha's Spring Gardening* (Burbank, CA: Warner Home Video, 2006).

7. *Canberra Times,* December 4, 1999, quoted in Adler, ed. *The World According to Martha,* 23.

8. *Albany Times Union,* September 24, 1995, quoted in Adler, ed., *The World According to Martha,* 65.

9. Byron, *Martha Inc.,* 329.

10. Byron, *Martha Inc.,* 269.

11. *New York Daily News,* April 19, 2000, quoted in Adler, ed., *The World According to Martha,* 173.

12. *Ottawa Citizen,* October 24, 1996, quoted in Adler, ed., *The World According to Martha,* 114.

13. Francis H. Cabot, *The Greater Perfection: The Story of the Gardens at Les Quatre Vents* (New York: Norton, 2001), 167. Inspired by a 1983 trip to Wakehurst Place, Sussex extension of Kew.

14. Cabot, *The Greater Perfection,* 311.

15. Robert Smithson, "Cultural Confinement," *Artforum,* October 1972, reprinted in Nancy Holt, ed., *The Writings of Robert Smithson: Essays with Illustrations* (New York: New York University Press, 1979).

16. Jack Nicklaus, *Nicklaus by Design:*

Golf Course Strategy and Architecture (New York: Harry N. Abrams, 2002), 8.

17.   Nicklaus, *Nicklaus by Design,* 76.

18.   Nicklaus, *Nicklaus by Design,* 83.

19.   Smithson, 71, *Down the Garden Path.*

20.   Paul Goldberger with host Kurt Anderson, *Studio 360,* WNYC, broadcast March 10, 2010.

BIBLIOGRAPHY

Adams, Henry. *The Education of Henry Adams*. New York: Modern Library, 1931.

Adler, Bill, ed. *The World According to Martha*. New York: McGraw-Hill, 2006.

Aguar, Charles E., and Berdeana Aguar. *Wrightscapes: Frank Lloyd Wright's Landscape Designs*. New York: McGraw-Hill, 2002.

Altshuler, Bruce. *Isamu Noguchi*. New York: Abbeville, 1994.

Amidon, Jane. *Moving Horizons: The Landscape Architecture of Kathryn Gustafson and Partners*. Basel and Boston: Birkhäuser-Publishers for Architecture, 2005.

———. *Radical Landscapes: Reinventing Outdoor Space*. Foreword by Kathryn Gustafson. New York: Thames & Hudson, 2001.

Amidon, Jane, and Dan Kiley. *Dan Kiley: The Complete Works of America's Master Landscape Architect*. New York: Bulfinch, 1999.

"An American." *American Husbandry, Containing an Account of the Soil, Climate, Production and Agriculture, of the British Colonies in North America and the West Indies*. London: Printed for J. Bew, 1775.

Andrews, Wayne. *Architecture, Ambition, and Americans: A Social History of American Architecture*. New York: Free Press, 1978.

Appleby, Joyce. *Thomas Jefferson*. New York: Times Books, 2003.

Aslet, Clive. *The American Country House*. New Haven, CT: Yale University Press, 1990.

Balmori, Diana, F. Herbert Bolton, Gordon Geballe, and Lisa Vernegaard. *Redesigning the American Lawn: A Search for Environmental Harmony*. New Haven, CT: Yale University Press, 1993.

Balmori, Diana, Diane Kostial McGuire, and Eleanor M. McPeck. *Beatrix Farrand's American Landscapes: Her Gardens and Campuses*. Sagaponack, NY: Sagapress, 1985.

Balmori, Diana, and Margaret Morton. *Transitory Gardens, Uprooted Lives*. New Haven, CT: Yale University Press, 1993.

Banham, Reyner. *Los Angeles: The Architecture of Four Ecologies*. New York: Harper & Row, 1971.

Bardeschi, Marco Dezzi. *Frank Lloyd Wright*. New York: Hamlyn, 1972.

Bartram, William. *Travels Through North and South Carolina, Georgia, East & West Florida, the Cherokee Country, the Extensive Territories of the Muscogulges, or Creek Confederacy, and the Country of the Chactaws*. Philadelphia, 1791.

Batey, Mavis, "The High Phase of English Landscape Gardening." *Eighteenth Century Life* 8 (January 1983): 44–49.

Bender, Steve, and Felder Rushing. *Passalong Plants*. Chapel Hill: University of North Carolina Press, 1993.

Bender, Thomas. *Toward an Urban Vision*. New York: Columbia University Press, 1975.

Beiswanger, William. "The Temple in the Garden: Thomas Jefferson's Vision of the Monticello Landscape." *Eighteenth Century Life* 8 (January 1983): 170–88.

Betts, Edwin Morris, and Hazlehurst Bolton Perkins. *Thomas Jefferson's Flower Garden at Monticello*. Charlottesville: University Press of Virginia, 1971.

Beveridge, Charles E., and Paul Rocheleau. *Frederick Law Olmsted: Designing the American Landscape*. New York: Universe, 1998.

Beyer, Teresa Gordon. "The Development of a California Style: Regionalism and the Spanish Colonial Revival in Southern California, 1880–1930." In Sheryl Kolasinski and P. A. Morton, eds., *Precis IV: American Architecture: In Search of Traditions*. New York: Rizzoli, 1983.

Blake, Peter. *God's Own Junkyard: The Planned Deterioration of America's Landscape*. New York: Holt, Rinehart & Winston, 1964.

Bisgrove, Richard. *The Gardens of Gertrude Jekyll*. Berkeley: University of California Press, 1992.

Bleam, Gregg. In Treib, ed., *Modern Landscape Architecture*, 1993.

Blodgett, Jeffrey, and Daniel Walker Howe, eds. *Victorian America*. Philadelphia: University of Pennsylvania Press, 1976.

Blomfield, Reginald. *The Formal Garden in England*. London: Macmillan, 1901.

Boorstin, Daniel. *The Lost World of Thomas Jefferson*. Chicago: University of Chicago Press, 1993.

Brechin, Gray. *Imperial San Francisco: Urban Power, Earthly Ruin*. Berkeley: University of California Press, 1999.

Bremer, Fredrika. *Homes of the New World: Impressions of America*. New York: Harper & Brothers, 1854.

Brown. Jane. *Beatrix: The Gardening Life of Beatrix Jones Farrand, 1872–1959*. New York: Viking, 1995.

———. *The Modern Garden*. New York: Princeton Architectural Press, 2000.

Brown, Kendall. *Japanese-Style Gardens of the Pacific West Coast*. New York: Rizzoli, 1999.

Bryan, John M. *Biltmore Estate: The Most Distinguished Private Place*. New York: Rizzoli, 1994.

Burton, Pamela. *Private Landscapes: Modernist Gardens in Southern California*. New York: Princeton Architectural Press, 2002.

Bushman, Richard. *The Refinement of America: Persons, Houses, Cities*. New York: Knopf, 1992.

Byron, Christopher. *Martha Inc.: The Incredible Story of Martha Stewart Living Omnimedia*. New York: Wiley, 2002.

Cabot, Francis H. *The Greater Perfection: The Story of the Gardens at Les Quatre Vents*. New York: Norton, 2001.

Cardwell, Kenneth H. *Bernard Maybeck: Artisan, Architect, Artist.* Santa Barbara, CA: Peregrine Smith, 1977.

Carr, Ethan. *Wilderness by Design: Landscape Architecture and the National Park Service.* Lincoln: University of Nebraska Press, 1998.

Catesby, Mark. *Natural History of Carolina, Florida, and the Bahama Islands.* Savannah: Beehive, 1974.

Chambers, Sir William. *Dissertation on Oriental Gardening.* Dublin: W. Wilson, 1773.

Chastellux, Marquis de. *Travels in North America in the Years 1780, 1781, and 1782.* Chapel Hill: University of North Carolina Press, 1963.

Church, Thomas Dolliver. "Architectural Pattern Can Take the Place of Flowers." *House Beautiful* 90, no. 1 (January 1948).

——. *Gardens Are for People: How to Plan for Outdoor Living.* New York: Reinhold, 1955.

——. "The Small California Garden; Chapter One, A New Deal for the Small Lot." *California Arts & Architecture,* May 1933.

——. "Transition: 1937–1948." In *Landscape Design.* San Francisco: San Francisco Museum of Art, 1948.

——. *Your Private World: A Study of Intimate Gardens.* San Francisco: Chronicle Books, 1969.

Clark, Clifford E., Jr. "Ranch-House Suburbia: Ideals and Realities." In Lary May, ed., *Recasting America: Culture and Politics in the Age of Cold War.* Chicago: University of Chicago Press, 1989.

Cleveland, Horace William. *Landscape Architecture, as Applied to the Wants of the West.* Pittsburgh: University of Pittsburgh Press, 1986.

Coffin, David R. "The Study of the History of the Italian Garden." In Michel Conan, ed., *Perspectives on Garden Histories.* Washington, DC: Dumbarton Oaks Research Library and Collection, 1999.

Colby, Vineta. *Vernon Lee: A Literary Biography.* Charlottesville: University of Virginia Press, 2003.

Conan, Michel, ed., *Contemporary Garden Aesthetics: Creations and Interpretations.* Washington, DC: Dumbarton Oaks Research Library and Collection, 2007.

——, ed. *Environmentalism in Landscape Architecture.* Washington, DC: Dumbarton Oaks Research Library and Collection, 2000.

——, ed. *Gardens and Imagination: Cultural History and Agency.* Washington, DC: Dumbarton Oaks Research Library and Collection, 2008.

Cook, Clarence. *The House Beautiful: Essays on Beds and Tables, Stools and Candlesticks.* New York: Charles Scribner's Sons, 1881.

Cooper, Susan Fenimore. *Essays on Nature and Landscape.* Athens: University of Georgia Press, 2002.

——. *Rural Hours.* Syracuse, NY: Syracuse University Press, 1995.

Corner, James. *Recovering Landscape: Essays in Contemporary Landscape Architecture.* New York: Princeton Architectural Press, 1999.

Cortissoz, Royal. *Monograph of the Work of Charles A. Platt.* New York: Architectural Book, 1913.

Cosgrove, Denis. *The Palladian Landscape: Geographical Change and Its Cultural Representations in Sixteenth-Century Italy.* University Park: Penn State University Press, 1993.

Cranz, Galen. *The Politics of Park Design: A History of Urban Parks in America.* Cambridge, MA: MIT Press, 1982.

Croly, Herbert. *The Promise of American Life*. Cambridge, MA: Belknap Press of Harvard University Press, 1965.

Curtis, William J. R. *Le Corbusier: Ideas and Forms*. London: Phaidon, 1986.

Darke, Rick. *In Harmony with Nature: Lessons from the Arts & Crafts Garden*. New York: Friedman/Fairfax, 2000.

Davis, Alexander Jackson. *Rural Residences*. New York: Da Capo, 1980.

Delaney, Topher. *Topher Delaney*. Gloucester, MA: Rockport, 2001.

Deverell, William. *Whitewashed Adobe: The Rise of Los Angeles and the Remaking of Its Mexican Past*. Berkeley: University of California Press, 2004.

Doell, M. Christie Klim. *Gardens of the Gilded Age*. Syracuse, NY: Syracuse University Press, 1986.

Domer, Dennis. *Alfred Caldwell: The Life and Work of a Prairie School Landscape Architect*. Baltimore: Johns Hopkins University Press, 1997.

Douglas, Ann. *The Feminization of American Culture*. New York: Knopf, 1977.

Downing, Andrew Jackson. *The Architecture of Country Houses*. New York: Dover, 1969.

———. *The Fruits and Fruit-Trees of America*. New York: Wiley, 1900.

———, ed. *The Horticulturalist*. July 1846–December 1875.

———. *Landscape Gardening and Rural Architecture*. With an introduction by George B. Tatum. New York: Dover, 1991.

———. *A Treatise on the Theory and Practice of Landscape Gardening*. New York: Dover, 1991.

———. *Victorian Cottage Residences*. New York: Dover, 1981.

Drexler, Arthur. *The Architecture of Richard Neutra: From International Style to California Modern*. New York: Museum of Modern Art, 1982.

Duchscherer, Paul. *Outside the Bungalow: America's Arts and Crafts Garden*. New York: Penguin Studio, 1999.

Duncan, Frances. "The Gardens of Cornish." *Century Magazine,* May 1906.

Duus, Masayo. *The Life of Isamu Noguchi: Journey Without Borders*. Princeton, NJ: Princeton University Press, 2004.

Dwight, Timothy. *Travels in New England and New York*. Cambridge, MA: Belknap Press of Harvard University Press, 1969.

Earle, Alice Morse. *Home Life in Colonial Days*. New York: Macmillan, 1898.

———. *Old Time Gardens*. New York: Macmillan, 1901.

Eaton, Leonard K. *Landscape Artist in America: The Life and Work of Jens Jensen*. Chicago: University of Chicago Press, 1964.

Eckbo, Garrett. "The Esthetics of Planting," In *Landscape Design*. San Francisco: San Francisco Museum of Art, 1948.

———. *Home Landscape: The Art of Home Landscaping*. New York: McGraw-Hill, 1956.

———. *Landscape for Living*. New York: Architectural Record with Duell, Sloan & Pearce, 1950.

———. *The Landscape We See*. New York: McGraw-Hill, 1969.

———. *Urban Landscape Design*. New York: McGraw-Hill, 1964.

Eliot, Charles W. *Charles Eliot, Landscape Architect*. Boston: Houghton Mifflin, 1902.

Elliot, Jared. *Essays Upon Field Husbandry in New England, and Other Papers, 1748–1762*. New York: Columbia University Press, 1934.

Ellis, Joseph. *American Sphinx: The Char-*

acter of Thomas Jefferson. New York: Knopf, 1997.

Ely, Helena Rutherford. *A Woman's Hardy Garden*. New York: Macmillan, 1903.

Emerson, Ralph Waldo. *The Essays of Ralph Waldo Emerson*. Cambridge, MA: Belknap, 1987.

———.*The Selected Lectures of Ralph Waldo Emerson*. Ed. Ronald A. Bosco and Joel Myerson. Athens: University of Georgia Press, 2005.

———. *The Selected Writings of Ralph Waldo Emerson*. New York: Modern Library, 1992.

———. *The Young American: A Lecture Read Before the Mercantile Library Association, in Boston, at the Odeon, Wednesday, February 7, 1844*. London : John Chapman, 1844.

Engel, David. *Japanese Gardens for Today*. With a foreword by Richard Neutra. Rutland, VT: C. E. Tuttle, 1959.

Esten, John. *Hamptons Gardens: A 350-Year Legacy*. New York: Rizzoli, 2004.

Etlin, Richard A. *Frank Lloyd Wright and Le Corbusier: The Romantic Legacy*. Manchester and New York: Manchester University Press, 1994.

Fay, James, et al. *California Almanac, 1985*. Novato, CA: Presidio, 1985.

Fell, Derek. *The Gardens of Frank Lloyd Wright*. London: Frances Lincoln, 2009.

Findlay, David. *Magic Lands: Western Cityscapes and American Culture after 1940*. Berkeley: University of California Press, 1992.

Fine, Jud. *Spine: An Account of the Jud Fine Art Plan at the Maguire Gardens, Central Library, Los Angeles*. Los Angeles: Los Angeles Library Association, 1993.

Fischer, David Hackett. *Albion's Seed: Four British Folkways in America*. New York: Oxford University Press, 1989.

Flam, Jack, ed. *Robert Smithson: The Collected Writings* (Berkeley: University of California Press, 1996).

Fleming, Nancy. *Money, Manure & Maintenance: Ingredients for Successful Gardens of Marian Kruger Coffin, 1876–1957*. Weston, MA: Country Place, 1995.

Fletcher, Valerie J. *Isamu Noguchi: Master Sculptor*. London: Scala, 2005.

Foster, Hal, and Gordon Hughes, eds. *Richard Serra*. Cambridge, MA: MIT Press, 2000.

Fox, Helen Morganthau. *Patio Gardens*. New York: Macmillan, 1929.

Francis, Mark, and Randolph T. Hester, Jr., eds. *The Meaning of Gardens*. Cambridge, MA: MIT Press, 1990.

French, Jere Stuart. *The California Garden: And the Landscape Architects Who Shaped It*. Washington, DC: Landscape Architecture Foundation, 1993.

Friedman, Alice T. *Women and the Making of the Modern House: A Social and Architectural History*. New York: Abrams, 1998.

Gebhard, David, *Schindler*. New York: Viking, 1971.

Gould, Lewis L. *Lady Bird Johnson: Our Environmental First Lady*. Lawrence: University Press of Kansas, 1999.

Greenlee, John. *The American Meadow Garden: Creating an Alternative to the Traditional Lawn*. Portland: Timber, 2009.

———. *The Encyclopedia of Ornamental Grasses: How to Grow and Use over 250 Beautiful and Versatile Plants*. Emmaus, PA: Rodale, 1992.

Grese, Robert E. *Jens Jensen: Maker of Natural Parks and Gardens*. Baltimore: Johns Hopkins University Press, 1992.

Griswold, Mac, and Eleanor Weller. *The Golden Age of American Gardens: Proud Owners, Private Estates, 1890–1940*. New York: H. N. Abrams, 1991.

Griswold, Ralph, and Frederick Nicholls. *Thomas Jefferson, Landscape Architect*. Charlottesville: University Press of Virginia, 1978.

Groening, Gerd, and Joachim Wolschke-Bulmahn. "Some Notes on the Mania for Native Plants in Germany." *Landscape Journal* 11, no. 2 (1992): 116–26.

Gustafson, Kathryn, et al. *Revelatory Landscapes*. San Francisco: San Francisco Museum of Modern Art, 2001.

Haeg, Fritz. *Edible Estates: Attack on the Front Lawn*. New York: Metropolis, 2008.

Halprin, Lawrence. *Changing Places: San Francisco Museum of Modern Art, 3 July–24 August 1986*. San Francisco: The Museum, 1986.

———. *The Franklin Delano Roosevelt Memorial*. San Francisco: Chronicle Books, 1997.

———. *The Sea Ranch: Diary of an Idea*. Berkeley: Spacemaker, 2002.

Halttunen, Karen. *Confidence Men and Painted Women: A Study of Middle Class Culture in America, 1830–1870*. New Haven, CT: Yale University Press, 1982.

Hanson, Archibald E. *An Arcadian Landscape: The California Gardens of AE Hanson, 1920–1932*. Los Angeles: Hennessy & Ingalls, 1985.

Harper, Glenn, and Twylene Moyer, eds. *Landscapes for Art: Contemporary Sculpture Parks*. Hamilton, NJ: ISC, 2008.

Harris, Diane. "Race, Class, and Privacy in the Ordinary Postwar House, 1945–1960." In Richard H. Schein, ed., *Landscape and Race in the United States*. New York: Routledge, 2006.

Harwood, Kathryn Chapman. *The Lives of Vizcaya*. Miami: Banyan, 1985.

Hatch, Peter. *The Gardens of Thomas Jefferson's Monticello*. Charlottesville: Thomas Jefferson Memorial Foundation, 1992.

Hawthorne, Hildegarde. *Lure of the Garden*. Illustrated in full color by Maxfield Parrish, Jules Guérin Sigismond de Ivanowski, Anna Whelan Betts, and others, and with photographs. New York: Century, 1911.

Hawthorne, Nathaniel. "Our Old Home: A Series of English Sketches." In *The Works of Nathaniel Hawthorne*. New York: Thomas Crowell, 1906.

Hays, Samuel. *Conservation and the Gospel of Efficiency: The Progressive Conservation Movement, 1890–1920*. Cambridge, MA: Harvard University Press, 1959.

Henriksen, Margot A. *Dr. Strangelove's America: Society and Culture in the Atomic Age*. Berkeley: University of California Press, 1997.

Hess, Alan, and Andrew Danish. *Palm Springs Weekend: The Architecture and Design of a Midcentury Oasis*. San Francisco: Chronicle Books, 2001.

Hill, May Brawley. *Grandmother's Garden: The Old-Fashioned American Garden, 1865–1915*. New York: Abrams, 1995.

———. *On Foreign Soil: American Gardeners Abroad*. New York: Harry N. Abrams, 2005.

Hine, Robert. *California's Utopian Colonies*. New Haven, CT: Yale University Press, 1966.

Hines, Thomas S. *Irving Gill and the Architecture of Reform: A Study in Modernist Architectural Culture*. New York: Monacelli Press, 2000.

———. *Richard Neutra and the Search for Modern Architecture*. New York: Rizzoli, 2005.

Hitchcock, Henry Russell. *Architecture of the 19th and 20th Centuries*. Harmondsworth, England: Penguin, 1968.

———, ed. *Contemporary Landscape Archi-*

tecture and Its Sources. San Francisco: San Francisco Museum of Art, 1937.

Hitchmough, Wendy. *Arts and Crafts Gardens*. New York: Rizzoli, 1998.

Holt, Nancy, ed. *The Writings of Robert Smithson: Essays with Illustrations*. New York: New York University Press, 1979.

Homberger, Eric. *The Historical Atlas of New York City: A Visual Celebration of Nearly 400 Years of New York City's History*. New York: Henry Holt, 1994.

Horn, Joan L., and Corporation for Jefferson's Poplar Forest. *Thomas Jefferson's Poplar Forest: A Private Place*. Forest, VA: Corporation for Jefferson's Poplar Forest, 2002.

Howard, Ebenezer. *Garden Cities of Tomorrow*. Cambridge, MA: MIT Press, 1965.

Howard, Hugh. *Thomas Jefferson, Architect: The Built Legacy of the Third President*. New York: Rizzoli, 2003.

Howard, Lucia, and David Weingarten. *Ranch Houses: Living the California Dream*. New York: Rizzoli, 2009.

Howett, Catherine. "Modernism and American Landscape Architecture." In Treib, ed., *Modern Landscape Architecture*, 1993.

Hunt, John Dixon. *The Afterlife of Gardens*. Philadelphia: University of Pennsylvania Press, 2004.

———. *Garden and Grove: The Italian Renaissance Garden in the English Imagination, 1600–1750*. Princeton, NJ: Princeton University Press, 1986.

———. *Gardens and the Picturesque: Studies in the History of Landscape Architecture*. Cambridge, MA: MIT Press, 1993.

———. *The Genius of the Place: The English Landscape Garden, 1620–1820*. London: Elek, 1965.

———. *Greater Perfections: The Practice of Garden Theory*. Philadelphia: University of Pennsylvania Press, 2000.

———. *The Picturesque Garden in Europe*. New York: Thames & Hudson, 2002.

———. "Pope's Twickenham Revisited." *Eighteenth Century Life* 8 (January 1983): 26–35.

Hunt, John Dixon, and Joachim Wolschke-Bulmahn, eds. *The Vernacular Garden*. Washington, DC: Dumbarton Oaks Research Library and Collection, 1993.

Hunter, Sam. *Isamu Noguchi*. Seattle: Bryan Ohno Editions in Association with the University of Washington Press, 2000.

Hyams, Edward. *Capability Brown and Humphry Repton*. New York: Charles Scribner's Sons, 1971.

Imbert, Dorothée. *The Modernist Garden in France*. New Haven, CT: Yale University Press, 1993.

Jackson, John Brinckerhoff. *Discovering the Vernacular Landscape*. New Haven, CT: Yale University Press, 1984.

Jackson, Kenneth. *Crabgrass Frontier: The Suburbanization of the United States*. New York: Oxford University Press, 1985.

Jaffe, Irma B., ed. *The Italian Presence in American Art, 1860–1920*. New York: Fordham University Press, 1992.

James, Henry. *The American Scene*. Bloomington: Indiana University Press, 1968.

———. *Italian Hours*. New York: Horizon, 1968.

James, Henry, Edith Wharton, and Lyall Harris Powers. *Henry James and Edith Wharton: Letters, 1900–1915*. New York: Scribner's, 1990.

James, John, trans. *The Theory and Practice of Gardening*. By A.-J. Dezallier D'Argenville. London: G. James, 1712.

Jefferson, Thomas. *The Garden and Farm Books of Thomas Jefferson.* Ed. Robert C. Baron. Golden, CO: Fulcrum, 1987.

——. *Writings.* New York: Literary Classics of the U.S., 1984.

Jekyll, Gertrude. *Colour Schemes for the Flower Garden.* Salem, NH: Ayer, 1983.

——. *Wood and Garden: Notes and Thoughts, Practical and Critical, of a Working Amateur.* London: Longmans, Green, 1910.

Jekyll, Gertrude, and Sir Lawrence Weaver. *Gardens for Small Country Houses.* New York: Charles Scribner's, 1927.

Jenkins, Virginia Scott. *The Lawn: A History of an American Obsession.* Washington, DC: Smithsonian Institution Press, 1994.

Jensen, Jens. *Siftings.* Baltimore: Johns Hopkins University Press, 1990.

Kaplan, Wendy. *The Arts and Crafts Movement in Europe & America: Design for the Modern World.* New York: Thames & Hudson, 2004.

Karson, Robin. *Fletcher Steele, Landscape Architect: An Account of the Gardenmaker's Life, 1885–1971.* Amherst, MA: Library of American Landscape History, 2003.

——. *A Genius for Place: American Landscapes of the Country Place Era.* Amherst, MA: University of Massachusetts Press, 2007.

——. *The Muses of Gwinn: Art and Nature in a Garden Designed by Warren H. Manning, Charles A. Platt & Ellen Biddle Shipman.* Sagaponack, NY: Sagapress, 1995.

Kassler, Elizabeth B. *Modern Garden and the Landscape.* New York: Museum of Modern Art, 1964.

Kaufmann, Edgar, Jr. *Fallingwater: A Frank Lloyd Wright Country House.* New York: Abbeville, 1986.

Kelly, Bruce, Gail Travis Guillet, and Mary Ellen W. Hern. *Art of the Olmsted Landscape.* New York: New York City Landmarks Preservation Commission and Arts Publisher, 1981.

Kennedy, Roger G. *Architecture, Men, Women, and Money in America 1600–1860.* New York: Random House, 1985.

Keswick, Maggie. *The Chinese Garden: History, Art, and Architecture.* Cambridge, MA: Harvard University Press, 2003.

Kimball, Fiske. *Thomas Jefferson, Architect: Original Designs in the Coolidge Collection of the Massachusetts Historical Society.* New York: Da Capo, 1968.

Kingsbury, Noël, and Tim Richardson. *Vista: The Culture and Politics of Gardens.* London: Frances Lincoln, 2005.

Kirsten, Sven A. *The Book of Tiki: The Cult of Polynesian Pop in Fifties America.* Koln: Taschen, 2000.

Kornwolf, James D. "The Picturesque in the American Garden and Landscape before 1800." *Eighteenth Century Life* 8 (January 1983): 93–106.

Krauss, Rosalind. "Sculpture in the Expanded Field." In *The Originality of the Avant-Garde and Other Modernist Myths.* Cambridge, MA: MIT Press, 1985.

Kruse, Kevin M., and Thomas J. Sugrue, eds. *The New Suburban History.* Chicago: University of Chicago Press, 2006.

Lamprecht, Barbara Mac. *Richard Neutra: Complete Works.* New York: Taschen, 2000.

Lancaster, Clay. *The Japanese Influence in America.* New York: W. H. Rawls, 1963.

Langley, Batty. *New Principles of Gardening.* New York: Garland, 1982.

Larkin, Oliver. *Art and Life in America.* New York: Holt, Rinehart & Winston, 1960.

Latrobe, Benjamin. "An Essay on Landscape." In Edward C. Carter II et al., eds., *The Virginia Journals of Benjamin Latrobe, 1795–1798.* New Haven, CT: Yale University Press, 1977.

Laurie, Michael. "Thomas Church, California Gardens, and Public Landscapes." In Treib, ed., *Modern Landscape Architecture,* 1993.

Lavin, Sylvia. *Form Follows Libido: Architecture and Richard Neutra in a Psychoanalytic Culture.* Cambridge, MA: MIT Press, 2004.

Lears, T. J. Jackson. *American Victorians and Virgin Nature.* Boston: Isabella Stewart Gardner Museum, 2002.

——. *Fables of Abundance: A Cultural History of Advertising in America.* New York: Basic Books, 1994.

——. *No Place of Grace: Antimodernism and the Transformation of American Culture, 1880–1920.* New York: Pantheon, 1981.

Leatherbarrow, David. *Uncommon Ground: Architecture, Technology, and Topography.* Cambridge, MA: MIT Press, 2000.

——. *Topographical Stories: Studies in Landscape and Architecture.* Philadelphia: University of Pennsylvania Press, 2004.

Leccese, Michael. *American Eden: Landscape Architecture of the Pacific West.* Paris: Vilo International, 2000.

Lee, Vernon. *Limbo, and other Essays.* London: J. Lane, 1908.

Lehrman, Jonas. *Earthly Paradise: Garden and Courtyard in Islam.* Berkeley: University of California Press, 1980.

Leighton, Ann. *American Gardens in the Eighteenth Century: "For Use or for Delight."* Amherst: University of Massachusetts Press, 1986.

——. *American Gardens of the Nineteenth Century: "For Comfort and Affluence."* Amherst: University of Massachusetts Press, 1987.

——. *Early American Gardens: "For Meate or Medicine."* Amherst: University of Massachusetts Press, 1986.

Lerer, Seth. *Children's Literature: A Reader's History, from Aesop to Harry Potter.* Chicago: University of Chicago Press, 2008.

Lewis, R. W. B. *Edith Wharton: A Biography.* New York: Harper & Row, 1975.

Lin, Maya Ying. *Boundaries.* New York: Simon & Schuster, 2000.

——. *Maya Lin: Systematic Landscapes.* New Haven, CT: Yale University Press, 2006.

Linden-Ward, Blanche. *Silent City on a Hill: Landscape of Memory and Boston's Mount Auburn Cemetery.* Columbus: Ohio State University Press, 1989.

Loewer, Peter. *Jefferson's Garden.* Mechanicsburg, PA: Stackpole, 2004.

Longstaffe-Gowan, Todd. *The London Town Garden, 1700–1840.* New Haven, CT: Yale University Press, 2001.

Longstreth, Richard, ed. *The Mall in Washington, 1791–1991.* New Haven, CT: Yale University Press, 2002.

Loudon, John Claudius. *An Encyclopaedia of Cottage, Farm, and Villa Architecture and Furniture.* New York: Worthington, 1883.

——. *Encyclopedia of Gardening.* London: Longmans, 1878.

Loudon, Mrs. *Gardening for Ladies, and Companion to the Flower Garden.* New York: Wiley & Putnam, 1843.

Lowe, David. *Lost Chicago.* Boston: Houghton Mifflin, 1975.

Lowell, Guy. *American Gardens.* Boston: Bates & Guild, 1902.

Lummis, Charles Fletcher. *Some Strange Corners of Our Country: The Wonderland of the Southwest*. New York: Century, 1892.

MacPhail, Elizabeth. *Kate Sessions, Pioneer Horticulturist*. San Diego: San Diego Historical Society, 1976.

Major, Judith K. *To Live in the New World: A. J. Downing and American Landscape Gardening*. Cambridge, MA: MIT Press, 1997.

Marranca, Bonnie, ed. *American Garden Writing: Gleanings from Garden Lives Then and Now*. New York: PAJ, 1988.

Martin, Peter, ed. *British and American Gardens of the 18th Century*. Williamsburg, VA: Colonial Williamsburg Foundation, 1984.

———. "'Long and Assiduous Endeavors': Gardening in Early Eighteenth-Century Virginia." *Eighteenth Century Life* 8 (January 1983): 107–15.

———. *The Pleasure Gardens of Virginia from Jamestown to Jefferson*. Princeton, NJ: Princeton University Press, 1991.

Martins, Susanna Wade. *The English Model Farm: Building the Agricultural Ideal, 1700–1914*. Macclesfield, England: Windgather, 2002.

Marx, Leo. *The Machine in the Garden: Technology and the Pastoral Ideal in America*. New York: Oxford University Press, 1964.

Mason, William. *The English Garden: A Poem*. New York: Garland, 1982.

MacDougall, Elizabeth, and George Tatum, eds. *Prophet with Honor: The Career of Andrew Jackson Downing, 1815–1852*. Philadelphia: Athenaeum of Philadelphia, 1989.

McCoy, Esther. *Five California Architects*. New York: Reinhold, 1960.

———. *Richard Neutra*. New York: Braziller, 1960.

McHarg, Ian. *Design with Nature*. Garden City, NY: Natural History Press, 1969.

McLean, Elizabeth. "Town and Country Gardens in 18th Century Philadelphia." *Eighteenth Century Life* 8 (January 1983): 136–47.

McPhee, John. *Annals of the Former World*. New York: Farrar, Straus & Giroux, 1998.

Meinig, D. W. *The Shaping of America: A Geographical Perspective on 500 Years of History*. New Haven, CT: Yale University Press, 1986.

Miller, Philip. *Gardener's Dictionary*. London: C. Rivington, 1733–39.

Miller, Wilhelm. *The Prairie Spirit in Landscape Gardening*. Amherst: University of Massachusetts Press, 2002.

Millhouse, Barbara Babcock. *American Wilderness: The Story of the Hudson River School of Painting*. Hensonville, NY: Black Dome, 2007.

M'Mahon, Bernard. *The American Gardener's Calendar*. Philadelphia: B. Graves, 1806.

Moore, Charles W., William J. Mitchell, and William Turnbull, Jr. *The Poetics of Gardens*. Cambridge, MA: MIT Press, 1993.

Morgan, Keith N. *Charles A. Platt: The Artist as Architect*. Cambridge, MA: MIT Press, 1985.

Morgan, Keith N., and R. W. Davidson. *Shaping an American Landscape: The Art and Architecture of Charles A. Platt*. Hanover, NH: University Press of New England, 1995.

Mumford, Lewis. *The Brown Decades: A Study of the Arts in America, 1865–1895*. New York: Dover, 1955.

———. *Sticks and Stones: A Study of American Architecture and Civilization*. New York: Dover, 1955.

Murmann, Eugene O. *California Gardens: How to Plan and Beautify the City Lot, Suburban Grounds and Country Estate.* Los Angeles: E. O. Murmann, 1914.

Nash, Roderick. *Wilderness and the American Mind.* New Haven, CT: Yale University Press, 1967.

Neumann, Dietrich, ed. *Richard Neutra's Windshield House.* New Haven, CT: Yale University Press, 2001.

Neutra, Richard Joseph. *Architecture of Social Concern in Regions of Mild Climate.* Sao Paulo, Brazil: Gerth Todtmann, 1948.

———. *Building with Nature.* New York: Universe, 1971.

———. Foreword to David H. Engel, *Japanese Gardens for Today.* Rutland, VT: C. E. Tuttle, 1959.

———. "Human Setting in an Industrial Civilization." In Joan Ockman, ed., *Architecture Culture 1943–1968: A Documentary Anthology.* New York: Rizzoli, 1993.

———. "Landscaping—A New Issue." In *Contemporary Landscape Architecture and Its Sources.* San Francisco: San Francisco Museum of Art, 1937.

———. *Life and Human Habitat.* Stuttgart: A. Koch, 1956.

———. *Life and Shape.* New York: Appleton-Century-Crofts, 1962.

———. *Mysteries and Realities of the Site.* Scarsdale, NY: Morgan & Morgan, 1951.

———. *Nature Near: Late Essays of Richard Neutra.* Ed. William Marlin. Santa Barbara, CA: Capra, 1989.

———. *Survival Through Design.* London: Oxford University Press, 1969.

———. *World and Dwelling.* New York: Universe, 1962.

———. Article in *Time,* August 15, 1949, 58–66.

Newton, Norman T. *Design on the Land: The Development of Landscape Architecture.* Cambridge, MA: Belknap Press of Harvard University Press, 1971.

Nicklaus, Jack. *Nicklaus by Design: Golf Course Strategy and Architecture.* New York: Harry N. Abrams, 2002.

Noguchi, Isamu. *Isamu Noguchi: Space of Akari and Stone.* San Francisco: Chronicle Books, 1986.

———. *The Isamu Noguchi Garden Museum.* New York: H. N. Abrams, 1987.

———. *A Sculptor's World.* Foreword by R. Buckminster Fuller. New York: Harper & Row, 1968.

Oliver, Richard. *Bertram Grosvenor Goodhue.* Cambridge, MA: MIT Press, 1983.

Olmsted, Frederick Law. *A Journey in the Back Country in the Winter of 1853–4.* New York: G. P. Putnam's Sons, 1907.

———. *A Journey in the Seaboard Slave States in the Years 1853–1854, with Remarks on Their Economy.* New York: G. P. Putnam's Sons, 1904.

———. *Walks and Talks of an American Farmer in England.* Ann Arbor: University of Michigan Press, 1967.

Olwig, Kenneth R. "Landscape, Monuments, and National Identity." In G. H. Herb and D. H. Kaplan, eds., *Nations and Nationalism.* Vol. 1, *1770–1880.* Santa Barbara, CA: ABC-CLIO, 2008.

O'Malley, Therese. "Mark Catesby and the Culture of Gardens." In Amy R. W. Meyers and Margaret Beck Pritchard, eds., *Empire's Nature: Mark Catesby's New World Vision.* Chapel Hill: University of North Carolina Press, 1998.

O'Malley, Therese, and Marc Treib, eds. *The Regional Garden in the United States.* Washington, DC: Dumbarton Oaks Research Library and Collection, 1995.

O'Neill, Frank. "The Great Iconoclast." *Garden & Gun,* Spring 2007, 71–79.

Orcut, Rev. Samuel. *A History of the Old Town of Stratford and City of Bridgeport Connecticut.* Vol. 2. Bridgeport, CT: Tuttle, Morehouse & Taylor, 1886.

Otis, Denise. *Grounds for Pleasure: Four Centuries of the American Garden.* New York: Harry N. Abrams, 2002.

Pack, Charles Lathrop. *The War Garden Victorious.* Philadelphia: Lippincott, 1919.

Padilla, Victoria. *Southern California Gardens: An Illustrated History.* Berkeley: University of California Press, 1961.

Parkinson, John. *A Garden of Pleasant Flowers (Paradisi in Sole, Paradisus Terrestris).* New York: Dover: 1976.

Peck, Amelia, ed. *Alexander Jackson Davis: American Architect, 1803–1892.* New York: Rizzoli, 1992.

Platt, Charles A. *Italian Gardens.* Portland, OR: Sagapress/Timber Press, 1993.

Poe, Edgar Allan. *The Collected Tales and Poems of Edgar Allan Poe.* New York: Modern Library, 1992.

Power, Nancy Goslee. *Power of Gardens.* New York: Stewart, Tabori & Chang, 2009.

Power, Nancy Goslee, with Susan Heeger. *The Gardens of California: Four Centuries of Design from Mission to Modern.* New York: Clarkson N. Potter, 1995.

Prest, John. *The Garden of Eden: The Botanical Garden and the Re-creation of Paradise.* New Haven, CT: Yale University Press, 1981.

Quest-Ritson, Charles. *The English Garden: A Social History.* Boston: David R. Godine, 2003.

Ray, Mary Helen, and Robert Nichols. *The Traveler's Guide to American Gardens.* Chapel Hill: University of North Carolina Press, 1988.

Reisman, David. *The Lonely Crowd: A Study of the Changing American Character.* New Haven, CT: Yale University Press, 1950.

Reps, John. *The Making of Urban America: A History of City Planning in the United States.* Princeton, NJ: Princeton University Press, 1965.

Reynolds, Ann. *Robert Smithson: Learning from New Jersey and Elsewhere.* Cambridge, MA: MIT Press, 2003.

Roberts, Jennifer. *Mirror Travels: Robert Smithson and History.* New Haven, CT: Yale University Press, 2004.

Robinson, William. *The English Flower Garden and Home Grounds.* New York: Charles Scribner's Sons, 1921.

——. *The Wild Garden.* Portland, OR: Sagapress/Timber Press, 1994.

Rogers, Elizabeth Barlow. *Landscape Design: A Cultural and Architectural History.* New York: Harry N. Abrams, 2001.

Rogers, George C. "Gardens and Landscape in 18th Century South Carolina." *Eighteenth Century Life* 8 (January 1983): 148–58.

Rose, James. *Gardens Make Me Laugh.* Baltimore: Johns Hopkins University Press, 1990.

Roth, Leland M. *McKim, Mead & White, Architects.* New York: Harper & Row, 1983.

Ruskin, John. *The Stones of Venice.* New York: Wiley, 1877.

Russell, Vivian. *Edith Wharton's Italian Gardens.* London: Frances Lincoln, 1997.

Rybczynski, Witold. *A Clearing in the Distance: Frederick Law Olmsted and America in the Nineteenth Century.* New York: Scribner, 1999.

Sargent, Charles Sprague. *Garden and Forest.* New York: Garden & Forest, 1888–97.

Schindler, Rudolf M. *Rudolph M. Schindler: R. M. Schindler House, Hollywood, California, 1921–22, James E. How House, Los Angeles, California, 1925.* Tokyo: A.D.A. EDITA Tokyo, 1999.

——. *The Architecture of R. M. Schindler.* Los Angeles: Harry N. Abrams, 2001.

Schoenbrun, David. *Triumph in Paris: The Exploits of Benjamin Franklin.* New York: Harper & Row, 1976.

Schuyler, David. *Apostle of Taste: Andrew Jackson Downing, 1915–1852.* Baltimore: Johns Hopkins University Press, 1996.

Schwartz, Martha. *The Vanguard Landscapes and Gardens of Martha Schwartz.* Ed. Tim Richardson. New York: Thames & Hudson, 2004.

Scott, Frank J. *The Art of Beautification of Suburban Home Grounds of Small Extent.* New York: Appleton, 1870.

Sedding, John Dando. *Garden-Craft Old and New.* London: K. Paul, Trench, Trübner, 1891.

Senie, Harriet F. *Contemporary Public Sculpture: Tradition, Transformation, and Controversy.* New York: Oxford University Press, 1992.

Sexton, Richard. *Parallel Utopias: Sea Ranch and Seaside: The Quest for Community.* San Francisco: Chronicle Books, 1995.

Sheine, Judith. *R. M. Schindler.* London: Phaidon, 2001.

Shenstone, William. *The Works in Verse and Prose.* London: J. Dodsley, 1791.

Shepheard, Peter. *Modern Gardens: Masterworks of International Garden Architecture.* New York: Praeger, 1954.

Simo, Melanie Louise. *Forest and Garden: Traces of Wildness in a Modernizing Land, 1897–1949.* Charlottesville: University of Virginia Press, 2003.

——. *Loudon and the Landscape: From Country Seat to Metropolis, 1783–1843.* New Haven, CT: Yale University Press, 1988.

Simo, Melanie Louise, and Peter Walker. *Invisible Gardens: The Search for Modernism in the American Landscape.* Cambridge, MA: MIT Press, 1994.

Sitwell, Sir George. *On the Making of Gardens.* New York: Scribner, 1951.

Smith, Ken. *Ken Smith, Landscape Architect: Urban Projects.* Ed. Jane Amidon. New York: Princeton Architectural Press, 2006.

Smithson, Robert. *Robert Smithson: The Collected Writings.* Ed. Jack Flam. Berkeley: University of California Press, 1996.

Smithson, Robert, et al. *Robert Smithson.* Berkeley: University of California Press, 2004.

St. John de Crèvecoeur, J. Hector. *Letters from an American Farmer.* New York: Dutton, 1912.

Starr, Kevin. *Material Dreams: Southern California Through the 1920s.* New York: Oxford University Press, 1990.

Steinberg, Theodore. *American Green: The Obsessive Quest for the Perfect Lawn.* New York: Norton, 2006.

Stewart, Martha. *Martha's Spring Gardening.* Burbank, CA: Warner Home Video, 2006.

——. *Martha Stewart's Gardening, Month by Month.* New York: Clarkson Potter, 1991.

Stilgoe, John. *Borderland: Origins of the American Suburb, 1820–1930.* New Haven, CT: Yale University Press, 1988.

Streatfield, David. *California Gardens: Creating a New Eden.* New York: Abbeville, 1994.

Tankard, Judith B. *Gardens of the Arts and Crafts Movement: Reality and Imagination.* New York: Harry N. Abrams, 2004.

———. *The Gardens of Ellen Biddle Shipman.* Sagaponack, NY: Sagapress, 1996.

———. *Gertrude Jekyll: A Vision of Garden and Wood.* New York: H. N. Abrams, 1989.

Thaxter, Celia. *An Island Garden.* Boston: Houghton Mifflin, 1988. First published 1978 by Heritage Books.

Thompson, Mark. *American Character: The Curious Life of Charles Fletcher Lummis and the Rediscovery of the Southwest.* New York: Arcade, 2001.

Tocqueville, Alexis de. *Democracy in America.* Ed. Phillips Bradley. New York: Knopf, 1945.

Torres, Ana Maria. *Isamu Noguchi: A Study in Space.* New York: Monacelli, 2000.

Treib, Marc, ed. *The Architecture of Landscape, 1940–1960.* Philadelphia: University of Pennsylvania Press, 2002.

———. *The Donnell and Eckbo Gardens: Modern California Masterworks.* San Francisco: William Stout, 2005.

———, ed. *An Everyday Modernism: The Houses of William Wurster.* Berkeley: University of California Press, 1995.

———, ed. *Modern Landscape Architecture: A Critical Review.* Cambridge, MA: MIT Press, 1993.

———. *Noguchi in Paris: The Unesco Garden.* San Francisco: William Stout, 2003.

———, ed. *Thomas Church, Landscape Architect: Designing a Modern California Landscape.* San Francisco: William Stout, 2003.

Treib, Marc, and Dorothée Imbert. *Garrett Eckbo: Modern Landscapes for Living.* Berkeley: University of California Press, 1997.

Tunnard, Christopher. *Gardens in the Modern Landscape.* New York: Scribner, 1950.

Turner, James. *The Politics of Landscape: Rural Scenery and Society in English Poetry, 1630–1660.* Cambridge, MA: Harvard University Press, 1979.

Uglow, Jenny. *A Little History of British Gardening.* New York: North Point, 2004.

Van Rensselaer, Mrs. Mariana Griswold Schuyler. *Art Out-of-Doors: Hints on Good Taste in Gardening.* New York: Charles Scribner's Sons, 1893.

Van Sweden, James. *Gardening with Nature.* New York: Random House, 1997.

Van Sweden, James, and Wolfgang Oehme. *Bold Romantic Gardens: The New World Landscapes of Oehme and Van Sweden.* Reston, VA: Acropolis, 1990.

Vaux, Calvert. *Villas and Cottages: A Series of Designs Prepared for Execution in the United States.* New York: Harper & Brothers, 1857.

Veblen, Thorstein. *Theory of the Leisure Class.* New York: Modern Library, 1934.

Vlach, John Michael. *Back of the Big House: The Architecture of Plantation Slavery.* Chapel Hill: University of North Carolina Press, 1993.

———. *The Planter's Prospect: Privilege and Slavery in Plantation Paintings.* Chapel Hill: University of North Carolina Press, 2002.

Walker, Peter. *Peter Walker and Partners: Defining the Craft.* San Rafael, CA: ORO Editions, 2005.

———. "The Practice of Landscape Architecture in the Postwar United States." In Treib, ed., *Modern Landscape Architecture,* 1993.

Warner, Sam Bass. *To Dwell Is to Garden: A History of Boston's Community Gardens.* Boston: Northeastern University Press, 1987.

Wechsler, Lawrence. *Robert Irwin Getty Garden.* Los Angeles: J. Paul Getty Museum, 2002.

Wedda, John. *Gardens of the American South: Grace, Beauty, History and Romance in Text and Pictures.* New York: Galahad, 1971.

Weidenmann, Jacob. *Beautifying Country Homes: A Handbook of Landscape Gardening.* New York: O. Judd, 1870.

Weitzman, Arthur. "An Eighteenth Century View of Pope's Villa." *Eighteenth Century Life* 8 (January 1983): 36–38.

Westmacott, Richard. *African-American Gardens and Yards in the Rural South.* Knoxville: University of Tennessee Press, 1992.

Wharton, Edith. *The Age of Innocence.* New York: Scribner, 1968.

———. *The Decoration of Houses.* New York: Norton, 1978.

———. *The House of Mirth.* New York: New York University Press, 1977.

———. *Hudson River Bracketed.* New York: Appleton, 1929.

———. *Italian Villas and Their Gardens.* New York: Century, 1903.

———. *The Valley of Decision: A Novel.* New York: Charles Scribner's Sons, 1902.

Whately, Thomas. *Observations of Modern Gardening.* London: West & Hughes, 1801.

Wiebe, Robert. *The Search for Order, 1877–1920.* New York: Hill & Wang, 1967.

Wilder, Louise Beebe. *Colour in my Garden.* Garden City, NY: Doubleday, Page, 1918.

Willis, Nathaniel Parker. *American Scenery Illustrated.* London: Virtue, 1837–38.

Wilson, Alexander B. *The Culture of Nature: North American Landscape from Disney to the Exxon Valdez.* Cambridge, MA: Blackwell, 1992.

Wolschke-Bulmahn, Joachim, ed. *Nature and Ideology: Natural Garden Design in the Twentieth Century.* Washington, DC: Dumbarton Oaks Research Library and Collection, 1997.

Wood, Jon, David Hulks, and Alex Potts, eds. *Modern Sculpture Reader.* Leeds, England: Henry Moore Institute, 2007.

Wrede, Stuart. *Denatured Visions: Landscape and Culture in the Twentieth Century.* New York: Museum of Modern Art, 1991.

Wright, Frank Lloyd. *Testament.* New York: Horizon, 1957.

Wyllie, Romy. *Bertram Goodhue: His Life and Residential Architecture.* New York: Norton, 2007.

Young, Terence. *Building San Francisco's Parks, 1850–1930.* Baltimore: Johns Hopkins University Press, 2004.

Zaitzevsky, Cynthia. *Frederick Law Olmsted and the Boston Park System.* Cambridge, MA: Harvard University Press, 1980.

Zapatka, Christian. *The American Landscape.* New York: Princeton Architectural Press, 1995.

INDEX